Imperialists, Nationalists, Democrats

Sarvepalli Gopal

Imperialists, Nationalists, Democrats

The Collected Essays

edited by

Srinath Raghavan

permanent black in association with ashoka UNIVERSITY

Published by
PERMANENT BLACK
'Himalayana', Mall Road, Ranikhet Cantt,
Ranikhet 263645
Email: perblack@gmail.com

in association with

ASHOKA UNIVERSITY

Distributed by
ORIENT BLACKSWAN PRIVATE LIMITED
Bangalore Bhopal Bhubaneshwar Chandigarh Chennai
Ernakulam Guwahati Hyderabad Jaipur Kolkata
Lucknow Mumbai New Delhi Patna
www.orientblackswan.com

First published in hardback 2013
Second paperback impression 2019

ISBN 81-7824-366-0

Printed and bound by Sapra Brothers, Noida, U.P.

Contents

ashoka UNIVERSITY

HEDGEHOG AND FOX

HISTORY AND POLITICS SERIES

"The fox knows many things, but the hedgehog knows one big thing"

General Editor RUDRANGSHU MUKHERJEE

MONOGRAPHS

Steven I. Wilkinson ARMY AND NATION
Thomas R. Trautmann ELEPHANTS AND KINGS
Partha Chatterjee, Sudipta Kaviraj, Nivedita Menon THE INDIAN IDEOLOGY
Nayanjot Lahiri ASHOKA IN ANCIENT INDIA
Nicholas B. Dirks AUTOBIOGRAPHY OF AN ARCHIVE
Vasudha Dalmia HINDU PASTS
Dipesh Chakrabarty THE CALLING OF HISTORY
Sunil Agnani HATING EMPIRE PROPERLY
Mahesh Rangarajan NATURE AND NATION
Bhavani Raman DOCUMENT RAJ
Sumit Guha BEYOND CASTE
Iqtidar Alam Khan INDIA'S POLITY IN THE AGE OF AKBAR
Linda Hess BODIES OF SONG
Charu Gupta THE GENDER OF CASTE
Ajay Skaria UNCONDITIONAL EQUALITY
Velcheru Narayana Rao TEXT AND TRADITION IN SOUTH INDIA
Udaya Kumar WRITING THE FIRST PERSON
Chinya V. Ravishankar SONS OF SARASVATI
Christian Lee Novetzke THE QUOTIDIAN REVOLUTION
B.D. Chattopadhyaya THE CONCEPT OF BHARATVARSHA
Sumit Sarkar ESSAYS OF A LIFETIME
Sudhir Mahadevan A VERY OLD MACHINE
Sanjay Subrahmanyam EMPIRES BETWEEN ISLAM AND CHRISTIANITY
Neeladri Bhattacharya THE GREAT AGRARIAN CONQUEST
Chetan Singh HIMALAYAN HISTORIES
Yogendra Yadav POLITICS, ELECTIONS, AND INDIAN DEMOCRACY
Arvind Krishna Mehrotra TRANSLATING THE INDIAN PAST
Francis Robinson THE MUSLIM WORLD IN MODERN SOUTH ASIA
Joya Chatterji PARTITION'S LEGACIES
Jennifer Dubrow COSMOPOLITAN DREAMS
Sumit Guha HISTORY AND COLLECTIVE MEMORY IN SOUH ASIA 1200–2000
Partha Chatterjee I AM THE PEOPLE

INDIAN HISTORY and POLITICS CLASSICS

Ranajit Guha A RULE OF PROPERTY FOR BENGAL
Ranajit Guha THE SMALL VOICE OF HISTORY
Romila Thapar THE PAST BEFORE US
Muzaffar Alam THE LANGUAGES OF POLITICAL ISLAM IN INDIA
Asok Sen ISWAR CHANDRA VIDYASAGAR AND HIS ELUSIVE MILESTONES
Rosalind O'Hanlon CASTE CONFLICT AND IDEOLOGY
Arvind K. Mehrotra, ed. A CONCISE HISTORY OF INDIAN LITERATURE IN ENGLISH
Ramachandra Guha AN ANTHROPOLOGIST AMONG THE MARXISTS
Partha Chatterjee DEAD MAN WANDERING
Partha Chatterjee EMPIRE AND NATION
Partha Chatterjee THE BLACK HOLE OF EMPIRE
M.S.S. Pandian BRAHMIN AND NON-BRAHMIN
Nayanjot Lahiri FINDING FORGOTTEN CITIES
Iqtidar Alam Khan THE MUGHAL NOBILITY
Srinath Raghavan WAR AND PEACE IN MODERN INDIA
Sudipta Kaviraj THE ENCHANTMENT OF DEMOCRACY AND INDIA
Sudipta Kaviraj THE IMAGINARY INSTITUTION OF INDIA
Sudipta Kaviraj TRAJECTORIES OF THE INDIAN STATE
Sudipta Kaviraj THE INVENTION OF PRIVATE LIFE
David Hardiman GANDHI IN HIS TIME AND OURS
Christophe Jaffrelot INDIA'S SILENT REVOLUTION
Sunil Kumar THE EMERGENCE OF THE DELHI SULTANATE
Christian Lee Novetzke, HISTORY, BHAKTI, AND PUBLIC MEMORY
Ramchandra Gandhi THE AVAILABILITY OF RELIGIOUS IDEAS
Brijen Kumar Gupta SIRAJ-UD-DAULAH AND THE EAST INDIA COMPANY
Francis Robinson THE ULAMA OF FARANGI MAHALL AND ISLAM IN SOUTH ASIA
Niraja Gopal Jayal CITIZENSHIP AND ITS DISCONTENTS
Michael J. Fisher COUNTERFLOWS TO COLONIALISM
Jahnavi Phalkey ATOMIC STATE
Ramachandra Guha THE UNQUIET WOODS
Rudrangshu Mukherjee AWADH IN REVOLT
Sarvepalli Gopal IMPERIALISTS, NATIONALISTS, DEMOCRATS

HISTORICAL SOURCEBOOKS IN CLASSICAL INDIAN THOUGHT

Patrick Olivelle, ed. A DHARMA READER
Sheldon Pollock, ed. A RASA READER
Johannes Bronkhorst, ed. A SABDA READER

INTERNATIONAL FICTION CLASSICS

Joan Sales UNCERTAIN GLORY
Jaan Kross THE CZAR'S MADMAN

Editor's Acknowledgements

This volume brings together all of Sarvepalli Gopal's essays not earlier published in any of the books he authored. The idea of putting it together came out of a conversation with Ramachandra Guha. Rukun Advani, who had edited Gopal's biography of Radhakrishnan and the abridged version of his biography of Nehru, promptly agreed to publish it. His patience and encouragement have been critical at every stage of this undertaking. Without Keshav Desiraju's enthusiasm and generosity this project would not have got off ground. He introduced me to Gopal's family and friends, secured access to Gopal's papers, and plied me with other material and suggestions. For all this I am deeply indebted. My greatest debt is to Indira Gopal. Even before I came along with the idea of this volume, she had painstakingly collected and filed Gopal's manuscripts, offprints, handwritten notes, letters, and other documents. She gave me free run of these and spent long hours discussing her husband's life and work. Her affection and warmth made my visits to their home 'Girija' a treat.

I had never met Gopal and my acquaintance with him was through his books and essays. But in compiling this volume and writing the Introduction I was fortunate in being able to consult people who knew Gopal personally or professionally. For their willingness to share their views with me I am grateful to Neeladri Bhattacharya, Sabyasachi Bhattacharya, Chandra Chari, Antony Copley, Sir Martin Gilbert, Uma Iyengar, Leela Kasturi, Rudrangshu Mukherjee, and Romila Thapar. Sir Christopher Bayly kindly sent me a copy of his obituary and appreciation of Gopal. The team at *Seminar*—Malvika Singh, Tejbir Singh, and Harsh Sethi—provided copies of Gopal's contributions to the journal unavailable elsewhere. Conversations with A.R. Venkatachalapathy helped me understand the intellectual and cultural context in Madras during the 1930s and 1940s. For their comments and suggestions on the Introduction I am particularly grateful to Keshav Desiraju, Ramachandra Guha, Sunil Khilnani, Mahesh Rangarajan, and Romila Thapar. Any surviving errors and inaccuracies are mine alone.

I have to the extent possible tried to track down the details of original publication or the occasion of these essays and lectures. These are shown in the copyright statement at the end of the book. Should any omissions in this regard be brought to notice, they will be rectified in subsequent printings.

Introduction

Sarvepalli Gopal: A Life in History

Srinath Raghavan

In the summer of 1946 the eminent American historian, Samuel Eliot Morison, published a short pamphlet for his students at Harvard. Titled 'History as a Literary Art', this ten-cent booklet had an unanticipated success. It was reviewed in respected periodicals and academic journals, including the *American Historical Review*. Soon, it found its way across the Atlantic and was widely circulated in Oxford, where its author had taught two decades earlier. Morison had been 'exercised over the bad English used by students of history . . . and over the dull, pedantic manner in which many historical monographs were being presented.'[1] His pamphlet intended to drive home to students of history the aesthetic demands of their discipline, for 'They have forgotten that there is an art of writing history.' He traced the problem to a 'chain reaction of dullness' triggered by professors who had 'risen to positions of eminence by writing dull, solid, valuable monographs that nobody reads outside the profession' and who encouraged their students to emulate them.

Morison sought to stem this tide by urging budding historians to cultivate a 'sense for style'. There was admittedly 'no royal road to style'. Much of his little book emphasized the virtue of vigour, vividness, and clarity. Historians could benefit much from studying

[1] 'History as a Literary Art', reprinted in Samuel Eliot Morison, *By Land and by Sea: Essays and Addresses* (New York: Alfred A. Knopf, 1954), pp. 289–98.

the techniques of novelists, who were 'superior to all but the best historians in characterization and description.' All this was agreeable, if pedestrian, advice. Morison's distinctive point, which he reserved for the end, was that 'the historian should have frequent recourse to the book of life.' He assured veterans of the Second World War, who were returning in droves and enrolling in universities, that their war years had not been wasted. 'Rather they should realize that the war gave them a rich experience of life, which is the best equipment for a historian.' Morison was emphatic that 'great historians, with few exceptions, are those who have not merely studied, but lived . . .' There was a self-referential tenor to this message: during the war Morison had been appointed—by none less than President Franklin Roosevelt—a rear admiral in the US Navy to be better prepared for writing its multi-volume official war history.

Among those who read this pamphlet was a student from India who had come up to Oxford in 1945 to read history. It is not certain that Morison's exhortations made any particular impression on the young Sarvepalli Gopal, but his subsequent life and work followed the track and embodied the qualities that Morison had identified as essential to the making of great historians.

II

Sarvepalli Gopal was born in Madras on 23 April 1923. He was the youngest of the six surviving children of the philosopher—and later president of India—Sarvepalli Radhakrishnan (1888–1975) and his wife Sivakamu (1893–1956). Of obscure parentage and humble origins, Radhakrishnan had grown up in a Telugu-speaking Brahmin household in the North Arcot district of the Madras presidency. By the time Gopal was born, Radhakrishnan had had a meteoric career as philosopher, writer, and academic, his most recent success being a prestigious professorship at Calcutta University. Sivakamu was the daughter of a railway stationmaster who had died during her infancy. Raised by her widowed and impecunious mother, she was not conventionally educated. But she was proficient in Telugu, and during Radhakrishnan's stint in Calcutta learnt to read and write

English with the help of a tutor. She was also fiercely determined to ensure that her children, especially her five daughters, should get the best modern education.

The boy was originally named Ramachandra, but the family's neighbours in Calcutta took to calling him Gopal. The name was formalized with the approval of Sir Ashutosh Mukherjee, the vice chancellor of Calcutta University and a patron of Radhakrishnan. As the youngest child—his eldest sister was fifteen years older—and only son, Gopal was the object of parental affection and ambition and doted upon by his sisters. His childhood was comfortable. The chair at Calcutta University had not only enhanced Radhakrishnan's professional and public stature, it had enabled him gradually to shake off the webs of poverty and debt in which his earlier life had been ensnared. When Gopal was five years old, Radhakrishnan bought his first car—an extravagance that enabled more frequent family outings. Gopal would later recall that 'A visit to Whiteaway's on Thursday afternoons for fruit salad and ice cream became an established treat.'[2]

In May 1931 Radhakrishnan was appointed vice chancellor of the Andhra University at Waltair. Away from the bustle of Calcutta and Madras, the family lived in a spacious house by the beach and the children managed to spend some time with their overworked father. Radhakrishnan was an affectionate if reticent parent. 'He created in the house', Gopal would write, 'an atmosphere of scholarship and human values and impressed on his children the necessity of faith and the virtue of kindness.' It would be years before Gopal immersed himself in the writings of his father, but almost by osmosis he soaked up the rationalism and liberal humanism that permeated Radhakrishnan's thought and work. More tangible was the influence of his father's large library, particularly his collection of English literature. By the time he entered his teens, Gopal was an omnivorous reader with a discriminating taste for prose and poetry. In the years ahead he would develop a particular interest in modernist literature, especially the

[2] Sarvepalli Gopal, *Radhakrishnan: A Biography* (New Delhi: Oxford University Press, 1989), p. 86.

work of Eliot, Forster, Woolf, Spender, and Auden, and would keep up with the torrential outpouring of literary criticism that flowed in the wake of their work.

Equally important to Gopal's intellectual development was his early exposure to the main currents of Indian nationalism. As a member of the Indian Educational Service, Radhakrishnan was in the employ of the Raj, and in June 1931 the viceroy, Lord Irwin, had even secured him a knighthood. Yet Radhakrishnan was deeply sympathetic to the nationalist cause—Gandhi and Tagore being among his long-standing correspondents. Britain, he averred in several speeches in the 1930s, should realize that it was time to replace paternalism with a partnership based on the free consent of self-governing peoples. This view of the relationship between Britain and India—as holding the potential for transformation, given political wisdom and foresight—would be central to Gopal's early historical work. The son's affinity with progressive nationalism was cemented by reading Nehru's *Autobiography* (1936): it 'gave me a set of public ideals and a value system which I was convinced any Indian worth anything should try to follow.'[3] These ideals and values animated Gopal's thinking and public engagement throughout his life.

In 1934, while still at Waltair, Radhakrishnan had purchased a plot of land in the prime residential area of Mylapore in Madras. By the following year a house had been constructed. 'Girija' is a magnificent two-storey brick-and-concrete bungalow with ample living space, a large kitchen and dining area, a back porch, and a front veranda with an elegant driveway and portico. There were only a few scattered houses in the vicinity, one of which belonged to C.S. Ayyar, the older brother of Sir C.V. Raman.[4] The decision to build a house in Madras was actually made by Mrs Radhakrishnan. Her husband's career was scaling new heights and he was much sought after for lectures and fellowships by universities abroad. She wanted an independent base

[3] Sarvepalli Gopal, 'Treasured Bookmarks', *The Hindu*, 11 October 1992.

[4] Radhakrishnan knew him well in Calcutta. C.S. Ayyar was also the father of Subrahmanyan Chandrasekhar, a future Nobel laureate in physics.

partly to ensure that the demands of his academic career did not affect the education of her daughter: a house in Madras would be ideal. The decision was perspicacious because, sure enough, Radhakrishnan took up, in the summer of 1936, the Spalding chair for the study of eastern religions and ethics at Oxford.

During his first year at Oxford, Radhakrishnan had his family with him. Mrs Radhakrishnan and the girls returned to India in mid-1937. Gopal stayed on in England to complete his schooling. Radhakrishnan had been keen to send him to Eton College, but this proved impossible at short notice and Gopal was admitted to Mill Hill School. Established in 1807 by a group of non-conformist merchants and ministers, Mill Hill is located atop a scenic ridge on the outskirts of London with commanding views of Epping Forest and the Northdowns, Harrow, and the Chilterns. The main reason for choosing Mill Hill was that the headmaster was the son of an old British friend of Radhakrishnan. Gopal spent three years at Mill Hill, finishing with a school certificate showing credits in English, History, Geography, Mathematics, Latin, and French. The headmaster noted that he had 'a brain of very good quality, is a hard worker and was very well liked by both masters and boys.'[5]

Schoolwork apart, Gopal was keen on cricket. Radhakrishnan had developed a special interest in the game during his tenure at Waltair and even sought to persuade the star batsman C.K. Nayudu to coach the varsity team. It was with his father that Gopal began watching cricket matches. His boyhood hero was Syed Mushtaq Ali, who had scored the first overseas test century by an Indian in a match against England in 1936—a match that Gopal could conceivably have watched. Decades later, when Radhakrishnan became president of India, it was apparently at Gopal's recommendation that both Nayudu and Mushtaq received their Padma awards.[6] Of his own cricketing

[5] Testimonial from T.K. Devy, Headmaster, Mill Hill School, 9 March 1940, Gopal Papers.

[6] Ramachandra Guha, 'Remembering Sarvepalli Gopal', *The Hindu*, 27 April 2003. Gopal's review of Ramachandra Guha's *Wickets in the East* (essay 29 herein), which includes this observation on Mushtaq Ali—'I have

abilities there is no record, but of his enthusiasm there is little doubt. On one occasion, when trying to reach a ball that had flown on to the roof, he fell a dozen feet through a skylight.[7] From his time in Mill Hill we can also date Gopal's abiding interest in writings on the game—cricket being the most literary of sports. Late in life, reviewing a clutch of cricket books, he casts aside the regal reserve of his final years to betray a passion for the game and deep admiration of those whose literary bent leads them to be its historians and raconteurs: 'To me, as no doubt to many others, the game and the English language have helped each other to increase the sum total of fascination. I still remember, for example, reading a long time ago a comment of Cardus on Duleepsinhji. "It is one of the delights", wrote Cardus, "of an English summer afternoon to watch Duleep's bat flash in the sun." That sentence, with all that it leaves unsaid, has haunted me through the years.'[8]

From Mill Hill Gopal was admitted to Oxford to read modern history. Since there were a couple of months to spare before the term began, he went back to Madras in August 1939. The outbreak of the Second World War the following month threw his academic plans out of kilter. Like many, Gopal found himself stranded by the disruption of transport between India and England. An anxious Radhakrishnan wrote to Joseph Franco, professor of history at Presidency College, Madras, asking if he would allow Gopal to attend the first year History honours class as a non-collegiate student to prevent his being idle at home. Gopal's teachers at Mill Hill also wrote to Franco, speaking 'almost extravagantly of his capacity and character'. The professor agreed and soon concluded that Gopal's teachers had 'not exaggerated his merits at all.' At the end of the academic year, the transport

watched him bat at Chepauk, and [he was] indisputably the most stylish batsman between Ranji and Viswanath'—suggests that Gopal did not in fact witness Mushtaq's Old Trafford century at Manchester on 26–27 July 1936, else he would hardly have failed to mention it here.

[7] Gopal, *Radhakrishnan*, p. 378.

[8] See the opening para in Sarvepalli Gopal, 'The Spell of Cricket' (essay 29 below).

difficulties persisting, the government decided that Indian students who were unable to continue their education in Britain should be given special consideration. Presidency College took up Gopal's case with Sir Mahomed Usman, the vice chancellor of the University of Madras, and sought permission to allow Gopal to continue the History honours course even though he had not passed the local intermediate examination.[9] Permission was granted and Gopal enrolled as a regular student at Presidency.

Now a mouldering institution, Presidency was then in its pomp. Within months of Gopal's joining, the college celebrated its centenary. It was justly proud of its alumni, among whom it counted distinguished politicians and administrators, writers and scholars—including a Nobel laureate. But the teaching of history in the college was vacuous and pedantic. Gopal excelled at it just the same, taking first place in the First Class in the final university honours examination and carrying off a clutch of prizes and medals at graduation. His teachers regarded him as 'a brilliant product of the History Department . . . one of the ablest students that has passed out of this College.'[10]

Gopal's views on history were shaped not so much by his teachers as by a book he read as an undergraduate: Christopher Hill's *The English Revolution 1640*. Published in 1940, it consisted in the main of a seventy-page essay written by the author just before being drafted. Hill would later explain that the book was 'written very fast' and aimed to be 'rather provocative'. It was to be 'my last will and testament'—he was sure he would die in the war.[11] Written from an explicit Marxist framework, the book's central argument—about a bourgeois revolution—is not particularly convincing: Hill conceded later that it was a 'first approximation, with all its crudities and over-simplifications.'[12] It was, all the same, a brilliant declaration of intent

[9] Testimonial from Professor J. Franco, 7 March 1944, Gopal Papers.

[10] Testimonials from Professor J. Franco, 7 March 1944, and H.C. Papworth, Principal of Presidency College, 13 August 1942, Gopal Papers.

[11] Cited in Donald Pennington, 'John Edward Christopher Hill', *Proceedings of the British Academy*, 130 (2005), p. 28.

[12] Christopher Hill, *The English Revolution 1640*, 3rd ed. (London: Lawrence & Wishart, 1955), pp. 4–5. Popular history by academic historians, like

and anticipated Hill's creative engagement with Marxism in the years ahead. But it was more the analytical frisson in the book that captured Gopal's imagination: '[the book] taught me that history was more than a series of chronicles that was being doled out to me in the lecture rooms and that proper understanding of the past required a knowledge of the interplay of societies, structures and ideas.'[13]

Even at this very early stage, Gopal's work stood out for its literary aspiration. 'He gave signs of an artistic taste', Franco noted, 'and his essays were always a pleasure to read.' Gopal's wider literary interest was sustained and encouraged by a legendary professor of English at Presidency College, K. Swaminathan.[14] Although he was not taught by Swaminathan, Gopal came to know him rather well. During these years he was active in amateur theatre as both playwright and actor: his 'histrionic abilities were of no mean order and he has considerable claims to youthful authorship.'[15] Indeed, Gopal's earliest surviving piece of writing is a satire on the Bengal famine that he wrote in 1943 with a close friend V. Abdulla, 'A Talk for Food, A Farce in Frustration'. The play was not only staged but published, with a preface in doggerel by Swaminathan.[16]

After graduating in the summer of 1942, Gopal joined the Madras Law College. The decision reflected neither his intellectual interests

---

popular science writing by reputed scientists (such as Sir Arthur Eddington and James Jeans), with all its inevitable simplifications, was finding a large market over these years. George Dangerfield's *The Strange Death of Liberal England* (1935) became a cult classic soon after its appearance, in large part because it was written with an astonishing literary panache which makes it readable to this day.

[13] Gopal, 'Treasured Bookmarks', *The Hindu*, 11 October 1992.

[14] K. Swaminathan acquired considerable subsequent renown as Chief Editor of Mahatma Gandhi's Collected Works. He is the subject of an elegiac essay by Ramachandra Guha: 'Gandhi's Editor: K Swaminathan', in Ramachandra Guha, *An Anthropologist Among the Marxists and Other Essays* (Delhi: Permanent Black, 2001), pp. 63–72.

[15] Testimonial from Professor J. Franco, 7 March 1944, Gopal Papers.

[16] TS copy of 'A Talk for Food, A Farce in Frustration'; 'K. Swaminathan: A Memoir', Gopal Papers.

nor thoughts about his future career, but the fact that the war was now at India's doorstep. Gopal was merely marking time before he could go up to Oxford. His listless interest in the law was not evident from his academic performance at the Law College. He graduated with a First Class in mid-1944 and took several college prizes besides.[17] But his academic ambitions were stymied by a war which showed no sign of stopping. On the contrary the Allies had just opened a second front in Europe with the Normandy landings, and the surrender of Germany lay almost a year ahead.

Gopal decided to try the competitive examination to the Indian Audit and Accounts Services. To those who knew him in later years, picturing Gopal as an accountant may strain the imagination. But the attempt was not quite as bizarre as it seems: Radhakrishnan's distinguished friend C.V. Raman had worked in the government as assistant accountant general before quitting the service for a professorship at Calcutta. In the spring of 1945, the results of the examination were announced and Gopal was placed seventh in the order of merit. Luckily for him, Germany and Japan surrendered soon after, sparing him the ordeal that C.V. Raman had shrugged off earlier. In October 1945, having waited six years, Gopal went up to Oxford to read for his BA in modern history at Balliol College.

III

Balliol was in many ways the natural choice. By the time Gopal joined it, the college boasted of a connection with India that dated back nearly a century. From the 1850s, Balliol men had toiled for the Eastern Empire. While Benjamin Jowett (1870–93) was Master, the college became virtually a finishing school for men wanting to join the Indian Civil Service (ICS). Between 1853 and 1947 no fewer than 345 Balliol men had worked in India, the bulk of them in the ICS. Three viceroys of India, including Curzon, had been at Balliol. Jowett had also made the college an attractive and welcoming destination for Indian students. From 1853 to 1947 the college had 88 Indians,

[17] Testimonial from K. Krishna Menon, Principal, Law College, Madras, 7 March 1944, Gopal Papers.

and from 1870 it had at least one Indian in residence every year.[18] A more personal consideration for Gopal was the presence in Balliol of Christopher Hill.

The Oxford to which Gopal came up was nothing like the inter-war idyll so memorably portrayed in Evelyn Waugh's *Brideshead Revisited*. The war had capsized not just the academic world of dons and students, but also the standard of undergraduate life in the university. Michael Howard, the distinguished historian and exact contemporary of Gopal, writes that 'Oxford was bleak: full of schoolboys and serious married ex-servicemen. There was even less to eat and drink than there had been during the war.'[19] The atmosphere in Philip Larkin's novel *Jill* (1946), which is set in wartime Oxford, communicates this perspective well, a later edition of it including the poet's recollection that 'Life in college was austere. Its pre-war pattern had been dispersed, in some instances permanently . . . Traditional types such as aesthete and hearty were pruned relentlessly back.'[20] Gopal's tutors at Balliol, Christopher Hill and Richard Southern, had served in the army and the foreign office over the previous five years, and, like other dons, may have found it difficult to settle back into the humdrum routines of university life. Notwithstanding the problems of war's aftermath, Gopal soaked up the intellectual and social life on offer.[21]

Post-war Oxford may have been drab, but the teaching of history there was very far from being that. A younger generation of dons tempered by wartime experiences and sensitized by left political leanings were impatient with prevalent modes of writing history

[18] Judith Brown, *Windows into the Past: Life Histories and the Historian of South Asia* (New Delhi: Oxford University Press, 2011), pp. 10–28; Noel Annan, *The Dons: Mentors, Eccentrics and Geniuses* (London: HarperCollins, 2000), pp. 61–78; personal communication from Professor Mahesh Rangarajan.

[19] Michael Howard, *Captain Professor: A Life in War and Peace* (London: Continuum, 2006), p. 124.

[20] Introduction in Philip Larkin, *Jill* (1946; rpnt London: Faber & Faber, 1975), pp. 11, 12.

[21] He seems to have remained forever loyal to his college: see Rudrangshu Mukherjee's recollection of a lunch for the new Master of Balliol in the mid-1990s, 'Good Night Sweet Prince', *The Telegraph* (Calcutta), 22 April 2002.

and eager to explore fresh approaches and new topics. Hill was closely involved in the historians' group of the Communist Party of Great Britain, which included Victor Kiernan, Rodney Hilton, Eric Hobsbawm, and E.P. Thompson. He was a major influence on Gopal during these years, and remained a mentor and friend thereafter. But though Gopal greatly admired Hill's erudition, acuity, and style, he did not embrace his tutor's Marxism. Hill, for his part, studiously refrained from privileging any approach to history in his teaching. A student recalls that 'in his tutorials he relied almost wholly on abrupt questions . . . He sat curled up in a curious hammock-like chair, beneath a picture of Oliver Cromwell, and made the pupils do all the work.'[22] Yet British Marxist historiography did leave an impress on Gopal's conception of history. He was attracted to it mainly because it sought to provide plausible explanations of historical change. History, Gopal held, 'is not the narration of events but an analysis of change.' At the same time he was not convinced of the primacy Marxism accorded—even if only 'in the final analysis'—to economic factors. The task of history, he felt, is to 'study the total activity of an entire people through time and of the ways in which it has altered.' This included their 'political, economic, and social development, their religion, ideas and attitudes.' All of these 'overlap and influence one another, so that distortion results from studying any in isolation.'[23] Gopal's willingness to consider multiple vectors of change meant that he was also open to several methods of studying history. In this sense he was from the outset a liberal historian.

A corollary to this was the premium he placed on 'precise, meticulous scholarship, devotion to accuracy and detail.'[24] From this the general imprint on him of the British empiricist historiographical tradition can be discerned, but it is also important to note the particular influence of another tutor, Cuthbert Collin Davies. A former officer in the

[22] Robin Briggs, 'Christopher Hill', *Oxford Dictionary of National Biography* (accessed on the internet).

[23] Lecture at Bhabha Atomic Research Centre Graduation Ceremony, n.d., Gopal Papers.

[24] Sarvepalli Gopal, 'A Sense of History', *Seminar* 39 (November 1962), p. 28.

Indian army who carried near his lungs a bullet from an Afghan rifle, Collin Davies was Reader in Indian History. He was in fact Oxford's sole academic link with Indian history at the time, and his special course on 'Warren Hastings and India' the only available exposure to the subject for a generation of undergraduates. Gopal took his course and the two established a good working relationship. Collin Davies insisted on 'an extensive use of first-hand materials, and a tight standard of accuracy.' He read his students' drafts more than once and urged them to use archival material with discrimination, pre-empting document fetishism.[25] Interpretation and explanation, Gopal later maintained, were the real task of the historian: 'An historian is, of course, the servant of the documents; but without his service the documents cannot speak.'[26]

A third precept of post-war British historiography that Gopal carried into his work, in keeping with his early inclination, was literary flair. Like Morison and Hill, Southern emphasized the need for clarity and style: 'for any piece of writing to prove finally effective and memorable depended on its author's having found the right voice and the right style.' He encouraged undergraduates to cultivate their prose by consulting the work of literary figures such as Quiller-Couch. Gopal would later echo these ideas, saying that the historian should 'state the evidence and the conclusions as lucidly as possible. The art of writing is as indispensable to the historian as the scientific method', and identifying the absence of 'craftsmanship' among Indian historians as a key reason for the decline of popular interest in history in their country.[27]

[25] C.H. Philips, 'Cuthbert Collin Davies: A Tribute', Donovan Williams and E. Daniel Potts (eds), *Essays in Indian History: In Honour of Cuthbert Collin Davies* (New York: Asia Publishing House, 1973), p. ix; Donovan Williams, *A History of the University College of Fort Hare, South Africa—The 1950s: The Waiting Years* (New York: Edwin Mellen Press, 2001), p. 575; Tapan Raychaudhuri, *The World in Our Time: A Memoir* (New Delhi: HarperCollins, 2011), pp. 214–18.

[26] Gopal, 'A Sense of History', p. 29.

[27] Ibid., pp. 28–9; Ved Mehta, 'Lightning and the Lightning Bug', in idem, *The Craft of the Essay: A Ved Mehta Reader* (New Haven: Yale University Press, 1998), p. xiii.

The early years at Oxford, then, firmly aligned Gopal's intellectual compass towards British historiography. Over the next decade and a half his view of Indian history, both in scope of interests and approach, would be almost entirely shaped by trends at Oxbridge, leading him in 1962 to the unkind, if not wholly unjust, observation that 'during the last 50 years this country has produced scientists, philosophers, mathematicians and economists who are of world class; but there has not been a single Indian historian who is anywhere as good as the best historians in other parts of the world.'[28] The young man had clearly set his sights high. The pull of Oxbridge accounted for the strengths as well as limitations of his early work.

Gopal's Oxford tutors regarded him as comfortably placed to take a First in Modern History Honours. But his performance in the examination was disappointing: he ended up in the Third Class. The result, Southern noted, 'was a great surprise' and seems accounted for by Gopal having taken unwell in the run-up to the examination. His illness most likely began in the 'bleak and cold . . . horrible winter of 1946–7': the historian Correlli Barnett recalled that 'blizzards began to sweep in across the country again and again through the rest of January and on through the coldest February for three hundred years.'[29] The result came as a blow, allayed to a degree by the announcement that his essay, 'The Permanent Settlement in Bengal and its Results', had been awarded the Curzon Memorial Prize.[30] It was subsequently published as a small book,[31] perhaps alleviating the injustice of the examination result. Gopal's choice of topic reflected Collin Davies' guidance and marked the beginning of his professional interest in policy studies, in particular the interaction of ideas and interests in the formulation of

[28] Gopal, 'A Sense of History', p. 29.

[29] Testimonial from R.W. Southern, Tutor, Balliol College, 30 June 1951; Testimonial from B.H. Sumner, Warden, All Souls College, 29 July 1947, Gopal Papers. On the winter of 1946–7, Howard, *Captain Professor*, p. 127; Correlli Barnett cited in Norman Stone, *The Atlantic and its Enemies: A History of the Cold War* (London: Allen Lane, 2010), p. 1.

[30] *The Times* (London), 1 March 1947.

[31] Sarvepalli Gopal, *The Permanent Settlement in Bengal and its Results* (London: Allen and Unwin, 1949).

policy. However, his treatment of the subject was also socio-economic, an orientation that reflected Hill's influence—though one which seems to have been conspicuously abandoned in his subsequent works on British policy. Equally important were Gopal's contemporary concerns. The essay is stamped by his outrage at the Bengal famine (a theme on which he had written his play) and the entire policy framework that enabled such devastation.

Written at the age of 23, the essay is now of interest mainly for tracing Gopal's intellectual trajectory. It has been superseded by a bulky literature on the permanent settlement, the best of which approaches the subject with greater detail, depth, and sophistication. The weaknesses in Gopal's handling of the topic are all too evident: his grasp of economics was uneven and his analysis of social relations insufficiently nuanced. Yet some qualities in it afford a preview of his future work. There is, to begin with, its sheer ambition. In just under 8000 words it analyses the formulation of the permanent settlement, its social and economic impact, and its subsequent modifications to the present. Its espousal of concision is supplemented by its lucidity and mordant judgements, many of them caustically phrased. It could not have been written by the standard Indian historian, or indeed the targets of Morisonian ire anywhere. Gopal's literary bent, and his immersion in the Oxonian ethos hot on the heels of the influence upon him of his father and Swaminathan's erudition, help create an elevated distance between the burgeoning historian and the bulk of his subcontinental counterparts.

The essay outlines the rural property order of Bengal during Mughal decline and the nurturing by its successor regime of an 'artificial intermediate class' of zamindars for supposed revenue optimization. It looks at the 'tangle of motives' that made Cornwallis implement the settlement and, in showing the influence upon him of Philip Francis (a key official of the time), anticipates Ranajit Guha's classic monograph on the subject.[32] Gopal traces the profoundly negative implications for the cultivator (*raiyat*) that flowed from the settlement. By the

[32] Ranajit Guha, *A Rule of Property for Bengal: An Essay on the Idea of Permanent Settlement* (Paris: Mouton, 1963).

time the Crown took over from the Company, he argues, 'the *raiyat* in Bengal had reached the nadir of his fortunes.' But the zamindars had prospered. The permanent settlement had enabled the rise of a 'wealthy aristocracy' and a 'fairly prosperous middle class, deriving its capital from the vast number of intermediate estates of minor value.' Both these classes 'quickly assimilated the ideas of the West and set Bengal in the van of Indian cultural movements.' The achievements of families such as the Tagores, Gopal writes wanly, are perhaps 'the greatest justification of the Permanent Settlement.'

Turning to the contemporary period, he notes that despite improvement in the legal position of the *raiyats*, the permanent settlement remains 'a hindrance to social progress'. The last paragraph of the essay contains an interesting declaration of his liberal political credo: 'in the modern world there is a new emphasis on the State as an organization to ensure each citizen those external conditions which are necessary for the fulfilment of his personality. Today famine relief is acknowledged to be a duty of the State; compulsory education is not regarded as an invasion of personal liberty; schemes of social security do not exude the aroma of revolution.' The essay closes with a call for government to 'acquire all intermediate interests in the land and establish direct relations with the cultivators of the soil. Until the State regains its executive rights, the people of Bengal will be unable to rise to the full stature of their being.'

IV

Upon returning to India Gopal managed to secure—on the strength of the Curzon Memorial Prize and glowing testimonies from his Oxford tutors—a lectureship in European history at Andhra University. Barely a year into this assignment, he was elected to a war memorial studentship by Balliol. This enabled him to return to Oxford for doctoral work in October 1949. By this time, Gopal was considered extremely eligible in Andhra circles. But it appears that he made it clear to his parents that he would marry whoever they chose and who met with his mother's approval.[33] Gopal married Kaveri Ramaswami

[33] Personal communication from Keshav Desiraju.

at the home of her parents Parvathamma and Dr H.V. Ramaswami on 29 May 1949. He was 26 to her 23. The early years were spent apart with Gopal returning to Oxford and Indira (as Kaveri was known in her husband's family) in Madras with her mother-in-law. Indira and Gopal would live together from 1952, when Radhakrishnan became vice president and Indira was the hostess first of 2 King Edward Road and then of Rashtrapati Bhavan.

Gopal's doctoral research on the viceroyalty of Lord Ripon was supervised by Collin Davies and completed in less than two years. Southern observed that this was 'almost a record time for a work of this quality and length.' It certainly dispelled any lingering doubt over his academic reputation by his performance in the BA.[34] Collin Davies regarded the thesis as 'a lucid, scholarly, and sympathetic account of a very difficult subject.' On his recommendation, it was published in early 1953 by the Oxford University Press.[35]

Gopal's decision to study the imperial mind by focusing on an individual was not common in those times. Academic historians in Britain tended to steer clear of political biographies. Writing in 1956, the historian J.H. Plumb would bemoan the fact that 'this last fifty years, which has seen such a rich development in psychology, has witnessed a further decline of interest in biography among professional historians in this country.'[36] Insofar as the biographical technique was employed, it aimed at developing collective thumbnail sketches to answer specific historical questions—a technique popularized by Lewis Namier and later dubbed 'prosopography' by Lawrence Stone. Gopal's adoption of the biographical approach reflected his liberal sensibility—liberals being more susceptible to individuals than ideologies or institutions. But it also signalled a departure from the socio-economic orientation of his prize essay on the Permanent Settlement. Indeed,

[34] Testimonial from R.W. Southern, Tutor, Balliol College, 30 June 1951, Gopal Papers.

[35] Letter from C.C. Davies to Oxford University Press, 5 November 1951, Gopal Papers; Sarvepalli Gopal, *The Viceroyalty of Lord Ripon 1880–1884* (London: Oxford University Press, 1953).

[36] J.H. Plumb, 'History and Biography', in idem, *Men and Places* (London: Pelican, 1966), p. 239.

these considerations were almost entirely absent from his early work on British viceroys and policy-making. Only much later was Gopal able to craft a way of combining his interest in the individual with the wider context of his subject's times. From the outset, though, Gopal's biographical approach owed something to the influence of a writer he never seems to have discussed: Lytton Strachey. Now primarily seen as a member of the so-called Bloomsbury Group,[37] Strachey's trenchant and iconoclastic studies of Victorian figures had set the tone for the modern form of historical biography. Although professional historians were uncomfortable with Strachey's attempt to reduce all history to personal history, the younger dons in post-war Oxford were drawn to his writings for their literary quality. Hugh Trevor-Roper observed, for instance, that Strachey had one quality which 'will preserve even his errors: style.'[38] Gopal certainly seems to have been influenced by Strachey's mode of historical biography—not least in embracing his penchant for irreverent and sarcastic observations.

The Viceroyalty of Lord Ripon is a study of 'the principles inspiring Ripon and the policies formulated in his time.' Sixty years on, it seems decidedly old-fashioned. Its almost exclusive focus is on the impulses and deeds of the viceroy. There seems an absence of analysis of the ideational context in which the policies were formulated; scant attention is paid to economic issues; the near-complete neglect of the impact (as opposed to the reception) of these policies on Indian society is conspicuous. Everything about it detracts from allowing it even marginal space within Indian historiography today. But it is

[37] The other stars of the group being Virginia and Leonard Woolf, Roger Fry, E.M. Forster, and John Maynard Keynes. The literature on this set of friends is fairly profuse. See, for example, S.P. Rosenbaum, *The Bloomsbury Group: A Collection of Memoirs, Commentary and Criticism* (London: Taylor and Francis, 1975).

[38] Hugh Trevor Roper, 'Lytton Strachey as Historian', in idem, *Historical Essays* (London: Macmillan & Co., 1957), pp. 279–84. Also see Virginia Woolf, 'The Art of Biography', *Atlantic Monthly* (April 1939), reprinted in David Bradshaw (ed.), *Virginia Woolf: Selected Essays* (Oxford: Oxford University Press, 2008), pp. 116–23; Michael Holroyd, *Lytton Strachey* (London: Chatto & Windus, 1994).

anachronistic to judge a work of history purely from the standpoint of current trends. The book was continuous with the concerns and methods of the prevalent historiography of direct rule in India by the Crown-in-Parliament. The emphasis in this tradition was on the history of British administration and policy—evident in the final volume of the *Cambridge History of India* published in 1932. The bulk of this latter volume focuses on the Indian government's internal and external policies, the structures of district and higher administration, the evolution of various departments, and the imperial legislature. By contrast, the Indian National Congress receives no more than a short chapter. The treatment of policy-making is based on some archival research, but rarely rises above the level of an impressionistic chronicle.[39] Gopal's work on Ripon (and on British policy as a whole) elevated this tradition to a much higher plane of analytical sophistication. The book was based on exhaustive research in 82 volumes of the Ripon papers, the private papers of his key associates, a host of provincial and central government documents, and contemporary newspapers. In just over 200 pages of supple prose it analyses the mainsprings of Ripon's internal and external policies, his successes and failures. Although it ranges across several domains of policy, it manages to capture underlying principles and ideas, and their effectiveness in implementation.

The choice of Ripon was interesting. It stemmed from Gopal's interest in the nature of the Indo-British encounter—a theme on which his views would undergo substantial evolution in the years ahead while remaining an abiding intellectual concern throughout. On the one hand it reflected his belief, echoing the views of his father, that the colonial relationship between Britain and India had been susceptible of transformation if only the former adopted liberal, wise, and far-sighted approaches. This was an influential tradition of liberal belief which had found its fictional apogee in E.M. Forster's *A Passage to India* (1924), a novel so popular among left-leaning liberals sympathetic to India that Gopal could not have escaped reading it even had he not been

[39] H.H. Dodwell (ed.), *Cambridge History of India VI: The Indian Empire, 1858–1918* (Cambridge: Cambridge University Press, 1932).

a known devourer of fiction; and in fact Gopal had read and deeply admired Forster's novels and essays.[40] On the other hand, the choice of Ripon was influenced by contemporary politics. That independent India had stayed on in the Commonwealth as a republic seemed to underscore the extent to which the Indo-British relationship had been drained of much of the bitterness that had accompanied the colonial enterprise. In Gopal's view, Ripon epitomized these altogether rare qualities and his policies helped make sense of the curious denouement of India's encounter with Britain.

Two chapters in the book, dealing with Afghanistan, underscore Gopal's growing interest in, and talent for, diplomatic history. In them Gopal deftly analyses Ripon's attempts to extricate the Indian government from the morass of Afghanistan—the '*damnosa hereditas* bequeathed to the new Viceroy' by his impetuous predecessor. In disentangling and splicing together the various skeins of Ripon's policy, he shows a sure grasp of the wider international context, party political jockeying in Britain, and tribal politics in Afghanistan. While he appreciates the viceroy's liberal instincts, he is not blind to the ruthless and disingenuous moves justified on the grounds of raison d'état. 'In his Afghan settlement', Gopal concludes, 'Ripon showed himself a man who combined foresight and calculation with a certain lack scruple.' Overall the viceroy, in Gopal's reading, was an unrepentant Gladstonian liberal 'who laid, perhaps unwittingly, the foundation-stone, of the edifice of Indo-British concord which is today so unbelievably a fact.' His 'chief title to statesmanship' lay in his realization of 'the necessity of some form of partnership, hierarchic at first, but gradually moving towards the formation of a society based on friendship between equals.' The four years of his viceroyalty, Gopal concludes, 'form one of the successful failures of history'. *The Viceroyalty of Lord Ripon* was in its time an important contribution

[40] This is evident in Gopal's review of Forster's *The Hill of Devi* (essay 27 below); his admiration for *A Passage to India* is made clear by this remark in his review of Sujit Mukherjee's *Forster and Further* (essay 28 herein): 'In fact, the sole Anglo-Indian novel which can even today stand on its literary worth alone is E.M. Forster's *A Passage to India*.'

to British liberal historiography on India. Although he remained a liberal historian, Gopal's subsequent work would show a progressively increasing critical distance from this tradition.

V

On completing his DPhil, Gopal returned to Andhra University. He held the position for a few more months while he prepared his book for publication. Although the book received very favourable notices,[41] Gopal quit his readership at Waltair in July 1952 and joined the National Archives of India as assistant director. The move to Delhi was prompted, in the first instance, by his mounting dissatisfaction with the state of academic history in India. Leading figures on that firmament, such as Jadunath Sarkar and G.S. Sardesai, struck him as akin to 'medieval monastic chroniclers of Europe', their work 'the raw material of historical writing rather than such writing itself.' 'The reputation of Indian historical scholarship', he would note some years later, 'has never been as low as it is today.'[42] Another reason was the election of Radhakrishnan as vice president of India and his move to Delhi. Mrs Radhakrishnan's health had deteriorated and she was unable to join her husband in Delhi. Consequently, Radhakrishnan wanted Gopal to move in with him.

In the national archives he worked for a little under two years before joining the ministry of external affairs as director of the historical division. This division had been formed at the suggestion of India's first foreign secretary, K.P.S. Menon. Kuruvilla Zacharia, a distinguished teacher of history at Presidency College, Calcutta, had held the position until 1953. He was succeeded for a brief period by J.N. Khosla, from whom Gopal took over in the summer of 1954. Here was a position that allowed him to combine his interests in history,

[41] 'Lord Ripon as Viceroy', *Times Literary Supplement*, 23 April 1954, p. 268; review by H.G. Rawlinson in *English Historical Review*, vol. 69, no. 272 (July 1954), pp. 505–6; review by A.B. McGrath in *Catholic Historical Review*, vol. 41, no. 2 (July 1955), pp. 212–13.

[42] Gopal, 'A Sense of History', p. 29.

the making of policy, especially foreign policy, and the intersection between history and policy—the former being the study of the past with an eye to the present, and the latter the examination of the present with an eye to the future. Gopal would hold the job for the next twelve years, and during his tenure the division would rise to the peak of its performance and influence. Gopal now became 'a prominent figure on the New Delhi scene.'[43]

Perhaps the greatest attraction of his positions at the national archives and the foreign office was the access to documents that were difficult, not to say impossible, for historians to consult. This privilege spurred Gopal's interest in contemporary history. The recent past had come into vogue in the inter-war years, even if its standing in the academic world was tenuous. In the Oxbridge milieu with which Gopal was closely associated, the study of modern history was dominated by great medievalists. Anything written on the previous couple of centuries was apt to be dismissed as journalism. But in Britain, and more broadly in the West, contemporary history had begun to flourish after the Great War, a cataclysm with scores of books in its wake. The best of these drew on voluminous 'blue books' published by belligerents eager to deflect blame from themselves for lighting the spark that led to the conflagration. The Second World War gave further impetus to contemporary history. Books such as *Diplomatic Prelude* by Lewis Namier and *The Last Days of Hitler* by Hugh Trevor-Roper showed how much historical insight was possible by writing about the recent past despite the paucity of documents and the persistence of *parti pris*.

For his maiden foray into contemporary history Gopal chose to study the viceroyalty of Lord Irwin (1926–31). The choice this time round was dictated by the same considerations that had led him to Ripon: here was another viceroy who had contributed to building goodwill between Britain and India. Like Ripon, Irwin had been despised by his contemporaries and judged harshly by historians. Working on this period, Gopal would recall, was 'a rash undertaking'.

[43] Inder Malhotra, 'Revive MEA's Historical Division', *The Hindu*, 2 May 2002.

The official and private papers pertaining to these years were closed in Britain. The Government of India allowed him to consult its files but insisted that he should not cite references with the required precision. Even such restricted access allowed him to go much further in his inquiries than any previous historian. He also managed to interview Lord Halifax (as Irwin was later known) as well as Sir Malcolm Hailey, governor of Punjab and the United Provinces in the 1930s. The fact that both men had known Radhakrishnan naturally helped. Yet the novelty of this methodological move should not be underestimated. Interviews and oral histories are now regarded as acceptable, if not unproblematic, sources for the historian. But in the mid-1950s few professional historians were bold enough to rely on them and risk unfavourable comparison with journalists.

Undeterred by such risks, Gopal believed all history was open to revision and correction in the light of fresh sources and analytical perspectives. 'The lack of comprehensive source material', he later noted, 'makes writings in contemporary history more tentative and the conclusions more provisional than in any other sector of historical analysis: but it does not follow that, therefore, the effort is of little worth.'[44] Besides, contemporaneity was 'a matter of mood as well as time.' The events that he wrote about may have occurred less than thirty years earlier, 'but are now as much a part of history as, say, the Norman Conquest.' It was possible, he insisted, to study the Irwin years 'with detachment and accuracy, setting aside prejudice and conjecture.'[45]

The Viceroyalty of Lord Irwin has a narrower focus than the book on Ripon. Gopal restricted himself to the viceroy's approach to Indian nationalists and their demands. His central argument is that Irwin, a sincere and devout Christian, made a deep personal impression on Indian opinion and more especially on Gandhi, and that he did so by managing to convince them that Britain was genuinely committed to

[44] Sarvepalli Gopal, 'History and the Search for Identity', presidential address at Indian History Congress, Hyderabad, 28–30 December 1978, published in *Mainstream*, 3 March 1979, pp. 27–30.

[45] Sarvepalli Gopal, *The Viceroyalty of Lord Irwin* (London: Oxford University Press, 1957), preface.

eventually granting independence to India. He traces the evolution of Irwin's attitude and policy on a series of issues: the Simon Commission, the Bardoli satyagraha, the civil disobedience movement, the talks and pact with Gandhi. He analyses the ideas and stances of various nationalist leaders, but even when discussing popular movements like the Bardoli agitation he seldom shifts his attention from the official mind and the nationalist elites. His conclusion, keenly reminiscent of the Forsterian conclusion of *A Passage to India*, reflects a central liberal realization of this period about the limits of personal relations: 'Two men in a fortnight cannot settle the relations between peoples. And yet the settlement has in British Indian history an importance far transcending that of its several items. It brought back to the forefront of the Indian effort for freedom the spirit of cooperation between the rulers and the ruled.' Irwin, in Gopal's appraisal, 'did more than most other men of his time to keep alive the faith of the two peoples in each other.'[46] Subsequently he admitted that his evaluation of Irwin had been too charitable. In light of the sources that became available later, he conceded that Irwin had no intention of catalysing the end of the Raj and that the decision to reach out to Gandhi had sprung partly from his desire to split the nationalist opposition. Yet Irwin's actions had helped in lifting 'the fog of suspicion at least for a while. Even when bitterness and conflict returned, the memory of the assessment of Irwin's term of office was not wholly erased from the Indian mind.'[47]

The Viceroyalty of Lord Irwin is stamped with a combination of economy and elegance: the increasingly recognizable signature of Gopal's prose style. Its narrative is lean, fast-paced, and garnished

[46] Ibid., preface. The liberal belief in personal relations as a solution to political difficulties, as well as the importance of politically influential personalities as the historian's desired subject, also strongly suggest Gopal's intellectual link to the literary ethos of left-leaning Bloomsbury writers such as Forster and Leonard Woolf (the latter having served the Empire in Ceylon), and to the stylistic historian of the group, Lytton Strachey.

[47] Sarvepalli Gopal, 'Drinking Tea with Treason: Halifax in India', in Wm. Roger Louis (ed.), *Adventures with Britannia: Personalities, Politics, and Culture in Britain* (Austin: University of Texas Press, 1995), pp. 145–58.

with sharply-etched pen-portraits and assessments. The Liberals, for instance, are 'able and endowed with legal and administrative talent, but they lacked support in the country and as political entities were splendidly null.' Well received when it appeared,[48] the book has naturally been surpassed by finer-grained studies. But it remains a landmark in Indian historiography as the first scholarly work of contemporary Indian history by any historian.

VI

In 1958 Gopal was appointed Rockefeller research associate by the School of Oriental and African Studies in London. This enabled him to take a sabbatical from the ministry and begin work on a book examining British policy in India from 1858 to 1905. But by early 1959 he had to interrupt his research and return to his official desk. The latent boundary dispute between India and China had come to the fore and the historical division had its work cut out. Over the next four years Gopal would play an important role in advising the prime minister on the historical dimensions of the boundary issue.

In the autumn of 1959 Nehru asked Gopal to consult the archives in London and prepare a thorough assessment of India's claims. Early the following year Gopal took Nehru through all the material. The prime minister was convinced of the historical case for India's boundary claims, on the strength of which Nehru hoped to work a compromise arrangement with China. This did not work out. The meetings between Nehru and Zhou Enlai in April 1960 failed to make any headway. The two premiers could only agree to constitute teams of officials who would present and assess the historical and legal material held by both sides.[49] The Indian team was led by Jagat Mehta, director of the China division in the foreign office. But the bulk of the work was done by Gopal and his associates from the historical division. The two sides met thrice in the following months. Unsurprisingly,

[48] Charles Heimsath, in *Journal of Asian Studies* 18: 1 (November 1958), pp. 156–7; *Times Literary Supplement*, 26 September 1958, p. 546; P.J. Griffiths, in *International Affairs* 34: 3 (July 1958), p. 396.

[49] Srinath Raghavan, *War and Peace in Modern India: A Strategic History of the Nehru Years* (Ranikhet: Permanent Black, 2010), pp. 261–6.

they failed to produce a joint report. Eventually, two separate reports were published together.

After the Sino-Indian war of 1962 the boundary dispute spawned a cottage industry of writings. Critics such as Alastair Lamb have pointed out that not all the pieces of evidence assembled by the Indian team were equally convincing and that there was a good historical case to let go of India's claims to Aksai Chin. The problems with these arguments are legion. Suffice it to note two points. First, the work done by Gopal was not one of pure scholarship but also of advocacy. The pudding was likely to be over-egged. Second, and more important, the report prepared by Gopal was far stronger than that of the Chinese. In fact, the Chinese could show no positive evidence to substantiate their claims over all of Aksai Chin. It is not at all surprising that, in the years since, China has sought a political bargain rather than a historical-legal discussion of claims.

VII

'No one who lived in India through the winter months of 1962', Gopal would write, 'can forget the deep humiliation felt by all Indians.'[50] He had had a ringside view of the collapse of Nehru's China policy, a debacle that deeply and perhaps indelibly coloured his perception of China. Almost two decades later, when Deng Xiaoping hinted at the possibility of improved relations with India, Gopal counselled caution. 'The loose talk widely prevalent in India of the opportunities for improving relations with China', he wrote, 'is not a testimonial to sentiment but a reflection on intelligence.' India should 'exercise patience and wait rather than weaken our positions by hurried and unthinking overturns.'[51] A more immediate consequence of the war was the accentuation of Gopal's weariness with the crushing official routine. The 'curse of the full in-tray' left him with little time to work on a book begun almost five years earlier. Besides, Radhakrishnan's recent election as president of India imposed additional filial demands. When Cambridge invited him in 1963 to spend a year in residence as

[50] Sarvepalli Gopal, *Jawaharlal Nehru: A Biography* 3 (New Delhi: Oxford University Press, 1984), p. 232.

[51] Sarvepalli Gopal, 'China and Us', *Seminar*, February 1980, pp. 27–9.

Commonwealth fellow, Gopal gladly took the opportunity to return to research and writing. In the agreeable environs of Trinity College, he got down to work and completed the book with remarkable speed.

British Policy in India was the capstone of Gopal's long-standing engagement with imperial statesmen and their policies in India.[52] It was also his most ambitious undertaking yet—'to examine the ideas, aspirations of British parties and statesmen, their ways and methods of implementing them and the consequences, both anticipated and unintended, of these efforts.' It presented a magisterial account of the key strands of British policy and their evolution during these years. In it Gopal broke new ground at three levels. He was the first historian to link policy-making in India to that in Britain. More importantly, he placed both sets of policy-makers in the context of British party politics during this period. This conceptual framework was not unproblematic, but it was illuminating. In analysing the workings of the official mind, Gopal drew on a mountain of private correspondence as well as official records. His extensive and skilful use of private papers served as a rich supplement to the prim politics and bland bureaucratese of the official archive. And he not only analysed particular policies but also showed the interconnections between superficially distinct strands of policy. This threw into bold relief the principal drivers of policy at various points in the period. Each of these ground-breaking moves stemmed from a deep and intimate familiarity with the structures and process of policy-making. A perceptive reviewer praised him by quoting Macaulay on Swift: 'to him the most important affairs of state are as familiar as his weekly bills.'[53]

The book spans a wide range of issues in both domestic and foreign policy. But its omissions are glaring. There is no sustained discussion of economic affairs: industrialization, foreign investment, and public works are not analysed in any detail. Nor is there a systematic examination of the larger discursive context in which policies were formulated. Gopal is aware of the importance of race, class, and

[52] Sarvepalli Gopal, *British Policy in India 1858–1905* (London: Cambridge University Press, 1965).

[53] Charles Petrie in *Illustrated London News*, 8 January 1966.

religion, but gives greater explanatory weight to party political affiliations and practical exigencies in the formulation of policy. The latter, in particular, were certainly important in the early years after 1857. More recent scholarship, however, underscores the importance of changing imperial ideology in the latter part of the nineteenth century.[54] Gopal's careful account of policy-making forces us, all the same, to consider questions that remain as yet unresolved—about the links between shifts in ideological attitudes and the evolution of policy, and about the functional relationship between them.[55] For all its deficiencies, *British Policy in India* remains the best study of the imperial mind at the high noon of the Raj. C.A. Bayly notes that 'it is impossible to teach or learn the subject in any depth without consulting this book.'[56] It is also one of those rare books on India's colonial history that can be read for pleasure as well as profit. It is filled with Stracheyan thumbnail sketches and assessments of the dramatis personae. On John Lawrence's viceregal tenure: 'The Viceroy fainéant in India appeared to the Secretaries of State in London as a senior foreman awaiting orders. Lawrence had been too long a civil servant to be able to resist the directives of the home government.' On Dufferin: 'No man seemed better suited than Dufferin to convert the high and commanding office of the Indian viceroyalty into a sedative. In him indolence had been developed into a virtue and tact raised to the level of a policy.' On Curzon's construction of the Victoria Memorial in Calcutta: 'it was a bizarre conception in marble—the Taj Mahal brought up to date. The building was to be ringed with statues of the Governors-General; and facing its entrance was to be that of Curzon. There is no doubt who, in Curzon's mind, was the greatest

[54] An excellent new study is Karuna Mantena, *Alibis of Empire: Henry Maine and the Ends of Liberal Imperialism* (Ranikhet: Permanent Black, 2010). Also see, Thomas R. Metcalf, *Ideologies of the Raj* (Cambridge: Cambridge University Press, 1998).

[55] For a recent, important study that wrestles with these issues without satisfactorily resolving them, see Partha Chatterjee, *The Black Hole of Empire: History of a Global Practice of Power* (Ranikhet: Permanent Black, 2012).

[56] C.A. Bayly, 'Obituary: Sarvepalli Gopal', St Antony's College Record (2002), p. 135.

of Queen's proconsuls in India.' A combination of aphoristic phrasing and pungent judgement distinguished Gopal's mature style. It would be showcased in his subsequent work in historical biography.

VIII

By the time he completed the fellowship at Trinity, Gopal was keen on getting back to academia. He was enthused by the emerging younger generation of Indian historians and found himself increasingly involved in the academic organization of Indian history, albeit from the sidelines. During these years he was a member of the history committee of the University Grants Commission, which sought to foster interaction between Indian historians and the stars of British and European history.[57] Gopal saw the glimmerings of a major transformation in the study of India's past. Having spent a decade in the ministry he also felt there was little more he could contribute to the historical division. During his tenure it had established itself as an indispensable think-tank of the ministry, comprising first-rate researchers and a fine library.[58] (Its subsequent decay and unlamented demise in the 1990s were much regretted by him.) Now the time was ripe for him to move on. This took a while, but in 1966 a suitable academic opening presented itself: the readership in Indian history at Oxford. Following Collin Davies' retirement in 1965, the position had been occupied in quick succession by H.T. Lambrick and Kenneth Ballhatchet. No sooner had Ballhatchet occupied the position than he decided to join the School of Oriental and African Studies. Gopal applied for the job and, unsurprisingly, secured it. In the summer of 1966 he moved to Oxford.

The readership in Indian history came with a professorial fellowship at St Antony's College and was held as a joint appointment with the Oriental Institute. Initially, Gopal was ill at ease with this arrangement and sought to locate himself either at his beloved Balliol or at All Souls. Neither option worked. But soon he began appreciating the

[57] Vina Mazumdar, *Memories of a Rolling Stone* (New Delhi: Three Essays Collective, 2010), p. 46.

[58] Malhotra, 'Revive MEA's Historical Division'.

cosmopolitan milieu of St Antony's, its eclectic faculty and graduate students. Given his 'explosive laughter and ironic sense of detachment', youngsters found his company particularly congenial and could be seen trooping up the stairs to the apartment he occupied above the old College Hall.[59] The college reciprocated his affection by electing him to an honorary fellowship after he returned to India, so ensuring that it remained his perch at Oxford. In the late 1960s, though, Oxford also harboured a considerable number of senior citizens oblivious of the dissolution of the British empire. Gopal punctured their pretensions so charmingly that very few of the victims realized what was going on. C.A. Bayly, a student of Gopal at St Antony's, recalls a hilarious encounter: 'On one occasion he was accosted by a common room pest who asked him why he was so tall and whiteskinned, implying that Tamils ought to be short and dark. He replied with mock seriousness that it was because, being Brahmins, his family had for generation upon generation employed servants to rub sandal-wood paste into their skins. The pest sidled off, apparently satisfied.'

Gopal's research interest had by this time shifted from British policy to the history of Indian nationalism, especially the Indian National Congress in the twentieth century. As if on cue, he was approached by the Jawaharlal Nehru Memorial Fund to write the official biography of the late prime minister. Indira Gandhi had taken her time deciding to commission it. Once she made up her mind, though, Gopal quickly emerged as the preferred candidate. His scholarly credentials coupled with his experience of working in government positioned him uniquely. Given the old association of their two fathers, Mrs Gandhi and Gopal also knew each other socially. When Gopal was appointed to the Oxford readership, the prime minister had sent a congratulatory telegram. Gopal sought and obtained an assurance that he would have free run of Nehru's papers, that no constraints would be imposed on his opinion and judgement. In January 1969 the biography was formally commissioned.[60]

[59] Bayly, 'Obituary', p. 136.

[60] 'Nehru: Daughter Picks Biographer', *The Times* (London), 30 January 1969.

Just over two years later, Gopal returned to India to join the new Jawaharlal Nehru University in New Delhi. The vice chancellor of the university, G. Parthasarathy, formerly ambassador to China, was an old friend. Gopal's decision to quit his position at Oxford surprised many of his friends and associates. The move seems to have been prompted by at least three considerations. The most important of these was personal: Radhakrishnan had retired from public life in 1967 and returned to Madras. His health and temperament had not coped well with the change. In consequence, Gopal had had to spend most of the time between terms by his father's side and he had found it increasingly difficult to juggle commitments between Oxford, Madras, and Delhi—where the Nehru papers were housed. The second reason was professional. Gopal rightly felt that the Oxford readership came with a glass ceiling. He had somewhat desultorily applied for the Beit professorship in the history of the British Commonwealth that had fallen vacant after the incumbent, John Gallagher, decided to move back to Cambridge. But the position was offered to Ronald Robinson who, in collaboration with Gallagher, had opened up new perspectives on the British empire. The third, and related, consideration was intellectual. The late 1960s were the formative period of the 'Cambridge school' of Indian political history. John Gallagher and Anil Seal (of Trinity College) were the impresarios of this group of young historians. Their thrust was to contest the importance of Indian nationalism in shaping the history of the late colonial period. Instead they emphasized the significance of local and provincial politics, which in their view was based on patron–client relationships between the government and its collaborators. The unity of Indian nationalism was a figment and its power hollow. The opposition to empire was putative and little more than collaboration by other means. What passed for nationalism was actually animated by a quest for the loaves and fishes of office rather than high-minded principles.[61]

[61] On the Cambridge school, see the manifesto by Anil Seal, 'Imperialism and Nationalism in India', *Modern Asian Studies* 7: 3 (1973), pp. 321–47. The methods and arguments of the Cambridge school owed a great deal to the work of C. Ernest Dawn, historian of the Ottoman empire, who argued

Gopal's relationship with Gallagher and his associates was ambivalent. He applauded their iconoclasm and irreverence but disapproved of their desire to drain Indian nationalism of all ideals and ideology. It would be some years before he would write his famous, devastating critique of the Cambridge school. 'Namier was accused of taking the mind out of politics . . . this school has gone further and taken not only the mind but decency, character, integrity and selfless commitment out of the Indian national movement.'[62] Although Robinson was not part of the Cambridge school, he was intellectually close to it (the notion of 'collaboration' loomed large in his work on imperial history). In any event, his appointment suggested that the Cambridge school perspective would dominate the historiography of India in England. By contrast, intellectual and institutional trends in India seemed favourable for the development of more sophisticated and less cynical approaches to Indian history. Gopal hoped that his biography of Nehru would not only contest the claims of the Cambridge school but form part of a new Indian historiography.

IX

His decision to embark on the biography was consonant with Gopal's historical interests and approach. His previous work on the imperial mind was all centred on high politics and policy-making with a particular focus on individuals. Now, his three-volume biography of Nehru built on that experience. The opening volume covered the first fifty-eight years of Nehru's life, up to Indian independence. The next

---

in a seminal essay (first published in 1961) that there was no ideologically driven Arab nationalist movement prior to 1914; he instead underscored the importance of Arab factional politics. This debt to Dawn remains curiously unacknowledged by the Cambridge historians. His essay was reprinted in C. Ernest Dawn, *From Ottomanism to Arabism: Essays on Arab Nationalism* (Urbana, Ill.: University of Illinois Press, 1973). Also see Dawn's reassessment in Rashid Khalidi, Lisa Anderson, Muhammad Muslih, and Reeva Simon (eds), *The Origins of Arab Nationalism* (New York: Columbia University Press, 1993), pp. 3–30.

[62] *Indian Economic and Social History Review* 14 (1977), p. 405.

two were devoted to the remaining seventeen years. Gopal was clear that, notwithstanding his important role in the Indian nationalist movement, Nehru would ultimately have to be judged as prime minister of the newly independent country.

To attempt a summary of these landmark volumes is futile. But their distinguishing features are worth highlighting. For a start, there was the biographer's peculiar relationship with his subject. Gopal conceded in the preface to the first volume that 'Jawaharlal was the hero of my youth.'[63] He had also regularly interacted with Nehru in the foreign office and been treated with much affection by the prime minister: Nehru apparently nicknamed him 'Peter Pan'. In itself, this need not have posed a problem for the biographer. Indeed, in the past such a personal connection was seen as an advantage, if not a necessity, Dr Johnson having remarked to Boswell: 'Nobody can write the life of man but those who have eat [*sic*] and drunk and lived in social intercourse with him.'[64] But Gopal gave considerable thought to this question and eventually decided to declare the provenance of his views on Nehru,[65] frankly admitting that 'to me his [Nehru's] image still glows.' Related to this was Gopal's particular approach to writing historical biography. His earlier studies had not emphasized the social and economic structures in which policy-makers functioned and which in turn were influenced by their decisions. But in his *Nehru* Gopal sought to place the man in the social and economic contexts of his time and demonstrate their impact on his thought and actions. He also strove to show how an individual, while remaining a product of his time, could shape the structures under which he operated. Of most consequence for generating a sense of the subject's weight was its author's view that the principal task of a historical biography was to use the life as a window to the times. 'The achievements of a country or society', he observed, 'cannot be epitomized in single persons.' The

[63] Sarvepalli Gopal, *Jawaharlal Nehru: A Biography* 1 (New Delhi: Oxford University Press, 1975).

[64] Cited in James Clifford, *Biography as an Art: Selected Criticism, 1590–1960* (London: Oxford University Press, 1962), pp. 40–3.

[65] Personal communication from Professor Romila Thapar.

study of the past was 'not a game of personalities but an analysis of the interaction of economic forces, social relations and thrusting as well as hegemonic ideas. In the evolution of these trends and patterns, representative and symbolic individuals may emerge, and a study of their leadership may cast some light on the whole.'[66]

These notions had first taken root in Gopal's mind during his encounter with heterodox British Marxist historiography, especially the work of Hill. Now in writing the life of Nehru he was strongly influenced by the biographical work of historians who owed some intellectual allegiance to the Marxist tradition. These included 'E.H. Carr on Bakunin, Christopher Hill on Cromwell, Edward Thompson on William Morris and, above all, Isaac Deutscher on Trotsky, Stalin and alas, the unfinished book on Lenin.' The form of historical biography that he admired attempted 'impersonal studies of personalities'.[67] Deutscher's celebrated three-volume biography of Trotsky provided a model. Gopal carefully re-read them, paying close attention to structure as well as style. Almost everyone who reviewed the Nehru biography complained that the man, as opposed to the statesman, never really came into focus. Gopal felt that this was true, but beside the point.

Biography and contemporary history nestled close in this approach. The best political biographies are those in which the biographer possesses a firm interpretive command over the political and historical terrain in which the subject operated. A thorough appreciation of the context and causalities that confronted the protagonist is indispensable to arriving at considered judgements. This, in turn, requires a high degree of development and sophistication in the historiography—a standard often difficult to meet when dealing with the contemporary period. Writing barely a decade after Nehru's death, this problem was considerably compounded for Gopal. No historical work on the Nehru years was worth the paper on which it was written. So, Gopal

[66] Sarvepalli Gopal, 'A Pot-Pourri', *The Book Review* 2:6 (November/December 1977).

[67] Ibid. Also see, idem, 'Science in India: New Vistas', *The Book Review*, 5: 5 (March/April 1981).

had practically to write the history of these years as well as the life of Nehru. This is one of the key reasons for the length of the project. Historians, with a few notable exceptions, tend to shy away from working on independent India. Gopal's *Nehru* dominates a virtually uncharted terrain and every scholar now tilling the field has to critically engage with it.

The other reason for the biography's persisting importance is the quality of Gopal's command over the sources. He had the benefit of untrammelled access to the Nehru papers, the bulk of which remain closed to most scholars even today. Gopal's was a deep and prolonged immersion in this cavernous archive. He was also able to access documents from the prime minister's secretariat and the foreign office. These were supplemented by research in foreign archives and interviews with Nehru's associates as well as wide and miscellaneous reading in contemporary periodicals and books. All this enabled Gopal to provide the most detailed and authoritative account of the public life of Nehru. Yet he did not get carried away by his treasure trove of untapped material. The three volumes of about 1000 pages are in fact a marvel of compression compared to the biographies of many a lesser (especially American) figure. Martin Gilbert, the leading biographer of Churchill, observed that Gopal's 'grasp of the detail of Nehru's story and its historical context was formidable, yet he never allowed it to overwhelm the narrative, or to obscure the interpretation.'[68]

The first volume begins with a brilliantly concise survey of the background to the emergence of Indian nationalism. Gopal paints a picture of British rule in India in the late nineteenth and early twentieth centuries that is at variance with his own earlier work on this period. Where he had previously empathized with the liberal strand of British policy, he now emphasizes the economic exploitation of India, the unwillingness to share power with progressive Indians, and the deliberate efforts to foster communal differences amongst Indians. Liberal statesmen he had earlier admired, including Gladstone, are now found wanting. There could be no better testimonial of the depth

[68] Personal communication from Sir Martin Gilbert. Churchill, of course, has all by himself spawned a whole biographical industry which has generated many thousands of pages.

of Gopal's liberalism, for few established historians have undertaken such a thorough revision of their own views. His willingness to do so is evidence of a rare intellectual openness and ability to engage with the work of younger, radical Marxist and Marxisant colleagues in Jawaharlal Nehru University on Indian economic history and nationalism, as well as the wider scholarship on the British empire.[69] It is equally evident that this volume was written to refute, if only indirectly, the Cambridge school interpretation of Indian nationalism as a grubby contest for the spoils of office. Gopal presents an acute and sensitive portrait of Nehru, tracing the competing pulls of his commitment to the ideals of freedom and anti-colonialism, of his desire to steer and uplift the ideology of the national movement, and of his emotional loyalty to and dependence on Gandhi.

The second and third volumes, dealing with the years 1947–56 and 1956–64, indicate a shifting of the biographer's preoccupations in tandem with his hero's career. International affairs and foreign policy are accorded pride of place in the second volume. Chapters on India's response to crises and conflicts in Kashmir, Korea, Tibet, Suez, and Hungary are topped up by a wide-ranging assessment of Nehru's approach to international problems. Gopal demonstrates unrivalled grasp of the diplomatic history of the Nehru years and demolishes an entire shanty town of myths and misinterpretations. By contrast, domestic political issues—the making of the constitution, the first general elections, internal struggles in the Congress party, challenges of governance, the movement for linguistic provinces—are given lower priority. This pecking order is maintained in the third volume, which has important chapters on Pakistan, Congo, Goa, and above all China. In contrast to its predecessor, though, this volume also deals at considerable length with the economic and social history of the period.[70]

[69] Among the latter, he was particularly impressed by the work of Eric Hobsbawm. Gopal had extended discussions with Hobsbawm during his visit to India in 1968 and also interviewed Hobsbawm for the Nehru biography. 'Notes of Interview with Hobsbawm', 8 January 1969, Gopal Papers.

[70] Sarvepalli Gopal, *Jawaharlal Nehru: A Biography* 3 (New Delhi: Oxford University Press, 1984).

In his choice of topics and treatment, Gopal stays close to Nehru's interests and attitudes. The effect, as Eric Stokes observed in a perceptive review, was akin to replaying 'a newsreel which had Nehru for camera man.'[71] This did not mean that he was uncritical or inclined to hagiography, for though he made no effort to conceal his admiration for Nehru's ideals and values, his assessments and judgements on the man could be trenchant and punitive. The even surface of his elegant and magisterial narrative is periodically punctuated by the sudden bolt of an astringent verdict. Of the young entrant to the national movement he says: 'There is, in all his letters of this time, the glow of virginal suffering and a complacent absence of reflection . . . He has made a cradle of emotional nationalism, and rocked himself in it.' Nehru's election to the presidency of the All India Congress Committee in 1929 is attributed to his being 'the malleable founder of the independence movement.' Indeed, Nehru 'was never happier than when under the influence of stronger characters.' And he 'drew sustenance from popular idolatry.' Unlike Gandhi, Nehru was not an original thinker. He was 'prone to be taken in too easily by glib thinking . . . and all too often his mind appeared in the grip of cliché.' Gopal made it clear that Nehru underestimated the importance of certain key issues in Indian politics: religion before independence, caste and language thereafter.

In international affairs, 'the warm, comfortable feeling of gratuitous virtue that underlay many of his speeches was irritating.' His economic policy comes in for severe criticism: 'from Nehru's efforts to build by stages a socialist utopia has emerged an India safe for businessmen to make profits in and for a new class of landlords to preserve its property and enforce social subordination.' Nehru's judgement of individuals was flawed. 'He had a weakness for flamboyant buccaneers . . . But even when his protégés were found out, Nehru was loath to discard them or take punitive action. Lack of care in selection was matched by lack of promptness in dismissal. His fidelity to his friends admitted of no question.' Taken all in all, if Nehru appeared a prophet frustrated,

[71] Eric Stokes, 'Jawaharlal Nehru in the Making', *Modern Asian Studies* 11:2 (1977), p. 295.

it was owing to 'the failures to follow up the courageous introduction of adult suffrage with a speedy enforcement of land distribution and tenancy reforms, a proper emphasis on education, a revision of the administrative apparatus and control of the population.' It is not surprising that Mrs Gandhi was somewhat disappointed by the product and felt that 'the biographer was not warm enough.'[72]

That said, the principal failing of the biography lies not in Gopal's adulation of Nehru but in his denigration of Nehru's colleagues and adversaries, regardless of their location in the political spectrum. Most often this stems from Gopal's propensity to see events and actions in the framework in which Nehru himself viewed them. In this sense, he was a thoroughgoing partisan unwilling to concede that some of Nehru's contemporaries may, on occasion, have got the measure of the man. In other cases, though, Gopal simply could not abide the individuals he so summarily disparaged. Whatever the species of bias, it skewed the narrative and called into question the reliability of his judgement.

Gandhi, for instance, is repeatedly presented as a 'conservative' on economic issues and his principal lieutenants—apart from Nehru—as 'proclaimed reactionaries'. Gandhi's resort to fasts apparently showed that his 'attitude was sheer revivalism against which cool thinking had no chance.' Subhas Bose was a 'dedicated yet egotistic, complicated, ill-fated being' who 'tended to see most events in relation to his own career.' Bose's autobiography is contrasted unfavourably with Nehru's: 'the ideas are jejune and the prose without flavour.' Jayaprakash Narayan was 'cross-grained, woolly-minded and exasperatingly self-righteous.' Rajendra Prasad is dispatched as 'of inferior intellectual quality and with a social outlook which belonged to the eighteenth century', and as 'prominent in the ranks of medievalism.' Kailas Nath Katju is scorned for his 'doddering ineptitude'. Nehru's cabinet colleagues after 1950 are collectively dismissed as 'mouldering mediocrities'. The harshest criticism is reserved for C. Rajagopalachari: 'deliberate perversity was a major facet of his intellectual arrogance'; 'a marked streak of linguistic bigotry'; 'inconsistency was to Rajago-

[72] H.Y. Sharada Prasad, 'Sons and Fathers', *Asian Age*, 24 April 2002.

pa-lachari [*sic*] always a cause of satisfaction'; the man had 'an attitude of cussed vindictiveness'. Gopal would later tone down or revise his views of many of the damned, but Rajagopalachari never rose in his estimation. His principal sin, in Gopal's reckoning, was to have supported the Muslim League's demand for self-determination in the early 1940s. The fact that he went on to become a prominent political opponent of Nehru's did not help his case. Reviewing a biography in 1997, Gopal would implausibly assert that 'Rajagopalachari, more than any single individual, made Partition of the country inevitable. This fact alone can never be forgotten or exonerate him.'[73]

Gopal's overarching purpose in the three volumes was not just to chart the transformation of Nehru from a 'dandified dilettante' to a leading statesman. Rather, he sought to underscore the continuing relevance of Nehru's central achievements: the preservation of national unity; the rooting of democracy and civil liberties in India; the emphasis on building a secular state; the introduction of economic-planning to realize an Indian version of socialism; and the adoption of a non-aligned foreign policy that at once advanced India's interests and fostered a world community. In so doing, Gopal was writing not just as a historian but as a citizen. The years that he worked on the Nehru volumes coincided with a dark phase in Indian democracy with Nehru's daughter at the helm. In a lecture delivered in 1979, Gopal noted that the 'developments of the two years from 1975 to 1977 have made the name of Nehru almost a dirty word in this country.'[74] He was concerned not merely about popular verdicts on the man, but the prospect of a wholesale abandonment of the ideals and aspirations that Nehru embodied.

X

The years of work on *Nehru* coincided with Gopal's tenure at Jawaharlal Nehru University. He was the first professor to be appointed

[73] Review of Rajmohan Gandhi's *Rajaji: A Life* in *The Hindu*, 7 December 1997.

[74] Sarvepalli Gopal, *The Mind of Jawaharlal Nehru* (New Delhi: Sangam Books, 1980), p. 2.

at the university's Centre for Historical Studies. Gopal's style of leadership was so informal and unbuttoned that it unsettled others used to traditional modes of hierarchy and deference. At his insistence, the faculty were all on first name terms irrespective of their location in the official pecking order. Gopal's approach to administrative and academic issues was democratic but also decisive. In faculty meetings he deployed his quiet wit to rein in the more aggressive colleagues and to defuse tensions when discussions reached the boiling point. He was closely involved in the Centre's attempts to frame an inter-disciplinary curriculum and to focus on new themes in Indian history. Under his leadership the centre attracted fine scholars and became a vibrant hub of research in the economic and social history of India.

His own chair in contemporary history, Gopal noted in his inaugural address, was the only one of its kind in India. But contemporary history was 'now being increasingly recognized in many parts of the world as a respectable branch of study.' The line between contemporary and modern history was admittedly 'a more artificial division than almost any other form of periodization and it is a moving line.' As a working definition, he suggested that it dealt with 'the immediate roots of the present and in that respect its student is on a conveyor-belt moving backwards.' A rough measure of when contemporary history began might be 'to date it from the time when official records are not open to scholars.'[75]

As part of his efforts to promote contemporary history, Gopal took keen interest in the acquisition of private papers for the National Archives and the Nehru Memorial Museum and Library. He also played a role in acquiring and hosting at his university the papers of the communist leader P.C. Joshi.[76] Perhaps his most important contribution was as editor of the *Selected Works of Jawaharlal Nehru*, a massive documentary collection (57 volumes and counting) that is

[75] 'The Formative Ideology of Jawaharlal Nehru', Inaugural address delivered at Jawaharlal Nehru University, 20 April 1976, Gopal Papers. An edited version was published under the same title in the *Economic & Political Weekly*.

[76] V. Ramakrishna, 'The Doyen of Indian Historians', *Frontline* 19: 9 (27 April–12 May 2002).

indispensable to every serious student of post-Independence India. In her preface to these volumes Indira Gandhi says they will only contain Nehru's personal correspondence, but Gopal ensured that the volumes on Nehru's years in office were packed with official letters, notes, and memoranda dealing with every aspect of policy and politics.

Although he exercised considerable influence at Jawaharlal Nehru University right to his retirement in 1983, Gopal shied away from senior administrative roles. On three occasions his name came up on the panel for vice-chancellorship, but each time he declined the nomination.[77] Similarly, whilst he liked interacting with students, he mostly found teaching onerous. Paradoxically, he could be a captivating lecturer. Each of his formal lectures was a performance: the effortless and unscripted delivery effectively masked the serious preparation that went into them. A student recalls his style in the classroom: 'At two minutes to nine one could hear him outside the door and lecture would begin sharp at nine. He would be crisp, clear and precise. In the middle of a lecture on historical method focusing on causation while we were deep into determinism or structuralism we would suddenly find that he had been finding his way towards a suitable note on which to conclude for the day. 9.50 and Professor Gopal would be out through the door.'[78]

During these years Gopal gradually began to emerge as a public intellectual. Like many individuals whose counsels are heard in the corridors of power, he preferred not to express his views on politics and policy in public or cold print. Three developments led him to shed his reticence. The first was the imposition of the Emergency by Mrs Gandhi. At the Indian History Congress session at Aligarh in 1975 Gopal moved the resolution opposing the Emergency, arguing that it was an assault on academic freedom. Then and later, several senior historians and academics were hesitant to come out so strongly against the government. For his quailing contemporaries, Gopal had nothing but contempt: in a letter to the *Times Literary Supplement* he

[77] K.N. Panikkar, 'Sarvepalli Gopal, 1923–2002', *Frontline* 19: 9 (27 April–12 May 2002).

[78] Vijaya Ramaswamy, 'Sarvepalli Gopal: 23 April 1923–20 April 2002', *The Book Review* 26: 6 (June 2002), p. 6.

dubbed them 'intellectual harlots'.[79] Gopal also played a leading role in organizing a representation by the academic community against the 42nd amendment to the constitution rammed through an emasculated parliament during the Emergency.

The second development was the move by the post-Emergency Janata government to withdraw three history textbooks published by the National Council of Education Research and Training (NCERT). Written by Romila Thapar, Bipan Chandra, Arjun Dev, Satish Chandra, and R.S. Sharma, these texts were held to be indulgent to the Muslim rulers, prejudiced against defenders of Hinduism, and worse, written by Marxist historians. The directive for withdrawal came from Prime Minister Morarji Desai, who thought that readers should not get 'wrong ideas about various elements of our history and culture'.[80] Gopal weighed in on this debate with a swingeing critique of the government's move, highlighting the dangers of rewriting history to suit the ideological purposes of the state and the importance of preserving academic freedom. Members of the ruling coalition, he noted, had attacked him in parliament as a fellow-traveller of communists. 'Marxist fellow historians will no doubt squirm to find me placed, however involuntarily, in their midst.' Yet the liberal historian put up a rousing defence of Marxist historiography. Marxism was 'a major intellectual influence in the world and throwing a *cordon sanitaire* round the Indian mind is not the answer. We need to have a dialogue with Marxism and not to suppress it . . . Without some Indian historians writing serious Marxist history, Indian historiography would be much the poorer.'[81] In the event, the Janata government did not last long enough to implement its decision. But the episode sensitized Gopal to the ideological and political resurgence of the Hindu Right, which gathered momentum in the years ahead.

[79] 'Inside India', *Times Literary Supplement* (1 July 1977), p. 804.

[80] For a detailed account of this controversy, see Michael Gottlob, *History and Politics in Post-colonial India* (New Delhi: Oxford University Press, 2011), pp. 18–27.

[81] Sarvepalli Gopal, 'The Fear of History', *Seminar* (January 1978), pp. 73–4.

Following from this was the third, and most important, development: the controversy over the Babri Masjid in Ayodhya. Gopal threw his weight behind a document, 'Political Abuse of History', which was signed by several leading scholars and which sought to set straight the historical record. Subsequently, he edited *The Anatomy of a Confrontation*, a collection of essays on the dispute. These were, he once confessed, 'depressing times'. Secularism was under siege, attacked not only by political forces of the Right but also by scholars who branded it an alien plant on Indian soil. In a series of essays and lectures delivered across India, Gopal sought to explain the origins and importance of secularism in the country.

In this period Gopal's own ideas on Indian secularism underwent a subtle evolution. Hitherto, he had adopted the high Nehruvian view which tended to equate secularism with state policy and practice: the removal of religion from public affairs, the separation of the state from all regions, and the granting of religious freedoms to all communities. Gopal now underlined the importance of another dimension of secularism. Secularism at this level had deep roots in Indian history and tradition. 'Secularism is more than laws, concessions and special considerations', he wrote in the preface to the volume on the Ayodhya controversy. 'It is a state of mind, almost an instinctive feeling, such as existed, by large for many centuries in India, when Hindus, Muslims, Christians and Parsis and followers of other faiths lived side by side in general harmony.'[82] Secularism at this level implied not the secularization of a multi-religious society but tolerance. This layered view of Indian secularism also stemmed from a larger project that Gopal was then pursuing—the biography of Radhakrishnan.

XI

'This is a son's book', wrote Gopal at the beginning of his biography of Radhakrishnan.[83] Indeed, Radhakrishnan himself had wanted Gopal

[82] Sarvepalli Gopal (ed.), *Anatomy of a Confrontation: The Rise of Communal Politics in India* (New Delhi: Viking, 1991).

[83] Sarvepalli Gopal, *Radhakrishnan: A Biography* (New Delhi: Oxford University Press, 1989).

to write his life. But the son did not rush into it, wondering 'whether I could curb my subjectivity enough to attempt writing this biography and I ultimately came to the conclusion that it was worth trying.'[84] The result was a triumph of the biographer's art, and Gopal's most satisfying biographical work.

As with the Nehru biography, Gopal situates Radhakrishnan's life in the larger historical context and uses the life to illuminate the times. The book is, in part, a study of cultural resistance to colonialism. The onslaught of colonialism had stripped bare 'the mind and spirit of the people': 'Bureaucrats, missionaries and racists were all finally on the same side.' In the struggle to salvage their identity and recover their dignity, the Indian people turned to tradition for solace and strength. Whilst tradition was often equated with belief and practice, at least some Indian intellectuals stressed the primacy of thought and philosophy. Given an educational system which was intended to service the lower bureaucracy and which frequently ended up producing 'half-and-half Indians', the best Indian thinkers understandably tried to 'revivify tradition with large doses of modernity'. The cultural response to colonialism, argues Gopal, was inherently political and prone to taking different forms. A seeming conformist might actually be subverting the colonial order. 'There were roads other than collaboration and direct resistance; and some of these feeder roads were invaluable, maybe even indispensable.'

Radhakrishnan began his career in this context and took one such road. He simultaneously advocated a return to the Vedantic corpus of Hinduism and openness to the modernity of the West. By emphasizing the spiritual and philosophical dimensions of religion, he sought to highlight the deeper unity that lay beneath the superficial differences between religions. A grasp of this underlying unity would, in turn, pave the way for a dialogic interaction amongst different faiths and cultures. Here lies the key to Gopal's mature reading of Indian secularism, one that emphasizes both state policy and an open-minded and creative engagement between cultures. The book traces the arc of Radhakrishnan's life from his humble origins in colonial India to his

[84] Letter to the editor of *The Indian Post*, 22 October 1989, Gopal Papers.

term as president of the republic. The Radhakrishnan that emerges from this biography stands alongside Gandhi, Tagore, and Nehru as one of India's great modern personalities.

The second half of the book, which deals with the post-Independence years, is richly informative on Indian and international politics of the period. The chapter on Radhakrishnan's tenure as ambassador in Moscow is easily the best available treatment of the early years of India's relations with the Soviet Union. Similarly, the account of Radhakrishnan's years as president is indispensable to understanding the tangled and shadowy politics after the successive demise of Nehru and Lal Bahadur Shastri. Gopal's assessments of Radhakrishnan's relations with his colleagues are for the most part judicious. Though he cannot resist side swipes at Rajendra Prasad ('stuffy and slow-going'), Abul Kalam Azad ('his preference for the education portfolio became a national disaster'), Indira Gandhi ('personal gratitude and general broadmindedness are not virtues to be expected of insecure prime ministers'), Radhakrishnan's former comrades in Madras ('the long line of extinct volcanoes'), and inevitably Rajagopalachari, the book differs from the Nehru biography in the attention paid to the private as well as public life of the subject. This is not just an 'impersonal study of personalities'. Taking on board the almost universal criticism for throwing a veil on Nehru the man, Gopal lays bare the inner recesses of Radhakrishnan's life. He begins by startling: Radhakrishnan was most probably born of an illicit relationship. He goes on to reveal the string of extra-marital relations in which Radhakrishnan indulged. 'Radhakrishnan', he writes, 'even enjoyed being double, a religious philosopher luxuriating in the company of women.' All this is narrated and analysed in an Olympian fashion. Only when discussing the death of his mother ('lacerated by his [Radhakrishnan's] non-marital wanderings') does Gopal's indignation seep through the carapace of detachment.

Gopal's candour drew, not unexpectedly, a good amount of ire and opprobrium from a prudish Indian audience. Why, several reviewers asked, was he sending the effigy of his father crashing from its plinth? *The Indian Post*, which published a review by M.V. Kamath, was inundated with hundreds of letters from readers who felt that Gopal had acted against all established norms of Indian culture and Hindu scriptures by holding fathers greater than gods. The editor joined the debate with a column that wondered whether 'we need to re-learn the lesson of objectivity'.[85] For once, Gopal responded to his critics. 'If what some of your correspondents describe as tenets of the Upanishads are to prevail', he wrote to the editor, 'then no proper biographical writing would be possible at all.' He added that Radhakrishnan had 'left me all his papers and would not have wanted me to be dishonest or conceal anything.' Rather than write hagiography, he had sought to portray Radhakrishnan 'not [as] a lifeless god or icon, but a very great human being, who, starting from below scratch, conquered his circumstances'. In the preface to the book, Gopal had claimed that he had 'shirked nothing'. Indeed, he had not—either as son or as scholar.

The book's central distinction is that it is exquisitely written. Always a careful stylist, here Gopal surpasses himself. The passages on Radhakrishnan's last years are poetic, luminous in their intensity. The 'late style' of writers and artists is meant to be marked by heightened levels of complexity.[86] This is not true of Gopal's prose, which in his father's biography is as limpid and pointed as a shard of glass. The term 'late style' is apposite in another way, though, for it turned out to be Gopal's last book.

In the remaining years Gopal stayed prominent in academic and public life. He continued to serve as general editor of the *Selected Works of Jawaharlal Nehru* and the *Towards Freedom* multi-volume documentary collection of the Indian side of the freedom struggle.[87] He was also one of the editors of UNESCO's *History of Humanity*. In fact, he had been elected to the board of UNESCO in the late 1970s and served for almost a decade. Owing to his association with UNESCO, Gopal frequently found himself in Paris and, despite

[85] 'Father and Son', *The Indian Post*, 23 September 1989.

[86] Edward W. Said, *On Late Style: Music and Literature Against the Grain* (London: Bloomsbury, 2006).

[87] The project was a counterpoint to the *Transfer of Power* volumes selecting documents from the imperial record under the chief editorship of Nicholas Mansergh.

his Anglo-Saxon orientation, came to admire prominent French intellectuals of this period: Sartre, de Beauvoir, and Foucault among others. Later, Gopal served as chairman of the Indian Institute of Advanced Study in Shimla (1993–8), the Institute of Social Sciences in Delhi (1995–8), and the Madras Institute of Development Studies (1995–7). Honours and awards poured in, including a DLitt from Oxford in recognition of his life's work and a Padma Vibhushan by the Indian government. But these years were beset by a prolonged illness which precluded all strenuous work. The valiant efforts of his wife, Indira, enabled him to write the occasional short essay or review until he succumbed on 20 April 2002.

His last published academic work was an article titled 'All Souls and India'.[88] This was a condensed version of two lectures that he had delivered as Chichele lecturer at All Souls in 1991. The lectures were characteristically well researched. In preparation, Gopal had written to Richard Bingle, the director of the India Office Library, for suggestions on archival material. He also worked through the Churchill archives at Cambridge and the Bodleian at Oxford. The lectures were a masterly survey of the involvement of the fellows of All Souls in the imperial project in India. They were also Gopal's final meditations on a subject that had been a central intellectual concern throughout his career: the nature of the Indo-British encounter. The choice of this theme for his valedictory essay was fitting. Gopal's own life encapsulated the ambiguities and complexities, the aches and tugs of this encounter.

XII

Looking back at Gopal's career, one is struck by the number of ways in which he stood out among his contemporaries. He was easily the most productive historian of his generation, writing no less than seven thoroughly researched books and scores of essays, apart from editing massive documentary collections. This is all the more remarkable when we recall that, formally, he began his academic career at the age of 43. Second, he was the pioneer in contemporary history and

[88] *Journal of Imperial and Commonwealth History* 27: 2 (May 1999), pp. 86–106.

the practitioner par excellence of the historical biography. Neither of these was fashionable in a rapidly professionalizing discipline that privileged the *longue durée* and deep structure, as well as economic and social history. Third, he was the only professional historian of his generation (and since) who had witnessed from close quarters politics and policy-making at the highest levels—an experience that lent considerable depth to his mature work. Gopal was also, alongside Ranajit Guha, the finest prose stylist among Indian historians, in great measure because, again like Guha, he was steeped in the literature of the language in which he wrote.[89] The historian, he believed, must aim to reach a large audience. This was one of the reasons why he chose biography as his mode of history—for biography has always held the widest appeal among the different ways of writing about the past. One measure of his success is the fact that every book of his was reviewed in the *Times Literary Supplement*. The desire for accessibility also reflected Gopal's larger conception of the role of the historian in public debates. The notion that the historian should act as a 'public educator' is not popular these days, but it was one that Gopal firmly held.

Gopal was, in sum, unique in being the great liberal historian of modern India, and arguably the finest. The unyielding commitment to liberal values in politics apart, his approach to history reflected a larger intellectual stance which a colleague describes as 'openness to ideas and other points of view, a faith in contestation in the domain of reason.'[90] He was a political historian who promoted economic and social history in his university and beyond; a biographer who stressed

[89] On account of their wide ideological divergence there is an irony in the similarity of this distinction that, one might have thought, neither would particularly want noticed. However, Ranajit Guha did in fact notice it. His review of an edited book includes this observation on Gopal's contribution: 'Take, for instance, S. Gopal's article, "Lord Curzon and Indian Nationalism, 1898–1905". This is easily the best piece of writing in the volume. But on a theme like this one has a right to expect more than a modicum of readable prose.' Ranajit Guha, 'The Movement for National Freedom in India', in idem, *The Small Voice of History: Collected Essays*, ed. Partha Chatterjee (Ranikhet: Permanent Black, 2009), p. 504.

[90] Sabyasachi Bhattacharya, 'He Made History Too', *Indian Express*, 25 April 2002.

the importance of studying structures and impersonal forces; a liberal historian who defended the contributions of Marxist historiography; a scholar who was open to revising his own ideas and approach in the light of criticism and fresh evidence.

The essays, addresses, and reviews collected in this volume reflect the range and diversity of Gopal's intellectual and political interests as well as his distinctive biographical approach to history. They are organized thematically in four sections. The first comprises his writings on the British empire in India, including essays on Gladstone, Curzon, Irwin, and Churchill. The second focuses on Nehru and his contemporaries, ranging from Tagore and Gandhi to de Gaulle and Edwina Mountbatten. The third brings together his writings and lectures on contemporary issues that continue to resonate today: democracy, secularism, language, and the use and abuse of history. The final section showcases Gopal's wider interests in science, literature, cricket, and travel.

Perhaps the most unusual piece herein is the diary he maintained during his trip to Israel in July 1973. The visit occurred, as it were, under the radar. For India had not accorded formal diplomatic recognition to Israel. The visit took place on the invitation of the Hebrew University of Jerusalem. In fact, Gopal had a standing invitation to visit Israel from 1967 on.[91] The date is significant. In the aftermath of the Arab–Israeli war of June 1967, Israel was keen to build bridges with India. During his visit Gopal was sought out by the Israeli government for his views on the possibility of developing bilateral ties. The diary shows Gopal as a curious, enthusiastic, and perceptive traveller. His observations on social divisions within Israel between the Ashkenazi and Sephardi Jews are shrewd. His views on Israel's settlement policy in the occupied territories are prescient. His assessment that 'there is hardly any hope of a settlement between Israel and Arabs' is accurate and timely. Exactly three months after Gopal's visit, the fourth Arab–Israeli war erupted.

[91] Daniel Argov to Gopal, 14 November 1967; Avraham Harman (President of Hebrew University) to Gopal, 30 May 1973; David Lazar to Gopal, 27 June 1973, Gopal Papers.

The writings and lectures gathered in this volume give us an excellent intellectual portrait of Gopal himself. The essayist speaks more forthrightly and personally, and over a wider and unexpected range of topics, than the historian. Gopal's personal and political convictions shine through more clearly here than in his major historical and biographical works. In these pieces we see Gopal as he really was: a complex man who was a scholar of the best type in being also a public intellectual and a committed liberal.

The purpose of this volume is to encourage the reader to engage afresh with Gopal's legacy, especially his two masterpieces—the biographies of Nehru and Radhakrishnan. In the world of academic history, Gopal is now a neglected figure. The reasons for this are not difficult to fathom. Political history is entirely out of fashion. In the years since Gopal wrote his major works, social and cultural historians have firmly occupied the centre ground of Indian history. A corollary to this is that the biographical approach to the writing of history remains unpopular. The advent of subaltern studies and post-colonial theory has meant that Gopal's work is regarded as unsophisticated. The snort of the theoretically-oriented scholar is audible, for instance, in Partha Chatterjee's review of the second volume of the Nehru biography, which claims that Gopal lacked 'the scientific apparatus' and 'theoretical reasoning' to throw real light on his subject.[92] Although the winds of theoretical fashion have since blown from different directions and contributed precious little to our understanding of early independent India, this unwarranted condescension towards Gopal's work persists. Also, contemporary history has failed to take off as a respectable academic discipline in India. With a handful of exceptions, scholars continue to toil in the fields of colonial and pre-colonial history. Finally, in the notoriously collectivist discipline of Indian history, Gopal did not found any 'school' that could carry forward his ideas and approach. He was too much of an individual and too short on self-importance to become a

[92] The review, originally published in 1979, is reprinted in Partha Chatterjee, *A Possible India: Essays in Political Criticism* (New Delhi: Oxford University Press, 1997), pp. 12–24.

guru. His work bore the watermark of his personality and style, and remains inimitable.

This situation of neglect is unlikely to last much longer. The methodological frontiers and temporal boundaries of history shift constantly. We are already witnessing a revival of narrative history, which ironically has now been adopted by scholars from the Subaltern Studies fold. Similarly, historians will sooner rather than later turn their attention to India after 1947. When they do, they will not avoid the political history of these years, so central has politics been to the fortunes of independent India. To those who hope to explain the history of these years without reference to the doings of political elites, one can only say 'good luck'. When future historians turn seriously to this period, they will have to grapple with the towering landmarks left behind by Gopal. This can already be seen in certain areas like diplomatic and international history, where his work has become the starting point for any substantial inquiry. If this welcome trend continues and intensifies, then Sarvepalli Gopal seems sure to come into his own again.

PART I

The British Empire in India

1

Gladstone and India

While many books and monographs have been written on almost every aspect of Gladstone's thought and activity, his views on India have suffered neglect. Morley, in his *Life of Gladstone*, made no reference to them. Professor Paul Knaplund, in his book on *Gladstone and Britain's Imperial Policy*,[1] has almost nothing to say about India. Dr Shannon, in a book published a few years ago,[2] goes so far as to say that Gladstone had no views on the subject. 'India seems hardly to have entered his thoughts.'[3] It is true that Gladstone was too preoccupied with, first Italy, and then Ireland, to give much sustained attention to India. Yet he never completely forgot her. One can trace, down the years, an interest and a point of view which had been carefully thought out; and this interest and viewpoint, because they were Gladstone's, had an influence on British policy in India.

Gladstone's attention seems to have been first drawn to India by the fortuitous circumstance that the subject for the Newdigate Prize in 1831, Gladstone's last year at Oxford, when he was twenty-two years of age, was *The Suttee*. Morley refers to an unsuccessful entry for the Newdigate Prize in 1829 but makes no mention of any second effort. Gladstone does not seem to have submitted a poem in 1831; but among the Gladstone Papers in the British Museum there is to

[1] London, 1927.

[2] R.T. Shannon, *Gladstone and the Bulgarian Agitation 1871* (London, 1963).

[3] Ibid., p. 8.

be found a draft of a poem on *The Suttee.*[4] It is clear that this was not meant to be the final version. It is not, in fact, good poetry; but it is of interest as indicating the early development of Gladstone's views on India. The poem runs into about 170 lines, but it is necessary to quote only a few lines as illustrative of Gladstone's outlook. A *sati* is a Hindu widow who immolates herself on her husband's funeral pyre. This practice of immolation, which had become a part of Hinduism in its days of decadence, was declared illegal by the governor general, Lord William Bentinck, in 1820. Gladstone, in his poem, first writes of the unity of mankind:

And voice serene of heav'ns unfading years
. . . gave to Time, his earth and sky and sea,
One frame divine, one living harmony.

Gladstone then commends the motives of the Hindu widow and asserts that she was not being forced to be a *sati* but was acting voluntarily:

She sate resolve—in death
Seal'd with a spouse's blood a spouse's faith,
And strove, nor vainly strove her soul, to prove
Tho' strong were torture, stronger yet was love.

Finally, Gladstone pays tribute to Bentinck:

Bentinck! 'Twas thine the bloodless crown to win
Proud victor over deeds of death and sin!
Spirit of England's fame, no longer dim,
A voice of thunder, thou didst speak in him,
Echoed the glad command from shore to shore
And murder's ghastly flame ascends no more!

These three strands: an assertion that all men were equal, an appreciation of the motives and sentiments of Indians, and an acceptance of British duties and obligations, together formed Gladstone's outlook on India throughout his public life.

[4] Add. Mss. 44721, folios 121 to 125, Gladstone Papers.

For many years after 1831, however, India seems to have faded from Gladstone's view; and the mind of the young Member of Parliament, when it looked beyond England, was seized of problems concerning other parts of the empire than India. Indeed, the promise of the Newdigate draft poem was shadowed by speeches in which Gladstone used the standard language of imperialism. For example, in 1837, speaking of Canada, he said: 'the time when a separation on the part of Canada might be beneficial had not certainly arrived at the present period, when her population was divided into two parties of different origin, and inflamed by their passions into continual collisions with each other. In this state of things, this country was enabled by her power to act as a mediator and umpire, and thus prevented contests which might be found still more fatal.'[5] On the other hand, he condemned the Opium Wars in China and appealed, to quote his words in the House of Commons in March 1857, 'to that which is older than Christianity, because it was in the world before Christianity—to that which is broader than Christianity, because it extends in the world beyond Christianity—and to that which underlays Christianity, for Christianity itself appeals to it,—I appeal to that justice which binds man to man.'[6]

In fact, in most problems concerning Britain's relations with other peoples, Gladstone was in these early years feeling his way; and India was no exception. 'The test of a good colonial policy', he stated in a memorandum written sometime during the years 1848 to 1850, 'is that it shall prepare colonies for independence and self-government; as it is the test of a good academy or college, that it shall prepare its pupils for the world.'[7] Nor was Gladstone inclined to apply this test only to colonies inhabited by people of the British race. He declared in parliament in June 1858, at a time when public opinion in Britain had been inflamed by reports of atrocities in India and the whole basis of British rule in India was being re-examined, that the British went to India not to become Indians and settle there permanently but to

[5] 22 December 1837, *Hansard*, vol. xxix, 1454.

[6] *Hansard*, vol. cxliv, 1799.

[7] Add. Mss. 44738, folio 247, Gladstone Papers.

remain strangers with the only duty of bringing forward Indians; and any such advance, if it were to be a true advance, should not be limited to social progress but should also envisage political development.[8] He stated this more explicitly in a private memorandum written a month later, in July 1858. The object, he wrote, of the Crown taking over the administration of India was 'to promote the practical equality before the law of the native population with the British, and to open to them impartially according to merit the honours and rewards of Government. India is to be governed for India; and as far as may be found practicable it is to be governed by India.'[9]

How was this to be done? Gladstone from the start placed his faith primarily, not in institutions or organization, but in man. He thought little more was required than to send out from Britain the right type of persons to govern India. His first experience in cabinet strengthened this view. In 1845 the governor general, Lord Ellenborough, annexed the province of Sind without securing the assent of either the British government or the court of directors of the East India Company. The Peel ministry reluctantly acquiesced in the annexation but could not prevent the directors from recalling Ellenborough for insubordination in this and other matters.[10] Gladstone saw in this further proof of the necessity of having reliable men at the head of the Indian administration. 'It may almost, I think', he wrote in 1847 to Dalhousie, who had served under Gladstone at the Board of Trade and had been nominated to the governor-generalship, 'be said that there is but one thing that can be done here for India, namely to send *just* and able men to govern it.'[11]

This weightage given by Gladstone to character in the viceroy was, to him, justified by the events of 1857 and 1858. In those years

[8] *Hansard*, vol. cl, 1621.

[9] Add. Mss. 44747, folio 180ff., Gladstone Papers.

[10] S. Gopal, 'Lord Ellenborough and the Home Authorities 1843–44', *Proceedings of the Indian Historical Records Commission*, 1953, pt II, pp. 32–5.

[11] Lee-Warner, *Proceedings of the Indian Historical Life of the Marquis of Dalhousie* (London, 1904), vol. I, p. 94.

of mutiny and revolt, the governor general was Gladstone's close friend, Charles Canning; and the high statesmanship of Canning in disregarding the fierce clamour for reprisals and asserting British power without surrender to vindictiveness delighted Gladstone. When in 1862, soon after his return to Britain, Canning died, Gladstone wrote, 'Few men have had such an opportunity as he had in India—of witnessing and striving for the things dearest to God, for justice, mercy and truth; fewer still have so used it.'[12] And over thirty years later, in 1895, Gladstone, looking back over the half century of British rule in India in his time, stated that Canning was the greatest viceroy he had ever known.[13]

Alongside Gladstone's interest in the social and political development of India under British guidance, which forms a consistent strand in his thought from 1831 to 1894, there was his deep interest in imperial finance. Hammond observed that Gladstone had Ireland in his heart, but he had in his brain a disturbing element of England, and of Treasury England.[14] The remark is pertinent to his attitude to India as well. He was convinced that the finances of India were mismanaged, and it was at his instance that Samuel Laing was sent out to India as Finance Member in 1860 to try to introduce sound principles of public finance.[15] Since Laing achieved little, Gladstone frequently, and throughout his years in office, suggested the extension of the principles of treasury control to Indian finances by the appointment of a treasury official to the India Council, the body of expert advisers attached to the secretary of state for India. He believed that it was essential to import British rules and ideas into Indian disbursement.[16] Gladstone

[12] P. Knaplund (ed.), *The Gladstone–Gordon Correspondence 1851–1896* (The American Philosophical Society, 1961), p. 41.

[13] Cited by Sir A. Godley to Lord Elgin, 19 September 1895, Mss. Eur. F.84, correspondence with persons in England, vol. 2, 114, Elgin Papers, India Office Library.

[14] J.L. Hammond, *Gladstone and the Irish Nation* (London, 1938), p. 86.

[15] Gladstone to Canning, 18 October 1860, volume of letters from ministers, 41, Canning Papers (in the possession of the Earl of Harewood).

[16] See, for example, his letter to Lord Kimbuley, 28 August 1893, E/6a, Kimbuley Papers (in the possession of the present Earl of Kimbuley).

was also concerned to relieve the British taxpayer, whom he regarded as burdened unduly by the liabilities of India. This worried him from the time the Crown took over from the East India Company the administration of India. 'The subject of English liability', he wrote in a private memorandum of 22 July 1859, 'for the charges of the Government of India is one of the most formidable ever introduced to the notice of Parliament.'[17] In 1867, when the allocation of expenses for the British expedition to Abyssinia was being debated, he commended the efforts to establish, in place of the existing system of 'give and take' between the two countries, a greater strictness of account and a greater definiteness of relation.[18]

By the time Gladstone formed his first government in 1868, he was too preoccupied with Ireland to take any direct interest in India. Indeed, if he thought of India at all it was as the country which provided the model for tenancy legislation in Ireland. In 1869, Sir George Campbell, the chief commissioner of the Central Provinces in India, visited Ireland and wrote a small book suggesting that the Bengal Tenancy Act of 1858, which recognized a right of occupancy for tenants and provided for compensation for improvements, could serve as a precedent for Ireland.[19] Morley revealed much later, in a private letter to Lord Ampthill in 1906,[20] that this book of Campbell first inspired the thought underlying the Irish Land Act of 1870, which recognized the tenant's right of occupancy in the form of a right to compensation for disturbance under certain circumstances. But apart from this, India did not figure at all in policy-making in London. Even the choice of the viceroy in 1869 was not Gladstone's; for the Disraeli government had, in their last days, appointed Lord Mayo as viceroy, and though Gladstone had considered cancellation of the appointment, he had refrained from doing so; and in India Mayo had carried out what was very much his own policy.[21]

[17] Add. Mss. 44748, folio 108, Gladstone Papers.

[18] *Hansard* (3rd Series), vol. cxc, 390ff.

[19] *The Irish Land* (London, 1869).

[20] 9 January 1906, Mss. Em. E. 233, vol. 13, Ampthill Papers, India Office Library.

[21] Sarvepalli Gopal, *British Policy in India 1858–1905* (Cambridge, 1965), p. 64.

The first viceroy appointed by Gladstone was Lord Northbrook in 1872. 'My own desires', Gladstone wrote to Northbrook soon after the latter's arrival in India, 'are chiefly these, that nothing may bring about a sudden, violent or discreditable severance, that we may labour steadily to promote the political training of our native fellow-subjects, and that when we go, if we are ever to go, we may leave a good name and a clean bill of account behind us.'[22] This, in a sentence, was the India policy of Gladstone; that while British rule might possibly be permanent, it was the chief duty of the British not to ensure that permanence but to train Indians to assume political responsibility. Gladstone believed, as did others like Macaulay and Munro before him, that the chief objective of an alien administration should be the teaching of its subjects to exercise authority. But Northbrook was hardly the man for the promotion of such a policy. A withdrawn and indeterminate personality, he sought to keep India static and to make no changes that were not absolutely necessary. Gladstone, as was to be expected, approved of Northbrook's decision to repeal the income tax which had been introduced by Mayo;[23] but on the other hand Gladstone was surprised at Northbrook's resistance—after the first Gladstone ministry had resigned—to the abolition of tariffs and the restoration of free trade.[24]

All in all, Gladstone's first term as prime minister had seen little advance in the furtherance of his views on India. Mayo and Northbrook had not shared them. They had been more concerned with maintaining the empire than with training Indians in public life and administration; and Gladstone had made no effort to assert his own principles. But when the Liberal Party was in opposition, the policies of the Disraeli government, and especially of the viceroy, Lord Lytton, revived Gladstone's sense of obligation to India.

In 1875, while he declared his displeasure at the British propensity to push financial generosity towards India beyond the bounds of

[22] 15 October 1872, Mss. Eur. C144, vol. 20, pt I, p. 74, Northbrook Papers, India Office Library.

[23] Ibid.

[24] Gladstone to Northbrook, 20 September 1875, Mss. Eur. C 144, vol. 23, folio 248ff., Northbrook Papers.

reason and justice, he stressed that unless British presence in India was beneficial to the people of India, the British had no business there at all.[25] Speaking in March 1876 on the Royal Titles Bill, he referred to the imperial power in India as 'that vast and curiously constructed fabric of which we are the stewards, and which it is our duty to maintain so long as any obligation connected with that power remains to be fulfilled.'[26] It was what seemed to be a gross abuse of this power by Lytton in passing the Vernacular Press Act that led Gladstone to raise the matter in the House of Commons in July 1878. Lytton's government had suspended the standing orders of the Indian legislature, secured approval by telegraph from the secretary of state and, in the course of a single day, enacted a measure imposing stringent restrictions on newspapers published in Indian languages. Gladstone condemned the Press Act as a betrayal of trust. He believed that the sole justification for British rule in India would be that India was ruled in the interests of the Indians and not of the British. The people of India, he said, realized this and that was why, despite sporadic dissent, their attitude was basically loyal. However, Lytton and his masters acted on the premise that the people of India resented British rule; and this was the basic flaw in their policy.[27] The issues involved in the Vernacular Press Act seemed to Gladstone of such importance that he insisted that the House vote on them.

Soon after, Gladstone expounded in detail his conception of England's mission in India. He emphasized the difficulties of the task. The British were in India travelling on a journey to which honour and duty inexorably bound them but on a route which plainly led into the unknown. It was 'a tutelage, unexampled in history'. Over a large population inhabiting a vast territory, the British held 'a dominion entirely uncontrolled, save by duty and by prudence, measured as we may choose to measure them.' But this dominion was exercised by a very few officials, and in Britain there was little interest. But the truth as to India could not too soon be understood. The Conservatives treated

[25] *Hansard* (3rd Series), vol. ccxxv, 1499.
[26] *Hansard* (3rd Series), vol. ccxxvi, 1759.
[27] *Hansard* (3rd Series), vol. ccxlii, 48ff.

India as a possession to be defended. Whereas in fact it was a trust to be fulfilled. If the masses of India could be convinced that the British were in their country with a mission and not merely to further their own interests, then there would be a chance of consolidating British rule. Indeed, this would form the best defence of the empire.[28]

In the Midlothian campaign of 1879 and 1880, Gladstone called upon British electors to choose between these rival conceptions of foreign and imperial policy; and he made the war in Afghanistan, on which the Conservative government had embarked, and Lytton's administration of India two of the main issues of contention. The Afghan war Gladstone described as, among other things, unjust, foolish, frivolous, dangerous and wanton, and he said the pulpit rather than the platform was the proper place from which to condemn it. He asserted that all men, British or Afghan, were equal and had the same rights and that in Afghanistan the British were in conflict with the sentiment of a free people. As for Lytton's administration, 'I cannot tell you', said Gladstone, 'how dishonouring to England I consider to have been the government of India during the last three years.' He accused Disraeli and Lytton of having failed to fulfil Britain's task in India—'the most arduous and perhaps the noblest truest that ever was undertaken by a nation.' The assumption of the higher title of Empress of India should have been accompanied by an increase of franchise or of privilege, by augmentation of benefits and by redress of grievances. Instead, the Indian people had been distrusted, the press had been gagged and funds, raised ostensibly for famine relief, had been spent on a ruinous war. By these means, said Gladstone, the Conservatives had impaired the foundations of the Empire and had forsaken their duty 'to consecrate the Empire to the Almighty by the strict application of the principles of justice and goodwill, of benevolence and mercy.'[29]

So in the four years of Lytton's viceroyalty Gladstone put forward the same principles which had inspired his Newdigate Prize poem

[28] 'England's Mission', *The Nineteenth Century*, September 1878, pp. 578, 580.

[29] *Political Speeches in Scotland* (Edinburgh, 1880), two vols.

of 1831—that the peoples of India and Asia had the same rights as those of Britain and Europe, that the sentiments and needs of the Indian people should be respected, and that Britain had a mission in India. These principles had by now become the policy to which the Liberal Party was committed and, with the Liberal victory in the 1880 elections, the policy to which the new government were committed. This was certainly the way in which Indian opinion regarded it, and Gladstone was aware of this. 'I know', he told the electors of Midlothian, 'the news of these elections has passed to India, reached the mind and the heart of many millions of your Indian fellow-subjects and I will venture to say that it has gladdened every heart among them.'[30] The new viceroy, therefore, would be regarded as the personal representative of Gladstone, sent out to give expression and effect in India to the new temper and energy of British Liberalism. So the selection of the right man seemed to the prime minister of more importance than ever, and it was only as a third choice that he selected Ripon, a man who deserved well of the Liberal Party but had irritated Gladstone by becoming a Roman Catholic.[31]

Ripon, however, was the right choice in so far that he wholeheartedly shared Gladstone's views. He withdrew British troops from Afghanistan and established friendly relations with its ruler. Acting on what was virtually a specific mandate from the prime minister, he repealed Lytton's Vernacular Press Act. Gladstone also suggested to Ripon that he should amend the Arms Act of 1878, which stipulated that no Indian could possess firearms without a license, for Gladstone believed that such special laws restricting the possession of firearms indicated, as did the Vernacular Press Act, a lack of trust in the people. But, despite the prime minister's support, Ripon's amending bill was smothered by official resistance.

This failure of Ripon to have his way on the Arms Act was a warning of what was to come in his handling of more important issues. The Afghan settlement and the repeal of the Press Act were only

[30] 2 April 1880, W.E. Gladstone, *The Midlothian Campaign* (Edinburgh, 1880), p. 194.

[31] Sarvepalli Gopal, *The Viceroyalty of Lord Ripon* (Oxford, 1953), pp. 2–3; Sarvepalli Gopal, *British Policy*, p. 129.

part of what Gladstone termed the 'great undoing process which the late Government bequeathed to us.'[32] When Ripon proceeded to undertake constructive measures, his efforts were virtually destroyed by lack of resolution. The viceroy sought to strengthen local self-government in the hope that it would serve as a means of political education, promote self-confidence among the educated classes of India, and train them for participation in government. Ripon thought also that the gradual admission of Indians to a larger influence in the administration, and a training to exercise that influence, would do more to secure the continuance of British rule in India than any policy of repression. It was not merely, therefore, the duty of Britain, but in her interest, to train educated Indians for public life and seek their support. Gladstone was cordially in favour of this policy of local self-government. It was in accordance with his theory that local responsibilities prepare men for national tasks; as he phrased it, it is liberty alone which fits men for liberty.[33] He was in sympathy also with Ripon's belief that the support of educated Indians would strengthen British rule and with the doctrine that it was Britain's duty to train Indians for self-government. 'We are pledged to India', he wrote to Ripon,[34] 'I may say to mankind, for its performance; and we have no choice but to apply ourselves to the accomplishment of the work, the redemption of the pledge, with every faculty we possess.' But Ripon's local self-government policy was not a great success. The officials showed little enthusiasm and Indians, while they appreciated the spirit of Ripon's endeavour, displayed scant interest. The policy only served to frighten the British community in India as being one more effort to introduce into India what they regarded as the subversive principles of Gladstone.

Ripon's government then introduced a bill removing racial discrimination in the sphere of criminal jurisdiction. Indian judges in the districts, i.e. outside the towns, were disqualified from hearing cases in which the accused were Europeans; and the government sought

[32] 13 March 1882, cited in Gopal, *British Policy*, p. 145.

[33] Letter to W.E. Forster, 12 April 1882, John Morley, *Gladstone*, vol. 3, p. 58.

[34] 24 November 1881, cited in Gopal, *British Policy*, p. 147.

to remove this anomaly. There was an immediate storm of protest, not so much because this was a major matter, as because it formed a convenient issue round which the British community's dislike of Ripon and of Gladstone could crystallize. To ignore and overcome the opposition would, of course, have been the right thing to do. Gladstone told Ripon that his interest in the matter was great and that his 'prejudice or conviction as to principles' was wholly and warmly with the viceroy—'wholly as to my understanding of the general view; warmly because in that general view great interests of the future seem to me to be at stake.'[35] But again Ripon showed himself lacking in determination. He believed in Gladstone's ideals but lacked Gladstone's moral stamina and reserve of underlying strength. Setting aside considerations of principle, he offered to reduce the scope of the bill. The prime minister was not pleased with this anxiety to compromise. He assured Ripon that he would accept whatever the viceroy decided, because it was for him to deal with the matter; but, Gladstone added, 'There is a question to be answered; where, in a country like India, lies the ultimate power, and if it lies for the present on one side but for the future on the other, a problem has to be solved as to preparation for that future, and it may become right and needful to chasten the saucy pride so apt to grow in the English mind towards foreigners, and especially toward foreigners whose position has been subordinate.'[36] Gladstone could never find any justification for racial arrogance; and he wrote to his son Henry, who was at this time in Calcutta and was one of the three or four Englishmen who supported the bill, that he had no patience with the 'narrow and domineering' spirit of the British community in India.[37]

On learning of Gladstone's staunch views on the subject, Ripon, in his weakness, sought to transfer responsibility to the Home Government; and he asked the cabinet either to take a decision on the bill or to submit the matter to the House of Commons. Gladstone

[35] 1 January 1883, Add. Mss. 43515, no. 26, Ripon Papers, British Museum. The number of the manuscript is as of 1951, when the papers were consulted.

[36] 17 April 1883, cited in Gopal, *British Policy*, p. 151.

[37] 6 February 1884; see F.W. Hirst, *Gladstone as Financier and Economist* (London, 1931), ch. xix.

sharply refused to do either. The cabinet was unanimous and firm in its general support of Ripon and the prime minister repeatedly gave expression to this in the House. But he was unwilling to go beyond such assurances of confidence in the viceroy and to take a specific decision on pending Indian legislation. In fact, the question was not even brought up before a full meeting of the cabinet. The principle, said Gladstone,[38] was beyond dispute; what was under discussion was a problem of Indian administration which had been initiated in India and should be settled there. Ripon could not therefore evade a decision, and virtually surrendered to the opposition. The bill was so modified as to become almost meaningless. Because of the personal failure of the viceroy, the principles of Gladstonian Liberalism suffered a severe reverse in India.

Ripon's successor was also chosen by the Gladstone government; but Dufferin was only nominally a Liberal and he had no intention, as he described it,[39] of 'Midlothianizing' India. Gladstone too had, in these years, no time for Indian details; and the experiment of administering India according to his principles, which had begun under such favourable auspices in 1880, petered out into insignificance.

However, in the years that followed, Gladstone was able to perform a few minor services for India. Dufferin had suggested that the legislative councils in India should be given the right of interpellation and authority to discuss the budget, and that the principle of election, in however dilute a form, should be utilized in the formation of these councils. The Salisbury government were opposed to this, and even Northbrook, who had served as one of Gladstone's viceroys, advised against any such legislation lest Indian and Irish politics get mixed and Gladstone use what Northbrook termed 'dangerous' language.[40] Finally, in 1892, for fear that if Gladstone returned to office he

[38] Gladstone to Granville, 28 September 1883, and Granville to Gladstone, 10 October 1883, A. Ramon, *The Political Correspondence of Gladstone and Granville 1876–86* (Oxford, 1962), vol. 2, nos. 1106 and 1107.

[39] To Sir Fitzjames Stephen, 28 July 1885, reel 525, Dufferin Papers (microfilm copy), India Office Library.

[40] Northbrook to Lansdowne, 1 March 1889, Mss. Eur. D558, series viii, vol. 1, pt I, no. 42, Lansdowne Papers, India Office Library.

might introduce a far more radical measure, the Salisbury ministry went ahead with legislation for Indian Council reforms. Their bill authorized the Government of India to nominate non-officials 'on the basis of recommendations' and empowered the authorities in India to make rules enabling the discussion of the annual budget and the asking of questions. The Indian National Congress, which had been formed some years earlier as the organization of politically conscious Indians, sent to Britain a delegation which sought Gladstone's support for the introduction of the principle of elections.[41] Gladstone promised to help, and his speech in the House was cleverly designed to secure this. He did not criticize the government for failing to provide explicitly for elections and assumed that the term 'nomination on the basis of recommendations' was a euphemism for elections. It would not, he said, be well or wise for parliament to proceed to particulars. 'It is not our business to devise machinery for the purpose of Indian Government; it is our business to give ample information as to what we believe to be sound principles of government . . . What I wish is that these first steps shall be genuine, and whatever amount of scope they give to elective principle shall be real. What we want is to get to the real heart and mind—at the most upright sentiment and the most enlightened thought of the people of India. We may be justified in expecting something more than a merely nominal beginning in this great and magnificent undertaking.'[42] Gladstone's speech delighted the government in that it had prevented a division in the House; but it satisfied Indian opinion in that it drew from the government a commitment to the principle of elections.

In 1892 Gladstone was back as prime minister. Lord Lansdowne, the viceroy, described it as 'a very serious misfortune' for India, because he expected Gladstone to resume his efforts of the1880s.[43] In fact, Gladstone's mind was far from India. He sent out as viceroy an unimaginative person, Lord Elgin, primarily on the ground that he

[41] S.N. Banerjea, *A Nation in Making* (Calcutta, 1963), p. 105.

[42] 28 March 1892, *Hansard* (4th Series), vol. iii, 78ff.

[43] Lord Cross, 19 July 1892, Mss. Eur. D.558, Correspondence with Secretary of State, vol. 4, pt II, no. 33, Lansdowne Papers.

was a close friend of Lord Rosebery. There was only one occasion when Gladstone in his last term showed a flicker of interest in India. It had for long been a demand of the Indian National Congress that examinations for recruitment to the Indian Civil Service should be held both in Britain and in India, so as to enable more Indians to compete and qualify without having to travel overseas. In 1893 the Liberal back-benchers in the House of Commons took the whips by surprise and passed a resolution recommending that examinations be held simultaneously in both countries. Gladstone desired that the Government of India should be warned against displaying a hostile spirit to this resolution.[44] He seems to have been genuinely anxious to meet the wishes of the House and of the Congress; but it was commonly believed that he wished merely to appease all sections of the Liberal Party in order to ensure the success of his Irish Home Rule Bill. 'When', wrote the Earl of Argyll to Lansdowne,[45] 'shall we get rid of this fanatical octogenarian, who has no interest in the future? He never did care for India, and, I *suspect*, would argue in private that it does us no good to keep it!'

Gladstone did not achieve much in India. The viceroys selected by him were men of slight calibre; and he himself was preoccupied elsewhere. Nor did he modify his ideas on finance even during Ripon's term. No critic of the Disraeli government had been more vehement in condemning British aggression in Afghanistan and the foisting of unnecessary expenditure on the Indian treasury; but when in office he was unwilling to sanction more than five million pounds as a grant from the British exchequer[46]—a sum which was less than half the total expenditure. In 1882 the Government of India were directed to despatch at their cost a contingent of troops to Egypt. When Ripon in India and Henry Fawcett in London protested, Gladstone yielded

[44] Gladstone to Kimbuley, 3 June 1893, vol. E/6a, Kimbuley Papers.

[45] 14 June 1893, Mss. Eur. D.558, series viii, vol. 5, pt I, no. 58, Lansdowne Papers.

[46] Gladstone to Lord Hartington, 23 October 1880 and 8 February 1881, and Hartington to Gladstone, 9 February 1881, Add. Mss. 44145, folios 135, 200, and 202, Gladstone Papers.

only to the extent of sanctioning a grant of £500,000 out of a total expenditure of nearly £1.3 million; and he silenced Ripon and Fawcett in order to secure a majority in the House on what he treated as a vote of censure.[47]

But despite the lack of results and his rigidity in financial matters, Gladstone succeeded in winning the confidence and affection of the Indian people. The experiment in Ripon's time to govern India in accordance with Gladstone's principles came, in practical terms, almost to nothing; but the immediate failure led to a later and more eventful triumph. For it kept alive the conviction that political and social advance in India should be a co-operative adventure of the rulers and the ruled. The emotional memory of Gladstonian Liberalism remained a prominent and a fertile element of the Indian scene right down to our own times.

[47] Fawcett to Gladstone, 15 September 1882, Add. Mss. 44156, folio 139, Gladstone Papers; Gopal, *Ripon*, p. 217, vol. ii, no. 1072; Gladstone's speech, 27 July 1883, *Hansard* (3rd Series), vol. cclxxxii, 806ff.; Gladstone to Granville, 28 July 1863, in A. Ramon *The Political Correspondence of Gladstone and Granville 1876–86.*

2

Lord Curzon and Indian Nationalism

Lord Curzon had been anxious, from the start of his public career, to be Viceroy of India. He was captivated by the allurements and the demands of the post, and he believed that he was destined to hold it. But Curzon was not inspired solely by personal ambition; he had also a sense of mission in India. He was convinced that it was the duty, 'laid on Englishmen from on high',[1] to maintain the Indian empire, which was 'the miracle of the world',[2] 'the biggest thing that the English are doing anywhere in the world.'[3] Curzon was also honest enough to recognize that this empire was of advantage to Britain. 'As long as we rule India we are the greatest Power in the world. If we lose it, we shall drop straight away to a third-rate Power.'[4] So duty and interest taken together made him

> an Imperialist heart and soul. Imperial expansion seems to me an inevitable necessity and carries a noble and majestic obligation. I do not see how any Englishman, contrasting India as it is with what it was or might have been, can fail to see that we came here in obedience to what I call the decree of Providence for the lasting benefit of millions of the human race. We often make great mistakes here; but I do firmly believe that there is

[1] Curzon to Sir Denzil Ibbetson, Member of the Viceroy's Council, 26 April 1904, vol. 209, pt ii, no. 1233, Curzon Papers, India Office Library.

[2] Curzon to Sir Francis Younghusband, 19 September 1901, vol. 182, pt ii, no. 23, Curzon Papers.

[3] Curzon to Balfour, 31 March 1901, vol. 181, pt ii, no. 211, Curzon Papers.

[4] Ibid.

no Government in the World [*sic*] that rests on so secure a moral basis, or is more fiercely animated by duty.[5]

Curzon was aware that 'a sort of national feeling' was slowly growing up in India; and he added, 'I sometimes wonder whether a hundred years hence we shall still be ruling India.' But he saw no reason why British rule should not continue indefinitely. He did not believe that the purpose of an alien administration was to prepare for its own withdrawal. India could be held by convincing the mass of the people that British rule was juster, purer and more beneficent than either any other foreign rule or the rule of Indians themselves. The viceroy should act as a benevolent despot, going everywhere, seeing everything, and treating his subjects with sympathetic impartiality. The government should secure the support of the loyal elements in the community, pursue the path of unwavering justice, redress grievances and anomalies wherever found, make British authority essential to the people by reason of its combined probity and vigour, insist upon a juster and more generous recognition of India by Britain, and perpetually build bridges over the gulf that separated the Indians and the British.[6]

To Curzon, therefore, the task of the Indian viceroyalty was essentially one of administration. To use his own phrase, he energized the government all along the line; and he raised the standards in every department of public affairs. He had no high opinion of Indians: 'They are very strange people, these natives; they have such an extraordinary respect for strength of decision and action that, if it be based upon sincere purpose, and expressed in sympathetic language, there is scarcely anything that they will not accept from their rulers, however contrary to their own previous utterances or prepossessions.'[7]

[5] Curzon to John Morley, 17 June 1900, vol. 181, pt ii, no. 119, Curzon Papers.

[6] Curzon to the Warden of Merton, 2 May, and to Morley, 17 June 1900, vol. 181, pt ii, nos. 92 and 119, Curzon Papers; Curzon to Balfour, 31 March 1901, vol. 181, pt ii, no. 211, Curzon Papers; Curzon to Salisbury, 21 June 1903, vol. 162, pt ii, no. 43, Curzon Papers.

[7] Curzon to Lord George Hamilton, Secretary of State, 25 January 1900, Hamilton Correspondence, D 510/4, folio73 ff., India Office Library.

But he attached particular importance to the improvement of relations between the two races and the removal of the impression that the British government were unjust or indifferent to India's interests. He shocked the officials of the India Office by sending a telegram of congratulations to the principal of a college at Poona on one of its students (R.P. Paranjpye, now Honorary Fellow of St John's College) securing the senior wranglership at Cambridge. He took the sternest view of cases in which Europeans were guilty of assaulting Indians. In 1899 and 1902, when the regimental and civil authorities sought to protect British soldiers accused of such crimes, Curzon had the regiments collectively punished and their commanding officers censured; and the civil authorities were publicly rebuked. Even the intervention on the second occasion of King Edward VII could not induce him to change his decision. 'If it be known that the Viceroy, backed by the Secretary of State, will stand up even against the crack regiment of the British Army, packed though it be with dukes' sons, earls' sons and so on—then a most salutary lesson will be taught to the army. If we yield to military and aristocratic clamour no viceroy will dare to go on with the work that I have begun.'[8]

Throughout his seven years in India, Curzon also persistently urged the British government and those who could influence British public opinion to show interest in, and regard for, the Indian people and not to practise an extortion 'that would shame the combined ingenuity of the usurer and the attorney'.[9] He desired that India should be lifted from the level of a dependency to the position which was bound one day to be hers, if it was not so already—that of the greatest partner in the British empire. Never did Curzon hesitate to plead India's case as he saw it. 'My first duty lies to my constituents and they are the people of India. I would sooner retire from my post than sacrifice their interest.'[10] He began the tradition of the British

[8] Curzon to Hamilton, 27 November 1902, D 510/12, folio 307ff., Hamilton Correspondence.

[9] Curzon to Lord Northbrook, 21 July 1902, vol. 182, pt ii, no. 103, Curzon Papers.

[10] Curzon to Sir Arthur Godley, Permanent Under-Secretary, India Office, 17 December 1903, vol. 162, pt ii, no. 94, Curzon Papers.

Indian government associating themselves wholeheartedly with the protests of Indian opinion against the policies of the South African governments. 'The name of South Africa', he wrote,[11] 'stinks in the nostrils of India.' During these years of Curzon's viceroyalty Gandhi was in South Africa and appreciated the viceroy's efforts. He wrote of Curzon in May 1901 as 'the strong and sympathetic Viceroy' and this letter was forwarded by the Government of India to Whitehall.[12] In 1902 Gandhi expressed a desire to wait in deputation on Curzon, but the viceroy thought that if he received Gandhi it might be resented as undue pressure.[13] On 20 May 1905, long after Curzon had become unpopular in India, Gandhi wrote an editorial commending Curzon's 'watchful guardianship' of the interests of Indians in South Africa.[14]

With this general goodwill which he had built up, Curzon was confident that he could ignore the demands for political advance. 'The real difficulty in India, my dear Godley, is this. I am thirsting after administrative reform in every direction . . . my one object being to make our administration equitable, and our dominion permanent. The advanced natives care about little but constitutional reform. They want to get a larger share of the government of the country; and they count justice, equity, sympathy, the even hand, as of little account compared with a larger control of the executive, for which they are as yet profoundly unfitted and which they will never get from me.'[15]

He disliked the Indian National Congress which had been founded in 1885 as the political organization of educated Indians, and regarded it as, if not actually disloyal, far from friendly to the government. Romesh Dutt, a retired member of the Indian Civil Service, was president of the Congress in 1899. He had communicated to Curzon

[11] Curzon to St John Brodrick, Secretary of State, 15 November 1903, vol. 162, pt ii, no. 87, Curzon Papers.

[12] *The Collected Works of Mahatma Gandhi*, vol. 3 (Delhi, 1960), p. 189.

[13] Curzon to M.C. Turner, 21 January 1902, vol. 205, pt ii, no. 73, Curzon Papers.

[14] *Indian Opinion*.

[15] Curzon to Godley, 9 April 1901, vol. 160, pt ii, no. 27, Curzon Papers.

his appreciation of the great importance which seemed to be attached by the viceroy to the conciliation of all sections of the Indian people; and in his presidential address he asked the government to secure the co-operation of Indians. Sir William Wedderburn, another retired member of the Indian Civil Service, who was prominent in the councils of the Congress, suggested to the viceroy that he establish a 'national Government' by winning for British rule the sympathy of educated Indians.[16] Lord George Hamilton advised that as it was difficult to meet the aspirations of 'young India' it was worthwhile encouraging 'older India'.[17] But Curzon saw no need to placate any Indians, young or old. He thought that India was filled with more loyal sentiments than at almost any previous time, and that the Congress was not the voice of India. From the start he treated that body as 'an unclean thing' and was determined to reduce it to impotence, by taking no notice of it.[18]

The Congress, which had developed as a body of loyalist Indian opinion, was embarrassed by the unqualified hostility of Curzon and made a fresh approach. Dinshaw Wacha, president of the Congress in 1902, appealed to the viceroy to consider the resolutions of the Congress with justice and sympathy, which, said Wacha,[19] were the two watchwords of Curzon's administration. To this letter there seems to have been no reply. Wedderburn wrote again, requesting Curzon for a friendly if informal recognition of the Congress as a responsible body expressing the Indian view on Indian affairs; and he was told that no co-operation was possible as the Congress tried both 'to guide the counsels of the respectable reforming party and at the same time to

[16] Dutt to Private Secretary to Viceroy, 15 September 1898, and Wedderburn to Curzon, 9 March 1900, vol. 181, pt i, nos. 51 and 98, Curzon Papers.

[17] Hamilton to Curzon, 5 January 1900, C126/2, folio 2ff., Hamilton Correspondence.

[18] Curzon to Wedderburn, 31 October 1900, vol. 181, pt ii, no. 160, Curzon Papers; Curzon to Ampthill, 15 June 1903, vol. 17, Ampthill Papers, India Office Library.

[19] Wacha to Private Secretary to Viceroy, 7 March 1902, vol. 205, pt i, no. 96, Curzon Papers.

keep in with the extreme men, who want something very different.'[20] But Curzon was dishonest in suggesting that the government would be willing to co-operate with the Congress if it remained a party solely of moderates. There was no Indian more distinguished for his moderation and rectitude than Gopal Krishna Gokhale, a member of the viceroy's legislative council. Curzon, on the recommendation of the Bombay government, gave Gokhale a title and wrote to congratulate him. Gokhale responded with enthusiasm: 'Your extremely generous terms will always be cherished by me, with profound gratitude; and they will be a source of constant encouragement to me in the work to which my best energies have been and will always be humbly devoted—bringing the two races closer together in this land, so that the purpose of Providence in bringing India under British rule may best be realized by both.'[21] Yet Curzon never sought to utilize the services of Gokhale.

In 1903 Curzon believed that he had begun to lose the support of educated Indians. 'No angel from Heaven could satisfy the Native party or escape being the victim of their incessant abuse.'[22] In fact Indian opinion was still hopeful, despite such indications of Curzon's political temper as the Bengal Municipalities Bill, that the viceroy would not regard equitable administration as an end in itself. The nationalist leader Bipin Chandra Pal wrote that the viceroy was the only man who had persistently sought to maintain British character in India.[23] Full disillusionment came only in 1904 when the viceroy made clear that he had no regard for the views and sentiments of Indians and that they should accept whatever Curzon believed was good for them. This change in the Indian attitude to Curzon was expressed in revealing terms by Wacha. 'The person who said that Lord Curzon was an *Asiatic* viceroy will prove true. He has forgotten

[20] Wedderburn to Curzon, 10 July 1902, and Curzon to Wedderburn, 15 August 1902, vol. 182, pt i, no. 121 and pt ii, no. 116, Curzon Papers.

[21] Gokhale to Curzon, 1 January 1904, vol. 209, pt i, no. I, Curzon Papers.

[22] Curzon to Salisbury, 21 June 1903, vol. 162, pt ii, no. 43, Curzon Papers.

[23] Article in *Hindustan Review*, Allahabad, June 1903.

English methods of governing India and is daily growing in love with *Asiatic* ways of ruling. What a fall is here. This Viceroy will leave the country the most odious and hated, aye, worse than Lord Lytton.'[24] The next year Wacha congratulated Gokhale on lying low in the legislative council 'the exalted python who has been so viciously doing mischief all round.'[25]

The final loss of faith in Curzon had been effected by his decision to partition the province of Bengal. To the viceroy it was essentially a measure of administrative reform. In April 1902 he had casually remarked that Bengal, with a population of 78.5 millions, was too large a charge for a single individual;[26] and when in the summer of 1903 he found that his officials were already at work on a scheme to divide Bengal, he gave it his general approval.[27] In December 1903 the proposals to transfer to Assam the three populous eastern districts of Bengal were published. There were certainly administrative advantages in this; but to public opinion in Bengal, partition appeared as an attempt to diminish the status of the province and to destroy the unity of the Bengalis. This was a correct assessment of official, if not of viceregal, thinking. The lieutenant governor of Bengal expected partition to weaken the influence of the eastern districts which were 'a hotbed of the purely Bengali movement, unfriendly if not seditious in character'. The home secretary to the Government of India wrote: 'Bengal united is a power; Bengal divided will pull several different ways. That is what the Congress leaders feel; their apprehensions are perfectly correct and they form one of the great merits of the scheme.'[28]

[24] Wacha to Gokhale, 4 February 1904, Gokhale Papers, National Archives of India. (Italics in original.)

[25] Wacha to Gokhale, 20 March 1905, Gokhale Papers.

[26] Curzon to Hamilton, 30 April 1902, D510/II, folio 59ff., Hamilton Correspondence.

[27] Viceroy's minute, 1 June 1903, Proceedings 149 to 160, Home Dept, Public A, December 1903, Government of India files.

[28] Letter of the Lieutenant-Governor, 6 April 1904 and note of the Home Secretary 6 December 1904, Proceedings 155 to 167, Home Dept, Public A, February 1905, Government of India files.

Meetings of protest were held throughout Bengal, but Curzon refused to pay heed. He declared that he could not find a single argument in the hundreds of articles and letters published and speeches made, and that, if the interests of sentiment and historical association were allowed to prevail, they would prevent all administrative reforms. In December 1904 he refused to receive a deputation of the Congress and interpreted the suggestion as a sign that the Congress was in a mood to accept defeat. The government went ahead with their plans, and the details of the partition scheme were published in July 1905. The agitation, far from dying out as Curzon expected, grew in intensity. In addition to meetings and processions, a boycott of British-manufactured goods was organized in Bengal. Even the British Chamber of Commerce lent its support to the agitation because of reports that Curzon's purpose in dividing the province was to weaken the Calcutta High Court.

The partition of Bengal was carried out in October 1905, on the eve of Curzon's departure from India, and two months after he had resigned as the result of a sharp controversy with the commander-in-chief, Kitchener, on an issue that is of no historical importance. Curzon's final comment on the agitation in Bengal was that it had only been saved from being formidable by being childish.[29] He failed to discern that Indian nationalism had now ceased to be purely intellectual and had attracted emotional support, that it had for the first time secured a grievance which agitated not politicians only but many men of thought and feeling, and that it had evolved revolutionary techniques other than terrorism. The agitation of 1904 and 1905 stung a new robustness into the politics of Bengal and India. It had been left to Curzon, who despised the Congress, condemned his predecessors for patting infant Indian nationalism on the back, and would have nothing to do even with moderates like Gokhale, to provide the occasion for the rise of a strong and virile opposition.

[29] Proceeding 302, Home Dept, Public A, September 1905, Government of India files.

3

'Drinking Tea with Treason'

Halifax in India

In the long public career of Lord Halifax, for much of which he has received a hail of severe criticism, there are two occasions when he merits commendation. In the summer of 1940, when the prime ministership of Britain was within his reach, he let it pass, in the national interest, to Winston Churchill; and nine years earlier, in the spring of 1931, towards the end of his term of five years as Viceroy of India, he signed an agreement with Mahatma Gandhi. That positive achievement has also been often condemned, at the time and since, as part of Halifax's general policy of appeasement; but in fact the approach to Gandhi was very different from the pusillanimity shown towards the European dictators. British policy in India, from the revolt of 1857 to the transfer of power ninety years later, was in essentials determined by governments; but there have been times when what was seen as the personal touch of understanding has helped. Lord Ripon in the 1880s testified by his actions that British rule was not always wholly unprincipled, and the personality of the last viceroy, Lord Mountbatten, enabled him to leave India to resounding cheers. But perhaps the most substantial contribution by any individual to the building of goodwill between India and Britain was made by Lord Irwin (as Lord Halifax was then known).

The five years of Irwin's viceroyalty, 1926 to 1931, seemed to me so seminal a period that thirty-five years ago, in 1957, I dared to write a book dealing with the events of those times.[1] It was a rash undertaking, because the records of the period in Britain were still closed and the Government of India, while it permitted me to read its files, insisted that no precise references should be given. Most of the collections of private papers in Britain and India were not accessible. On the other hand, I had the advantage of being able to talk to Lord Halifax and to discuss what I had written with Lord Hailey, one of the key officials in India at that time. Since then, Lord Halifax and several others have published their memoirs, there have been quite a few authorized biographies, and the primary sources now open to scholars are legion. How do the analyses and conclusions in my book of long ago stand up in the light of all this fresh evidence?

The main drive of my argument at that time was that Irwin's character, with its sincerity and religious dedication, made a marked impression on Indians and especially on Mahatma Gandhi, and convinced them, for the time being at any rate, that, as Irwin was the spokesman of British authority, it could be accepted that the British were genuinely committed to withdraw ultimately from India. I now believe that the additional evidence does not invalidate this analysis but adds many nuances. Irwin was certainly a man of honest purpose but he had no intent to hasten the end of British rule; and his keenness to reach a settlement with Gandhi was, I now realize, to a considerable extent motivated by a desire to divide the forces of the opposition, He was a devout Christian but a Christian imperialist who, like many of his friends at All Souls College at Oxford, acted on the assumption that the British empire was a part of the divine order. This feeling is summed up by the reported comment of Leopold Amery, who incidentally was no great admirer of Irwin: 'The empire is not external to any of the British nation. It is something like the Kingdom of Heaven within ourselves!'[2]

The selection of Edward Wood to go to India as viceroy in April 1926 was to British public opinion generally a surprise. He had no

[1] Sarvepalli Gopal, *The Viceroyalty of Lord Irwin* (Oxford: Oxford University Press, 1957).

[2] Quoted in W. Studdert-Kennedy, *British Christians, Indian Nationalists and the Raj* (Delhi: Oxford University Press, 1991), p. 195.

obvious qualifications for the job nor was he himself, with an old father and very young children, anxious to spend five years out of Britain. But in a general consideration of possible choices his name floated to the surface. He was a personal friend of the prime minister, Stanley Baldwin, who was not keen on letting him go; but King George V, once his own candidate, Lord Haig, was ruled out, supported the selection of Wood; and Lord Birkenhead, the secretary of state for India, agreed to it but with no great enthusiasm. 'How much better in life', he observed to Lord Reading, Wood's predecessor as viceroy, 'and how much more paying it is to be blameless than to be brilliant, and it certainly pays in such a connection never to have attacked anyone.'[3]

When Wood landed in Bombay as Lord Irwin, the urgent issue in Indian public life was not the meaning to be attached to British acceptance in 1917 of the progressive realization of responsible government as the objective of their rule and the pace at which this commitment should be implemented. It was the growing tension between Hindus and Muslims which dominated the scene, and Irwin's first speech as viceroy, devoted to this topic, enabled him to show India how deeply religious a person he was and what religion meant to him. He appealed for toleration not only in the name of Indian national life but also in that of religion, because he said he could appeal to nothing nobler, and because religion was the language of the soul and it was a change of soul that India needed. All religions assumed a sense of personal deficiency in the mind of the individual, a consciousness of failure to apprehend more than a fraction of life's mystery, leading to an irresistible yearning to reach out for higher things. Achievement was hard and the attempt would result in a wide tolerance of the deficiencies of others. There could be no greater tragedy than that religion, which should be the expression and the support of man's highest instincts, should be prostituted by an alliance with actions through which these instincts were distorted and disgraced.[4]

This was no definition of religion in any narrow, denominational

[3] Lord Birkenhead, *Birkenhead: The Last Phase* (London: Thornton Butterworth, 1935), p. 250.

[4] Speech at Simla, 17 July 1926, Lord Irwin, *Indian Problems* (London: G. Allen & Unwin, 1932), p. 231ff.

sense. Though 'a Christian who really believed in Christianity',[5] Irwin in this speech gave utterance to broad aspirations and human values which would appeal to men and women of religious feeling whatever their particular creeds. While the speech had little immediate consequence because rioting continued despite the efforts of Indian leaders to improve the atmosphere, Irwin had presented to the Indian public his credentials as a viceroy who was concerned with more than mere execution of policy and management of the administration. However, any good that this speech may have done was soon overlaid by a decision taken in 1927 for which Irwin himself bore the major responsibility. Trust in British declarations about their role in India had been destroyed by General Dyer's wanton slaughter in Amritsar in 1919 and, even more, by the widespread support in Britain for his action.[6] Reading, as viceroy, did little to rebuild such trust. He favoured the long game and, rather than take firm stands, let matters slide. Could Irwin do any better? The chance came when the British government decided not to wait for ten years as stipulated by the Government of India Act of 1919 but, in order to prevent the decision being taken by a possible Labour government, to appoint in 1927 a commission to inquire into the working of the act and recommend what, if any, further steps should be taken. Birkenhead believed in the British empire as almost a fact of nature and did not think that India would ever attain Dominion Status. In a potboiler, *The World in 2030*, which he wrote in 1930, he assumed without argument that even by the year 2030 India would be under British rule. But in 1927 even Birkenhead was prepared to consider the appointment of a commission with British and Indian members and it was Irwin who advised him against it. The viceroy had as yet little knowledge of India and no imaginative comprehension of her people, their problems and their attitudes; and he was guided mainly by Sir Malcolm (later Lord) Hailey, whose experience till then was confined mainly to the Punjab.

[5] Penderel Moon, *Gandhi and Modern India* (London: English Universities Press, 1968), p. 125.

[6] For an analysis of the causes for this support, see Derek Sayer, 'British Reaction to the Amritsar Massacre 1919–1920', *Past and Present* (May 1991), pp. 130–64.

Their recommendation to Birkenhead was that the inclusion of Indians would make the commission unwieldy and probably result in two separate reports; so it would be far better to confine the choice to members of parliament, thereby making the exclusion of Indians seem not a deliberate decision but a fortuitous circumstance. Birkenhead, who had felt that the arguments against exclusion of Indians were a priori very strong, now acquiesced. He added that he was concerned about a boycott of such a purely British commission, which would be disastrous to its prestige and authority; but Irwin assured him that such a general boycott was in the highest degree improbable.[7]

In my book I had described as 'the first and greatest mistake of Irwin's Viceroyalty' what I had assumed to be his acceptance of Birkenhead's diehard decision to exclude Indians from the commission. Now we know that Irwin's was the prime responsibility. The general resentment roused by the announcement of the commission and the widespread boycott faced by the commission on its arrival took Irwin by surprise. Because Gandhi, released in 1924 on grounds of health even before his sentence had been completed, felt himself morally bound to refrain from political activity, Irwin concluded that his power as a political force had suffered a great decline. He did invite Gandhi to see him and Gandhi came all the way from the far south; but at the interview neither made any impression on the other. Irwin was reticent and found Gandhi remote: 'It was like talking to someone who was spending three weeks in this planet from another.'[8]

If Irwin too readily wrote off Gandhi and at this point took little trouble over him, it was because he attached scant importance not only to Gandhi but also to the Congress party which he saw as losing support and riven by dissension between the sober elements and the younger radicals. Primarily under Hailey's influence, he looked forward to the emergence with increasing authority of alternative political groupings, such as the Liberals and the landowners; and the

[7] Irwin to Birkenhead, 19 August 1926, Birkenhead to Irwin, 23 March and 12 May 1927, and Irwin to Birkenhead, 6 January and 26 May 1927, Mss. Eur. C152, vols 2 and 3, Halifax Papers, India Office Library.

[8] Irwin to Hailey, 6 November 1927, Mss. Eur. E220, vol. 11, Hailey Papers, India Office Library.

spreading rancour among Hindus and Muslims seemed to hold out hopes of some Muslim leaders moving away from the boycott. 'I think', Irwin wrote to Birkenhead in 1929, over a year after the commission's first arrival and with the boycott showing no signs of yielding, 'it is really very much like a child refusing to eat its supper. There comes a point when it is no good pleading or reproaching any longer and when, if its tempers are ignored, it may return to eat it on its own.'[9] Various concessions were offered to make it easier for the political parties to change their attitude; and both Gandhi and his senior colleague, Motilal Nehru, thought that this might well happen.

However, the boycott held. The chairman of the commission, Sir John Simon, lacked the personality and the political flair to weaken the ostracism; and the general bitterness was intensified by the publication at this time of *Mother India*, a vicious attack on Indian society by an American journalist who was suspected of having received official assistance. Irwin began to realize that the Congress was not to be despised nor Indian politicians ignored; and the lesson was underlined by developments in a corner of Gujarat, at that time part of the Bombay presidency. In an agricultural country, land revenue is an obvious danger-point, and Bardoli was an area which Gandhi had accustomed to no-tax campaigns. The land was held by relatively prosperous peasant proprietors and Irwin, on a visit in 1927 to witness flood relief measures, had been impressed by the consideration shown by these landholders to the poor.[10] Yet now the Bombay government ordered an enhancement of land revenue in this area, where settlements were made once in thirty years, on the basis of a rough-and-ready recommendation by the settlement officer and despite the protests of his superior, the settlement commissioner. The landholders retorted by refusing to pay anything until the enhancement had been cancelled. Thereupon the Bombay government attached crops and movable property and considered forfeiture of occupancy rights; but the peasant proprietors, under Congress leadership, stood firm. In the

[9] Quoted in Lord Birkenhead, *Halifax* (London: Hamish Hamilton, 1965), p. 255.

[10] Irwin to Lord Goschen, Governor of Madras, 11 July 1928, vol. 22, Halifax Papers.

face of this, the Bombay government planned to seize, if necessary, the whole cotton crop and to move troops into the area. But at this point Irwin decided to intervene. He thought that the case for the provincial government was weak and realized that the eyes of political India were on him. If he hesitated, then official rigidity, coming in the wake of the inept decision about the composition of the commission, would take the viceroyalty beyond the point of no return into the desert of mindless repression. So, before it was too late, Irwin directed the Bombay government to reach a compromise. Prisoners were released, forfeited lands restored and, after a public inquiry conducted by experts, the land revenue rates were considerably reduced. Even Hailey was concerned that, by seeming to yield to the Congress on an issue regarding the peasants, the viceroy might be opening up dangerous possibilities in the future.[11] But in fact this was the turning point of the viceroyalty. Relying on his own instincts and strength of character, Irwin was moving towards an answer to the key question of how Britain could regain the trust of Indian opinion.

Though Irwin had not given up hope of building up loyalist parties as a counter to the Congress,[12] he recognized that, for the time being at any rate, there was no alternative to it. But the Congress was no monolithic body. A committee presided over by Motilal Nehru produced a report in the summer of 1928 asserting that Dominion Status was the immediate objective and demanding the transfer of 'full responsible government' to the people of India. The secretary of the committee was Jawaharlal Nehru, Motilal's son. He signed the report with reluctance, for a few months earlier, at the session of the Congress in Madras in December 1927, he had pushed through a resolution declaring the goal of the Indian people to be complete independence. He was, of course, aware that there was no substantive difference between Dominion Status and independence; but he attached importance to the mental attitudes which these two concepts indicated, and was determined that India should break completely with the past and with the British connection. Gandhi and other senior

[11] Hailey to Sir C. Rhodes, 5 July 1928, vol. 12, Hailey Papers.

[12] Irwin to all Governors of Provinces, 7 September 1928, vol. 22, Halifax Papers.

Congressmen did not take the independence resolution seriously; but its significance lay not in itself but as a reflection of the non-compromising stance of the younger elements in the party.

This caused concern to the British authorities. Not that they worried about the empty debates regarding the relative merits of Dominion Status and independence; but it troubled them that Jawaharlal Nehru's Independence for India League advocated not only complete independence but also economic change on socialist lines. A Communist party had been formed in India and the Government of India, in an attempt to scare the Indian public by painting in dark colours what a Communist society would mean, arrested some leading Communists on charges of conspiracy and started legal proceedings not in any major city where Communists were active but in Meerut, a small town just outside Delhi. The reason for this was to avoid trial by jury—a petty subterfuge which does no credit to a government of which Irwin was head. But even had this lengthy trial succeeded in stifling the Communist party, there remained, from the official viewpoint, the danger of nationalism and socialism converging under the leadership of Jawaharlal Nehru; and if Nehru and his supporters extended their influence from the urban areas, in which the Congress had till now largely functioned, to the countryside and roused the peasantry to defiance and rejection of their economic wretchedness, then, as Hailey never tired of warning Irwin, the *raj* would be shaken to its foundations. It was in this mood of alarm that in October 1928 Irwin's government directed the provincial administrations to scan Jawaharlal Nehru's speeches carefully and in December suggested that the Bombay government consider prosecuting him for a speech in his usual vein, castigating British imperialism and calling for a revolt against evil and for the establishment of a cooperative, socialist commonwealth. But the Bombay government, with a greater sense of reality, replied that everyone would agree with much of what Nehru had said and it would be difficult to prove that he had advocated not just socialism but communism and revolution.

Official hopes that the Congress would split in 1929 were defeated by the compromise which Gandhi effected at the annual session of the party in Calcutta in December 1928. It was resolved that if the British government did not accept by the end of 1929 the Nehru report seeking Dominion Status, then the Congress would initiate a campaign of civil disobedience in order to gain independence. So those supporting Motilal Nehru envisaged months of negotiation while Jawaharlal Nehru and his followers looked on 1929 as a year of preparation. The younger Nehru's position appeared to be strengthened by the viceroy's prompt and public response to the resolution of the Congress that, while the Nehru report was doubtless entitled to serious consideration, the British parliament could never agree to being reduced to merely endorsing the opinions of others. He also told Vithalbhai Patel, the president of the Central Assembly, with the intent that the message should be passed on to the leaders of the Congress, that the Calcutta resolution had created an impossible situation from which, so far as he could see, there was no issue.[13] But Irwin did not intend to leave matters at that. Motilal Nehru told Geoffrey Dawson, the editor of *The Times*, then on a visit to India, that what was really wanted was an assurance that Dominion Status was on the way;[14] and he informed the chief justice of the Allahabad High Court that the Congress would be content with Dominion Status of any quality and however limited a degree so that Indians could prove themselves responsible and deserving of more powers.[15] So too Gandhi, when he met Irwin at a social function in Delhi in February 1929, said that if India had the predominant voice in constitution-making, she would astonish Britain by showing how much she would desire to leave in British hands through lack of self-confidence.[16] Dominion Status with reservations, while logically contradictory, obviously formed the immediate aspiration of the larger part of Indian political opinion. It sought a firm recognition of full rights to come rather than a major constitutional advance at once; and this seemed to Irwin worthy of consideration.

In England on leave in the summer of 1929, the viceroy found his

[13] Birkenhead, *Halifax*, p. 257.

[14] Dawson's memorandum, 25 March 1929, Evelyn Wrench, *Geoffrey Dawson and Our Times* (London: Hutchinson, 1955), p. 272.

[15] Sir G. Mears to Irwin, 26 March 1929, vol. 23, Halifax Papers.

[16] Irwin to Lord Peel, Secretary of State for India, 21 February 1929, vol. 5, Halifax Papers.

authority increased by a change of government. Labour was now in office and the prime minister, Ramsay MacDonald, was committed publicly to seeing India becoming a Dominion within months. But the government was weak and preferred to leave the initiative to a Conservative viceroy who could rely on the personal support of Baldwin, the Leader of the Opposition. Irwin proposed that, to redress the affront caused to Indian opinion by the composition of the Simon Commission, a round table conference of British and Indian delegates be convened to consider India's constitutional future; and that it be clearly affirmed that Dominion Status was the goal. There was considerable opposition to this in the Conservative and Liberal parties and Baldwin, on learning that the Simon Commission had not been consulted, withheld the support of the Conservative party and cabled to the viceroy, now back in India, not to make any such public statement. But Irwin went ahead and made his announcement on 31 October 1929, with the approval of the Labour government and in defiance of the leadership of his own party.

The declaration of itself surrendered no ground. It committed the British government merely in the sphere of ultimate purpose. The objective was Dominion Status but no immediate transfer of any measure of authority was contemplated. Indeed, Irwin believed that the declaration would ensure that the essential mechanism of power would remain in British hands as long as one could foresee and with the support of all Indians except the few who advocated independence. But it was more than a mere reaffirmation of earlier British statements about their objectives in India. Coming as it did after Balfour's definition of Dominion Status in 1926, it was taken by Indian opinion as a firmer commitment than any made before by the British government; and this understanding was underlined by the criticism of Irwin in Britain, especially by Simon, Reading, and Birkenhead. 'Refusal', wrote Irwin bluntly to Reading, 'to make our purpose plain affords ground to our enemies to say that we intend India to occupy a permanently subordinate place in an Empire of white nations.'[17]

[17] Irwin's note to Reading enclosed with letter to Wedgwood Benn, Secretary of State for India, 14 November 1929, vol. 5, Halifax Papers.

The crucial question, however, was whether Irwin, by this clear proclamation of British good faith, would succeed, as he hoped, in dividing the Congress and tearing apart the compromise which Gandhi had achieved in Calcutta. Hailey had approved of the viceroy's declaration in 'that it seems to me wisdom to provide an occasional landing stage for more sober people to rest on while the extremist is being swept down the tide;'[18] but would the declaration in fact serve such a purpose? Gandhi reacted positively, for, as Hailey noted, while the British thought of Dominion Status objectively as a state of things, Gandhi thought of it subjectively as a frame of mind, 'a special kind of political kiss-in-the-ring.'[19] He associated the Congress with the Liberals and others in signing a joint manifesto offering cooperation if the government adopted a policy of general conciliation, granted an amnesty to political prisoners, ensured that progressive, political organizations were adequately represented at the conference with the Congress having predominance, and acknowledged that the conference was not for discussing when Dominion Status was to be established but was for framing a scheme of a Dominion constitution suited to India's needs.

Gandhi even persuaded Jawaharlal Nehru, the president-designate of the Congress, to sign the manifesto, which marked a retreat by the party; for, far from preparing for a struggle for independence and even from insisting on a full acceptance of the Nehru report, the Congress was now willing to hold negotiations with the British government without the latter making any precise offer. Tej Bahadur Sapru, the Liberal leader, and Hailey suggested to Irwin that he might make some reciprocal gesture, such as the release of those prisoners who had not advocated violence.[20] But Irwin took no such action, presumably because he had by now gathered that, after the first warm response, the attitude of the Congress was stiffening. Sherwood Eddy, a young American who had just spent three days with Gandhi, reported to the viceroy that Gandhi was no longer looking for a compromise. This was not, as was thought at the time, primarily due to Jawaharlal

[18] Hailey to Sir M. O'Dwyer, 4 November 1929, vol. 14, Hailey Papers.
[19] Hailey to Irwin, 4 December 1929, vol. 23, Halifax Papers.
[20] Ibid.

Nehru, who was drafting his presidential address in terms which left no room for negotiations. It was the criticism in Britain of the viceroy's statement which led Gandhi and the Congress to believe that little purpose would be served by relying on a single individual, however sincere, with the backing of a weak government in London. Irwin, in his memoirs published many years later, conceded 'that the situation had chilled and hardened under the impact of the unfriendly debates in Parliament.'[21] When Gandhi and Motilal Nehru, along with some others, met the viceroy on 23 December 1929, the break was clear. Gandhi said that he doubted the sincerity of British intentions though he recognized that of individuals; India and not parliament ought to frame India's future and unless the establishment of Dominion Status could be presumed as an immediate result of the conference he could not attend. Irwin replied that there was no common ground and reported to London that Gandhi and Motilal Nehru had been 'very impossible'.[22]

So attention shifted to the session of the Congress. Irwin considered banning the session but then thought better of it. The Congress pledged itself to the goal of independence and a campaign of civil disobedience under the leadership of Gandhi. The government decided to wait and watch developments and rejected the suggestion of the Punjab administration that Jawaharlal Nehru be prosecuted for his presidential address. The official assessment of the situation was summed up by a writer from India in *The Round Table* that Gandhi and the Nehrus were isolated not only from all other political parties but even from the right and left wings of the Congress party.[23] On 26 January 1930 the Independence pledge was administered at meetings held throughout the country, but Gandhi vetoed processions and speeches so as not to precipitate a crisis; and the government refrained from action. Then, towards the end of February, Gandhi decided to initiate civil disobedience by collecting salt from the sea and challenging the imposition of the salt tax. Setting out from his ashram

[21] Lord Halifax, *Fullness of Days* (London: Collins, 1956), p. 145.
[22] Irwin to Wedgwood Benn, 26 December 1929, vol. 5, Halifax Papers.
[23] *The Round Table*, xx (January 1930).

in Ahmedabad with a band of disciplined followers on 12 March, he reached the seashore after twenty-four days and picked up salt. Irwin thought that the issue was so trivial and the incidence of the tax so minimal that Gandhi should be allowed to become a figure of ridicule rather than be converted into a martyr by arrest, when he might well embarrass the government by starting a fast. The viceroy did toy with the idea of putting Gandhi and his followers in lorries and transporting them back to the ashram;[24] but even this proposal, intended to show contempt, he abandoned in favour of doing nothing. The belief that civil disobedience, which had ended in 1922 in tragedy,[25] would in 1930 end as farce showed a deficiency in imaginative understanding. In fact, Gandhi's march to the sea has a high place in the history of the Indian freedom movement and indeed of freedom in the world.

But by now Irwin, even if as yet he lacked a full grasp of the situation, had gained enough confidence to act on his own. Hailey, with long years of service in the country, was worried that inaction would reduce the authority of the Government of India. 'I myself see the Central Government, and I suppose most other people in India now see it, as presenting the picture of a person once dignified if unwieldy, but now entirely without position or respect, because its beard is pulled and its hat knocked over its eyes by every urchin in the street . . . The East has far more respect for a ruler who misuses his powers than for one who allows his authority to be flouted.'[26] The viceroy too seems to have doubted his own judgement as the march proceeded with public interest not evaporating and with no popular resistance to Congress actively developing. For there is a tinge of frustration as well as an element of banter in his report to the secretary of state. 'The will power of the man must have been enormous to get him through his march, which must have been a very severe physical strain. I was always told that his blood pressure is dangerous and his heart is none too good,

[24] Irwin's telegram to Sir F. Sykes, Governor of Bombay, 15 March 1930, vol. 24, Halifax Papers.

[25] In 1922 Gandhi called off civil disobedience after a police station was set on fire and a number of policemen burnt to death.

[26] Hailey to Sir A. Hirtzel, 4 April 1930, vol. 17, Hailey Papers.

and I was also told a few days ago that his horoscope predicts that he will die this year, and that this is the explanation of this desperate throw. It would be a very happy solution.'[27]

Two events in April, a raid on armouries in Bengal and the temporary loss of control of Peshawar in the predominantly Muslim North-West Frontier Province, forced Irwin's hand. He took drastic action to assert the authority of the government, causing Gandhi to condemn what he described as a veiled form of martial law, in face of which even Dyerism paled into insignificance. He himself was arrested on 5 May. For the rest of the year there was no slackening of official efforts to break the campaign of civil disobedience. Considering later criticism in Britain that Irwin had been a weak and appeasing viceroy, it is worth mention that he virtually set aside ordinary law and ruled by ordinance, imposed tight control of the press and placed about 60,000 political workers in prison. He was also not above minimizing to his British superiors the rigours of his rule in India in 1930. On one occasion, for example, some British and American journalists, who witnessed the beating back of an attempt to enter a salt depot, reported that they had been sickened by police brutality. But, in writing to the king, Irwin sounded a different note. 'Your Majesty can hardly fail to have read with amusement the accounts of the severe battles for the Salt Depot in Dharsana. The police for a long time tried to refrain from action. After a time this became impossible, and they eventually had to resort to sterner methods. A good many people suffered minor injuries in consequence; but I believe those who suffered injuries were as nothing compared to those who wished to suffer an honourable contusion or bruise, or who, to make the whole setting more dramatic, lay on the ground as if laid out for dead without any injury at all.'[28]

While taking stringent steps to hold civil disobedience at bay, Irwin was surprised and impressed by the influence in the country, which the campaign revealed, of Gandhi and the Congress. As the correspondent of *The Times* reported in May 1930, the 'Gandhi spirit' had obtained a great hold;[29] and thereafter it showed no signs

[27] Irwin to Wedgwood Benn, 7 April 1930, vol. 6, Halifax Papers.
[28] Birkenhead, *Halifax*, p. 284.
[29] Report of the correspondent on 18 May in *The Times*, 19 May 1930.

of loosening. This led Irwin, even as he took strong action against civil disobedience, to encourage in August the Liberals, Sapru and M.R. Jayakar, to talk to Gandhi in prison. Special arrangements were also made for the two Nehrus, themselves in prison in the United Provinces, to join Gandhi to see if any compromise could be worked out between the government and the Congress. These talks failed; but the first session of the Round Table Conference, where a surprising, if temporary, consensus of agreement emerged between the princes and the delegates from British India, made even clearer than before the need to bring the Congress into the constitutional discussions. As Irwin told the secretary of state, logically there were only two alternatives, to govern without consent or to make terms with Gandhi, and the concept of the knock-out blow had become futile.[30] So, by the end of the year, he decided, rather than relying on the mediation of others, to plan for direct negotiations with Gandhi; and, as officials in the Foreign Office of London noted in later years when Halifax was foreign secretary, although he took a long time to reach a decision, once it was reached his mind hardened like cement.[31] He had also learnt by 1931 the right approach to Gandhi. Banking on his reputation as a deeply religious person, Irwin addressed the Central Assembly on 17 January 1931 in what one may call the Christian style of imperialism. While deploring Gandhi's policy, he recognized the spiritual force impelling him, thought he would be as willing to recognize that the British were sincere in their attempt to serve India, and suggested that ultimate purposes differed little if at all. Two days later the prime minister, Ramsay MacDonald, followed this up by offering full provincial autonomy and a central executive responsible to a federal legislature; some safeguards would be provided but only for a period of transition and in the interests of the minorities. And then, to cap it all, on 25 January Gandhi and his chief colleagues were released and the notification declaring the Working Committee of the Congress an unlawful body was withdrawn.

It was now for Gandhi to respond. Jawaharlal Nehru pressed him

[30] Irwin to Wedgwood Benn, 5 September and 3 November 1930, vol. 6, Halifax Papers.

[31] Birkenhead, *Halifax*, p. 419.

not to be carried away by these gestures of the government which to Nehru amounted to nothing; but Gandhi knew that the Congress party was suffering from war-weariness and that the businessmen who supported the Congress were by now keen on calling off civil disobedience. His first move, however, gave nothing away. He wrote to Irwin demanding an inquiry into police excesses during the previous year and, when Irwin refused, proclaimed his disappointment.[32] But he was persuaded by the Liberals to see the viceroy, 'to meet', as he wrote in his letter, 'not so much the Viceroy as the man in you.' Irwin agreed, and set out not to convince Gandhi on any subject but to gain his confidence. He succeeded in that Gandhi came back from the first interview with the feeling that Irwin's sincerity was beyond question. Thereafter they had seven more sessions and talked in all for a little less than twenty-four hours. Irwin was struck by Gandhi's force of character and his immensely active and acutely working mind, a singularly winning directness accompanied by a subtlety of intellectual process which could be disconcerting.[33] Gandhi on his part was impressed by Irwin's understanding and frankness. At this time, unlike in December 1929, he did not worry about the sharp attacks on Irwin in Britain. The 'change of heart' to which he attached much importance and which he thought he saw in the viceroy was sufficient for him not to insist on any of the fundamentals of the Congress programme.

In contrast to his stand during the talks with Sapru and Jayakar in August 1930, Gandhi now made no demands on the constitutional issue and accepted responsibility with safeguards or, as he preferred to call them, adjustments, provided they were in the interests of India and could be discussed with Britain on equal terms. The talks moved to the verge of a breakdown on the question of an inquiry into police excesses, but finally Gandhi gave way when Irwin told

[32] Interview with Robert Bernays, 12 February 1931, Robert Bernays, *Naked Fakir* (London: Gollancz, 1931), p. 86.

[33] Irwin to the King, 13 March 1931, in Harold Nicolson, *King George the Fifth* (London: Constable, 1952), pp. 507–8; Halifax, *Fullness of Days*, p. 146.

him the government could not afford to weaken the morale of the police for the Congress might resume civil disobedience and then the police would be needed again. On picketing and the manufacture of salt Irwin made minor concessions. He permitted peaceful picketing for economic objectives in the belief that if it were not a political weapon it would be dead in three weeks. As for salt, he agreed to its collection for domestic consumption and for sale within the villages where it could be found. But on every other point the government had its way.

After the settlement had been reached, Gandhi asked Irwin to commute the death sentences, which were to be executed that week, on those held responsible for the murder of a police officer in Lahore. This would have made it easier for Gandhi to secure support for the agreement at the session of the Congress due to be held in Karachi. Irwin replied that a reprieve was not possible and to postpone the hanging till after the session of the Congress would be dishonest. So the three men were hanged on the eve of the meetings at Karachi. This made Gandhi's task even more difficult than expected; but he said publicly, in accordance with his promise to Irwin, that, while he had pleaded for the lives of these men—'Charity never faileth'—he did not see what other course Irwin, from his point of view, could have taken. The whole episode is evidence of the uprightness of both men and the high level of their negotiations.

By transforming the conversations from parleys between implacable political opponents into discussions between two spiritually sensitive individuals, Irwin had gained the advantage on most points. The Working Committee of the Congress, and particularly Jawaharlal Nehru, were deeply critical of what they regarded as surrender and ratified the settlement only out of personal loyalty to Gandhi. The major gain to the Congress lay not in any clause of the settlement but in the tacit recognition that it was the voice of the people and that the government had been obliged to deal with it as almost an equal partner. It was this which horrified Irwin's critics in Britain. His whole attitude, said Winston Churchill, had been an apology; he had not shown sufficient confidence in Britain's work in India. British civil and military officials in India too, for the most part, disliked Irwin's approach of, in Lord Lloyd's phrase, 'drinking tea with treason', and, after Irwin's departure from India in April 1931, the Government of India rapidly and with relief reverted to its traditional policy of confrontation with Indian nationalism.

Irwin himself contended that even by negotiating with Gandhi he had not deviated from this policy of seeking to weaken and thwart nationalist forces in India. On his return to London, he claimed at a private meeting of the Conservative party that his settlement would ensure the loyalty to Britain of Gandhi and the older politicians and that it had built a breakwater against the dangerous agrarian forces which were being harnessed by the younger Nehru and would cause the serious problem of the future.[34] Dividing the Congress was an objective of which he never lost sight. Later, as ambassador in Washington during the war years, he regularly reiterated the stock arguments in favour of British imperialism in India; and one of his speeches in April 1942 was so extreme that Sir Stafford Cripps, negotiating in India, was driven to protest.[35] Some amends for this Halifax made five years later by his speech in the House of Lords supporting Attlee's plan for the transfer of power. He was not prepared, said Halifax, to condemn the government's action unless he could honestly recommend a better solution. This speech changed the temper of the debate and infuriated Churchill.

Irwin's viceroyalty was more important in improving the atmosphere of relations between India and Britain than in the day-to-day course of events. Remarkable testimony to the impact of his seeming sympathy and understanding was the suggestion in December 1931 by Vithalbhai Patel, then president of the Congress, that Irwin be invited to give a ruling as to whether it was the government or the Congress which was violating the settlement. Irwin had an earnest, unspeculative and unimaginative mind. He never broke through the accepted British view of the indispensability of empire and had no far-sighted vision of the relations between the British and the Indian peoples. On coming to India he made grave mistakes, but he grew in

[34] Lord Butler, *The Art of the Possible* (London: Hamilton, 1971), p. 41.

[35] Cripps to Secretary of State for India from New Delhi, 22 April 1942, *Transfer of Power*, vol. I, no. 600.

the job and gradually realized that he had to deal with the Congress party and particularly with its 'super-president', Mahatma Gandhi. He saw, what all his successors except Mountbatten failed to see, that it was in Britain's interest to win Gandhi over. In dealing with Gandhi, the fact that Irwin was a devout believer helped a great deal. Gandhi, and hence the Indian public, accepted Irwin as an honest viceroy with decent impulses; and this lifted the fog of suspicion at least for a while. Even when bitterness and conflict returned, the memory of the assessment of Irwin's term of office was not wholly erased from the Indian mind.

For Irwin too the negotiations with Gandhi, begun on grounds of expediency, soon gained deeper significance. He who had the previous year lamented that Gandhi was 'regrettably hale and hearty',[36] now warmed to Gandhi's personality and spiritual strength. 'I shall always', he wrote in 1949 after Gandhi's death,[37] 'be thankful for the opportunity of knowing and being, I hope, a friend of Mr Gandhi . . . I can think of no person whose undertaking to respect a confidence I should have been more ready to take than his.' Nor was this just a tribute born of hindsight after India had become independent and Gandhi had been assassinated. When, while the talks were proceeding, a senior official asked Irwin if Gandhi had been tiresome, the viceroy replied, 'Some people found Our Lord very tiresome.'[38] On 6 March 1931, after the settlement had been reached, he wrote to Gandhi a letter which merits quotation in full.

> Dear Mr Gandhi,
>
> I want to write you a personal note of my own very great thanks to you for all you have done, while we have been working together during these last difficult days.
>
> It has been a great privilege to me to be given this opportunity of meeting and knowing you; and I hope that, either before I leave India or in England, you will give me the pleasure of seeing you again.

[36] Irwin to Wedgwood Benn, 26 March 1930, Halifax Papers, vol. 6.

[37] Article in S. Radhakrishnan (ed.), *Mahatma Gandhi: Essays and Reflections* (G. Allen & Unwin, Memoral edition, London 1949), p. 396.

[38] Birkenhead, *Halifax*, p. 299.

I do pray—as I believe—that history may say you and I were permitted to be instruments in doing something big for India and for humanity.

Believe me, with again much thanks and with deep understanding,

Yours very sincerely,
Irwin.[39]

This unique document in viceregal correspondence forms a fitting conclusion to Irwin's years in India and does much to correct the balance as against the several shortcomings of his tenure.

[39] Halifax Papers, vol. 26.

4

All Souls and India

The 1920s

There have been quite a few Fellows of All Souls in this century who have had links with India. Apart from those, British and Indian, who happened to have been born in that country, there are three viceroys of the British period as well as a president of free India, several judges, civil servants and scholars, even a novelist. Some, without having served in India, have played a role in formulating India policy. To go through this list would be interesting enough; but in these two essays [this chapter and its successor] I shall consider a general issue. The main development in India from the 1920s till 1947 was the growing force of Indian nationalism under the general leadership of Mahatma Gandhi and the Indian National Congress. The question before British policy-makers was how to deal with this problem. Should one try to thwart, arrest, defeat, even crush the nationalist sentiment or should one work with it, especially as Britain was committed from 1917 to the progressive realization of responsible government? And what were the attitudes in All Souls during these years to this question?

In the early years of this century some Fellows of All Souls were members of Milner's Kindergarten in South Africa and they worked on the premiss that the greatest contribution they could make to the world was to maintain the British empire and develop it on what they regarded as the right lines. There was for a long time almost a faith that the British empire was a part of the divine order. But the specific interest of this group in India really stems from the ideas and work of

Lionel Curtis, who was a Fellow from 1921 till his death in 1955, and was frequently spoken of in Oxford as the ancient mariner of All Souls. But Curtis had thought out and expounded his views even before he became associated with this college. He believed that Britain and the 'White' Dominions were the custodians of the 'highest civilization' yet evolved and were therefore justified in imposing restrictions on the immigration of people of Asian origin. Though honest enough to recognize that this smacked of racism and was a violation of human rights, he asserted that these Dominions had no other option if they were not to be swamped by 'the more backward and more numerous societies' of mankind. Active in the enforcement of this policy in South Africa, he came into contact and into conflict with Gandhi, then organizing the Indian community to assert their rights as equal citizens; and this did not make Curtis popular with Indians.

Curtis, however, was not concerned only with South Africa. Throughout his life he was an advocate of the idea of a world state, but in these early years he combined it with a justification of empire, on the ground that only those should participate in government who had proved themselves capable of doing so; and it appeared to Curtis that the peoples of European origin, with the possible exception of the Japanese, had alone shown themselves equal to the task of self-government. Among the peoples of Europe the British were to Curtis pre-eminent and he considered it providential that the task of ruling vast communities, which he believed could not as yet govern themselves, had been accepted by Britain, a country which was mainly identified with the principle of self-government.[1]

For the British empire in India in particular Curtis put forward a novel justification. From the sixteenth century India had been overrun by European adventurers, and the rulers and institutions of Indian society had been powerless to resist them. They could only be controlled by fellow Europeans who represented the 'moral forces' of a 'higher civilization'; and of these forces the British were to Curtis the best, because they understood better than others the meaning of

[1] L. Curtis, *The Problem of the Commonwealth* (London: Macmillan, 1916), p. 200.

freedom. As contacts with Europe had rendered the Indian people unable to govern themselves in the way they had been doing till then, inclusion in the British Commonwealth, where the rule of law was better understood and observed than in any European state, was the best alternative open to them.[2]

So, according to Curtis, Britain had established an empire in India in order to protect Indians from British and European marauders. But he believed in freedom as not just a Western but a human ideal, and he was sure that Britain's empire could not endure unless it fulfilled what Curtis defined as the principle of its being, which was self-government. The contradiction between dominance and liberty he sought to surmount by thinking in terms of training Indians to govern themselves, a process which he expected to need for completion not years or decades but centuries. He toured India in the winter of 1916–17 and drafted proposals which won the approval of Edwin Montagu, the secretary of state for India, and later of the viceroy, Lord Chelmsford, himself a former Fellow of All Souls and years later the Warden. Curtis's scheme, while leaving the Central government undisturbed and under unqualified British control, suggested the transfer in the provinces to Indian ministers answerable to the legislatures certain subjects which were deemed peripheral to the maintenance of British authority, such as education, sanitation, and local self-government. This seemed to Curtis the proper first step on the very long road to freedom. The rationale he offered was that Indians, working side by side with British officials who continued in charge of the crucial portfolios like law and order, would gain experience of administration, while Indian voters would know how the persons they had elected were functioning and whether they merited the confidence of the electorate.

This was the system of dyarchy, as it was known, introduced into India by statute in 1919. It operated in the provinces for eighteen years, till 1937, and thereafter was informally adapted to the central government. Though later Austen Chamberlain and Sir William

[2] L. Curtis (ed.), *The Commonwealth of Nations* (London: Macmillan, 1918), pp. 159–62 and 180.

Duke, a retired Indian civil servant, each claimed the credit for having first thought of it, there is no doubt that dyarchy in its complete form was the brainchild of Lionel Curtis. It was not popular with anybody. The British governors of the provinces disliked it as cumbrous. They preferred a unitary government under their tight control rather than an unwieldy two-tier combination. Lord Ampthill, who had once been governor of Madras, denounced Curtis in parliament as 'a globe-trotting doctrinaire with a positive mania for constitution-mongering',[3] while Lord Sydenham, who had served as governor of Bombay, wrote of 'the disastrous Mr. Lionel Curtis' who was the author of 'one of the most crazy constitutions ever concocted.'[4] Nor was Indian opinion more favourable. Dyarchy had the appearance of a swamp in which nationalist aspirations would be bogged down for an incalculable time to come; and transfer of certain subjects which were regarded by both British and Indians as relatively insignificant seemed to serve little purpose. It has been reported that in Burma during these years, if anyone wished to abuse another, a general term of vituperation was, 'you are a dyarchy.'[5]

It must be said in fairness to Curtis that the results might have been better, and his efforts would certainly have been more appreciated in India if, along with the principle of dyarchy, Montagu and Chelmsford had adopted some of the other suggestions of Curtis. He had regarded the development of awareness among Indian voters as even more important than the political education of Indian ministers by association with British administrators. He wanted the Indian electorate to grow over time in size and in responsibility; and for this reason he wished to see greater use in public life of the Indian languages. Reading today his writings of over seventy years ago, one is struck by his prophetic insight on many matters. He envisaged the

[3] Quoted in L. Curtis, *Dyarchy* (Oxford: Clarendon Press, 1920), p. xxviii.

[4] Lord Sydenham, *Studies of an Imperialist* (London, 1928), quoted in Studdert-Kennedy, *British Christians, Indian Nationalists and the Raj*, p. 224.

[5] M. Collis, *Into Hidden Burma* (London: Faber & Faber, 1953), p. 165.

indefinite continuance of British rule in India; but he also recognized that a great obstacle to the effective extension of popular government in India was the practice of conducting business in the English language. He was aware of the weaknesses of Indian society, but he added that the British had themselves become another caste. India was full of chasms which divided one class from another, but the most dangerous of all chasms was that which divided British officials from educated Indians. Engrossed in administration these officials were apt to forget that governance was at best a means to an end. The British had made themselves unlovable in India, and the first step towards mending their ways was frankly to accept that they needed mending.

Above all, Curtis appealed to Montagu and Chelmsford to revoke the decision of John Morley and Lord Minto ten years earlier to create separate electorates, whereby only Muslim voters exercised their franchise to elect Muslim candidates. Curtis realized that separate constituencies based on religious divisions would, more than anything else, hamper and delay the development of responsible government in India. It would lead to Muslims depending on artificial protection instead of catching up with the rest of the Indian community; and he therefore regarded the decision of Morley and Minto to be 'the greatest blunder ever committed by the British government in India.' He added, with what one can only term penetrating foresight, that separate electorates would eat into the unity of Indian nationhood and in the end would require civil war for their eradication. So he urged 'that we shall be guilty of an unpardonable crime against India if we fail now to make provision whereby these fetters, in which we have allowed her to bind herself, can be loosed.'[6] Had the governments of India and Britain at that time set aside immediate prospects of selfish advantage and paid heed to the warning of Curtis, the later history of India might have been very different.

Over the years, Curtis's thought developed in stages. He hoped that the British empire would broaden into a commonwealth of the self-governing 'white' Dominions, with an imperial parliament and cabinet. Other European countries and the United States could also

[6] Curtis, *Dyarchy*, p. 441.

join; and Curtis was prepared to consider the entry into this federation of territories under British authority when, at some remote period, they attained full self-government. The ultimate goal, lying far in the future, was a world state. Curtis strove, throughout his life, to win over public opinion in Britain, the 'white' Dominions, and the United States to the acceptance of these objectives; and strength and purpose were lent to his crusading instincts by his conviction that he was in fact seeking to build the Kingdom of God on earth. He had no doubt that this was the best way to carry out the teachings of Jesus Christ. The plan to transform the British empire into a Commonwealth leading on to the elimination of national sovereignty throughout the world was, in Curtis's eyes, the translation of the Sermon on the Mount into political terms. The Christian Church appeared to him to lay too much emphasis on the salvation of the individual soul; but the best way to carry out the divine purpose was to build up a system of human relations based on the law of God, which stressed the duty of each person to all humanity. 'My own conclusion is that if we could now ask the founder of Christianity to say whether in any degree his idea of the Kingdom of Heaven had been realized he would surprise us by pointing to the sphere of the state rather than of the church.'[7]

A devout Christian who believed that Christianity was the real force not only behind Western civilization but behind all civilization truly so called, it would have been logical for Curtis to have been an advocate of evangelization and missionary activity. Indeed, Gilbert Murray thought it necessary to point out to him the dangers of such a step. To argue that such principles as justice, cooperation and the brotherhood of man were worthless unless they were combined 'with a belief in the divinity of Jesus, the Virgin birth and Lord knows what other bizarre and speculative beliefs' was not just, wrote Murray, essentially irrelevant; it was 'pernicious rubbish, leading straight to the renewal of the wars of religion and the persecution of heretics.'[8] But Curtis was careful not to tread such a narrow road. Though the ultimate values

[7] L. Curtis to Olaf Caroe, 15 September 1932, Curtis Mss., Box 8, Bodleian Library.

[8] Gilbert Murray to L. Curtis, 10 February 1939, Curtis Mss., Box 13.

were to him Christian values, he did not insist on others accepting these values only for this reason. But believing Christians, more than others, could be expected to act on them. So when Edward Wood, a Fellow of All Souls who had shared rooms with Curtis—a man of Christian dedication but with a commitment, expressed in his maiden speech in the House of Commons, to maintaining the position and fulfilling the functions of 'a superior race'—was appointed viceroy of India in 1926, the anticipation that these values which were regarded as Christian would be applied to the sustenance of empire was keen.

The selection of Wood to go out to India as Lord Irwin was to British public opinion a surprise. He had no obvious qualifications for the job and in a general consideration of possible choices his name had floated to the surface. 'How much better in life', observed Birkenhead, the secretary of state for India, 'and how much more paying it is to be blameless than to be brilliant, and it certainly pays in such a connection never to have attacked anyone.'[9] The urgent issue at this time in India appeared to be not the working of dyarchy, or the meaning to be attached to the British acceptance in 1917 of the progressive realization of responsible government as the objective of their rule, or the pace at which this commitment should be implemented. It was the growing tension between sections of Hindus and Muslims which seemed to dominate the scene, and Irwin's first speech as viceroy, devoted to this topic, enabled him to show India how deeply religious a person he was and what religion meant to him. He appealed for toleration not only in the name of Indian national life but also that of religion, because he said he could appeal to nothing nobler, and because religion was the language of the soul and it was a change of soul that India needed. All religion assumed a sense of personal deficiency in the mind of the individual, a consciousness of failure to apprehend more than a fraction of life's mystery, leading to an irresistible yearning to reach out for higher things. Achievement was hard and the attempt would result in a wide tolerance of the

[9] Lord Birkenhead, *Frederick Edwin Earl of Birkenhead: The Last Phase* (London: Thornton Butterworth, 1935), p. 250.

deficiencies of others. There could be no greater tragedy than that religion, which should be the expression and the support of man's highest instincts, should be prostituted by an alliance with actions through which these instincts were distorted and disgraced.[10]

This was no definition of religion in any narrow, denominational sense. Though, as Penderel Moon later commented, Irwin was 'a Christian who really believed in Christianity',[11] in this speech he gave utterance to broad aspirations and values which would appeal to men and women of religious feeling whatever their particular creeds. While the speech had little immediate consequence, Irwin had presented his credentials to the Indian public as a viceroy who was concerned with more than mere execution of policy and management of the administration.

However, the good that this speech may have done was soon overlaid by a decision taken in 1927 for the substance of which Irwin himself bore the major responsibility. Trust in British declarations about their role in India had been destroyed by General Dyer's wanton slaughter in Amritsar in 1919 and, even more, by the widespread support in Britain for his action. Could Irwin start the process of rebuilding that trust? The chance came in 1927. The Government of India Act of 1919 had laid down that a commission should be appointed after ten years to inquire into the working of the act and recommend what, if any, further steps should be taken. The British government decided not to wait till 1929 but to appoint a commission in 1927 itself—primarily to prevent the decision being taken by a possible Labour government. Irwin advised the British government to exclude Indians from the commission because their presence would make the body unwieldy and probably result in two separate reports; it would be far better to confine the choice to members of parliament, thereby making the exclusion of Indians seem not a deliberate decision but a fortuitous circumstance. Irwin had as yet little knowledge of India

[10] Speech at Simla, 17 July 1926, in Lord Irwin, *Indian Problems* (London: Allen & Unwin, 1932), p. 231.

[11] P. Moon, *Gandhi and Modern India* (London: English Universities Press, 1968), p. 125.

and no imaginative comprehension of her people, their problems, and their attitudes; and he was guided by officials with limited experience. It should be added that Curtis also was for a commission consisting only of members of parliament, because he believed that the practice prevalent in the days of the East India Company of parliament securing its own information rather than being dependent on others should be resumed.[12]

Accepting Irwin's advice with some misgivings, Birkenhead appointed as chairman of the statutory commission his friend and colleague at the Bar, Sir John Simon, whom Birkenhead knew to share his views that India would and should remain for long, if not for ever, under British rule. Simon had visited India a year earlier and had returned, according to Leo Amery,[13] very much with the conviction that the Indian was not really adapted to parliamentary government. Now Simon took up the chairmanship, confident that he would have the cooperation of the viceroy, if only because he and Irwin were both Fellows of All Souls and belonged, as Simon later described it, to 'a band of brothers'.[14] He might in a sense be said to have deserved the support of the viceroy, for it was Irwin's preference for a wholly British commission that led to general resentment in India and to a widespread boycott of Simon and his colleagues. But Irwin believed that the boycott would die out for lack of momentum. 'I think', he wrote in 1929, a year after the commission's first arrival in India, 'it is really very much like a child refusing to eat its supper. There comes a point when it is no good preaching or reproaching any longer and when, if its tempers are ignored, it may return to eat it on its own.'[15] Of the Congress party Irwin had no great opinion; and as for Gandhi, Irwin after his first meeting with him in 1927 shared the assessment of Curtis, who had known Gandhi in South Africa and had met again

[12] L. Curtis to T.B. Sapru, 31 December 1927, Curtis Mss., Box 3; L. Curtis, *Civitas Dei*, vol. 2 (London: Macmillan, 1937), pp. 271–2.

[13] John Campbell, *F.E. Smith: First Earl of Birkenhead* (London: Jonathan Cape, 1983), p. 750.

[14] Lord Simon, *Retrospect* (London: Hutchinson, 1952), p. 38.

[15] Quoted in Lord Birkenhead, *Halifax* (London: Hamish Hamilton, 1965), p. 255.

in India in 1916, that 'the smart young Johannesburg lawyer had completely vanished in the typical ascetic of the East.'[16]

However, the boycott held. Simon lacked the personality and the political flair to weaken the ostracism. As Irwin described him, Simon was accustomed to 'keeping all his personality within locked doors while inviting other people to disclose theirs.'[17] We have had recently several assessments of Simon. Lord Blake has written that he was a clever cold fish who was 'indefinably unlikable',[18] and Lord Jenkins has described him as 'ingratiating and unctuous'.[19] Lord Hailsham, however, has reminded us that there was another side to Simon and has quoted Lord Attlee, who, as a member of the commission, knew Simon well, as saying that there was always 'a little pink quivering Simon struggling to get out.'[20] But this more human aspect of Simon, if it did exist, was not discerned in India. His bitterness at the humiliation of the boycott deepened his dislike of India and Indian politicians. India did not appear to him in any sense a nation,[21] and he thought Indians were lacking in courage 'and moral courage most of all—there is more of it in Kathleen's little finger than in three hundred millions of people in India, and this is what will be their undoing.'[22] But Simon was disappointed in his hope that the viceroy would give him full backing. Irwin had little personal regard for Simon and ironically, on the one occasion in these years when Fellows of All Souls held two the highest posts in Indian affairs, they could not get on with each other. Irwin also gradually realized that he had erred in excluding Indians from the commission and in under-rating Gandhi and the Congress party. So the Government of India carefully distanced themselves from the

[16] Foreword of Curtis to a book on South Africa, Curtis Mss., Box 10.

[17] Irwin to Neville Chamberlain, 15 April 1929, quoted in A. Roberts, *'The Holy Fox': A Biography of Lord Halifax* (London: Weidenfeld, 1991), p. 23.

[18] *The Times*, 21 May 1992.

[19] *The Observer*, 31 May 1992.

[20] Lord Hailsham, *A Sparrow's Flight* (London: Collins, 1990), p. 86.

[21] To F.W. Hirst, 19 March 1929, Simon Papers, Box 62, Bodleian Library.

[22] Simon's note on his talk with Ramsay MacDonald, 1 May 1930, Simon Papers, Box 64. Kathleen was Lady Simon.

commission; and in Simon's view the most successful demonstration against him and his colleagues was in Delhi, where it had been handled 'about as badly as it could be.'[23] He later complained that Irwin had joined the boycott and was talking to Gandhi and the Congress even while the commission was being stoned.[24]

It was too much, however, for Simon to expect that Irwin's government would suspend all operations on the political front till his commission had submitted its report. Events in themselves made this impossible. In a part of Gujarat, in the Bombay presidency, the provincial government ordered an enhancement of the land revenue without a proper investigation, and the peasant proprietors under Congress leadership refused to pay anything until the enhancement had been cancelled. Coercive measures failed to break their resistance. The case of the Bombay government was weak and if the viceroy failed to intervene, then official rigidity, coming in the wake of the inept decision about the composition of the commission, would take the viceroyalty beyond the point of no return into the desert of mindless repression. So, before it was too late, Irwin directed the Bombay government to reach a compromise. He thereby got his administration back on the road and, two years after his arrival in India, started moving towards an answer to the key question of how Britain could regain the trust of Indian opinion.

By now also Irwin, though he had not given up hope of building up loyalist parties as a counter to the Congress, recognized that as yet there was no alternative to it. But the Congress was no monolithic body. A committee presided over by Motilal Nehru produced a report in the summer of 1928 asserting that Dominion Status was the immediate objective. The secretary of the committee was Jawaharlal Nehru. He signed the report with reluctance, for a few months earlier, at a session of the Congress in December 1927, he had pushed through a resolution declaring the goal of the Indian people to be complete independence. He was aware that there was no substantive difference

[23] Simon to Ramsay Macdonald, 11 December 1928, Simon Papers, Box 6.

[24] Simon to J.L. Garvin, 17 September 1930, Simon Papers, Box 66.

in practice between Dominion Status and independence; but he attached importance to the mental attitudes which these two concepts indicated, and was eager that India should break completely with the past and with the British connection. Gandhi and other senior Congressmen did not take the independence resolution seriously; but its significance lay not in itself but as a reflection of the non-compromising stance of the younger elements in the party.

To Irwin and his advisers this seemed to open up prospects of dividing the Congress and weakening the section which was unqualifiedly hostile to the *raj*. Official expectation that the Congress would split in 1929 was defeated by the compromise which Gandhi effected in December 1928. It was resolved that if the British government did not accept by 1929 the Nehru report seeking Dominion Status, then the Congress would initiate a campaign of civil disobedience in order to gain independence. Irwin promptly and publicly replied that the British parliament could never agree to being reduced merely to endorsing the opinions of others. But in contrast to Simon, who rejected the Nehru Report out of hand as 'a very empty performance' and 'a shoddy piece of work',[25] Irwin saw in the emphasis placed by the Nehru Report on Dominion Status an opportunity to be exploited. Motilal Nehru told Geoffrey Dawson, the editor of *The Times*, then on a visit to India, that what was really wanted was an assurance that Dominion Status was on the way;[26] and Gandhi told Irwin that if India had the predominant voice in constitution-making, she would astonish Britain by showing how much she would desire to leave in British hands through lack of self-confidence.[27] Dominion Status with reservations, while logically contradictory, was clearly the immediate aspiration of the larger part of Indian public opinion. It sought a firm recognition of full rights to come rather than a major constitutional advance at once; and this Irwin felt required consideration.

[25] Simon to Ramsay MacDonald, 11 December 1928; Note of 24 April 1929, Simon Papers, Box 62.

[26] Dawson's memorandum, 25 March 1929; E. Wrench, *Geoffrey Dawson and Our Times* (London: Hutchinson, 1955), p. 272.

[27] Irwin to Lord Peel, Secretary of State for India, 21 February 1929, Halifax Papers, Mss Eur. C. 152, vol. 5, India Office Library.

In Britain on leave in the summer of 1929, the viceroy found his authority increased by a change of government. Labour was now in office and the prime minister, Ramsay MacDonald, was committed publicly to India becoming a Dominion within months. But the government was weak and preferred to leave the initiative to a Conservative viceroy who could rely on the personal support of Baldwin, the leader of the opposition. Irwin proposed that, to redress the affront caused to Indian opinion by the composition of the Simon Commission, a conference of British and Indian delegates be convened to consider India's constitutional future; and that it be clearly affirmed that Dominion Status was the goal. There was considerable opposition to this in the Conservative and Liberal parties. Baldwin, on learning that Simon had not been consulted, withheld the support of the Conservative party and cabled to the viceroy, by now back in India, not to make any public statement on these lines. Nevertheless, Irwin made the announcement on 31 October 1929, with the approval of the Labour government and in defiance of the leadership of his own party. Simon blamed Wedgwood Benn, the Labour secretary of state, for this 'light-hearted folly',[28] but in fact it was Irwin's decision.

The declaration in itself from the British viewpoint surrendered no ground. It committed the British government merely in the sphere of ultimate purpose. The objective was Dominion Status but no immediate transfer of any measure of authority was contemplated. Indeed, Irwin was confident that the declaration would ensure that the essential mechanism of power would remain in British hands as long as one could foresee and with the support of the Congress except for those few members who advocated independence. But it was more than a mere reaffirmation of earlier British statements about their objectives in India. Coming as it did after Balfour's definition of Dominion Status in 1926, it was taken by Indian opinion as a more precise commitment than any made before by the British government, and this reading was underlined by the criticism of Irwin in Britain, especially by Simon, Reading and Birkenhead. 'Refusal', wrote Irwin sharply to Reading, 'to make our purpose plain affords ground to

[28] Note of Simon, 1 May 1930, Simon Papers, Box 64.

our enemies to say that we intend India to occupy a permanently subordinate place in an Empire of white nations.'[29]

It was in fact the reaction in Britain which led Gandhi and the Congress to retract from their immediate positive response and to feel that little purpose would be served by relying on a single individual, however sincere, with the support of a weak government in London. Irwin, in his memoirs published many years later, conceded that the situation had chilled and hardened under the impact of the unfriendly debates in parliament.[30] The Congress now pledged itself to the goal of independence and a campaign of civil disobedience under the leadership of Gandhi. With this mandate, Gandhi set out in March 1931 from Ahmedabad in western India to the seashore in order to challenge the imposition of a tax on salt. Irwin thought that the issue was so trivial and the incidence of the tax so minimal that Gandhi should be allowed to become a figure of ridicule rather than be converted by arrest into a martyr. This attitude again showed a deficiency in imaginative understanding, for in fact Gandhi's march to the sea has a high place in the history of the Indian freedom movement and indeed of freedom in the world. Irwin himself seems to have realized, as Gandhi's march proceeded with public interest not evaporating and with no popular resistance developing to civil disobedience, that he might have been mistaken in taking no action. For there is a tinge of frustration as well as an element of banter in his report to the secretary of state. 'The will power of the man must have been enormous to get him through his march, which must have been a very severe physical strain. I was always told that his blood pressure is dangerous and his heart none too good, and I was also told a few days ago that his horoscope predicts that he will die this year, and that this is the explanation of this desperate throw. It would be a very happy solution.'[31]

Ultimately Gandhi was arrested and, to smother the campaign

[29] Irwin's note to Reading enclosed with letter to Wedgwood Benn, 14 November 1929, vol. 5, Halifax Papers.

[30] Lord Halifax, *Fulness of Days* (London: Collins, 1956), p. 145.

[31] Irwin to Wedgwood Benn, 7 April 1930, vol. 6, Halifax Papers.

of civil disobedience, Irwin virtually set aside the ordinary law and ruled by ordinance, imposed tight control of the press and placed about 60,000 political workers in prison. But he was surprised and impressed by the influence in the country, which the campaign had revealed, of Gandhi and the Congress; and this convinced him that it was necessary to bring the Congress into the constitutional discussions. Logically, he told Benn, there were only two alternatives, to govern without consent or to make terms with Gandhi; and the concept of the knock-out had become futile.[32]

The basis for such constitutional discussions would normally have been the Simon Commission's report, which was published in the summer of 1930. But in assuring both the king and Simon that this would be so, the viceroy, as Penderel Moon has written, was being 'untruthful'.[33] The Declaration of October 1929, which Simon had so disliked, had in fact left him high and dry. When some members of the commission had at that time threatened to resign, Simon had held his group together by securing the king's intervention; and he now produced an unanimous Report by tailoring the recommendations to fall in line with the views of the most reactionary members—a process no doubt made easier by the fact that he himself shared those views. No mention was made of Dominion Status, it was doubted if parliamentary government was suited to India, no changes were suggested in the central government, a step back was taken by proposing indirect elections for the central assembly, and in the provinces dyarchy was sought to be replaced by autonomy with heavy safeguards. This 'very obvious and deliberate' refusal, in Irwin's words, of Simon 'to take the bandage off his eyes'[34] robbed the report of all relevance. It presented a clear survey of the history of British administration in India without taking any notice of the growth of nationalist sentiment in the country. So the report was dead before it was born and Irwin

[32] Irwin to Wedgwood Benn, 5 September and 3 November 1930, vol. 6, Halifax Papers.

[33] P. Moon, *The British Conquest and Dominion of India* (London: Duckworth, 1989), p. 1044.

[34] To Wedgwood Benn, 20 June 1930; Birkenhead, *Halifax*, p. 287.

made clear to the Indian public, within three days of its publication, that he would take no notice of it. Knowing this, Simon appealed to the British members of the Viceroy's Executive Council to have the report circulated in India under the auspices of the government.[35] This too leading to no response, Simon turned to All Souls for help. He complained to the college warden about Irwin, requested Geoffrey Dawson to cable to the viceroy suggesting that he give the report more respectful attention, and asked Reginald Coupland to write to *The Times* supporting the report.[36] But the warden did not react and the others politely shied off. The crowning blow was when the Labour government, on Irwin's advice, refused to invite Simon and the members of the commission to the conference of British and Indian delegates which met later that year.

The path Irwin took on his own initiative during the last month of his term in India was that of direct negotiations with Gandhi; and by now he knew the right approach. Banking on his reputation as a deeply religious person he publicly, on 17 January 1931, while deploring Gandhi's policy recognized the spiritual force impelling him, thought that Gandhi would be as willing to recognize that the British were sincere in their attempt to serve India, and suggested that ultimate purpose differed little if at all. Prime Minister Ramsay MacDonald followed this up two days later by offering full provincial autonomy and a central executive responsible to a federal legislature; some safeguards would be required but only for a period of transition and in the interests of the minorities. And then, to cap it all, Gandhi and his chief colleagues were released unconditionally.

Gandhi in reply, after some hesitation, sought an interview, 'to meet', as he wrote, 'not so much the Viceroy as the man in you.' Irwin agreed, and set out not to convince Gandhi on any subject but to gain his confidence. He succeeded in that Gandhi came back from their first meeting with the feeling that Irwin's sincerity was beyond

[35] Simon to Sir George Schuster, Finance Member, and to Sir William Birdwood, Commander-in-Chief, 25 June 1930, Box 64, Simon Papers.

[36] Simon to the Warden of All Souls and to Geoffrey Dawson, 30 June 1930; and to R. Coupland, 1 July 1930, Box 65, Simon Papers.

doubt. Thereafter they had seven more sessions and talked in all for a little less than twenty-four hours. At this time, unlike in December 1929, Gandhi did not worry about the sharp attacks on Irwin by Churchill and his supporters in Britain. Indeed, the 'change of heart' to which Gandhi attached much importance and which he thought he discerned in the viceroy was sufficient for him not to insist on any of the fundamentals of the Congress programme. He put forward no demands on the constitutional issue and accepted responsibility with safeguards or, as he preferred to call them, adjustments, provided they were in the interests of India and could be discussed with Britain on equal terms. The talks moved to the verge of a breakdown on the question of an inquiry into the alleged excesses of the police while combating civil disobedience in 1930; but finally Gandhi gave way when Irwin said that the government could not afford to weaken the morale of the police, for the Congress might resume civil disobedience and then the police would be needed again. On picketing and the manufacture of salt Irwin made minor concessions; but on all other points the government had their way. By transforming the conversations with Gandhi from parleys between implacable political opponents into discussions between two spiritually sensitive individuals, Irwin had gained the advantage on most issues.

After the settlement had been reached, Gandhi asked Irwin, as 'a great Christian', to commute the death sentences which were to be carried out that week on three men held responsible for the murder of a police officer. This would have made it easier for Gandhi to secure ratification of the settlement by the Congress. Irwin replied that he could find no grounds for a reprieve and to postpone the hangings till after the session of the Congress would be dishonest. So the three men were hanged, making Gandhi's task at the session more difficult than expected; but he said publicly, in accordance with his promise to Irwin, that while he had pleaded with the viceroy in the language of the New Testament that 'charity never faileth', he could not see what other course Irwin, from his point of view, could have taken.

Simon while refraining from public comment was in private a severe critic of Irwin's policy. He blamed the viceroy for letting matters 'slide and glide' without taking a stand *somewhere*. He had allowed himself to be surrounded by persons who told him that he was the only saviour of India. Irwin was being rapidly turned into 'a British Gandhi', and in his desire always to agree with what any Indian politician said, had descended to 'the depths of shivering apology'.[37] That Irwin had dealt with Gandhi on almost equal terms upset not only diehard opinion in Britain but also many British officials in India, and after Irwin's departure in April 1931, the Government of India rapidly, and with relief, reverted to their traditional policy of confrontation with Indian nationalism. But Irwin contended that he was not compromising with nationalist forces but planning to weaken them by adopting a more sophisticated approach. He told the Conservative party that the day was past when India could be held by Churchill's 'possessive instinct . . . That conception of imperialism is finished and those who try to revive it are as those who would fly a balloon that won't hold gas . . . The thing just won't work.'[38] Later, on his return to London, he claimed at a private meeting of the Conservative party that his settlement would ensure the loyalty to Britain of Gandhi and the older politicians and that it had built a breakwater against the dangerous agrarian forces which were being harnessed by Jawaharlal Nehru and would cause the serious problem of the future. Dividing the Congress was an objective of which Irwin never lost sight.

Irwin had an earnest, unspeculative and unimaginative mind. He never doubted the indispensability of empire and he had no farsighted vision of the relations between the British and the Indian peoples. On first coming to India he made grave mistakes. But he grew in the job and gradually realized that he had to deal with the Congress and particularly with Mahatma Gandhi. He saw that it was in Britain's interest to win Gandhi over; and in dealing with Gandhi he was helped by the emphasis he laid on the fact that both of them were

[37] Simon to Lord Linlithgow and to R. Coupland, 1 July 1930, Box 65, Simon Papers; Simon to J.L. Garvin, 17 September 1930, Box 66, Simon Papers. Emphasis in original.

[38] Irwin to J.C.C. Davidson, quoted in J. Charmley, *Lord Lloyd and the Decline of the British Empire* (London: Weidenfeld & Nicolson, 1987), p. 172.

devout believers. Gandhi, and hence Indian opinion, accepted Irwin as an honest viceroy with decent impulses. Testimony to his impact was the proposal by the Congress in December 1931 that he be asked to give a ruling, which they would accept, as to whether it was the government or the Congress who were violating the settlement. The most important aspect of Irwin's years in India was perhaps the improvement in the atmosphere of relations between India and Britain. Even when bitterness and conflict returned, the memory of its assessment of Irwin's term of office was not wholly erased from the Indian mind.

5

All Souls and India

The 1930s and After

So, at the end of the 1920s, two schools of imperialist doctrine could be found at All Souls: what one might term the Christian approach favoured by Curtis and Irwin, and the diehard rigidity symbolized by Simon. Curtis saw in Irwin the successor to Milner, providing moral and intellectual leadership to promising young men so that they would devote themselves to serving the empire.[1] But it was the Simon approach which was gaining ground in the college. When in 1929 some Fellows proposed that the college spend part of its surplus income on studying the problems of the empire, including 'problems connected with the government of subject races', the scheme was struck down by a majority in the college, and one reason advanced was that All Souls was already being criticized for, to a large extent, identifying itself with a particular school of imperialist thought.[2] This school was clearly the one of extreme conservatism. But in the 1930s All Souls was not as prominent in policy-making for India as it had been in the years of Irwin and Simon. Its chief link with that country was Maurice Gwyer, the main draftsman of the Government of India Act of 1935, which was not negotiated with Indian leaders as had

[1] See draft letter (probably not sent) of Curtis to Irwin, 3 June 1931, Curtis Mss, Box 5.

[2] All Souls College Minute Book 1926–1946, vol. 1, memorandum IV of October 1929 and record of subsequent discussion.

been planned in 1931 but was imposed on India and as such did not commend itself to much of Indian opinion. Even Penderel Moon, at this time a junior civil servant in the Punjab, did not approve of the method,[3] while Hodson later described the act as being far behind the times for which it was legislating.[4]

Gwyer came out to India in 1937 as the first chief justice of the federal court to keep a judicial eye on the implementation of the Act. In that capacity Gwyer did not hesitate on occasions to strike down executive decisions. His legal knowledge was respected and his impartiality was never doubted. Gandhi accepted Gwyer's arbitration in a dispute between himself and a petty ruler in Gujarat. Gwyer also, not having much judicial work, took on in 1938 the vice-chancellorship of Delhi University, and, after retirement from the court in 1943, stayed on in India for another seven years, primarily because he was crippled by arthritis and the climate of the country suited him. But, throughout his long stay in India, Gwyer remained, to the Indian people, a somewhat remote figure; and he cannot be said, despite twelve years as vice chancellor of Delhi University, to have made any major contribution to India's system of higher education. Gwyer himself never at any time felt fully at home in India. His term as chief justice ended with acrimonious correspondence with the viceroy. He was piqued at not having been consulted about the choice of his successor and was outraged that the India Office should have selected not an Indian but a Conservative back-bencher with no great reputation in the British courts of law. Gwyer wrote to Linlithgow that he was no longer as convinced as he had been that the British government were sincere in their desire to grant India the equal status that she coveted.[5] Nor did conditions in India lighten Gwyer's sense of gloom. The British seemed to him to have lost interest, heart and faith, while India had yet to acquire the stable foundations for a sovereign

[3] Moon to his mother, 3 August 1932, Moon Mss., Mss. Eur. F. 230, India Office Library.

[4] H.V. Hodson, *The Great Divide* (London: Hutchinson, 1969), p. 60.

[5] Sir M. Gwyer to the Viceroy, 4 November 1942, L/PO/8/89, India Office Library.

state.[6] So Gwyer watched from the sidelines with increasing pessimism as India stumbled through rioting and bloodshed to partition and independence. The only relieving factor to Gwyer was Gandhi's courageous stand against this general drift to savagery. Gwyer had not at the start been drawn to Gandhi but was converted by the time Gandhi was assassinated in January 1948. 'I found myself at the end feeling a real affection for him and his like will not be seen again.'[7]

It is with the appointment of Leo Amery as secretary of state for India in the Churchill government of 1940, and his continuance in that office till the end of the war, that All Souls College once again comes prominently into the Indian picture. Amery was a good All Souls man. It is not necessary for me to deal in detail with Amery for Professor Roger Louis, in his Chichele Lectures of 1990, provided a comprehensive survey of Amery's views and policies. By contrasting them with Churchill's crude imperialism Professor Louis suggested that Amery had a radical outlook with a firm commitment to the freedom of India. He certainly never failed in his pronouncements during the war years to state that he envisaged a time when Britain would withdraw from India. But in fact he believed in an enduring empire and regarded All Souls, as Professor Louis brought out so clearly, as representing the almost spiritual essence of the British empire. In interpreting that essence, Amery leant heavily on the side of Simon, and had a poor opinion of Irwin whom he described, long before the years of appeasement, at a time when the viceroy was probing for a settlement with Gandhi, as 'a dignified exterior who says nothing'.[8] He was willing to accept Dominion Status as the objective for India provided its attainment was indefinitely postponed. As secretary of state, he regarded Irwin's settlement with Gandhi in 1931 as a precedent to be rejected. He refused to act on the basis that the Congress under the leadership of Gandhi was the main protagonist in Indian politics and he was all for the policy of a knock out blow to the party which sought to see the end of British rule.

[6] Gwyer to Moon, 12 June 1943, File 28, Moon Mss.

[7] Gwyer to Moon, 16 February 1948, File 29, Moon Mss.

[8] Amery MS. Diary, 9 November 1930, quoted by Louis in his Chichele Lectures.

In defence of this change of tack, it was argued that the situation in India had changed considerably during the 1930s. Elections to the provincial assemblies had been held in 1936 and the Congress, while opposed to the Government of India Act of 1935, had contested the elections and won clear majorities in seven of the eleven provinces. The Muslim League, claiming to represent the interests of the Muslim voters, fared less well, and even in the constituencies with separate electorates, won much fewer seats than it had expected. So the Congress, rejecting the League's offer to form coalition ministries, formed governments on its own. It asserted that it was a national and not a Hindu party and had many Muslim members; and several Muslim Congressmen took office as ministers. But it was easy to coalesce two facts, that the Congress had won substantial majorities and that the Hindus formed a substantial majority in India, and to contend that the Congress was a Hindu party. British governors later testified that the Congress, while in office in the provinces from 1937 to 1939, had been careful to respect the interests of religious minorities. But charges were made and believed that Muslims were being oppressed and Islam was in danger; and tension between Hindus and Muslims took on a deeply political tinge.

As secretary of state, Amery was careful not to emulate his prime minister, Winston Churchill, who stated explicitly that tension between Hindus and Muslims was the mainstay of British rule in India, for if the Hindus and Muslims got together they would join in showing Britain the door. But Amery accepted the conventional understanding of British officials in India that India was a plural society divided by religion and that this division was age-old and deep-seated. Hindus and Muslims were thought to be, and always to have been, fiercely opposed to each other, with the animosities of centuries never ceasing to smoulder beneath the surface. So the Congress and Gandhi were not treated by Amery, as Irwin had treated them, as the most important factors on the Indian scene, but only as bit-players along with several others. Nor did Amery regard nationalist aspirations as forming the main issue in Indian politics. It was the Hindu–Muslim conflict that to him was the crux of the Indian problem. So the fact that the Congress could win majorities by electoral process was to Amery irrelevant. Sensitiveness to public opinion was acceptable only in a homogeneous society, which to Amery India was not. She could only be governed democratically on the basis of agreement between Hindus and Muslims. The appeal of the Congress to secular parliamentary traditions had to be resisted vigorously, for to Amery this outlook was at bottom totalitarian. Amery recognized that the expectation of the Congress, as the largest and most effectively organized party in India, to govern would be normal in any democratic society; but in India he regarded the claim as untenable. The adoption by the Muslim League in March 1940 of a resolution demanding the creation of a separate state of Pakistan, consisting of those provinces in India with Muslim majorities, strengthened Amery's conviction that the Congress would have to be put down firmly.[9]

So, while immediately after assuming office Amery told the viceroy that he was considering how best to bring Jawaharlal Nehru, with his known sympathy for the Allied cause, into closer association with the government, his first public statements were a clear rejection of the Irwin approach. Stress was laid on the rift between the Hindus and Muslims and the Congress charged with being unrepresentative of Indian opinion as a whole. In August 1940 Amery announced the offer of the British government to appoint a few 'representative Indians' to the Viceroy's Executive Council and to arrange for the framing of India's future constitution by a small body 'representative of the principal elements in India's national life'; and these elements would include the princes and British commercial interests. The Muslims were assured that power would not be transferred to their disadvantage; and it was made clear that any decision of the body framing the constitution would be subject to the fulfilment of Britain's 'obligations' in India.

This offer, not surprisingly, satisfied no section of Indian opinion and Hodson, at that time an official in the ministry of information in London, found it difficult to explain it to the press. He has since commented that in the offer there was hardly a sentence without a

[9] Amery's speeches, 14 August 1940, 21 November 1940, and 22 April 1941, L.S. Amery, *India and Freedom* (Oxford: Oxford University Press, 1942); also Amery's letters to R. Coupland, 10 August 1942 and 8 February 1943, Mss. Brit. Emp. S. 403, Box 5, Coupland Papers, Rhodes House Library.

qualifying or balancing clause, creating the general impression of taking as much with one hand as was given with the other. The note of boldness or imagination or generosity was wholly absent.[10] Yet Amery defended the offer as very far-reaching and going a long way to meet the hopes of Indian nationalism, and contended that the Congress had rejected it because the party wished to seize power immediately so as to be able to control future constitutional developments.

Thereafter the purpose of Amery was to thwart the Congress and conciliate the Muslim League. Professor Louis has suggested that he was one of the key figures within the British government favouring the tilt towards a separate Muslim state. When Churchill, in a sudden, startling, change of mood in 1942 offered to fly out to Delhi or at least to broadcast to the Indian people in an effort to reach agreement, Amery, supported by the viceroy, headed Churchill off for fear that he might take a position sympathetic to the Congress. Instead, Stafford Cripps went out to Delhi with a declaration which, as Churchill explained to Amery, was essentially a pro-Muslim and reasonably Conservative policy. It offered no more than for the present collaboration in defence and for the future Dominion Status with possible partition of the country. It was Amery who was responsible for the clause which gave provinces the right to secede. But even this declaration Amery did not wish to see accepted, and was relieved when the viceroy, with Churchill's backing, ensured that Cripps failed in his mission. 'I . . . feel', Amery wrote in his diary, 'like someone who has proposed for family or financial reasons to a particularly unprepossessing damsel and finds himself lucky enough to be rejected.'[11]

The Congress and the British government were now on a collision course and Amery, who believed that nothing could be of greater benefit to India than that the Congress should disintegrate,[12] wholeheartedly approved the decision to arrest Gandhi and other leaders

[10] Hodson, *The Great Divide*, p. 86.

[11] J. Barnes and D. Nicholson, *The Leo Amery Diaries*, vol. 2 (London: Hutchinson, 1988), p. 794.

[12] Amery to Linlithgow, 28 May 1942; N. Mansergh and P. Moon (ed.), *Transfer of Power*, vol. 2, document 95.

of the Congress and wished them to be kept in custody till the end of the war. His positive suggestions veered between declaring India, still largely run by officials, a Dominion as soon as the war was over and the convening of a conference without the participation of the Congress and the Muslim League to frame proposals for a future constitution. The first suggestion was rejected as unrealistic by the cabinet and the second, for the same reason, by the Government of India. The inspiration behind both proposals was a desire to ignore the Congress, even if it meant bypassing the League as well.

Amery planned to build up a kindergarten of his own and chose Fellows of All Souls to wander about India and suggest what should be done in the way that Milner's young men had promoted the cause of empire in South Africa.[13] Professor Coupland went out in the autumn of 1941 to study the constitutional problem and H.V. Hodson was appointed reforms commissioner, leading Lord Linlithgow to comment that any further All Souls influence might lead the next viceroy, his successor, if new to India, straight up the garden path. Coupland kept in close touch with Amery and his report, published in 1944, bears the imprint of Amery's views. He thought that Irwin's declaration in October 1929 about Dominion Status being the objective should have been made much earlier and he believed that the faults of the *raj* had been mainly negative: an insular aloofness, insensitiveness, and want of imagination. The most regrettable features of British rule was the difficulty white men often found not to feel and to betray a sense of superiority to coloured persons. Too many Englishmen had claimed from Indians a deference inconceivable on any grounds but those of race and, even worse, they had sometimes enforced the claim with unpardonable insolence.[14]

But to Coupland, as to Amery, the major and urgent issue was not Britain's attitude to Indian nationalism but the differences between

[13] See Amery's remarks to L. Curtis in August 1940; Barnes and Nicholson, *The Amery Diaries*, vol. 2, p. 661.

[14] R. Coupland, *The Future of India: The Third Part of a Report on the Constitutional Problem in India* (London: Oxford University Press, 1944), p. 175; idem, *India: A Restatement* (London: Oxford University Press, 1945), p. 68.

Hindus and Muslims. No two philosophies of thought and conduct could be more discordant, in his view, than those of Hinduism and Islam, and the clashes between the followers of these two religions was the outcome of two sharply contrasted faiths and of the social systems and ways of life that they had inspired. If this longstanding tension had recently acquired a political colouring, Coupland held the Congress wholly responsible. He agreed with the contention of Curtis many years earlier that the creation of separate electorates had been a flagrant breach of democratic principle; but he felt that the Muslims had a strong case to justify such a breach. Britain had not lit the fire of rancour between Hindus and Muslims, nor done the devil's work of stoking it. He accepted Amery's description of the Congress as totalitarian, and it was this totalitarianism, along with what Coupland called the dictatorship of Gandhi, which to Coupland were responsible for rousing the fears of the Muslims in India and transforming the idea of Pakistan from an empty slogan into a real possibility. He acknowledged that the Congress ministries, which had functioned in the provinces from 1937, had on the whole done well and had established that the Congress party could perform constructively and was more than an organization for resistance. But he accused these ministries of creating the impression of the Congress being the natural successor to the *raj*, of being responsible to the central executive of the party rather than to the provincial legislatures, and of being unable to break away from the personal authority of Gandhi. Even worse than the ministers seemed to Coupland to be the backbench supporters of the party, who were said to strut around the villages claiming to be wielders of authority and sometimes even talking in terms of raising a private army.

Coupland, writing in 1944, did not suggest that what he described as the totalitarian mentality of the Congress party was akin to that of the Nazi and Fascist parties; but he argued that the essence of totalitarianism was not in its methods but in its principle, and the Congress was following the totalitarian principle of one-party government by refusing to form coalitions with the Muslim League. To the contention that one-party governments are a normal feature of democracies in the Western world, Coupland's reply, like that of Amery, was that these countries were homogeneous societies with educated electorates. In India, where caste and illiteracy impeded democracy from taking root and religion created a deep cleft in public life, attempts to run governments on Westminster lines would only result in aberrations of democracy. The charge of the Muslim League that the Congress was not a secular but a Hindu party was accepted. It followed that to Coupland parliamentary government, or government by political parties securing a majority of the votes, was not acceptable in India; it would always have to be government by coalition and compromise between parties which, whatever their professions, in fact in Coupland's view represented religious communities.

Coupland in his report, therefore, elaborated on the lines of Amery's thinking, and his interpretations were at the time endorsed by Hodson. He too was of the view that the Congress party, which Irwin had recognized as the main vehicle of Indian nationalism, had arrested the processes of democratic functioning by making the provincial governments answerable to a party executive which itself was under the thumb of Gandhi, whom Hodson characterized as a 'man of remarkable personality and nihilistic outlook.'[15] In his book written many years later Hodson toned this down and distanced himself from the criticism. The Congress, he wrote, was a tightly disciplined national organization, and its structure, combined with its claim to represent all Indians, gave rise to charges, both in India and abroad, of dictatorship and totalitarianism. These were particularly dirty words in democratic countries in the thirties, but if they did apply to the Congress they applied in a fundamentally different sense from the totalitarian dictatorships of Europe, for the Congress ethos, if not always its practice, was essentially democratic. But Hodson still blamed the Congress for debasing provincial autonomy as envisaged in the Act of 1935 and for implying that in the future majority rule would be Congress rule, exercised from the centre which would be dominated by the Hindu majority through an organization which brooked no opposition and refused to share its power.[16]

[15] H.V. Hodson's review of the second volume of Coupland's report, *The Spectator*, 7 March 1943.

[16] Hodson, *The Great Divide*, pp. 63–4 and 75.

There was, however, one Fellow of All Souls who had come out to India on his own much before those sent out by Amery. Penderel Moon had been elected a Prize Fellow in 1927 and was described by Curtis some years later as the most brilliant of the young men elected since the war, with a mind naturally mature but flexible.[17] Encouraged by Curtis and Coupland, Moon joined the Indian Civil Service and reached India in 1929 with the twin aspirations of doing what he could for the poor and facilitating the transition to full self-government. The officials at the India Office in London regarded such idealism as misplaced and told Moon that the British remained in India to safeguard the £1000 million of capital invested in that country and not to teach Indians how to govern themselves. Disregarding this advice, Moon proved himself an outstanding district officer in the Punjab, touring extensively and concerning himself with the details of administration. But such total involvement brought with it its own sense of disillusion. He became convinced that the British, whatever the hopes of the best of them in the nineteenth century and whatever the good work they might have done, had by the 1930s become, in the phrase of Lord Ellenborough, a governor general of the mid nineteenth century, 'strangers in India', creators of parasite classes and themselves parasitic, obstructionists because they stuck to the ruts and resisted new ideas. The revenue, taxation, and judicial systems were all cumbrous and wholly unsuited to India and were smothering her.[18] Nor could India afford these gigantic structures. Travelling, on his first arrival in India, from Bombay to Lahore by train, Moon was struck by the sterility of the country. 'I am surprised', he wrote to his mother, 'not at the poverty of Indians but at their continued existence.'[19] This first impression was confirmed by his later experiences. India was basically a poor country and the British were doing hardly anything to change this. They seemed to have neither the will nor the ideas to initiate even the beginnings of an economic transformation, such as

[17] Curtis to A.D. Bell, September 1933, Box 9, Curtis Papers.

[18] Moon to his mother, 23 February and 25 June 1930, File 1, Moon Mss.; P. Moon, *Strangers in India* (London: Faber & Faber, 1944), p. 22ff.

[19] 2 December 1929, File 1, Moon Mss.

the promotion of industrialization or cooperative farming. It could even be that such changes were beyond the capacity of an alien government; if so, it was all the more reason for hastening the day of Indian independence.

Indeed, Moon believed that British rule in India had continued too long and should have ended at least fifteen to twenty years before it was withdrawn in 1947. He had no use for Simon's lifeless report, supported fully Irwin's policy, and described as an amazing stroke of luck the selection by the Conservative party of such a comparatively rational man as viceroy.[20] But Moon would have liked the British government to have acted promptly on Irwin's declaration about Dominion Status rather than to lose themselves in the 1930s in the interminable process of seeking a constitutional provision for every possibility and thereby postponing full self-government. Moon's explanation for this was that the British were in two minds; they had promised India self-government but did not really want to relax their hold and did not have much faith in the form of self-government that was being considered. This made the British seem untrustworthy; it had certainly led to Indians losing faith in them.[21]

Moon had no respect for the men in high places in Lahore and Delhi in the late 1930s and made no attempt to conceal his contempt. He had also little regard for most Indian politicians, especially those who became ministers in the provincial governments in 1937. British officials in India had become no more than 'mercenaries' in an administration which was, in Moon's opinion, daily getting more and more shady and in another five years would be wholly corrupt. The British 'mercenaries' would then have no alternative but to pocket their pride and their honour along with their pay.[22]

After a long discussion with Coupland in India in the spring of 1942, Moon reported that they were in agreement as to the main lines on which a solution should be sought.[23] It is true that they were

[20] To his mother, 13 August 1930, File 2, Moon Mss.

[21] Moon, *Strangers in India*, p. 165.

[22] To his father, 10 April 1938, File 13, Moon Mss.

[23] To his father, 1 March 1942, File 17, Moon Mss.

both thinking at this time in terms of satisfying the demands of the Muslim League without shattering the unity of India by grouping provinces together with a weak government at the centre. They both had their doubts about parliamentary government for India, and they agreed that much economic progress could not be expected under foreign rule. But on other major issues Moon's position was very different from that of Coupland. Moon was of the view that Irwin's policy of dealing with the Congress and Gandhi should continue. So strongly did Moon feel about this that it led to his leaving the service in 1943. While fully supporting the action taken by the government in arresting the leaders of the Congress, he wrote to the Punjab government condemning the harsh treatment, 'which smacks of the concentration camp' of Congress workers in prison. 'I really think,' he commented to his father, 'that old Hitler has more excuse for his various atrocities in the occupied territories than we have for our barbarities out here.'[24]

But it was not just the contrast to the principles of freedom for which the British were supposed to be fighting the war that worried Moon. To him ill-treatment of members of the Congress was also poor policy; for, despite the strengthening of the Muslim League after 1937, the Congress represented India more nearly than any other party and when, after the war, the Indian problem was again considered, it would be impossible to ignore the Congress. It was the party of the future, bound to come again to the front as the active leaders of the country, and wisdom required that if its members had to be interned, this should be done with the minimum of harshness. So the Punjab government's reply to Moon's protest that Congressmen deserved to be shot as traitors and would have been in a free country, so angered Moon that he passed on the government's reply to an Indian friend, describing it as a shameful story. The letter was intercepted by the censor and the Punjab government, supported by the Government of India, proposed to get rid of Moon, whom they had always found difficult and never reluctant to taunt senior officers. Amery, who knew Moon's family and had met him frequently in college, tried to

[24] To his father, 15 November 1942, File 17, Moon Mss.

find employment for him outside the Punjab, but Linlithgow, the viceroy, refused to consider this; nor were the officials of the India Office willing to accommodate Moon in London. Moon, who had from 1938 been toying with the idea of leaving India and going into politics in Britain, now resigned, unapologetic and refusing to apply for a proportionate pension or to claim all the leave to which he was entitled.[25]

On the Hindu–Muslim problem also the viewpoints of Moon and Coupland differed sharply. Moon held that the desire for posts and power, which had developed in recent years, formed the basic cause for differences between Hindus and Muslims. The divergent beliefs and ways of life stretching back for centuries, on which Coupland laid stress, no doubt existed; yet, despite these differences, the fact was that Hindus and Muslims were closely intermingled, lived and worked side by side, and were hardly at all distinguished by race; and those belonging to the same area spoke the same language and shared a common provincial patriotism. The British had not created the divisions, but their mere presence had kept these differences alive, and both consciously and unconsciously the British had made use of them for their own purposes.[26] In particular, he regarded the continuation of separate electorates to have been a very grave mistake;[27] but this opinion which he held in the thirties and forties he changed towards the end of his life in the light of the deteriorating situation and considered separate electorates to be a regrettable but necessary evil.[28] However, he adhered consistently to the view that it was the responsibility of the British to make some efforts to bring about agreement between the Hindus and the Muslims; and when the Muslim League adopted the Pakistan resolution in 1940 Moon was in favour of encouraging leaders in the Congress and the League

[25] L/SG/6/3601 of 1943, India Office Records.

[26] Moon, *Strangers in India*, p. 103; P. Moon, *The Future of India* (London: Pilot Press, 1945), p. 23.

[27] To his father, 17 August 1932, File 5, Moon Mss.

[28] P. Moon, *The British Conquest and Dominion of India* (London: Duckworth, 1989), p. 953.

known for their moderation to get together and bypass both Gandhi and Jinnah, the uncompromising leader of the Muslim League. At that time secretary to the governor of the Punjab, Moon persuaded the governor to write to the viceroy on these lines; and he also joined a group of British civil servants in the Punjab who wished to wait on the viceroy to urge the same approach. But Linlithgow was following a policy, once the war broke out, of strengthening the League in order to weaken the Congress; and he therefore refused to take any steps to promote agreement between the two parties and frowned on all attempts to induce Muslim leaders to disown Jinnah.

To Coupland the viceroy's attitude was understandable and the Congress was to be blamed for the deadlock which lasted throughout the war years;[29] and to Hodson Linlithgow ranks in history as an outstanding viceroy.[30] But to Moon Linlithgow's attitude seemed, even at the time, indefensible. He became a severe critic and described Linlithgow as 'probably the most unpopular Viceroy there has been for nearly a century. I don't know which speak worst of him, Indians or English.'[31] He had played an easy hand so amazingly badly that he had driven Gandhi and the Congress, who were eager to support Britain in the war, into opposition; and by his ineptitude he had forced the Hindu–Muslim problem, which need never have been raised at all, into the forefront. On the other hand, had the cooperation of the Congress been secured at the start of the war, a national government would have come into existence of its own accord and Hindu–Muslim questions and the demand for Pakistan would have melted away. Thanks to the viceroy, the chance of a settlement between moderate members of the Congress and the League had been lost. The only course now left for the British was to go all out for the strong support of the Muslims, leading either to the establishment of the Muslims as unquestionably the dominant political power in India or to the division of India.[32] To

[29] Coupland, *India: A Restatement*, pp. 197–8.

[30] Hodson, *The Great Divide*, p. 109.

[31] Moon to his father, 23 February 1941, File 16, Moon Mss.

[32] Moon to his father, 5 and 19 November 1939, File 14, Moon Mss.; 31 January and 13 October 1940, File 15; 3 December 1942, File 17.

avoid this Moon, after his resignation, advocated the imposition of a settlement by the British, even if need be by force. The Hindu–Muslim conflict was still open to the influence of human will and effort; for few even of the leaders had really decided in their own minds the minimum demands which they had in all circumstances to obtain and the maximum concessions which they could make and beyond which they could in no circumstances surrender.[33]

While Moon saw an element of artificial contrivance in the Hindu–Muslim problem and did not share Coupland's view that it was solely a product of history, he agreed that it had in recent times been allowed to develop such proportions as to make parliamentary government in India a mockery. Asserting that democracy in India did not have to be on the basis, best known in Britain, of elected governments answerable to legislatures, Moon was inclined, like Gandhi, to think in terms of autonomous village communities and a chain of councils from the village upwards with indirect elections. But he did not see why self-government need mean democratic government. In All Souls during the inter-war years and after, there was a strong streak of sympathy for the monarchical principle in India and much support for the Indian princes. Rushbrook Williams was their staunchest champion and for six years had the odd designation of 'foreign minister' of one of the minor states—odd because these states had no foreign relations at all. Amery thought in terms of strengthening these princes by improving their bloodstock. 'If India', he wrote to the viceroy, 'is to be really capable of holding its own in the future without direct British control from outside, I am not sure that it will not need an increasing infusion of strong Nordic blood, whether by settlement or intermarriage or otherwise. Possibly it has been a real mistake of ours in the past not to encourage Indian princes to marry English wives for a succession of generations and so breed a more virile type of native ruler. Perhaps all that may yet come about.'[34] He also suggested to Coupland that in any future settlement the states could form a Dominion of their own, for no secretary of state could ever inform parliament that these states

[33] Moon, *Strangers in India*, p. 87; Moon, *The Future of India*, p. 27.

[34] 1 October 1943, Linlithgow Papers, Mss. Eur. F. 125, vol. 12, India Office Library.

were being handed over to anyone else against their will.[35] But on this point Coupland did not follow Amery's lead and, while listing the advantages which might have accrued if the British had retained the monarchical tradition in India, did not favour a Dominion consisting of the princely states, and advised them to adapt themselves to the progress of democracy and seek constitutional arrangements with the rest of India.[36] Irwin, as viceroy, was firm in dealing with the princes but he too believed that the sentiment for monarchy was strong in India and suggested to Prime Minister Attlee in 1947 that the king and queen should go to Delhi to formally say goodbye—a proposal which Attlee sensibly brushed aside.[37]

Moon too, surprisingly, thought that the princes could have a major role to play in the future. The absorption of the states into the rest of India seemed to him to be out of the question, and attempts to force their ruling families, several of whom were well established in the affections of the people, would only result in Hindu–Muslim clashes and convulsions which were unlikely to succeed. Far better to leave the princes to adapt themselves to the times and to draw on their political wisdom which Moon believed other parts of the country, under the influence of Western ideas and institutions, to have lost. Even the least powerful of the princes could, as a pensioned and titled nobility, continue to be influential members of a recognized and respected ruling class—a class which Moon thought India badly needed. Moon went further and suggested that the states should absorb the provinces under British rule rather than the other way round, and that the princes should take the place of British governors as heads of the provinces. So he concluded that 'in the backward obsolete states, the objects of so much misplaced scorn, there perhaps lies the secret of India's future and her best hopes.'[38]

[35] Amery's note on the future of the States, Box 5, Coupland Papers.

[36] Coupland, *The Future of India*, pp. 150–4; Coupland, *India: A Restatement*, pp. 79 and 279.

[37] Halifax to Attlee, 12 June 1947 and Attlee's reply, 15 June 1947, *Transfer of Power*, vol. 11, document 222, enclosures.

[38] Moon, *Strangers in India*, pp. 65–7 and 164; Moon, *The Future of India*, p. 36.

With the departure from India of Linlithgow in 1943, it was possible to steer Moon back into direct concern with Indian affairs. He first worked at Chatham House on Indian problems and then, early in 1946, returned to Delhi on a contract as secretary of the development board. The grounds for his resignation earlier were by now well known in India and ensured his general popularity. No other British official, after several years in pre-Independent India, served first Pakistan and then India in various capacities and was well regarded by both countries. But by the time he returned in 1946 the situation had so developed as to leave all his speculations about the future of India far behind. The scheme with which he had been associated in 1938, linking some provinces together with a weak central government, and Coupland's scheme of 1944, of four regions, two with a Hindu majority and two with a Muslim majority, with an inter-regional centre, clearly influenced the plan of the Cabinet Mission which came to India in the summer of 1946. The idea of sections and groups for provinces was taken up but, unlike in Coupland's scheme, there would be a central government responsible to a legislature and not merely an executive which would by statute be a coalition chosen by the head of state. But this plan too fell to the ground and the creation of Pakistan appeared unavoidable. Moon, whose years of service in the Punjab had convinced him that the unity of that province should not be broken, was keen that the Sikhs, who formed a large minority in this Muslim-majority area, should be given sufficient assurances to make them feel secure in Pakistan; and to this end he tried to bring together Sikh and Muslim leaders and also, in 1947, got in touch with Lord Mountbatten's staff.[39] But this hope of a united Punjab within Pakistan proved illusory and Moon, watching the massacres and migrations which followed the bisection of the province by Cyril Radcliffe, blamed equally Gandhi, Jinnah, and the British for the lack of wisdom and statesmanship which had led to the tragedy. The Congress, obsessed by the desire to get rid of the British, had given insufficient attention to the growing menace of Muslim separatism;

[39] Moon to Lord Ismay, 27 June 1947, *Transfer of Power*, vol. 11, document 371; P. Moon, *Divide and Quit* (London: Chatto & Windus, 1961), p. 84.

Jinnah had given hardly any thought to the consequences of creating Pakistan and to the need to win over Sikh opinion; and the British should have hastened to transfer power, made it clear that they would never consider the division of the country and, above all, as Moon saw it, not thought in terms of parliamentary democracy in India.

The divergent approaches of Halifax and Simon to India continued till the end of empire and even beyond. In February 1947 Halifax spoke in the House of Lords supporting the plan for the transfer of power. He said he was not prepared to condemn the Labour government's policy unless he could honestly recommend a better solution. This speech changed the temper of the debate and infuriated Churchill. Two years later, when it was decided that India would continue, as a republic, to be a member of the Commonwealth, Amery, after initial hesitation, accepted the position. But Simon was even less enthusiastic. 'The truth is', he wrote to Churchill, 'that Nehru and Cripps have won. The agreement may be the best way out but the fact remains that Cripps has attained his ambition to "dissolve the British Empire" and Nehru, like Costello, gets all the advantages without any of the responsibilities.'[40] However, despite Simon's advice, Churchill wholeheartedly supported the decision.

'Between all that is best', wrote Curtis in 1920, 'of the British in India and of Indian nationalism there remains no wall but only the phantom of a wall, which will presently vanish.'[41] A comment in similar vein was made in Delhi many years later, in 1954 by Sarvepalli Radhakrishnan, who said that history is not what we remember but what we choose to remember; and India remembered the positive aspects of British rule and elected to forget the rest. Radhakrishnan had been elected a Fellow of All Souls in 1940 and lived here for two terms every year from 1945 till 1952, when he took up full-time assignments in India and was elected an Honorary Fellow. The connection with the College was of special importance to him. To Zhou Enlai in 1954, for

[40] Amery's letters to Churchill, 14 and 29 April 1949, and Simon's undated note but obviously of April 1949, CHUR 2/44, Churchill Archive, Churchill College Library, Cambridge. Costello was the prime minister of Ireland.

[41] *Dyarchy* (Oxford: Clarendon Press, 1920), p. xxxiv.

example, he spoke with a touch of mischief of the delights of All Souls common room. 'The last subject', reported *The Times* correspondent in Delhi, 'is said to have confused the Chinese Prime Minister.'[42] As for the college, its first Indian Fellow was a philosopher of religion, who could have been expected to be concerned almost wholly with matters which had nothing to do with everyday life. But Radhakrishnan was not, and had never been, a secluded philosopher. He was always fully involved in the world even if not in the rough and tumble of political life. His early writings are set in the context of British rule in India, with Christianity appearing as an ally of imperialism and an alien ideological force and with many European scholars writing off the thought of India as a crass combination of the crude and the fatuous with nothing positive to contribute to the world. In reply, Radhakrishnan set himself the task of interpreting Indian thought in terms which related it to the Western tradition so that it could be seen as a bright chapter in the history of the human mind, become a part of every person's heritage, and enter into the bloodstream of world culture. His attempt to establish that Indian thinkers had grappled with the basic problems and formulated theories which had not lost their value helped Indians, smarting under foreign rule, to recover their intellectual self-esteem. But Radhakrishnan also made clear to Indians that this long and rich tradition had been arrested and required innovation and further evolution. While he elucidated Hinduism at its highest levels and renewed its dignity, he stressed that it had to cast off much that was corrupt and abhorrent.

The commitment to society, the crusading tone even in his scholarly writings, the modern note in his interpretation of classical texts and his intellectual resistance to the deforming pressures of colonialism gave Radhakrishnan by the 1930s a distinct public image both in Britain and in India. He was convinced that even non-political endeavour could not thrive in the absence of political freedom. Foreign rule could not evoke any living response from the people. Intellectual sterility in India was to no small extent due to the shame of subjection. No nation could be trusted with the charge of another. It was Britain's duty to grant freedom to India, and if she did so with

[42] 3 July 1954.

intelligent sympathy the friendship between Britain and India would be enduring. To speak of Hindu–Muslim differences as the obstacle was to accept the deficiency of British rule; for, in Radhakrishnan's view, it was the government which had promoted this rift among a generally harmonious people.

Not surprisingly, Radhakrishnan approved of Irwin's settlement with Gandhi in 1931, for he saw in Gandhi a leader armed with the strength of spirit who was developing non-violence as the moral equivalent of war. He missed no opportunity, even when Gandhi was in prison, to speak and write explaining Gandhi's work and thought. In 1922, when the synod of bishops of the Church of England in India denounced Gandhi's non-violence as unchristian and called on Christians in India to obey the government unquestioningly, Radhakrishnan replied in a series of articles that Christ had called on his followers to resist evil but to do so, as Gandhi did, in a non-violent manner. The bishops would do better spending their time promoting a reconciliation between India and Britain. When Gandhi was murdered, Radhakrishnan, addressing the memorial meeting held in the Codrington Library of All Souls College, spoke of the faith in humanity which had made Gandhi the leading prophet of the moral and spiritual revolution without which the world would not find peace.

With India free, the priorities in Radhakrishnan's intellectual objectives shifted. His position now moved closer to that of Curtis, but he was more interested in promoting a world community rather than a world state. He did not share Curtis's vision of the British empire as the nucleus of a world federation; and he saw the basis for a world community not in Christian teachings but in human values and inter-religious understanding. He crisscrossed the world asserting that to regard one's own country as the centre of the universe was an outmoded idea and one should learn to admit the possible worth of values and ways of life which were not acceptable to oneself. Appointed India's ambassador in Moscow in 1949, he saw his task, at the height of the cold war, as one of seeking a better understanding of each other's viewpoint, without compromising on principles or weakening his own commitment to democracy and the freedom of the individual.

Irwin was the first Fellow of All Souls to live in the viceroy's house built by Lutyens in New Delhi; and Radhakrishnan, nearly forty years later, was the second. By then both the name of the house and the designation of the occupant had been changed. But these were more than mere changes in nomenclature. They reflected a change in the basis of the relations between Britain and India. In turn, over these years, the nature and spirit of the Indian connection of All Souls had also been transformed.

6

Churchill and India

Anyone writing the article on India at a symposium on Winston Churchill is in the unenviable position of finding himself in a minority of perhaps one, for this is not an issue on which Churchill on the whole comes out well. It is symbolic that on the day he landed at Bombay in 1896 he suffered an injury which was to cause him pain throughout his life, for India has injured his reputation just as much. During the ten months he spent in India as a young army officer he saw little of the country except military barracks, polo grounds, and government houses; but the views he formed of India then remained the basis of his policies throughout his political career. Britain was doing great work in India and carrying out 'her high mission to rule these primitive but agreeable races for their welfare and our own'. The task was virtuous, the exercise invigorating, and the result profitable. But he did not care much for the British community in India; and as for the Indians, he did not come into contact with any except the servants, whom he found wholly subservient. 'For a humble wage, justice and a few kind words, there was nothing they would not do.'[1] That Britain had a duty to perform in India which was also to her advantage, and that the empire could last for ever with the Indian people having no right to think of freedom while they had the good fortune of living under British administration—these ideas, rooted in Churchill's mind at this time, remained with him till the end of his days, unshaken by the many changes of the twentieth century.

[1] Winston Churchill, *My Early Life* (London: Thornton Butterworth, 1930), pp. 101–2; Randolph S. Churchill, *Winston S. Churchill: Youth* (London: Minerva, 1966), vol. 1, p. 297.

He did, however, while leading a pleasant if boring life in the Indian army, recognize the strength of military influence in Anglo-Indian life and, in the controversy which surfaced in 1903 between the viceroy, Lord Curzon, and the commander-in-chief, Lord Kitchener, as to civilian control of military policy, Churchill was wholeheartedly in Curzon's side.[2] The same principle inspired his initiative, as secretary of state for war in 1920, in refusing further employment to General Dyer, who had been condemned by an official commission for opening fire in Amritsar on an unarmed crowd which had no means of escape and killing a large number. Though, in his evidence before the commission, Dyer admitted that his action was not required to save the Raj but was intended to strike terror not only in Amritsar but throughout the Punjab, there was considerable sympathy for him in Britain; and this was reflected in the ranks of the Conservative party when the matter was debated in the House of Commons. So Churchill decided to intervene. He told the House that he had informed the Army Council, which had unanimously supported Dyer's dismissal, that he held himself perfectly free (whatever the Council's decision might be) and would, if the cabinet so decided, recommend Dyer's retirement from the army. Whatever the provocation, the massacre at Amritsar was a monstrous event without precedent or parallel in the recent history of the British empire, an event 'which stands in singular and sinister isolation'. Dyer had failed to ask himself the standard questions: was the crowd attacking, was it armed with lethal weapons, and was he using more force than was necessary to maintain law and order? Moreover, Dyer had resorted to the doctrine of 'frightfulness', the inflicting of great slaughter in order to terrorize not merely the rest of the crowd but the whole district, even the whole country. 'Frightfulness is not a remedy known to the British pharmacopoeia. This is not the British way of doing business.' British rule in India did not stand on the basis of physical force alone, and it would be fatal to try and make it so. Close and effectual co-operation with the people of India was essential, 'that spirit of comradeship, that sense of unity and

[2] See Churchill to Curzon, 22 August 1905, Mss Eur F 111, vol. clxxxiii, pt I, no. 134a, Curzon Papers, India Office Library (IOL), London.

of progress in cooperation, which must ever ally and bind together the British and Indian peoples.'[3] Churchill's speech not only changed the tenor of the debate. This was one of those rare occasions when he was in line with nationalist sentiment in India, and his popularity in India was never again to touch this peak.

As a member of the Conservative government from 1924 to 1929, Churchill seems to have taken little interest in Indian affairs; nor did he need to, as for the most part the secretary of state for India was his friend Lord Birkenhead, whose views on India were the same as those of Churchill, and there was no aspect of the government's India policy with which Churchill disagreed. Nor was India an issue in the general elections of 1929. It is said that, had the Conservatives returned to office, Baldwin had intended to move Churchill from the Exchequer to the India Office.[4] There would then, in the 1930s, have been not even a semblance of change in India policy. But it was Labour that formed the government and in December 1929 the viceroy, Lord Irwin (later Lord Halifax), appointed in 1926 by the Baldwin government, announced, with the backing of the Labour government, that Dominion Status was the objective of British policy in India. The statement in itself gave away nothing, and in fact Irwin believed that it would ensure that the essential mechanism of power would remain, as far as one could foresee, in British hands. But Churchill believed that Baldwin, in supporting the viceroy's statement, was acting on the assumption that the times were too far gone for a robust assertion of British imperial greatness and was throwing away with both hands the British position in India.[5] He told Baldwin that he cared more about the Indian issue than anything else in public life; and Baldwin felt that Churchill, becoming 'once more the subaltern of hussars of '96', wished to go back on all British commitments and govern India

[3] Martin Gilbert, *Winston S. Churchill: World in Torment, 1917–1922* (London: Heinemann, 1975), vol. 3, pp. 404–12.

[4] Robert Rhodes James, *Churchill: A Study in Failure, 1900–1939* (London: Weidenfeld and Nicolson, 1970), p. 186.

[5] Winston S. Churchill, *The Second World War: The Gathering Storm* (London: Cassell, 1948), vol. 1, p. 31; Carl Bridge, *Holding India to the Empire* (New Delhi: Sterling Publishers, 1986), p. 43.

with a strong hand.[6] An after-dinner joke of Churchill during these years was that Gandhi should be bound hand and foot at the gates of Delhi and trampled on by an enormous elephant ridden by the viceroy.[7] The element of banter may have strengthened the general feeling that Churchill was only using the India issue to rally the right wing of the Conservative party so as to replace Baldwin as leader.[8] It is indeed difficult to take seriously his speeches in 1930, picturing an India in which the Labour government had handed over complete control to the dictatorship of a Congress Brahmin oligarchy, which would hire an army of white janissaries with German officers to secure the armed ascendancy of the Hindus. But Churchill strongly believed that unless Gandhi and his movement were crushed, India would be lost and the downfall of the British empire consummated, just as he was convinced that the national interests of Britain required the removal of Baldwin.

So, when, early the next year, the viceroy released Gandhi and started negotiations with him, Churchill, in protest against Baldwin's support of Irwin's failure to assert 'the majesty of Britain', resigned from the shadow cabinet on 27 January 1931. But in his speeches he stressed not only the glory but also the necessity of empire; the loss of India would, in his view, mean famine in Britain and the final ruin of Lancashire. Better remembered in India than his denunciation of the doctrine of 'frightfulness' over ten years earlier was one of his perorations at this time, which considered it 'alarming and also nauseating to see Mr Gandhi, a seditious Middle Temple lawyer, now posing as a fakir of a type well-known in the East, striding half-naked up the steps of the Viceregal Palace, while he is still organizing and conducting a defiant campaign of civil disobedience, to parley on

[6] Churchill to Baldwin, 24 September 1930, and Baldwin to J.C.C. Davidson, 13 November 1930, both quoted in John Barnes and David Nicholson (eds), *The Empire at Bay: The Leo Amery Diaries, 1929–1945* (London: Hutchinson, 1988), pp. 92 and 97, respectively.

[7] Duff Cooper, *Old Men Forget* (London: Rupert Hart-Davis, 1953), p. 103; Alistair Horne, *Macmillan* (London: Macmillan, 1988), vol. 1, p. 110.

[8] Carl Bridge, 'Churchill and Indian Political Freedom: The Diehards and the 1935 Act', *Indo-British Review* (July–December 1987), pp. 26–30.

equal terms with the representative of the King-Emperor.'[9] It has been estimated that nearly half of the Conservative party in parliament shared Churchill's conviction that the British must make clear their intention to remain effective rulers of India for a very long and indeed indefinite period, and were suspicious of Baldwin's seeming indifference in this matter. On 1 March Baldwin decided to resign but reversed his position within twenty-four hours; soon after came news of Irwin's settlement with Gandhi and Baldwin's speech in the House justifying his support of the viceroy, which confirmed his leadership of the party.

Even so, Churchill believed that the Conservatives would be locked in this controversy for several years, and it would become the dividing line in England.[10] Therefore, though his hopes of ousting Baldwin steadily receded, he did not give up the fight. He denounced Irwin's settlement with Gandhi as 'such humiliation and defiance as has not been known since the British first trod the soil of India',[11] and described British policy in India as 'a hideous act of self-mutilation' being performed to the astonishment of every other civilized nation.[12] When Gandhi came to Britain that autumn he sought out Churchill, but Churchill declined to meet him.[13] But after the general elections in October 1931 Churchill's sympathizers in the Conservative party in the House of Commons dropped from almost half to less than a quarter. In two votes on India only forty-four voted with him. So now Churchill, even as he carried on a sustained campaign in parliament against the Government of India Bill, which was no revolutionary measure, took the battle to the country and with greater success. At

[9] Churchill's speech at the West Essex Unionist Association, 23 February 1931, *The Times*, 24 February 1931.

[10] Churchill to Irwin, 24 March 1931, cited in Bridge, *Holding India to the Empire*, p. 65.

[11] Speech in the House of Commons, 12 March 1931.

[12] Speech at the India Empire Society, 18 March 1931, *The Times*, 19 March 1931.

[13] Clare Sheridan (Churchill's cousin), 'The Great Little Mahatma', in Sarvepalli Radhakrishnan (ed.), *Mahatma Gandhi* (London: George Allen & Unwin, rev. ed. 1949).

the annual party conference in 1933 he got a third of the votes, and in 1934 nearly half. He could not stop the bill being passed, but pledged to put an end to this 'bogus Act' which had been forced on them. Meanwhile, with the rise of the dictators in Europe, he claimed to find in Britain in the later 1930s a new climate of opinion, a sterner temper in the air; the 'languorous slothfulness' of the recent past had passed, and even in India, 'as if to strike a note of realism to Pandits, Mahatmas and those who now claim to speak for the helpless Indian masses, the Frontier is astir; and British officers and soldiers are giving their lives to hold back from the cities and peace-time wealth of India the storm of Pathan inroad and foray.'[14]

When, with the outbreak of war in September 1939, Churchill joined the cabinet, he soon made his views on India felt. He insisted that no measures should be undertaken in India to associate Indian political parties with the war effort which would weaken the supreme power of the viceroy and Britain's freedom to deploy forces in India; nor should any constitutional legislation be initiated till the war was over or promises be made that would bind parliament after the war. India had just to be kept quiet for the duration of the war. He also asserted in cabinet that he did not share the anxiety to encourage and promote unity between the Hindu and Muslim communities; for, if it were brought about, the immediate result would be that the united communities would join in showing Britain the door. The Hindu–Muslim feud was the bulwark of British rule in India.[15]

So, with Churchill becoming prime minister in May 1940 with no colleague able to influence his judgement on India, it could be taken for granted that any substantial change in policy in this regard was out of the question till the war was won. Halifax lamented that he found Churchill impossible to reason with on India; and Amery, whom Churchill appointed secretary of state for India, though no radical himself and prepared to take only such steps as would confirm the British presence in India, was driven to protest that Churchill had

[14] Winston S. Churchill, 'The New Phase in India', *Evening Standard*, 16 April 1937.

[15] R.J. Moore, *Churchill, Cripps and India 1939–1945* (Oxford: Clarendon, 1979), pp. 21–3, 28; Bridge, *Holding India to the Empire*, p. 153.

no notion of the problem at all and 'is really not quite normal on the subject of India.'[16] While the Indian National Congress became more accommodating with every military reverse suffered by the British in the summer of 1940 and offered to assist in defence if a fully national government were established without any long-term commitment by the British government, Churchill would not allow the viceroy, Lord Linlithgow, to go further than appoint a few 'representative Indians' to the Viceroy's Executive Council, set up a War Advisory Council, and declare that the future constitution of India should be framed by a body 'representative of the principal elements in India's national life' (including the princes and British commercial interests), and any decision of that body would be subject to the fulfilment of Britain's obligations in India (whatever these may be).

The Congress found this offer disappointing and, rejecting it, soon saw many of its leaders back in prison. This did not worry Churchill; and nationalist opinion in India, seeing no glimmers of hope from London, began to look for support from President Roosevelt in Washington. The pledge of Britain and the United States in the Atlantic Charter in August 1941, to respect the right of all peoples to choose their form of government, raised expectations; but within a month of signing the charter, on 9 September 1941, Churchill informed parliament that this clause applied only to European nations under Nazi rule; and it would seem that Roosevelt had agreed that no wider interpretation should be given.[17] Professor Reginald Coupland, visiting India at this time, thought that it was Churchill's categorical announcement which led to a spreading of a new and uncomfortable suspicion of British intent even beyond nationalist circles.[18]

In December 1941 the Government of India favoured the release of all Congressmen in jail, and the war cabinet, for once overruling

[16] For Halifax's comments, see Amery's diary entry for 26 July 1940 in Barnes and Nicholson (eds), *Amery Dairies*, p. 636; and for Amery's own views, diary entries for 12 July 1940 and 24 November 1941, ibid., pp. 633, 750.

[17] Churchill to Roosevelt, 9 August 1942, in Martin Gilbert, *Churchill: The Finest Hour* (London: Heinemann, 1983), vol. 6, p. 1164.

[18] Reginald Coupland, *The Cripps Mission* (London: Oxford University Press, 1942), p. 22.

the prime minister, supported this view, with Churchill deploring 'surrender at the moment of success' and muttering something to the effect 'when you lose India, don't blame me.'[19] But with Japan's entry into the war, pressure rose from public opinion in the United States, from Chiang Kai-shek, and in Britain from the Labour party to win Indian support for the war. Churchill at first resisted this pressure; 'the rule of the Congress and Hindu priesthood machine' would paralyse defence and would not be tolerated by 'the martial races' of India who, in his opinion, were predominantly Muslim.[20] Then, for a fleeting moment, Churchill's romantic imagination prevailed over his fossilized prejudices, and he formulated a scheme for expanding the defence council in India, offered to broadcast to India recommending it, and even planned to fly out to Delhi. Amery and Linlithgow smothered this scheme as amateurish and weighted against the Muslim League in favour of the Congress; and Churchill without protest reverted to his usual attitude. But the idea of seeking a settlement with Indian political parties was accepted. Stafford Cripps was sent out to India with a set of proposals, whose main points were the convening after the war of a constituent assembly elected on a system of proportional representation by freshly elected provincial assemblies; the recognition of the possibility of Pakistan, by conceding the right of any province that was not prepared to accept the new Dominion constitution to retain its existing constitutional position; and the collaboration while the war lasted of Indian parties with the British government, who would continue to bear the full responsibility for India's defence.

Churchill assented to these proposals because they seemed to him 'essentially a pro-Moslem and reasonably Conservative policy.'[21] He

[19] Lord Glendevon, *The Viceroy at Bay* (London: Collins, 1971), pp. 208–12.

[20] Churchill to Attlee from Washington, 7 January 1942, in Nicholas Mansergh (ed.), *The Transfer of Power 1942–47* (London: Her Majesty's Stationery Office, 1970), vol. 1, no. 6; Churchill to Chiang Kai-shek, 3 February 1942, ibid., no. 62; Averell Harriman's report of conversation with Churchill, 26 February 1942, quoted in M.S. Venkataramani and B.K. Shrivastava, *Roosevelt, Gandhi, Churchill* (Delhi: Radiant, 1983), pp. 16–17.

[21] To Amery, 8 March 1942, in Barnes and Nicholson (eds), *Amery Diaries*, pp. 785–6.

was right, for all that the proposals offered were collaboration in defence and not control, which Churchill was determined to retain, and in the future a Dominion constitution with possibly a partition of the country as demanded by Jinnah and the Muslim League. But Nehru and the Congress were willing to set aside their objections to the long-term aspects of the proposals if they could collaborate in defence to meet the immediate crisis; and Cripps secured Churchill's approval for rewording the paragraph on defence arrangements. It was now affirmed that the task of organizing the defence of India must be the responsibility of the Government of India with the co-operation of the peoples of India. But at this point the viceroy stepped in and toned down the cooperation in the military effort to mean merely the appointment of an Indian to some office connected with defence without in any way impinging upon the functions and duties of the commander-in-chief. Even this Cripps was optimistic enough to hope could in practice prove satisfactory to the Congress; but the commander-in-chief, Lord Wavell, refused to be responsive. Churchill, with the support of the war cabinet, refused to back Cripps and informed Linlithgow and Wavell that he would not approve any steps taken by Cripps unless they were unqualifiedly endorsed in separate cables by the viceroy and the commander-in-chief. Thus strengthened, Linlithgow and Wavell saw to it that all Cripps's efforts to reach an arrangement with the Congress came to nothing. The threat of Cripps to hand the matter over if he were not trusted was sharply repelled by Churchill, and Linlithgow was directly informed that there was no question of any convention, such as had been suggested by Cripps, limiting in any way his powers under the existing constitution.[22]

With the failure of the Cripps Mission, the critics of Churchill's India policy in the United States and Britain were silenced, and Churchill was strengthened in his determination to take no further steps. Knowing that Roosevelt's personal representatives in India, Louis

[22] For details of the Cripps Mission, see the documents in *Transfer of Power*, vol. 1; General G.N. Molesworth, *Curfew on Olympus* (Bombay: Asia Publishing House, 1965); Moore, *Churchill, Cripps and India*, pp. 104–26; Sarvepalli Gopal, *Jawaharlal Nehru* (London: Jonathan Cape, 1975), vol. 1, pp. 278–87.

Johnson and then William Phillips, were dissatisfied with such a freeze, the prime minister enlisted the services of Harry Hopkins to ensure that Roosevelt did not raise the matter again. A national government in India, he told Hopkins, would certainly recall all Indian troops from the Middle East and make an armistice with Japan on the basis of free transit for Japanese forces and supplies across India, in return for which the Japanese would give the Hindus the military support necessary to impose the will of the Congress party upon the Muslims, the princes, and the depressed classes.[23] Then, when the Congress, under Gandhi's leadership, in desperation planned a movement to force the British to quit India, Churchill and the war cabinet supported the viceroy in summarily arresting the leaders of the Congress and outlawing the party. Churchill was particularly allergic to Gandhi and would seem to have been convinced that he was following a pro-Japanese line. But his dislike of Gandhi and the Congress extended by now to cover the Indian people as a whole. 'I hate Indians. They are a beastly people with a beastly religion.'[24] For eighty years Britain had given India such peace and prosperity as she had never known in her history and it was thoroughly wrong to follow a policy of scuttle at the insistence of some mischief-makers. Though Britain gained nothing from India she would continue to do her duty there at any cost. For twenty-five years the Conservative party had gone along the wrong tracks in India, but Churchill was not prepared for 'the humiliation of being kicked out of India by the beastliest people in the world next to the Germans.' If he were pushed much further he would drop everything else and go round the country rousing the Conservatives against this.[25] 'We mean to hold our own. I have not become the King's First Minister in order to preside over the liquidation of the British Empire.'[26]

[23] Churchill to Hopkins, April 1942 (n.d.), in Venkataramani and Shrivastava, *Roosevelt, Gandhi, Churchill*, pp. 33–4.

[24] Churchill to Amery, 9 September 1942, in Barnes and Nicholson (eds), *Amery Diaries*, p. 832.

[25] Record of Churchill's talk with A.R. Mudaliar and others, 10 September 1942, *Transfer of Power*, vol. 3, document 2, enclosure; Churchill to Amery, 12 November 1942, Barnes and Nicholson (eds), *Amery Diaries*, p. 842.

[26] Speech at Mansion House, 10 November 1942.

In February 1943 Gandhi started a fast for twenty-one days. Churchill approved of the viceroy's decision not to release Gandhi and prepared for Gandhi's possible death in detention. The British government was moving forward victoriously on the war fronts and this was 'not the time to crawl before a miserable little old man who had always been our enemy'.[27] Gandhi managed to survive the fast and the deadlock continued. That summer in Washington, when Phillips, Roosevelt's representative in India, saw Churchill with the president's encouragement and observed that Indians wanted power in the central government, Churchill exploded. 'My answer to you is: Take India if that is what you want! Take it by all means! But I warn you that if I open the door a crack there will be the greatest blood-bath in all history; yes, blood-bath in all history. Mark my words, I prophesied the present war, and prophesy the blood-bath.'[28] Wavell, meeting Churchill before taking up the viceroyalty as Linlithgow's successor, felt that while Churchill knew nothing about the problem, he 'hates India and everything to do with it.'[29]

At the British government's farewell dinner to Wavell, Churchill expressed his 'subdued resentment' at the world's failure to appreciate Britain's great achievement in India. 'If the day should come, as I pray it may not, when we cast down for ever our responsibilities there and vanish from the scene, this episode in Indian history will surely become the Golden Age as time passes . . .'[30] Whatever the merits of British rule, the stated preference of the prime minister for its indefinite continuance ran so contrary to numerous political commitments that the India Office ensured that Churchill's speech was not reported. But Churchill saw to it that at least while the war lasted the Indian problem was kept on ice. He agreed to Gandhi's release in the summer of 1944 because of the opinion of the doctors that Gandhi would not be fit

[27] Churchill to Viceroy and Amery to Viceroy, both 8 February 1943, *Transfer of Power*, vol. 3, nos. 424 and 437.

[28] Record by Phillips of interview with Churchill, 22 May 1943, Venkataramani and Shrivastava, *Roosevelt, Gandhi, Churchill*, p. 156.

[29] 27 July 1943, Penderel Moon (ed.), *Wavell: The Viceroy's Journal* (London: Oxford University Press, 1973), p. 12.

[30] 6 October 1943, *Transfer of Power*, vol. 3, nos. 424 and 437.

again for active politics, and was annoyed that, far from dying, Gandhi succeeded in drawing Wavell into a correspondence. Gandhi even wrote to Churchill: 'You are reported to have the desire to crush the "naked faqir", as you are said to have described me. I have been long trying to be a faqir and that naked—a more difficult task. I therefore regard the expression as a compliment, though unintended. I approach you then as such and ask you to trust and use me for the sake of your people and mine and through them those of the world.'[31] This letter, which Gandhi signed 'your sincere friend', the Government of India, through whom it was sent, claimed to have miscarried; so two months later Gandhi sent a copy. The officials at Delhi and Whitehall were for ignoring this letter; but Churchill, with better manners, had a formal acknowledgement sent.

Such formal correctness in personal dealings had nothing to do with policy, which remained as intractable as ever. Indeed, Wavell was courageous enough to complain to the prime minister that the British government were treating the vital problems of India 'with neglect, even sometimes with hostility and contempt.' Churchill might believe that in a mistaken view of Indian conditions and with an entirely misplaced sentimental liberalism Britain had taken the wrong turn with India twenty-five or thirty years earlier; but the clock could not be put back and the present attitude was aggravating the mischief.[32] But Churchill, who by now was regretting his appointment of Wavell as viceroy, was not to be moved. He had no compunction in denuding India of food supplies because of the need for shipping in other theatres of war, for he believed that the starvation of Bengalis, who were anyhow underfed, was less serious than that of sturdy Greeks.[33] He did, under pressure from Wavell, request Roosevelt for a special allocation of ships to move wheat from Australia to India; but when

[31] Gandhi to Churchill, 17 July 1944, *Transfer of Power,* vol. 5, no. 20, enclosure 5.

[32] Wavell to Churchill, 24 October 1944, *Transfer of Power,* vol. 5, no. 64.

[33] Amery's diary entry for 24 September 1943, in Barnes and Nicholson (eds), *Amery Diaries,* p. 943; Wavell to Amery, 25 February 1944, *Transfer of Power,* vol. 4, no. 401; C.B.A. Behrens, *Merchant Shipping and the Demands of War* (London: Her Majesty's Stationery Office, 1955), pp. 359 and 434–5.

the United States replied that this could not be managed Churchill felt that nothing more could or need be done. Lord Mountbatten, in command in South East Asia, on his own diverted 10 per cent of the shipping at his disposal for import of foodgrains into India, but Churchill, who seemed to regard famine relief as 'appeasement' of the Congress, vetoed this and reduced the shipping at Mountbatten's disposal by 10 per cent. But Mountbatten persisted and transferred 10 per cent of his reduced shipping to food imports for India.[34]

With the war drawing to an end, diverse and contrary thoughts floated through Churchill's mind as to the future of India. In resisting total withdrawal from that country at any time Churchill would seem to be reflecting the general mood of the Conservative party. He told Amery that once the war had been won there was no obligation to honour promises made at a time of difficulty and not taken up by the Indians.[35] Contemptuous of Indian politicians at various times during the war, he sought to divert attention from problems of constitutional change to a vigorous policy of social reform,[36] or the creation of large collectivized farms on the Soviet model to replace the existing system of fragmented land tenure. It would really pay the British to take up the cause of the poor peasant, to confiscate the lands of rich Congressmen and divide them up.[37] But Churchill did not follow up these ideas and probably did not take them seriously, knowing that, in spite of him, the British might well, in his own phrase, chatter themselves out of India.[38] At the time of the Cripps Mission he cabled to Mackenzie King in Canada: 'We have resigned ourselves to fighting our utmost to defend India in order, if successful, to be turned out.'[39] Later, just

[34] Mountbatten to Wavell, 7 September 1944, in Moon (ed.), *Wavell*, p. 89; Mountbatten to the author, 28 May 1970.

[35] 4 August 1944 in Barnes and Nicholson (eds), *Amery Diaries*, p. 993.

[36] Amery to Linlithgow, 30 October 1942, *Transfer of Power*, vol. 3, no. 128.

[37] Amery to Linlithgow, 1 September 1942, and to Wavell, 9 August 1944, *Transfer of Power*, vol. 2, no. 673 and vol. 4, no. 634, respectively.

[38] R.A. Butler's report to Samuel Hoare of conversation with Churchill, 27 November 1942, quoted in Moore, *Churchill, Cripps and India*, p. 137.

[39] 18 March 1942, *Transfer of Power*, vol. 1, no. 346.

before the detention of Gandhi, he amazed the king by informing him that his colleagues and both, or all three, parties in parliament were quite prepared to give up India to Indians after the war. Cripps, the press, and American opinion had all contributed to reaching the conclusion that British rule in India was wrong and had always been wrong for India; and British political parties had already been talked into giving up India.[40] He normally had a regard for the Indian army which he believed (wrongly) was recruited mostly from among the Muslims, and he told Chiang Kai-shek that if the British withdrew their troops from India the Hindu parliamentarians would be rapidly dominated by the 'Muslim warriors'.[41] But he also some months later expressed to Amery his conviction that the Indian army was only waiting to shoot the British in the back.[42] Out of this effervescing, confused welter of comments and suggestions, what emerges is that, while Churchill would have liked to maintain the empire in India, or even hold on to a bit of the country, he was not hopeful of it. But he agreed with Jinnah that a united India was a British creation which could not survive under Indian rule. Pakistan was perhaps the only answer because Muslims and Hindus would never live together peacefully; and Churchill envisaged a situation where Britain could sit on top of a tripod—Pakistan, Princely India, and the Hindus.[43]

The general election of 1945 saved Churchill from taking decisions. His reactions to Attlee's policy were determined by his opposition to what he termed 'the handing over of India to Hindu caste rule.'[44] He stressed that the British should not be seen to be letting down the

[40] King George VI's diary, 28 July 1942, in John Wheeler-Bennett, *King George VI, His Life and Reign* (London: Macmillan, 1953), p. 703.

[41] Churchill to Chiang Kai-shek, 26 August 1942, *Transfer of Power*, vol. 2, no. 637.

[42] 21 June 1943, Barnes and Nicholson (eds), *Amery Diaries*, p. 895.

[43] Record by Phillips of conversation with Churchill, 11 December 1942, Venkataramani and Shrivastava, *Roosevelt, Gandhi and Churchill*, pp. 70–1; minute of Churchill, 9 December 1944, *Transfer of Power*, vol. 5, no. 146; R.A. Butler, *The Art of the Possible* (London: Hamilton, 1971), p. 111.

[44] Churchill to Jinnah, 3 August 1946, cited in Martin Gilbert, *Winston S. Churchill: Never Despair 1945–1965* (London: Heinemann, 1988), vol. 8, p. 248.

princes, the Muslims, and the scheduled classes, and kept in touch with Jinnah and with B.R. Ambedkar, the leader of the Harijans or 'untouchables'. He was in favour of making India a party issue, but Eden and Butler, while going along with Churchill in insisting that the British government should not take sides with any of the parties in India, declined to make India a partisan matter in British politics.[45] They could not, however, prevent Churchill from periodically airing his views in the House of Commons. By now Nehru had replaced Gandhi as the prime mover on the Congress side, and Churchill's attitude to him was mixed. In 1937 he had described Nehru as 'communist, revolutionary, most capable and most implacable of the enemies of the British connection with India.'[46] But Nehru's speeches and writings in Britain in 1938 advocating collective security and condemning the dictators and the Munich agreement seem to have won Churchill's approval, and in 1939, on the eve of Nehru's visit to China, Churchill sent him a message of goodwill through the Chinese ambassador in London.[47] Then in 1940, when Nehru was given a savage sentence of imprisonment for four years, Churchill instructed Amery to telegraph at once to the viceroy expressing the hope that the actual rigour of the sentence would be moderated and Nehru not treated like a common criminal.[48] But events thereafter were such that Churchill thought Nehru had good reason to be Britain's bitterest enemy;[49] and Churchill, while claiming to have nothing personal against Nehru, and giving him credit for ordering the army to open fire on Hindu mobs,[50] denounced the British government

[45] Lord Pethick-Lawrence's record of talk with R.A. Butler, 27 November 1946, *Transfer of Power*, vol. 9, no. 105; Butler to Wavell, 5 December 1946, Moon (ed.), *Wavell*, p. 390.

[46] 'The New Phase in India', *Evening Standard*, 16 April 1937.

[47] Jawaharlal Nehru, *Discovery of India* (Calcutta: Signet Press, 1945), p. 439.

[48] Amery to Linlithgow, 14 November 1940, Mss Eur F 125, Linlithgow Papers, vol. ix, IOL.

[49] See Churchill's speech in the House of Commons, 6 March 1947.

[50] Churchill in House of Commons, 12 December 1946. In fact there had been no occasion for Nehru to give any such order.

for having brought the Congress into the Interim Indian government in September 1946 with Nehru as vice president of the Viceroy's Council. 'It was a cardinal mistake to entrust the government to Mr. Nehru . . . In handing over the Government of India to the so-called political classes, you are handing over to men of straw of whom in a few years no trace will remain.' Rather than utilize the services of Lord Mountbatten to carry through an Operation Scuttle, Churchill asserted that the government should consider inviting the aid of the United Nations.[51]

The hostility was toned down when Mountbatten succeeded in persuading the Congress to accept Dominion Status if the date for the transfer of power were brought forward; and Churchill was willing to support the government if Pakistan would also agree to be a Dominion. As Jinnah was avoiding any commitment on this issue, Mountbatten sought Churchill's support in bringing Jinnah into line. 'By God', Churchill is reported to have remarked, 'he is the one person who cannot do without British help.' He advised Mountbatten to threaten Jinnah by recalling all British officers from the units of the armed services transferred to Pakistan, thereby making it clear that it would be impossible to run Pakistan without British help. He also authorized Mountbatten to give Jinnah the message, 'This is a matter of life and death for Pakistan, if you do not accept this offer with both hands.'[52] It is not clear from the record whether Mountbatten passed on this message to Jinnah; but certainly Jinnah realized that with India becoming a Dominion, it would be hazardous for Pakistan to keep out, and on 15 August 1947 the establishment of the two Dominions received the support of all parties in Britain.

Churchill had encouraged Mountbatten to stay on as governor general of India even though he was not to have a similar position in Pakistan as well.[53] But Churchill's goodwill for India (which he insisted on calling Hindustan) was short-lived. He berated Mountbatten,

[51] Churchill in the House of Commons, 6 March 1947.

[52] Record of Mountbatten's interview with Churchill, 22 May 1947, *Transfer of Power*, vol. 10, no. 513.

[53] Churchill's message to Mountbatten, *Transfer of Power*, vol. 11, no. 26.

with the conflict in Kashmir in mind, for having supported Britain's enemies against the Muslims, who were Britain's friends, and advised Mountbatten to get out quickly and not involve the king and his country in further backing traitors.[54] He was critical of India's police action in taking over the administration of Hyderabad and urged Eden to oppose as strongly as possible the Labour government's acquiescence in this, which was 'about the most odious of transactions as any in which a British Ministry has ever been implicated.'[55] But there was again a sharp shift in Churchill's attitude to independent India in the spring of 1949, when Nehru suggested that a way should be found for India, even after becoming a republic, to continue as a member of the Commonwealth. Drawing on his sense of history, Churchill found a precedent in Roman times for the presence of a republic in the Commonwealth and thought in terms of the king becoming the president of India.[56] After a formula was found in April 1949 for India's continuance in the Commonwealth, Churchill expressed a desire to call on Nehru. The Indian prime minister went round himself and at their first meeting Churchill was emotional, saying something to the effect: 'Sir, I have done you great wrong. You are like the prodigal who has returned to the fold of the family.'[57] He advised the Conservative party that it was absolutely necessary for it to have a policy which was not unfavourable to the new India,[58] and when Smuts cabled from South Africa deploring India's continuance as a republic in the Commonwealth, Churchill replied: 'When I asked myself the question, "Would I rather have them in, even on these terms, or let them go altogether", my heart gave the answer, "I

[54] 19 November 1947, in Philip Zeigler, *Mountbatten* (London: Collins, 1985), p. 461.

[55] Churchill to Eden, 12 September 1948, in Gilbert, *Churchill*, vol. 8, 431.

[56] V.K. Krishna Menon (High Commissioner of India in London) to Nehru, 11 March 1949, Nehru Papers, Nehru Memorial Museum & Library (NMML), New Delhi.

[57] Nehru's report of conversation in Jagat S. Mehta, 'The Nehru We Loved to Serve' (mimeo paper, University of Texas, Austin).

[58] Dictation notes, 2 May 1949, in Gilbert, *Churchill*, vol. 8, p. 743.

want them in." Nehru has certainly shown magnanimity.'[59] Later that year, when Nehru was passing through London on his way to Washington, Churchill met him and said he would have liked to have had the opportunity to introduce Nehru to audiences in the United States. When Nehru was curious to know what he would have said, Churchill replied that he would have presented Nehru as the man who had 'conquered two great human infirmities: you have conquered fear and you have conquered hate.'

From this time, Churchill, whatever his attitude to Indian nationalism before 1947 and his continuing disappointment that the Indian empire had become a part of history, developed a personal relationship with Nehru over which the shadow of the past did not fall. As prime minister from 1951 he was appreciative of Nehru's standing and significance in the world, paid attention to his views on Africa, and agreed with him on the anomaly of Portuguese imperial policy. Finding himself standing next to Nehru and his daughter while waiting for their cars after the coronation service at Westminster Abbey in 1953, he said to Indira Gandhi, 'You must have hated the British for the treatment meted out to your father. It is remarkable how he and you have overcome that bitterness and hatred.' When Mrs Gandhi replied, 'We never hated you', Churchill observed, 'I did, but I don't now.'[60]

That same year the British government sought Nehru's aid in recasting their relations with Egypt. At Cairo on his way back from London, Nehru advised Nasser and his colleagues not to use harsh language against Britain even while standing firm on the issue of sovereignty. The tone of their speeches became milder thereafter, making discussion with Britain easier, and Churchill acknowledged Nehru's assistance. 'Thank you so much for your message and for the help you gave us over Egypt and Israel. Winston.'[61] He was,

[59] Quoted in Hugh Tinker, *Separate and Unequal* (London: C. Hurst, 1946), p. 388.

[60] K. Natwar Singh, 'Jawaharlal Nehru and Winston Churchill', *Secular Democracy* (Delhi), August–September 1989.

[61] Telegram forwarded by British High Commissioner in Delhi, 1 July 1953, Nehru Papers, NMML.

throughout his prime ministership in the 1950s, careful not to do anything which might give offence to the Government of India, for India was in a position to exercise a moderating influence in Asia, and it was especially important for India and Britain to be in the closest possible association in the handling of all major international problems.

In 1955 Churchill retired, and his farewell exchanges with Nehru show that he realized the significance of India seeking to better herself by democratic means, and felt that India's prime minister could play a crucial role in world affairs. 'I hope you will think of the phrase, "The Light of Asia". It seems to me that you might be able to do what no other human being could in giving India the lead, at least in the realm of thought, throughout Asia, with the freedom and dignity of the individual as the ideal rather than the Communist Party drill book.' And then again, a few months later:

> One of the most agreeable memories of my last years in office is our association. At our conferences your contribution was a leading and constructive one, and I always admired your ardent wish for peace and the absence of bitterness in your consideration of the antagonisms that had in the past divided us. Yours is indeed a heavy burden and responsibility, shaping the destiny of your many millions of countrymen, and playing your outstanding part in world affairs. I wish you well in your task. Remember 'The Light of Asia!'[62]

It is difficult to say that Churchill was wholly serious about all this. One gathers from Lord Moran that Churchill was telling Nehru what he thought Nehru wished to hear.[63]

From start to finish Churchill was unshaken in his conviction that British rule in India was both good for India and advantageous to Britain. He could be just and generous, as in July 1920, imaginative, as momentarily in February 1942, or sentimental, as in April 1949; but basically he could not accept either that Indians genuinely

[62] Churchill to Nehru, 21 February and 30 June 1955, ibid.

[63] Lord Moran, *Winston Churchill: The Struggle for Survival* (London: Sphere Books, 1966), pp. 630–1.

wanted self-government or that Britain was no longer able to sustain an empire. He got to like Nehru personally and made the best of a bad job in maintaining good relations with a free India, even if this was contrary to his set views. As he once observed to de Gaulle: 'My conscience is a good girl. I can always come to terms with her.'[64] If Tom Paulin's interpretation of Larkin's lines in 'The March Past' is correct and the reference is to the loss of the British Empire,[65] they represent accurately Churchill's feelings, for the poet speaks of being overcome by a . . .

> . . . blind
> Astonishing remorse for things now ended
> That of themselves were also rich and splendid
> (But unsupported broke, and were not mended)

'History will record', Churchill told Eisenhower and Dulles at Bermuda in December 1953, 'that Britain's desertion of her duty in India was the most serious political blunder of the past decade. I may personally not live to see all of the unfortunate results that will flow from that tragedy, but there are people around this table who will come to see that this act is certain eventually to bring grief and sorrow to the entire Western World.'[66] A few months later he reiterated to Dulles his bitterness at the 'giveaway' of India. The Labour government had done it to the accompaniment of plaudits from the United States, but the result was something the Western powers would have to live with painfully for a long time.[67] His last words to his last cabinet in April 1955 included the wish that his colleagues would weave 'still more closely the threads which bound together the

[64] Quoted in Francois Kersaudy, *Churchill and de Gaulle* (London: Fontana, 1990), p. 200.

[65] Tom Paulin, 'Into the Heart of Englishness', *Times Literary Supplement*, 20–26 July 1990.

[66] Report of Joh Foster Dulles on the Bermuda conference, 4–8 December 1953, Eisenhower Papers, Dwight D. Eisenhower Library, Abilene, Kansas.

[67] Memorandum of Dulles on a conversation at dinner with Churchill, 12 April 1954, ibid.

countries of the Commonwealth or, as he still preferred to call it, the Empire.'[68] The refusal to part mentally and emotionally with empire made India Churchill's blind spot. The isolated instances of policy or improvements in personal relations with Nehru which bring him out in a better light deserve mention; but they cannot efface the shadow thrown on a glorious reputation.

[68] I owe this reference to Dr Anita Inder Singh.

7

The 'Cambridge School' and South India

A colleague of mine, guiding a seminar on the politics of various countries, whenever he was obliged to whip up a flagging discussion, would fall back confidently on the comment, 'But wasn't it different in the south?' It is a question that is particularly pertinent to any discussion on India, be it in a discussion on history or on contemporary conditions. That the south is different is the most obvious, if most superficial, conclusion to be drawn from the latest elections in India; but this is no new conclusion, British administrators thought so too. Historians of India seem to have shared this opinion; indeed, so different did the south appear that to many it was hardly worth studying at all. A curious feature of recent South Indian historiography is that much of the research has been done by foreign scholars—from Malaysia, Australia, the United States and Britain. The corpus of work published by two young Cambridge scholars, David Washbrook and Christopher Baker, deserves particular mention;[1] for, whatever one may think about the analysis, gratitude cannot be withheld for the thoroughness with which detail has been collected from the most varied official sources.

To the credit of Washbrook and Baker, they do not assume that the south is different. They set out to establish in the South Indian

[1] C.J. Baker and D.A. Washbrook, *South India: Political Institutions and Political Change 1880–1940* (Delhi, 1975; hereafter B.&W.); C.J. Baker: *The Politics of South India 1920–1937* (Delhi, 1976; hereafter B.); D.A. Washbrook, *The Emergence of Provincial Politics 1880–1920* (Delhi, 1977; hereafter W.).

context what has now become a well-known assertion about Indian nationalism, that it was not an autonomous entity with inherent strength but was a purely reactive phenomenon to British governmental actions. It is seen as no more than a conglomeration of factions, held together by patronage, clientage and linkages. Those who claim to be nationalists are really indulging in no more than, in Baker's phrase, 'antics' (B. 25). They are said to have neither idealism nor ideology and to be inspired by nothing nobler than a desire for office and jobs and a self-interest which leads to an incessant shifting of loyalties and a constant hopping on bandwagons. Namier was accused of taking the mind out of politics; this school has gone further and taken not only the mind but decency, character, integrity, and selfless commitment out of the Indian national movement.

Washbrook is slightly more responsive to reality than Baker, but it is not unfair to speak of a Washbrook–Baker model of South Indian politics. Supported by an overkill of political, economic and social data which may stun, even if it does not convince, the reader, the authors contend that at the start the British government in Madras were only interested in the collection of revenue and the maintenance of law and order; for the rest, administration was carried on by or in the interests of men who independently possessed a large share of authority in society. The clientage network of these leaders was vertical rather than horizontal to the social order. Non-Brahmin magnates had Brahmin lawyers, clerks and priests and there was, particularly in the Andhra districts, considerable fraternizing among the various castes. These cross-caste structures were little influenced by the caste categories in which the government were beginning to think for administrative convenience.

Meantime, as even our authors cannot fail to see, a new national sentiment was beginning to spread in Madras presidency as in the rest of India. Washbrook accepts this, as well as the fact that the government promoted politicization of caste in an effort to weaken the Congress. But at this point the baton passes to Baker, and his interpretation is more imperceptive. He argues that the Justice party, which was brought into existence in 1914 with active official encouragement as a protagonist of non-Brahmin interests, was, like the Congress, only interested in jobs at the municipal, district board and provincial level. To sustain the contention that the Justice party did not take caste feelings seriously, attention is focused on old personal friendship between the leaders of the Justice party and members of the Brahmin community. All the activities of the party while in office to build up the narrow interests of the non-Brahmins are pushed under the carpet of the party manifestos, which utter the same radical objectives as the Congress party. The loyalism of the Justice party is explained away as no more than a front. To minimize the hostility of the non-Brahmins as a whole to the Brahmins, emphasis is laid on the rivalries and antagonism between various sub-castes among both the Brahmins and the non-Brahmins.

So much for the Justice party; but for the model to be sustained it is necessary to fit the Congress party to this Procrustean bed as well. For this purpose one has to reduce the significance of the mass campaigns which the Congress organized in various parts of the presidency after 1920. So the no-tax campaign in Guntur in 1920–2 is attributed to local grievances and the conduct of discontented village and forest officials (B.&W. 98–141). Hardly anything is said in any of the books about the Veikom Satyagraha of 1925. Rajagopalachari is stated to have utilized non-cooperation to build up a career (B.&W. 129)—a charge which even his most severe critic would regard as ridiculous. In the ding-dong tussle for office which Baker regards as the basic explanation for Madras politics from 1920, the Congress is seen as finally coming out on top in the 1937 elections because of better use of local men of prestige and its all-India contacts—the last being the only concession Baker makes to nationalism.[2]

In a sense, one wishes that all this were true. It would be more pleasing to Indian chauvinist vanity if South Indian society had not been caste-ridden and had lacked a social basis for a lasting non-Brahmin movement, if it had been faced with problems cast on modern lines, if politicization of caste had not been a serious phenomenon, and if caste confrontation had been mostly a matter of rhetoric. The truth,

[2] C. Baker: 'The Congress at the 1937 Elections in Madras', *Modern Asian Studies*, October 1976, pp. 557–89.

of course, is very different. The people of South India during the last two hundred years were not as forward-looking as Baker and Washbrook suggest, nor the British rulers as innocent of political machinations. For centuries Brahmins had held a dominant position in the religious, economic and political life of this part of the country, and throughout these many years South India formed a multi-caste society with one dominant caste—the Brahmins. The high ritual status of the Brahmins was nowhere more unchallenged than here. Especially in the Tamil-speaking areas, the religious services of the Brahmins could not be dispensed with by raising the status of priests of lower-ranking groups, and the Brahmins were able to extort their price, which was acceptance of the primacy of their ritual status, grants, exemption from taxes and other perquisites. So the Brahmins secured both deference and privilege. This was supported in the heart of the Tamil country—the districts, in the British period, of Madurai, Thanjavur, and Salem—by Brahmin ownership of land. The Brahmin population of this area was six to seven times higher than elsewhere and much richer. It formed about a third of the *mirasidar* elite and its marriage and kinship network spread out over a wide area. The Brahmin landowners would not, of course, themselves plough the land and had this done by subordinate tenants and labourers. All the other castes derived their living by a dependent relationship upon the dominant Brahmin caste. Even in villages where the Brahmins were not the landowners, they secured a special position; they were not tenants of the non-Brahmin landlords but had independent rights to maintenance from temple lands and were only subject to the jurisdiction of their caste assembly.

To round off their ascendancy, the Brahmins maintained, despite the best efforts of the local kings, their grip on village administration. The law too was codified by them and they assisted in its enforcement by the courts; but they themselves were regarded as above the general law and could only be tried by their own caste panchayats. The coming of the East India Company made no difference to this. In 1816 the British created the office of village headman with police and judicial functions and in 1836 revenue collection was added to his duties. But in fact the village headman, frequently a Brahmin, functioned as merely one member of the Brahmin panchayat which administered the villages till the end of the century.

Not being a static elite, the Brahmins were quick to take advantage of education in the English-teaching schools and colleges which sprang up in the nineteenth century. To ritual status, traditional literacy, landownership and official influence they now added the asset of the new learning. South India was the earliest field of missionary endeavour and attracted the largest share of missionary enterprise; and by 1850 there was a wide network of schools, seminaries, and printing houses, covering almost every district and even extending into remote villages where the influence of the *raj* was almost imperceptible. As the missionaries concentrated more on schools than on colleges, Madras was more advanced in primary education and more backward in higher education than the other presidencies. The Brahmins did not allow their religious commitment and orthodoxy to inhibit their utilization of missionary institutions or their access to the occupational opportunities which a knowledge of English would provide. Even Christian proselytization did not worry them much, and it was the higher non-Brahmin castes who appear more resentful of this. There is a revealing description provided by the *Madras Native Herald*, a newspaper run by non-Brahmins, in August 1861 of the Scottish Free Church Mission School in Madras city; 'the Sebastopol of southern India, the citadel of Satan, the centre of caste, pride and Brahminism.'

By 1870 the Madras presidency had caught up in higher education, and here again it was the Brahmins who were in the forefront. By the end of the century, constituting about 3.6 per cent of the population, they provided about 69 per cent of the graduates, while the non-Brahmin Hindus, who formed about 88 per cent of the population, had about 20 per cent of the graduates. This lop-sidedness was reflected in the public services and the professions. The decision of the Madras government in 1858 that recruitment to all posts, barring the lowest, should be by competitive examination facilitated this. Few Brahmins from Madras entered the Indian Civil Service because they were unwilling to cross the seas; but below the top level they secured a disproportionate share of the posts.

For long the British government did not mind this Brahmin domination of education and official employment, for the Brahmins were basically loyal. As Sykes reported from Salem in 1853, 'A Brahmin never considers himself of any nation; he is "twice-born" and by virtue of this is bound by no such ties . . . He and his father . . . have had nothing to do with one nation more than another. And whoever may rule India, he fully believes that all financial affairs will be administered as hitherto . . . through those "twice-born".' The first stirrings of political awareness in Madras were among the high-caste non-Brahmins, who first set up a branch of the British Indian Association and then, disliking its attitude, established their own Madras Native Association. Had this channel of political and social articulation remained open and gained strength, it might have precluded the later major development of Madras politics along caste lines. But the government and the missionaries in alliance thwarted this effort. Thereafter, for many years the government had little to worry about from either the Brahmins or the non-Brahmins; as Washbrook observes so sensitively, 'between 1895 and 1916, scarcely a single anti-British dog barked on the streets' (W. 233). But the Brahmins were, from the 1890s beginning to take an interest in politics and to join the Congress party. In 1909 they secured nine out of the ten elected seats in the councils, and in 1916 they held 14 out of 15 seats allotted to the Madras presidency in the All-India Congress Committee. With the Congress transforming itself from a moderate into an agitational party, the government had at last to sit up and take notice. Tilak's activities in Maharashtra brought home to the officials that Brahmins were not above sedition; and in Madras itself Brahmins were enrolling themselves in considerable numbers in the Theosophical Society and the Home Rule leagues. Mrs Besant was bringing together nationalist sentiment, Hindi revivalist feeling, and a general support of Brahmin authority.

To combat this growing strength of the Congress, the authorities in Madras could not utilize communal and provincial issues. The Muslims and Sikhs were too few to matter, and migrations from other provinces hardly existed. It is true that the Madras presidency was multilingual, but antagonism between Malayalis, Andhras, and Tamils still lay below the surface. However, caste rancour was an obvious lever for promoting political dissension. The Brahmin monopoly of power, prestige, and property was glaring even as late as 1918. In what was broadly a three-tier structure of Brahmins, non-Brahmins, and adi-Dravidas, a strong dislike of Brahmin hegemony was beginning to develop among the other two sections of society. They were not anti-religious or anti-Hindu but anti-Brahmin. This feeling was not submerged by rivalries among the non-Brahmin castes, an acceptance of Brahmin ritual status and utilization of Brahmin services. The British were not loath to further this feeling for their own purpose. The Justice party was formed with their energetic support. In 1916 Tyagaraya Chetty attacked the Home Rule movement as a scheme devised by Brahmins who were not content with a virtual monopoly of official posts throughout the country but wished to take over the government. Washbrook tries to explain this attitude by stating that Chetty's anti-Brahminism 'was more political than racial' (W. 214). This sentence, as it stands, is meaningless. It is astonishing that in a book with pretensions to scholarship and published in 1977 it should be assumed that caste difference could possibly have a racial basis. To be charitable, what Washbrook presumably wants to say is that politicization of caste differences had occurred, which is true enough. In 1917, at the first non-Brahmin conference, T.M. Nair asked why a political non-Brahmin movement had come to the surface, and gave the answer: 'We felt that we ought to give the British Government all the support we can in crushing out any movement in this country which is calculated to undermine their influence and much more to completely sever their connection as rulers of this country.'[3] Willingdon, on coming out as governor of Madras in 1919, failed to understand the motivation of British policy and thought the stress on caste feeling overdone. 'I really think', he wrote to Montagu,[4] 'it is largely artificial'. A few months later he was expressing his intense dislike of the non-Brahmins: 'These non-Brahmins are certainly the

[3] Reported in *Justice*, 22 August 1917.

[4] 20 May 1919, Mss. Eur. F 93, vol. 4, Willingdon Papers, India Office Library.

dirtiest, meanest devils I've ever come across, and again I say why the d-l they were allowed this most unfair advantage (of separate representation) which they are most unfairly exploiting, I can't think.'[5] But then came non-cooperation and the evidence of the Congress under Brahmin leadership gaining mass support. Washbrook recognizes this, grants that the vote-pulling capacity of the Congress had become so great that some local elections were practically decided in the Congress district offices, and points out that Brahmins like Venkatapayya in Bezwada and Kaleswara Rao in Guntur stood at the head of political networks (W. 182-3). Willingdon at the time saw this too, and his distaste for the non-Brahmins gave way to political considerations. Just over a year after drenching the non-Brahmins in invective he is reporting to Montagu: 'politically, the non-Brahmin is the most steady of our politicians and this should keep our presidency all right.' All two weeks later, 'Gandhi goes on organizing and is to my mind catching hold as there is no counter-propaganda. I am trying hard to get the non-Brahmins to start a counter-campaign.'[6]

Washbrook and Baker might have been more discerning in this matter if they had paid more attention to the Malayalam-speaking district of Malabar as well as the neighbouring states of Travancore and Cochin. There the local Brahmins enjoyed a very high status in the social hierarchy; and the same status was claimed by the non-Malayali Brahmins, who appeared in these areas in increasing numbers from the early eighteenth century, secured most of the jobs and dominated trade and money-lending.[7] From 1817 to 1877 they held the diwanship of Travancore without a break, and for long stretches even thereafter. This Brahmin dominance was resented by the educated Nayars wanting employment. By the end of the century, Malabar was one of the most literate districts in the presidency. Many of these Nayars, failing to get jobs in Travancore and Cochin, migrated to Madras city and helped to fan anti-Brahmin agitation in the presidency as a whole.

[5] 5 February 1920, ibid.

[6] 6 and 21 March 1921, ibid.

[7] For further details, see R. Jeffrey, *The Decline of Nayar Dominance* (Delhi, 1976).

So, while one is thankful to the industry of Washbrook and Baker, many facts which they have unearthed go against their own interpretation and suggest that politics cannot be explained by politics alone. That the Congress and the Justice party are both interested in jobs and patronage, that they voice identical slogans and set forth similar aims and intentions in their party documents do not add up to the total answer. The social antagonisms of caste had begun to seep into politics, and the British promoted and took the fullest advantage of this. One cannot run away from the fact that Brahmins and Congress and nationalist leadership in Madras tended to overlap, just as the Justice party became synonymous with non-Brahmin interests as well as loyalism. In 1923 the chief secretary of the Madras government reported, in a matter-of-fact way, that there was a fairly well-defined ministerial party composed of non-Brahmins, and the opposition consisted entirely of Brahmins.[8] Goschen, Willingdon's successor as governor, reported seriously to the secretary of state, Birkenhead, in 1925 that as Tyagaraya Chetty lay unconscious and dying, he kept saying, 'Swarajists are humbugs, be loyal to the throne.'[9]

In Madras presidency, unlike in other parts of India, with the spectacular exception of the Mapilla rebellion, peasant unrest neither erupted sporadically nor influenced provincial politics to any marked degree. These were, except for the peaks of Congress mass campaigns, broadly a matter of limited constitutional activity and elections on a restricted franchise. They could, therefore, be enclosed and articulated in a caste idiom. It was the political community of caste which, surmounting class differences, kept together Andhra landholders, Tamil businessmen and educated Malayalis; and it was the incongruity of this situation that, to a large extent, explains the defeats of the Justice party in 1934 and 1937 at the hands even of narrow electorates. The Congress boycotted the elections in 1920. But in all elections thereafter, despite limited suffrage, the Congress steadily increased its

[8] 16 July 1923, Parliamentary Papers 1924–5, vol. 10 (cmd. 2361), 266, House of Commons.

[9] 13 May 1925, Mss. Eur. D. 595, vol. 2, Goschen Papers, India Office Library.

vote. This establishes that the nationalist groundswell was growing incessantly among even the non-Brahmins, despite the Justice party enjoying the advantages of office and the support of the officials. To underrate these trends and to seek full explanations on the basis of other categories is to miss many of the nuances, and some even of the deep tides, of Madras politics.

PART II

JAWAHARLAL NEHRU AND HIS CONTEMPORARIES

8

The Mind of Jawaharlal Nehru

The subject I have chosen for these lectures might seem limited and inconsequential. Why talk of the mental development of an individual, that too someone who has been dead for over thirteen years and who, if he has left any mark on this country at all, has left it, as many nowadays claim, for the worse? Such an approach has first to be justified before we get to the substance of our topic.

Individuals do matter in history, not in the old-fashioned sense of changing the course of history, for history is not epitomized in an individual; it is not a game of personalities but the interplay of social forces, economic relations, and new or hegemonic ideas. However, even Marxist scholars today accept that individuals can be significant and representative figures in history, and some of the most important work of contemporary Marxist historians has been in the field of biography. The question then arises, was Nehru such a significant and representative figure? Deservedly or not, he played a more crucial role than most Indians of his generation. His mind, unusually convoluted and sophisticated, symbolized the thinking of a large number of his educated countrymen at a time when, because of circumstances, their thinking mattered more than was normal. The cross-currents and contradictions in Nehru's mind were shared, to a lesser or greater degree, by the many Indians who found in him their spokesman both before and after 1947.

Nehru, then, mattered; but did he matter for the bad? The developments of the two years from 1975 to 1977 have made the name of Nehru almost a dirty word in this country. The *Economic and Political Weekly*, writing at the height of the Emergency, had this to say: 'What one sees is not a departure from the path set by Nehru, but a continuation along the same lines, more purposeful and self-assured, and less encumbered by Hamletian attitudinisations.'[1] Even after the end of the Emergency, this tendency to blame Nehru has continued. We are told from high quarters that he was the wrong choice as prime minister and that his policies have led logically to disaster. In one of the recent books on these two years, Mr C.G.K. Reddy, whose own resistance to authoritarianism has earned him the right to be heard, states, 'It is only now . . . that the country is willing to abandon the myth of Nehru as a great democrat, socialist and adventurer, and has begun, to see the vanity, pettiness and the Machiavellian quality of the man.'[2]

It can, of course, from the other side be argued that the electoral defeat of dictatorship was, in a sense, the posthumous achievement of Nehru, that he had so well educated the Indian people in the rights of citizenship, taught them, through a series of general elections, that the franchise is the ultimate weapon, so firmly rooted the democratic system in India that, in 1977, in the crisis of its existence, it had the last laugh—that, in fact, it was the Nehru inheritance that could not be uprooted and that he defeated his enemies from the grave. But it is not my purpose, in these lectures, to get entangled in this debate. I only wish to notice that this debate still continues and that an analysis of the mind, thought, and achievement of Nehru is still valid, still immediate and relevant. It is also a topic which, though current, calls for historical treatment for two reasons. Various influences and traditions, prevalent ideas as well as thinking of previous times, came to play on Nehru's responsive intellect. Moreover, Nehru's mind was one which evolved; in fact, it never ceased evolving, and I hope to show that all his analyses and policies were the result of ceaseless shaping—of thought that was never rigid and of continuous development. His was a mind of many layers—over the years it took in much and rarely

[1] 13 November 1976.
[2] *Baroda Dynamite Conspiracy* (Delhi: Vision, 1977), pp. 12–13.

sloughed off anything. I do not intend to go into all aspects of his various policies or list his diverse achievements. This would be both tedious and impractical. I shall only follow the main strands of his mental development to the extent that they are relevant to his actions and pertinent to our recent history.

Formative Ideology

The framework of thought that Nehru formulated for himself over a long stretch of years upto 1947, which influenced his policies as prime minister—policies which were accepted by the large number of Indians who followed his lead—had some ambivalences which often became weaknesses. This was because there was no leaning to a readymade ideology worked out by others and adapted to India, but a putting together of bits and pieces. Looking back today at the ideology of Asian and African nationalism, with the integrated drive of Mao and the clear and sharp ideas of Fanon and Cabral before us, Nehru appears eclectic, contradictory, and fumbling. His efforts at formulating a coherent body of thought and practice seem weak, halting, incomplete and, as Nehru himself thought, perhaps circumscribed by his class background. The Mahatma, though he borrowed much from the West, had the advantage of internalizing all his ideas and actions in the Indian experience, whereas Nehru was always in a way the outsider. He was always conscious of this, and it was one of the main elements in his deference to Gandhi. Nehru saw himself as an upper-class figure, who cared for the people, whom the people loved, but who lacked the common touch such as Gandhi had.

This is where Nehru has suffered from both his own self-criticism and the historian's hindsight. To do him justice, it should be remembered that he was also the pioneer of a new phase of 'third world' nationalism. So long as the national movement in India was the comfortable monopoly—as it was till 1920—of the middle class, there was no need to strive for a well-thought-out philosophy of action. That class was aware of its own interests and realized, without much close argument, what to demand or to concede, when to resist, where to push. But once Gandhi broke the monopoly of the middle class, effected peasant mobilization in politics, and made Indian nationalism a heterogeneous social movement, it became Nehru's burden to find for this new phase of nationalism an ideology which would hold the various classes together. Denying himself the easy, because total, answer of Marxism, he worked out a more untidy and complex analysis, and it is worth reminding ourselves that most of the more clear-sighted exponents of nationalist thought in Asia and Africa are, in a sense, standing on Nehru's shoulders.

So it can be argued that the shakiness, hesitancies, and faltering nature of Nehru's thought are not to be scorned at. But why did he reject Marxism in its completeness? The answer is a compound one, of personality, context, and mental attitudes. There is, first of all, the romanticism which was one of the deepest layers of his mind. His emotions had to be stirred and involved before he could react. This explains why it required the massacre of Amritsar to draw him fully into the national movement; and thereafter the emotional commitment was always predominant. In the early 1920s, he thrilled in jail-going and hugged the fact of sacrifice. In his diaries and letters of those days, echoes of romantic poetry and precedents drawn from the Italian Risorgimento blend with a complacent absence of reflection. Even in later years, after he had nourished his intellect to robustness, this streak of romanticism was not submerged. In the late 1920s he informed a British official that his only ambition was to be buried in the foundations of free India. At Ahmednagar Fort in 1942, he noted in his diary a sentence of the Buddha, 'I would enter a blazing fire but I would not enter my home with my goal unattained', and Nehru added that as he came across this sentence by chance, 'a thrill passed through me, almost an electric shock.' The romanticist element is prominent also in *The Discovery of India*. Written in one of the dark periods of Indian nationalism, when Nehru loyally went to prison but doubted if the Congress had taken the right decision, the book is an emotional comprehension of India's past, a stress on her continuous culture, vitality, and staying power through all ups and downs. It is a throwback, however sensitively formulated, to the cultural nationalism of the nineteenth century, and it is this which makes the *Discovery* poor in historical analysis. Soaked in Western culture but wishing to idealize all things and thought 'Indian', Nehru found a compromise in quoting such Western scholars as approved of and applauded India's past.

As prime minister, Nehru remained a romanticist, who was kept going by his faith in the Indian people. Unlike the Mahatma, who was a strong man providing strength to others, Nehru drew strength from popular idolatry. He was no longer, as in the days of the freedom struggle, embarrassed by this affection of the people; he was not so much overcome by a sense of his unworthiness as, forced by the death of Gandhi to stand on his own feet, seeking support from popular acceptance. He still could not get close to others, either as individuals or in a crowd; but the people of India became a mystique with him. 'My heart', he wrote in 1955, after watching the civil and military parade on Republic Day in Delhi, 'was filled with pride and joy at the sight of our nation on the march, realising its goals one by one. There was a sense of fulfilment in the air and of confidence in our destiny.'[3] This same romanticist sense of affinity with the Indian people, of fellow-travelling with them, gave him self-confidence in his dealings in foreign affairs. 'And if I speak to the great people of the earth, leaders of other nations, who probably are much cleverer than I am, maybe more experienced than I am, I am not bowled over by their greatness or by their cleverness. Because my mind is fairly clear and frank and I say what I have to say and I want to be friends with them, but anyhow I am not afraid of what they might do or say.'[4] This confidence and assurance did not last through the 1950s, and the crumbling of Nehru's romanticist images and the weakening of Nehru's policies, interacting on each other, speeded up the damage each wrought on the other. But the involvement with the Indian people and faith in their destiny never totally disappeared. 'I do not despair. Although sometimes I feel a little angry at our own failings and weaknesses, I have faith in our people and in the future of India; also in a better-ordered world. It is because of this faith that I carry on as, I presume, most of us carry on. Life would be hollow emptiness

[3] Nehru to chief ministers, 26 January 1955, Nehru Papers, Nehru Memorial Museum & Library, New Delhi (hereafter NMML).

[4] Address to Congress Parliamentary Party, 29 May 1956, Tape M-17/C, Nehru Papers, NMML.

without that faith in the future and faith in ourselves to face that future.'[5] From most other men all this would seem cliché, but Nehru converted platitude into inner conviction.

Such romanticism, though persistent, cannot of course be taken in isolation; there was also the ever-widening intellectual outlook. To begin with, Nehru was just one more of the ordinary run of conforming nationalists, an unquestioning follower of the Mahatma. He accepted unquestioningly not only non-cooperation but all the other teachings of Gandhi—*khaddar*, spinning, faith in God—and what made it worse was that, unlike Gandhi, he had at this time little sense of humour. He believed that to enter the national movement with a mathematical mind was to hinder it; it was no time to weigh losses and gains; the existing system was to be destroyed; there was no middle course left. But he combined this lack of reservation in objective with an unqualified adherence to the mildest of methods. There could be no half-measures, he said in the midst of the civil disobedience campaign in 1921, and added that he had discovered no new method of driving the English out of India except *swadeshi*. He did not agree with those who advocated violence; *swaraj* could be won and retained only by the use of *swadeshi* cloth. Finding himself in jail he wrote solemnly, 'Now I understand a little what Jesus meant when he asked us to forsake the world and save our soul.'

Involved by accident, in 1920, with the *kisans* of the United Provinces, Nehru had no clear ideas about peasant participation in politics. If this activity was important to him, it was because he found it satisfying psychologically; it gave Nehru the feeling that he was re-Indianizing himself and functioning in a wholly Indian situation. But he had made no study of economic and land problems, and he had no economic ideology to offer. He had as yet no thought of providing a revolutionary dimension to Indian nationalism, and he was certainly not thinking in terms of a peasant revolt. In fact, in the general conflict then going on in the United Provinces between the government and the *zamindars* on the one hand and the *kisans* on the other, his influence, like that of the Congress, was thrown on the side of moderation, in telling the

[5] To chief ministers, 6 March 1961, Nehru Papers, NMML.

kisans to be quiet and peaceful and to abide by whatever orders the officials might issue. Often, after Nehru had spoken, men got up to confess to looting and other violent crimes, knowing well that this would lead to their arrest. In the early 1920s, Nehru glamorized the *kisans* and pictured them as brave men uncontaminated by city life or a textbook education; but he was not deeply moved by their economic wretchedness. He saw in them a sturdy peasantry which would be the backbone of a successful nationalist movement, and he wished to enlist them for the political struggle as it was being waged by the Congress; but he did not encourage the coordination of these scattered outbursts against local misery and the development of large-scale peasant resistance. He agreed with Gandhi that the *kisans* should pay their rents and devote their full attention to the non-violent struggle for *swaraj*. He even preached *kisan–zamindar* unity; and on the issue of ejectment which, more than any other, agitated the *kisans* of the United Provinces, Nehru's comment was a meaningless one, that the ejectment of the *kisan* was but a minor part of the major issue of ejectment of the British from India.

At this time Nehru had not considered carefully whether economic and social change should be part of, or even parallel to, the political revolution; and he accepted unthinkingly the escapist suggestion that economic issues should not hinder political activity. Peasants were told that, till *swaraj* was attained, they should not complain about their economic disabilities. In the early 1920s, Nehru's idea of freedom was purely political—ridding the British of their control over the police, the army, and finance. Freedom was spinning, the wearing of hand-spun cloth, justice, prohibition, removal of untouchability, and all such moral virtues; and foreign rule was the opposite of these. There was very little economic connotation. The contrast, for example, with Mao, coming to prominence at about the same time in China, is clear. Mao had had an early anarchist phase; but he had soon moved on from that. He organized peasant associations which, though they did not undertake drastic land reforms, at least attacked the social domination of the landlords.

But it did not strike Nehru and his colleagues in the Congress to take even such initial and unexceptionable steps as setting up village schools and cooperatives and reactivating village *panchayats*—three institutions to which Nehru much later, as prime minister, was to attach much importance—or demanding the minimum redressal of the wrongs of the *kisans*. Nehru did not see that, apart from anything else, this would strengthen the political affiliations of the tenants; but then Nehru's political ideas too were at this time in a narrow groove, and were merely an unformed mixture of anarchism and village government, of the ideas of Gandhi and Bertrand Russell. Nehru at this time was a great believer in devolution and in as little centralization as possible. *Swaraj* was to him *panchayat raj* and he favoured giving these village councils considerable powers in a free India. He thought at this time that representative institutions and democracy as found in Western countries had proved failures; but orthodox socialism also did not give him much hope, and to him the lesson of the First World War was that an all-powerful state was no lover of individual liberty. Life under socialism would be a joyless and a soulless existence, regulated to the last detail by bureaucratic orders. Bolshevism and fascism were the ways of the West; they seemed to Nehru basically alike and representing different phases of violence and intolerance. For his part, he preferred the Gandhian path, as generally delineated in *Hind Swaraj*. 'The choice for us', he wrote in 1923, 'is between Lenin and Mussolini on the one side and Gandhi on the other. Can there be any doubt as to who represents the soul of India today?'[6]

With self-education, however, which started in the mid-1920s, there came the evolution of a personal voice. The influence, not so much of the British as of the European intellectual tradition, grew. First of all, he developed a belief, which stemmed from the eighteenth century, in the perfectibility of man. This comes out most clearly in the *Glimpses of World History*, written in the early 1930s. The history of humanity did not strike him as pleasant; yet Nehru thought it possible to see the silver lining of progress right through the long and dismal record of man's selfishness and quarrelsomeness and inhumanity. While in later years this optimism of Nehru was dimmed, it was not wholly

[6] Presidential Address at UP Conference, 17 October 1923, *Selected Works of Jawaharlal Nehru*, vol. 2 (New Delhi: Orient Longman, 1972), p. 210.

erased. 'My own reaction', he wrote in 1958, 'to events in India or the world is not pessimistic and some faith, which I cannot analyse or explain, fills me with hope for the future. Perhaps this is due to the good fortune that has attended me in a large measure.' Of the philosophy that underlay *Glimpses* he wrote thirty years later that ever since he had written that book 'I have been repeatedly disillusioned about many things and even now the outlook is not a promising one. Yet I feel that, in the balance, progressively the good forces in the world will prevail over the evil forces. It is difficult to justify all this by logic. But I still think that it is true.'[7]

This belief in the future strengthened Nehru's hopes of realizing in India his vision of a rational, educated, and forward-looking society based on modernization, industrialization and a scientific temper. The influence of Bertrand Russell is more than ever prominent. It seemed to Nehru practical to take advantage of the experience of the West rather than go through the same stages and to move quickly in bringing a society, whose central fact was backwardness, on a par with Europe and the United States. He thought this could be done mainly by developing the two aspects of science, which to him was the central fact of life: the scientific approach, the calm search for truth, which should permeate all spheres of thought and action and result in the triumph of reason and tolerance; and the partnership of science and industry, the application of science to remove poverty and hunger.

This was a facile optimism expecting too much, and such a theory of modernization was too naïve, a credulous belief born of pure reason. Nehru was too much a legatee of the European age of enlightenment to be effective in India. His intellectualism and his total confidence in science having an immediate impact on both mental attitudes and the economic problem ignored the darker aspects of the Indian situation. The belief in perfectibility, and in rapid progress to it, hindered full awareness of the rigidity of tradition, the strength of the forces of resistance and the propensity to violence.

To this faith in human capacity Nehru added what he derived from Britain, its liberalism and nonconformity: an acceptance of civil

[7] To an American correspondent, 17 January 1963, Nehru Papers, NMML.

liberty as an absolute value, to be safeguarded at all cost. This was not a position which Nehru thought necessary to justify or argue about. From 1927 he was an admirer of Soviet achievements, but not of the coercive methods associated with these achievements. If the Soviet system were to be extended to India, it should be without drilling: 'because the costs of such drilling are too great; it is not worthwhile; it is not desirable from many points of view.' In 1936, immediately after a passionate presidential address to the Congress advocating socialism, he established a civil liberties union on non-party lines. After 1947, the organizer of the civil liberties union was not lost in the prime minister. He ensured the precise elaboration in the constitution of the rights of the individual, and the vesting of the courts with full authority to protect those rights. He was reconciled to keeping in preventive detention those whom he regarded as enemies not so much of the state as of society, especially those spreading communal animosity; but even in such cases he insisted that such detention should be for short periods and never longer than necessary. He sanctioned the withdrawal of advertisements from journals and newspapers only in cases of scurrilous writing and not for criticizing, however vehemently, Nehru or the government.

The big blot, of course, on this record was the detention of Sheikh Abdullah, for which Nehru bore the ultimate responsibility. He continuously pressed the Kashmir government to consider Sheikh Abdullah's release but, unwilling to interfere with their policy and order them to do so, he had to live with this failure. To Abdullah himself he virtually apologized for his helplessness. 'We, who are in charge of heavy responsibilities, have to deal with all kinds of forces at work and often they take their own shape. We see in the world today great statesmen, who imagine they are controlling the destinies of a nation, being pushed hither and thither by forces beyond their control. The most that one can do is to endeavour to function according to one's judgement in the allotted sphere.'[8] And one of his valedictory acts of policy in 1964 was to secure the release of Sheikh Abdullah and seek a settlement with him.

[8] To Sheikh Abdullah, 8 April 1955, Nehru Papers, NMML.

On top of the belief in man and commitment to liberty came a conversion to the Marxist interpretation of history. In this respect Nehru regarded himself as a full-blooded Marxist. He accepted that the class which controls the means of production is the ruling class, and that history is the history of class struggles. One could only understand the past, deal with the present, and face the future with confidence, if class conflicts and social struggles were taken into account. Instead of merely condemning British imperialism as alien domination, he tried to comprehend the motives, manner, and methods of its functioning. He gave new emphasis to the interlinking of economics and politics, of capitalism and imperialism, and from the 1930s his quarrel was not just with the foreign ruler but with systems.

However, Nehru could never be an unqualified Marxist. For him Marxism was not a logical construction but primarily an intellectual impulse based to a considerable extent on emotional sympathy. It was not so much a rational or even a political approach but an aesthetic reaction to the evils of capitalist society, an abhorrence of its ugliness and squalor. He was more responsive to a writer like William Morris than to the conventional exponents of Marxist thought. Morris was so affected by the degradations and impoverished human relationships which industrial capitalism involved that he moved on to a frontal attack on class exploitation; and Nehru's thinking was on similar lines. Even where British rule was concerned, he was always drawing attention to its vulgarity and the coarsening it involved to both the rulers and the ruled. In 1952, as prime minister, a sight of the hovels in which the workers of Kanpur lived caused him such intensity of shame that he developed a sort of fever. 'I have no need', he told a meeting of industrialists soon after, 'for any industrialisation which degrades a human being and sullies his honour.'[9]

Then again, while Nehru accepted the Marxist analysis of the past, he was not convinced by the Marxist diagnosis of the future. Because of his commitment to civil liberties, he rejected the concept of the dictatorship of the proletariat. Marx had written in the early

[9] Speech to the Federation of Indian Chambers of Commerce and Industry, 29 March 1952, *National Herald*, 30 March 1952.

days of industrialization in Western Europe, when revolutionary violence, which was in the tradition of Europe, appeared to offer the only way to change; but the world, and capitalism, had changed, and Marxism would have to be adapted to new conditions. Nehru was not being unrealistic in this. A development for example, such as Eurocommunism, with its acceptance of political pluralism and its rejection of revolutionary dictatorship, is on parallel lines to Nehru's efforts. Whether such an adaptation can be still regarded as Marxism or has changed it beyond recognition is a matter for debate; for Marx thought that a drastic, forcible reorganization of society was necessary for socialist transformation. The working class or its leader, the Communist party, could not simply take hold of the readymade state machinery and wield it for its own purposes. Between capitalist and communist societies there had, according to Marx, to be a period of revolutionary shift: there could not be a peaceful transition. Yet it should be added that Marx himself provided no complete political theory or programme: all his writings were in response to specific episodes and under pressure of immediate events: and he did not rule out the occasional transformation by peaceful methods.

Democracy and Socialism

So Nehru had acquired, and maintained throughout his life, a half-liberal, half-Marxist position, though Marxists would say that half-Marxism is no Marxism at all. You cannot have the icing without the cake; it cannot be decorative rather than permeating. But this did not worry Nehru; he did not borrow an ideology but built up an ideology for himself. He saw himself as a libertarian Marxist, and his idea of socialism encompassed at every stage a large and irreducible measure of civil liberty. One could have neither democracy nor socialism without the other; in fact, each thrived on the other. Nehru rejected any mechanical view of human nature and looked forward to a socialist society which, by removing economic and social obstacles and inhibitions, would provide greater scope for individual freedom. But enduring, undistorted socialism could itself only be the result of voluntary and willing effort. It was not inevitable nor could it be imposed. He had no use for the argument that democracy and socialism are contradictory and that democratic socialism is only a façade to cloak a disinclination to alter the status quo. Socialism could only come to India when the country was ready for it and the great majority of the people desired it. It was not a question of forcing the pace but of winning over opinion. The task was to educate the people so that they would be in a better position to decide when the issues came up. Then perhaps the socialist utopia would be attained, with the support of the vast majority and the least harm to anyone.

Beneath the theorizing there was also the compulsion. Given the size, the problems, the developed pluralism, the regional pulls, and the conflicting demands of religion and language, the only long-term way in which India could be held together was by democracy. In the abstract, one can think of more authoritarian grips over even large societies; in practice too, it can be argued that the British had, over 200 years, drawn India together by what was largely executive government. Nehru could have, bearing in mind the legacy of viceregal rule as well as his own personal standing with the people, thought in terms of avowed one-man rule, justified by plebiscite. But even if this had worked, it could only have worked in his lifetime. Nehru was thinking much further ahead; and, therefore, working against the drive of his own personality and the eager subservience of those around him, he promoted the spirit and nurtured the institutions of a democratic system. He exploited his personal dominance to create such a political atmosphere in the country as would ensure that no one else would be able to dominate Indian politics as he had done. One of Nehru's greatest successes was the preclusion of a successor in any real sense.

About the type of democracy, there was really little discussion. There was no political planning before 1947 as there had been organized thinking on economic matters. Gandhi had not favoured parliamentary democracy and his mind had run along lines of village administration and trusteeship. Nehru in the 1930s had criticized Gandhi in terms of Marx and contended that there was a structural violence in-built into capitalist society, just as he had rejected, from the Gandhian viewpoint, the coercion innate in Marxism. But parliamentary democracy did not appear to him to be inseparable from capitalism and seemed more acceptable than communism and fascism, which in those days appeared as the alternatives. So Nehru made no effort to reverse the trend of constitutional thinking before 1947 or to resist British influence. Like most middle-class Indians of his generation, Nehru had his roots in two countries. It has been suggested that this was in itself a drawback. Mr Malcolm Muggeridge, for example, has argued that Nehru was too British in outlook to achieve anything worthwhile in India. Meeting Nehru a few months before his death, Mr Muggeridge described him as 'a man of echoes and mimicry; the last Viceroy rather than the first leader of a liberated India.'[10] This criticism has not as yet been justified; indeed, all the facts so far point the other way and bear out the validity of Nehru's faith that parliamentary democracy can bear a transplant into a backward and underprivileged society. Ignoring all conventional wisdom, Nehru gave adult suffrage to a people, the large majority of whom were illiterate. Professor Raj has asked us to consider that this could have been a way of strengthening conservative elements in Indian society, for it is well known that peasants usually support the existing state of things, as against the radicalism of the urban poor.[11] He has cited the precedent of Louis Bonaparte in France; universal suffrage was then, in Proudhon's words, counterrevolution, and assisted in the overthrow of a republic. This thought, for all I know, might have prevailed in Nehru's subconscious; but what influenced his thinking process was the logical extension of democratic principle. And it worked; the people grew accustomed to political participation, they learnt what a French writer of the eighteenth century regarded as the most dangerous thing, that they had a mind; and Nehru taught them to apply that mind. All his public speeches, both before and after 1947, were part of a sustained programme of adult education. Over the years Nehru helped to transform the political value structure of the Indian people. It was an unseen revolution.

[10] *The Chronicles of Wasted Time, Part I: The Green Stick* (London: Purnell, 1972), p. 115.

[11] 'Contribution of Nehru to Parliamentary Democracy in India', *Mainstream*, 12 November 1977.

Elections and election campaigning are, of course, not enough; Nehru had also, as part of this democratizing, to build up the whole complex of parliamentary institutions. He took seriously his duties as leader of the Lok Sabha and of the Congress party in parliament, sat regularly through the question-hour and all important discussions, treated the presiding officers of the two houses with extreme deference, sustained the excitement of debate with a skilful use of irony and repartee, and developed parliamentary activity as an important sector in the public life of India. The tone of his speeches in parliament was very different from that which he adopted while addressing public meetings. He still sometimes rambled, but sought to argue rather than teach, to deal with the points raised by critics and to associate the highest legislature in the country with deliberations on policy. Rather than administer by ordinance or decree, he transferred some of his personal command to parliament by preferring to function through it, and thereby helped the parliamentary system to take root. The only criticism that can be made of him is that in a federal system he should have given effect to proportional representation. It was not that he was blindly following the British system. But, apart from his feeling that in countries where it had been tried proportional representation had resulted in unstable governments, Nehru was sure that it was impractical in India, being too intricate to be understood by the ordinary voter.

Outside parliament, Nehru also saw to it that no hindrance was placed in the way of a free press and an independent judiciary. On the one occasion when he slipped by publicly criticizing a judge who was conducting a commission of inquiry, he quickly sent an apology. But his main problem was the strengthening of democratic government. His theory was faultless. Such government was a fine art, the achievement of cooperative working in a series of expanding circles so that everyone had a sense of participation:

> The main thing is teamwork of those in the Government and the organization; secondly, division of responsibility and at the same time close coordination of all activities; thirdly, the building up of cadres of workers with responsibility; fourthly, creating good reactions in the public about the work of the Government and the organization. Above all, there *must*

> be the strengthening of your position, not some kind of a rival of others, but as the undisputed head of responsible colleagues who work as a team, supporting each other and frankly discussing every important matter.[12]

But, especially after the death of Patel, he himself was unable to make cabinet government a reality. He insisted that all important matters should at some stage be brought up in the cabinet; there were numerous cabinet committees and consultation was frequent; but there was deficiency in spirit and animation. All he could do was to establish the postures of collective policy-making in the hope that life could be poured into them after his death.

It was often suggested to him, particularly by Jayaprakash Narayan, that his best contribution to democratic functioning would be to function as a national rather than as a party leader. Nehru replied that it was not clear what this meant. If in practical terms it implied leaving the Congress he was not prepared to do so. It was not just a matter of loyalty to the past. The Congress had both a positive and a negative advantage. No other party could rival it in national spread and depth and it could still serve as a cementing mixture. It also had no particular ideology and he was confident that, as before 1947, he could give it gradually an economic orientation. The disadvantage of a party label Nehru sought to overcome by seeking a consensus in favour of his policies even outside the ranks of the Congress. He insisted that his foreign policy was not his brainchild or a party approach but in the best interests of India, to be followed by whichever party was in office; and we see today the result of his foresight, when non-alignment has not gone down with the party ship. In domestic politics he saw himself, if not as the national leader in Jayaprakash's terms, at least as the national appeaser, enclosing various conflicting elements in a broad pattern of agreement. Seeking to add economic sovereignty to political independence and resisting communal reaction and social conservatism need not be narrow party doctrines.

However, indispensable to democratic government is the flourishing of an effective opposition. 'I do not want India to be a country in which

[12] To Bakshi Ghulam Mahomed, Chief Minister of Kashmir, 15 August 1956, Nehru Papers, NMML.

millions of people say "yes" to one man, I want a strong opposition.'[13] But one cannot create an opposition; the moment the government gives another party a protected position which it has not earned, that party will lose such weight as it carries with the people.'

Nehru gave every opportunity to the other parties to function, to explain their views, to contest elections in fair conditions and to try to convert people to their own standpoint. It was he alone, among the senior Congress leaders, who made it possible for the Communist party to form the government in Kerala in 1957; and the dismissal of that government two years later caused him much heart-searching. He was particularly friendly with Jayaprakash and the other leaders of the Socialist party and was eager to see it develop as the second, the alternative, party in India. As early as 1948, he wrote to Pant that Jayaprakash is 'apt to go astray very often and act in an irresponsible manner. But he is one of the straightest and finest men I have known and if character counts, as it does, he counts for a great deal. It seems to me a tragedy that a man like him should be thrust, by circumstances, into the wilderness.'[14] He tried to maintain a friendly relationship with the Socialists and sought broad cooperation without compromise of the individuality of either the Congress or the Socialists. In 1955, after the Congress had committed itself to a socialist pattern of society, some Socialist leaders approached him on the ground that there was now no basic principle dividing the two parties. But Nehru declined to recommend their return to the Congress, because he still believed that the Socialists had a role to play as a responsible opposition party; and he was probably also influenced by the desire not to hurt Jayaprakash.

Ruling India democratically also involved inner-party democracy, the art of human management. Holding together the Congress as a coalition of opinion within a broad framework of agreement was one of his chief preoccupations; while giving the party broadly a leftist orientation he kept both flanks, on left and right, open, so that the party would gain an increasingly wider base, and draw in support

[13] Speech at Trivandrum, 2 June 1950, *National Herald*, 3 June 1950.
[14] 1 July 1948, Nehru Papers, NMML.

from both sides. He allowed the provincial parties to choose their chief ministers and supported them till they lost the confidence of their followers. Power and personality patterns in the states were allowed to resolve themselves.

Decentralization was, in Nehru's eyes, the foundation of parliamentary democracy; 'it is not good enough to work *for* the people, the only way is to work *with* the people and go ahead, and to give them a sense of working for themselves.'[15] His hopes lay in the community development programme and the national extension service. Nehru saw in these twin programmes the possibility of a great revolutionary change carried out peacefully and without conflict. Local democracy would provide support to the constitution. Nehru's mind went back to his ideas of the 1920s, and he talked once again of the ultimate objective of a cooperative commonwealth. It was only the forward movement of a whole people, a sense of participation not just in political activity but in economic and social development as well, that could justify, and even prevent from languishing, the parliamentary system in a country like India. Democracy in its fullest sense was the chance given to people to decide for themselves on all basic issues rather than merely securing acquiescence in decisions taken by others. Modernization can, of course, be imposed from above. Kamal Ataturk achieved it in this manner in Turkey. Even in our own times, democratic decision is not always regarded as a necessary element in the ideals of modernization. But to Nehru participation was an integral part of modernization and that which vested it with endurance. It was because the community development programme involved the masses and gave them considerable initiative and responsibility that it evoked in Nehru the crusader's zeal; and it is the relative decline and crumbling of this programme that he would have thought the long-term weakness of the democratic system in India.

However, even if this base of decentralization had been strong, democracy cannot be sustained in political isolation. In the West, liberal democracy had developed gradually, leading even to the theory that it can endure in its clearest form only in the setting

[15] To B.C. Roy, 25 December 1949, Nehru Papers, NMML.

of capitalist industrialization. So the experiment of establishing democratic institutions in a conservative society and, even worse, a backward society was not only almost a superhuman effort; it could also be regarded as anti-historical. If such democracy was not to be 'premature', it should—as it could not follow social and economic advance—at least be intertwined with it. Democracy, to have a chance of permanence in India, would necessarily have to be democratic socialism. Today, mainly because of recent events in our country, few in the world hold the patronizing view that the poor are only interested in economic issues. But it does not follow that economic issues can be ignored.

From the late 1920s, Nehru regarded himself as not only a full-blooded Marxist but also a full-blooded socialist. The world could only escape disaster if it took to socialism; and in India, if independence meant keeping all the vested interests intact, this would not even be the shadow of freedom. But he never defined precisely his concept of socialism. He rejected Gandhi's 'muddled humanitarianism' but did not specify what he wished in its place and how it was to be achieved. His was a radical, principled, and emotional rather than an ideological mind. Though he claimed to use the word 'socialism' not in a vague way but in a scientific, economic sense, to him it was always more a tendency than a definable body of doctrine. It was an outlook, a blend of science and humanism, a philosophy of life; and it would have to be adapted to Indian conditions and speak in the language of the country. Particularly as, before 1947, there was no working class leadership or even an elite leadership which could serve as an alternative to the Congress under Gandhi, Nehru was reconciled to proceeding very slowly and was content with making the Congress aware of economic issues. Even the planning committee before 1947 was deliberately unclear in its aim and, under Nehru's guidance, did no more than lay down a broad trend for expanding the presence of state ownership or control. It was as if Nehru hoped to lead the Congress and the Indian middle classes generally to socialism without their knowing it. But even after 1947 he maintained this pragmatic, undefined approach. When Jayaprakash asked him how he hoped to build socialism with the help of capitalists and expressed his concern at Nehru's proneness to run down all forms of socialist thought and practice, Nehru replied that he did not pretend to be a socialist in any formal sense of the word and surely socialism was not the monopoly of any particular group. In public, Nehru argued that it was a question not of theory but of hard facts, of raising the living standards of the people. The attitude was logically impeccable. The disowning of theory has the advantage of flexibility; but it also carries the danger of robbing policy of any hard core of objective and commitment.

The dangers of pragmatism losing a sense of long-term direction can be seen in Nehru's ideas on economic policy after 1947. At the very start, radical theories of distribution gave place to an emphasis on production, and the importance which Nehru attached to nationalization diminished. He was prepared for it only if it did not impede production or upset the existing structure. It was no longer a question of holding certain views but of timing, priorities, and the manner of implementation. Progress should be gradual, taking into account the availability of trained personnel and with the greatest amount of goodwill. Seeking what was clearly a move away from what even Nehru had described as no more than 'a strong tendency towards socialism', he pleaded in 1948 that there was never a clean slate in life, and a sudden and complete upsetting had to be discarded because it was inconsistent with any intelligent approach. In private Nehru had no doubt that this was the wrong direction, but, for the time being at any rate, felt there was little to be done. Two years later, in 1950, with the institution of the Planning Commission, Nehru hoped to transfer emphasis from production to distribution and also to stress the expansion of industrial development in the public sector, 'balance the various social forces at work in India, and pay more attention to what might be called the vital forces which will ultimately lead to progress.'

In line with this, Nehru secured in 1955 the commitment by the Congress to the building of what was termed, in an odd, half-hearted, phrase, 'the socialistic pattern of society'. The words seem to have been chosen deliberately to indicate that the country was accepting not a rigid or doctrinaire framework of ideology but certain methods of economic and social change. The socialism to which Nehru was pointing was not so much a certain desirable set of social relations as a way of solving social problems. 'I will not rest content', Nehru had said in 1953, 'unless every man, woman and child in this country has a fair deal and attains a minimum standard of living.' It was as a major step towards this that the Second Five Year Plan was cast on qualitatively different lines from the First. It was meant to effect structural changes in the national economy and to lead towards a society which gave priority to equality. The ways in which this socialism was to be made possible were very similar to those which Anthony Crosland formulated for Britain a year later. India was striving to move ahead from a low stage of economic backwardness whereas Britain was an advanced capitalist society, and the programme was necessarily very different. But the approach which Nehru favoured was on the lines of British left-wing thinking. The ownership of industry was in itself unimportant and nothing was gained by nationalizing existing industries solely in order to gain control. But it was important for the state to control the strategic points of production. Any discussion on the relative merits of the public and private sectors was unrealistic; for the argument that the private sector was sacrosanct no longer held good, and there was no doubt that the public sector would grow and gradually dominate the scene. But both sectors had their roles in increasing production within the broad limits of general control by the state and could even help by healthy rivalry in keeping each other up to the mark. As technology and monopoly had not in India reached the stage which endangered society as a whole, the steps necessary in Western countries to control monopoly capitalism were not as yet required in India. There was enough time for the public sector to grow both absolutely and relatively, and by stages secure control of the whole economy. So the economic foundations of a socialist society could be gradually laid and, without a major and immediate assault on private enterprise, steps would be initiated to reduce disparities in income and wealth, weaken private monopolies, and disperse the concentration of economic power in the hands of a few individuals.

In a sense, this willingness to tolerate the private sector and the attempt to attain socialism through a mixed rather than a wholly state-owned economy reflected Nehru's changing views on the class war. In his early days of left-wing enthusiasm, he had argued that the class struggle could not be shirked. The final aim could only be a classless society; everything that came in its way would have to be removed, gently if possible but forcibly if necessary; and there seemed to him then little doubt that coercion would often be necessary. The democratic method had many triumphs to its credit, but it had not succeeded in resolving any conflict about the basic structure of the state or of society. However, as Nehru mellowed with the years, he saw no reason why this should not be possible. Particularly in India, with the examples of the integration of the princely states and *zamindari* abolition, where well-established systems in favour of a privileged few had been broken up, Nehru was hopeful that class conflict could be resolved through peaceful methods. Western precedents had no bearing on our problems, and India would have to work out her own solutions. A note written on 13 July 1958 has a curious ending: 'In considering these economic aspects of our problems, we have always to remember the basic approach of peaceful means; and perhaps we might also keep in view the old Vedantic ideal of the life force which is the inner base of everything that exists.' And perhaps in one of the very last things he wrote before he died, on 25 May 1964, he observed that in India it was important to profit by modern technical processes and increase production, 'but in doing so we must not forget that the essential objective to be aimed at is the quality of the individual and the concept of dharma underlying it.'

So there was a gradual change in the nuances of Nehru's understanding of democratic socialism. At the start the emphasis was on socialism, and democracy if possible. But as may be expected, considering the importance he attached to democracy, he was clearly uneasy about this; and then he became happier with the thought that, especially in India, it would be practicable to harmonize democracy and socialism. He was pleased when a journalist wrote in 1955 of 'Nehruism: India's Revolution without Fear'—a socialist revolution by consent, without class war, heretics, or victims. The business class, which had been frightened in the years from 1947 to 1952, could by the late 1950s breathe more freely. In fact, one had reached the possibility of democracy precluding socialism: Nehru's efforts at revolution by participation and agreement were in danger of being converted by vested interests into a revolution by revisionist methods, thereby reducing it to virtually no revolution at all. So the experiment, unprecedented in world history, has not yet succeeded. The dream which has haunted every forward-looking person, even someone so distant from Marxism as William Beveridge who summed it up in 1940—'I would very much like to see communism tried under democratic conditions'[16]—still remains a dream. But its feasibility seems more likely in India than elsewhere, not because the class war is less of a reality or more amenable to reasonable settlements, but because of the very fact of under-development; for in India socialism has to be very different in its basic approach from that known in the West. Here it has to be a rapid movement towards industrialization rather than the liberation of an industrial proletariat from bureaucratic organization. So, while the experiment of democratic socialism has not yet succeeded, it has also not yet failed; and the question is still very much with us, as put by the *New Statesman* a year ago: 'How is it possible to devise a form of government which ensures domestic peace, invites popular participation in conditions of freedom, and also creates conditions for an assault on intolerable poverty?'[17]

Internationalism

Nehru's ideas on foreign policy were as pragmatic and practical as his socialism. This policy was firmly based on national interests and current realities in the world. Though, especially in the later years, he often expounded the moral virtues of non-alignment and, in his efforts to explain to his own people he annoyed other governments by seeming to claim a great deal for India, there was not so much a priggish parading of principle or a messianic universalism as a strengthening of India's position. It was part of the search for self-reliance, required to buttress political independence.

[16] Jose Harris, *William Beveridge* (Oxford: Clarendon Press, 1977), p. 366.

[17] 8 July 1977.

Non-alignment was not a product of Nehru's whims but the expression of the state of mind prevalent among the newly-free countries of Asia after the Second World War. In March 1947, just when the 'cold war' was developing in Europe, Nehru gave expression to this viewpoint at the Asian relations conference: 'For too long we of Asia have been petitioners in Western courts and chancelleries. That story must now belong to the past. We propose to stand on our own feet and to cooperate with all others who are prepared to cooperate with us. We do not intend to be the playthings of others.'[18] For centuries India and the other countries of Asia had been treated as the outer fringes of the great powers of Europe and America, and though these Asian peoples had no problems or divisive interests among themselves, they had had extraneous conflicts and decisions thrust upon them. They had now no intention of continuing to inherit the problems of other peoples; but they could not, even if they wished, opt out of the world. Since 1945, passivity as a foreign policy has been out of the question for most countries. So Nehru set himself the task of working towards the assertion of certain principles which were not only good in themselves but in India's interests—anti-colonialism, anti-racism, the concerted move-away from economic under-development, the building of ever-widening areas of peace. Even on 'cold war' issues India could exercise independence of judgement if her specific interests were not involved; such an attitude would be proper on grounds of principle as well as work to her special advantage. It was 'not a wise policy to put all your eggs in one basket purely from the point of view of opportunism, if you like, a straightforward, honest policy, an independent policy is the best.'[19]

The realistic element in Nehru's foreign policy stands forth clearly when we look at specific problems. India's membership of the Commonwealth was not the result of Nehru's liking for all things British. Immediately after 1947, the Soviet Union regarded India as

[18] *Asian Relations* (Proceedings of the Asian Relations Conference, Delhi, 1948), pp. 20–7.

[19] Speech in Constituent Assembly, 8 March 1948, Jawaharlal Nehru, *India's Foreign Policy* (New Delhi: Publications Division, 1961), p. 35.

still a camp-follower of the West, condemned all the policies of the Government of India and directed the Indian Communist party to rebellion. Such Soviet antipathy drove India to lean more and more on the Western powers. At the conference of Commonwealth prime ministers in October 1948, Nehru, while critical of the aggressiveness of the United States, particularly in economic matters, added that the Asian peoples had no sympathy for Soviet expansionism and recommended that publicity be given to this aspect of Soviet policy rather than to criticism of communism as an economic doctrine or a way of life. This, taken with Jinnah's efforts to tease India out of the Commonwealth and India's military weakness and economic dependence, made it worthwhile remaining in the organization; and it would also relieve India from over-dependence on the United States, In 1949, Nehru does not even seem to have expected the Commonwealth to remain in existence for long; for in reply to Jayaprakash's criticism that membership suggested a lack of self-confidence and an implicit commitment to one of the power blocs, Nehru spoke of the great practical help that India's association would secure for at least two or three years at very slight cost. The future was free as air, but for the time being membership of the Commonwealth would be useful. 'We are apt', he warned Jayaprakash, 'to be too sure of our stability, internal and external. Taking that for granted we proceed to endeavour to remodel the world.'[20]

The Commonwealth, of course, has lasted longer than expected; and once India's stability had been assured, the organization had to be used by India unsentimentally, to further her policies without inhibiting them. Nehru converted it into one of the great junctions of world affairs and harnessed it in support of his China and Korea policies. In the early and mid-1950s, he held the key position in the Commonwealth. But, where major issues were involved, he did not allow it to deflect him from the path he had chosen. Suez is well known; but a less publicized problem was Africa. To Nehru Africa was a neighbour across the sea and of direct concern to India. So, while he regretted the Mau Mau movement and the recourse to

[20] 14 May 1949, Nehru Papers, NMML.

violence in Kenya, he came round to the view that, in the face of British provocation, the Africans had really no alternative to resistance. 'How any decent person who is an African can be a "loyalist" passes my comprehension.'[21] Talk of the different races living together, condemnation of terrorism, and emphasis on the interests of the Indian communities in Africa were all meaningless in the face of the heavy offensive that the British were mounting against the African people. 'We are all for the multiracial society, but I am getting a little tired of the repetition of this phrase when the African is being kicked, hounded and shot down and the average Indian prays for safety first.'[22] The conviction of Kenyatta was a purely political act which the Africans could not be expected to accept. Nothing that the Africans had done was as bad 'as the racial domination of the white settlers, and preaching to the African was an impertinence when his house was on fire and he himself in agony and torture. I am not interested at present in petty reforms for the Africans; that is a matter for them to decide. I am interested in standing by people who are in great trouble and who have to face tremendous oppression by a powerful Government. I should condemn of course every species of violence and give no quarter to it. But I shall stand by the Africans nevertheless. That is the only way I can serve them and bring them round to what I consider to be the right path.'[23]

Public statements on these lines evoked the wrath of the British government, but Nehru would not shift his position, and when the British continued to object, Nehru sent a sharply worded rejection. 'Our Government is not used to being addressed in this way by any Government and I can only conclude that he [the British Commonwealth Secretary] has for the moment forgotten that he is addressing the independent Republic of India . . . It has been our constant endeavour not to embarrass the British Government and we have tried to cooperate with them to the largest possible extent subject to

[21] Nehru's Note, 25 March 1953, Nehru Papers, NMML
[22] Ibid.
[23] Nehru to Apa Pant (Indian Commissioner in East Africa), 20 April 1953, Nehru Papers, NMML.

adhering to our own principles and policies. We shall continue to do so, but we are not prepared to change these principles and policies because of any pressure exercised on us by an outside authority.'[24] Throughout his years in office, Nehru, despite India's membership of the Commonwealth, did not fail to keep faith with the African people and to press his views on British policy-makers.

Another little-known string of events in 1955 also shows Nehru's matter-of-fact approach as well as the usefulness and the limitations of nonalignment. The Asian–African conference at Bandung in April 1955 was not specifically a conference of non-aligned countries, but those countries which were represented there gained a greater cohesion. Though Nehru was by now severely critical of many aspects of American policy, particularly military aid to Pakistan, he still sought to avoid leaning more in favour of one side in the 'cold war'. He assured the United States of lack of hostility but suggested that the world crisis should be interpreted not in terms of communism or anti-communism but as the consequence of large, dynamic countries inevitably trying to expand in various ways. The approach to world affairs of Dulles was squarely in confrontation with that of Nehru, while the Soviet Union's emphasis on peaceful coexistence led to a convergence of policy with India. Even so, on a visit to the Soviet Union that summer, Nehru was concerned to put forward the case for the United States. When Bulganin and Khrushchev accused the United States of adopting aggressive attitudes, Nehru commented, 'I don't see why a strong man should always go about showing his muscles.' It was a remark seemingly made in agreement with Soviet criticism but, in fact, it had a double edge. Nehru then drew attention to the more hopeful elements in United States policy: the eclipse of McCarthy, the differences between Dulles and Eisenhower, and the more conciliatory attitudes of the president, and the general friendliness of the people of the United States. But on leaving the Soviet Union, Nehru saw his task as being that of conveying to the Western powers his understanding that there had been a real change of outlook in Moscow. The new

[24] Message to British Government, 25 April 1953, Nehru Papers, NMML.

leaders of the post-Stalin period were keen on coexistence, but they could not be pushed beyond a certain point. So Nehru spoke up for the United States in the Soviet Union, and expounded the Soviet cause in his dealings with Western governments. Although nothing came of the summit conference at Geneva later in the year, all the four powers agreed that Nehru's interpretation of each side to the other had helped.

Credit is not claimed for Nehru for even the temporary lifting of the clouds. Great powers know their own interests and act on them. But Nehru had helped to convey nuances and impressions, to act in the interstices of great power relations and to improve mutual comprehension. As he once said about the role of non-alignment: 'There are no affirmatives and negatives about it. There are fine shades of opinion, hints thrown out, general impressions created without commitments, reactions awaited and so on. If a reaction is favourable, one takes another step forward. Otherwise one shuts up . . . What do we try to do? To soften and soothe each side and make it slightly more receptive to the other.'[25]

A similar sense of realism is to be found, despite general belief, in the formulation of Nehru's China policy. His romanticist fantasies about traditional friendship did not basically impinge on his handling of relations between the two countries. From the 1920s Nehru had been of the view that Chinese communism was more nationalist than communist and, when the communists came to power in 1949, the attitude of foreign governments appeared to him crucial in determining in which direction China would develop. Hostility of the Western and other non-communist states would result in correspondingly closer relations between the Soviet Union and China, but a different policy might well lead to loosening of even existing ties between these two countries. So he advocated an attitude of 'cautious friendliness'. The exchanges on Tibet in 1950 left no room for any illusions, and even in Korea he knew that the Chinese government was exploiting his world influence. He made allowances for the Chinese view of the world,

[25] Nehru to G.L. Mehta (Indian Ambassador at Washington), 1 June 1955, Nehru Papers, NMML.

'Chinese psychology, with its background of prolonged suffering, struggle against Japan, and successful communist revolution, is an understandable mixture of bitterness, elation and vaulting confidence to which the traditional xenophobia and present-day isolation from outside contacts have added fear and suspicion of the motives of other powers. For inducing a more balanced and cooperative mentality in Peking, it is essential to understand those psychological factors.'[26]

But such understanding did not necessarily mean a neglect of India's interests. An attempt would have to be made for friendly relations tions with China, if only because conflict, or even fear of conflict and preparation for it, would grossly distort India's economy. But Nehru did not assume such friendship; the basic challenge between India and China, as he remarked in 1952,[27] ran along the spine of Asia. 'Our attitude towards the Chinese Government', he instructed his ambassador later that year,[28] 'should always be a combination of friendliness and firmness. If we show weakness, advantage will be taken of this immediately.' Chinese expansionism had been evident during various periods for about a thousand years, and a new period of such expansionism was, thought Nehru, perhaps imminent. His meetings with Chou-en-lai and other Chinese leaders in 1954 weakened the element of uneasiness in his attitude to that country, and he felt it no longer necessary to answer fully, one way or the other, the question of cooperation or conflict between India and China. For a third position seemed to have emerged, of containment of China through friendship, by the creation of an environment in which China would find it difficult to be hostile. Perhaps Nehru overestimated the importance of India, and India's support, to China's leaders in the long term; and there were also inadequacies in diplomacy and administration which brought his China policy to ruin. But there was no basic flaw in the analysis or the assessment.

In many ways, it is in the evolution of Nehru's policy on the Goa

[26] Nehru to Ernest Bevin, 20 November 1950, Nehru Papers, NMML.

[27] Frank Moraes, *Witness to an Era* (Delhi: Vikas Publishing House, 1973), pp. 200–1.

[28] Telegram to N. Raghavan, 10 December 1952, Nehru Papers, NMML.

question that one sees the relative strength of various influences of ideas and principles and how, gradually, some prevailed. Before 1947 Nehru, more than any other nationalist leader, had regarded the expulsion of the Portuguese and the merger of Goa with India as part of the freedom struggle. For this purpose, he relied, after becoming prime minister, on local and international pressures. The government and people of India themselves should not intervene, for economic sanctions might hurt the inhabitants of Goa more than the Portuguese authorities, and military action, though easy, should be on principle avoided as long as possible. The people of India, being mature and not 'children at play', would quietly wait.

Goans settled in India were not stopped from entering Portuguese territory, but all other Indians were discouraged from supporting what should essentially be regarded as a freedom movement within Goa. When the Portuguese shot down some Indian volunteers who sought to cross into Goa, the Government of India did not react to such brutality, nor did they permit the establishment in India of a provisional government of Goa. 'We have to take not only the right steps', Nehru told the chief ministers,[29] 'but also in the right way. We have also to keep in view our general world policy because we cannot isolate one action from another. I have no doubt that we shall win in Goa. But I am anxious to do so without giving up in the slightest the basic policy that we claim to pursue.'

So it was a policy of inaction and of patience, waiting for the popular movement in Goa to gain strength, for the colonial economy to weaken, for the sympathy of world opinion to prevail. The Government of India were not pacifist but they would only go to war in case of an armed attack. 'If you are under the impression that the Government will take police action or use force to liberate Goa from Portuguese domination, you are entirely mistaken. I am not going to do any such thing.'[30] But such commitment to peace and principle was regarded abroad as weakness, and the very belief in Nehru's dedication to international ethics slackened the pressure that foreign

[29] 3 September 1954, Nehru Papers, NMML.

[30] Speech at Poona, 4 June 1955, *Times of India*, 5 June 1955.

governments were willing to exert on Portugal. Those who had faith in Nehru would not take seriously his assertion that India would not accept indefinitely the continuance of Portuguese rule in Goa. So gradually it became increasingly clear that, because of the adamancy of the Portuguese and the failure of other powers to interfere, the dilemma could not be resolved by Nehru's methods. It would have either to be broken at the cost of Nehru's principles or the Portuguese left undisturbed in defiance of Nehru's commitments.

In 1957, for the first time, in a letter to Vinoba Bhave commenting on the futility of a peace brigade and the impracticality of reducing the size of the Indian army,[31] Nehru reckoned reluctantly with the possibility of having to take armed action in Goa. He could not but recognize that his Goa policy was a singular record of failure and the situation, instead of improving, had in many ways deteriorated. There was a total deadlock and India had no policy beyond that of waiting. He still believed that events in the world were working against the Portuguese and that the situation was developing in India's favour; but at the back of his mind was the growing unease that ultimately action would have to be taken by India. When the Portuguese threatened to enforce a right of passage to the enclaves of Dadra and Nagar Haveli, Nehru welcomed the prospect as providing an occasion for occupying Goa in retaliation; but the Portuguese took no action. So when, in Nehru's phrase, the cup was full and began to spill over, he sanctioned military action in the national interest and at the expense of his general principles: 'Ultimately', he wrote to President Kennedy, 'we had to face what might be called the choice between two courses both of which were undesirable from various points of view. We chose what to our thinking was the lesser evil.'[32]

I have tried in these lectures to draw attention to the formative influences on Nehru as well as, with experience and growing responsibilities, the slow erosion of old assumptions and the subtle progression of new ideas. I have selected three main groups of concepts and problems, and sought to discern, if possible, the development

[31] 4 May 1957, Nehru Papers, NMML.

[32] 29 December 1961, Nehru Papers, NMML.

of his mind, symbolic of a whole generation of thinking Indians and reflected in a nation's policies. Democracy, as adapted to an underprivileged society; socialism, indistinct in outline, but not necessarily therefore disadvantageous, and not conceived as a backward and poverty-stricken socialism but linked with production rather than distribution; and finally a nationalism poised on internationalism but not sucked into it before the world had become a fully international community.

It is not possible to categorize Nehru: for he was a Marxist who rejected regimentation, a socialist who was wholly committed to civil liberties, a radical with a preference for non-violence, and a world citizen who combined his international obligations with a total involvement in India, saw the necessity of self-reliance even in a shrinking world, and stressed the need to adapt every ideology to the Indian condition. Above all, he was a leader who believed in carrying his people with him even if it slowed down the pace of progress. In 1936, when Krishna Menon wrote from London complaining that Nehru was not forceful enough in securing the acceptance of his views, he replied: 'Try to imagine what the human material is in India. How they think, how they act, what moves them, what does not affect them. It is easy enough to take up a theoretically correct attitude, which has little effect on anybody. We have to do something much more important and difficult and that is to move large numbers of people, to make them act . . .'[33] Nearly twenty years later, as prime minister, his approach was very similar: 'A leader must always have a sense of the public. He cannot do some things, because he senses they would create difficulties . . . We have to deal with human beings as individuals and in the mass, and we must know the art of getting into their minds and hearts and not merely imagine that any logical argument must prevail.'[34] It is, I think, this compulsive motivation to keep in step with the people of India, and his faith that if he followed this policy he could not go wrong, that explain both Nehru's achievements and

[33] 28 September 1936, *Selected Works of Jawaharlal Nehru*, vol. 7 (New Delhi: Orient Longman, 1975), p. 470.

[34] To B.K. Kaul, 29 October 1953, Nehru Papers, NMML.

his failures. It was said of a general in the last world war that to say that he made mistakes was merely to say that he made war. Nehru too made mistakes; but he made them in the process of making the India that we know and have. As for his opponents and those who today have the opportunity to carp and criticize, they function in a world he changed.

9

Nehru, Religion, and Secularism

The idea of a secular India is today under siege, and doubts are being raised even about its roots. Distinguished sociologists and political scientists argue that secularism cannot endure in India because it is an alien cultural ideology, imposed on a country to which it is not suited primarily by India's first prime minister, Jawaharlal Nehru. It is contended that Nehru believed there was no religious understanding of the cosmos and expected it would yield to a more rational approach as a scientific temper and economic growth gained ground.[1] But this is to oversimplify and thereby misinterpret Nehru's views on religion as well as the basis of secularism in India.

In youth and early middle age, Nehru was a conventional believer, and some of his public utterances would have done credit to a religious chauvinist. Speaking at Jhansi in 1921, for example, at a meeting over which the Sankaracharya of Puri presided, he called on Hindus to support the Khilafat campaign, because 'if the English succeeded in destroying the Muslim religion, they will try to destroy your religion, our religion, the Hindu religion.' He then, while commending non-violent non-cooperation, conceded that if 'there is anybody who unsheathes his sword to save his country or his religion, you cannot call him a coward.'[2] But thereafter, in the mid-1920s, a reading of Marx and Bertrand Russell led him to reject dogma and the dogmatic

[1] T.N. Madan, 'Secularism in its Place', *Journal of Asian Studies* 46:4 (November 1987), pp. 747–59; A. Nandy, 'The Politics of Secularism and the Recovery of Religious Tolerance', in V. Das (ed.), *Mirrors of Violence* (Delhi: Oxford University Press, 1990), pp. 69–93.

[2] 13 June 1921, *Selected Works of Jawaharlal Nehru*, First Series (henceforth

mentality, and to perceive the social and political abuse of religion. The growing communal rancour in India reinforced this attitude, and he saw the need for scotching 'our so-called religion', for secularizing the intelligentsia at least, and for proceeding on secular lines in politics. 'How long that will take I cannot say but religion in India will kill that country and its politics if it is not subdued.'[3]

Nehru had by this time no use for conventional or organized religion and gave up temple-going and participation in rituals. A mild agnostic who prided himself on a pagan outlook and approved of the ancient practice of an altar-to the unknown God, he had scorn for priests and theologians who took firm positions on what was bound to be unknown, quarrelled fiercely with each other, and testified to the truth by breaking heads. The founders of the world's religions had been among the greatest and noblest of men whom humanity had known, but those who came after them had been far from great or good. Religion, meant to make people better, in fact had made them behave like beasts; instead of bringing enlightenment, religions had often tried to keep people in the dark; they had not broadened people's minds but frequently made them narrow-minded and intolerant. Many great and fine deeds had been performed in the name of religion, but in its name millions had also been killed and every possible crime committed. Preaching elevation of the immortal soul had gone alongside reducing the mortal body to ashes.

Nor was Nehru impressed with talk of the other world. There was enough work to do in this world without bothering about the next. 'There is too much', he told Indians on his return from Europe at the end of 1927, 'of what is called religion in our life and politics. The less we talk of and worry about the next world, the more good we are likely to do our fellow countrymen and country.'[4] Those whose

---

SWJN-FS), vol. 1, pp. 177, 183. The speech was delivered in Hindi and the only report we have is the English version prepared by police reporters; hence there may be distortions, but the text we have generally represents Nehru's viewpoint at this time.

[3] To Syed Mahmud from Geneva, 15 July 1926, *SWJN-FS*, vol. 2, p. 235.

[4] Statement to the press, Colombo, 19 December 1927, *SWJN-FS*, vol. 3, pp.1–2.

actions were prompted by hopes of going to heaven after death were like children whose behaviour was inspired by promises of being rewarded with jam puffs.[5] The methods of reason and of science were sufficient for clear thought and correct action in this world, and left no room for the authoritarianism and encouragement of superstition and backwardness associated with religions. In the West, such rejection had taken the form of a struggle for freedom of conscience, but in India this had not seemed to be necessary because in the early days there had been no compulsion and men and women had been free to believe what they liked. But gradually the rites and obscurantism of a degraded religion became dominant and reduced the people to slaves of the 'sacred books', customs, and conventions. The chains of retrograde ideas and outworn prejudices were far worse than the chains which tie up bodies, and men and women, though unaware of these invisible bonds, were in fact held in their terrible grip.[6]

Religion not only fettered the mind; it also allowed itself to be exploited by political and economic interests. But getting rid of religion in India did not seem to Nehru to pose a serious problem. He knew, of course, the causes that contributed to the continuous strengthening of the religious element in Indian politics: the social backwardness among all sections of the Indian people, the uneven nature of economic development in and between various parts of India, the advantage taken by the British of the prevalent social disharmony and their support of conservative elements, the Hinduized outlook of Indian nationalism and the widely accepted concept of Hindus and Muslims co-operating as two distinct communities rather than acting together as Indians. But he believed that religion in politics would disappear of its own, as had happened in Europe, with the spread of education and with industrialization replacing religious strife with economic conflicts. So, for the time being, he thought it sufficient to incorporate in the Resolution on Fundamental Rights, at the Karachi Congress in March 1931, clauses asserting that every

[5] Letter to his daughter from jail, 20 January 1931, *Glimpses of World History* (henceforth *Glimpses*; Kitabkhana: Allahabad, 1934), pp. 37–8.

[6] Letter to his daughter, 28 June 1932, *Glimpses*, p. 241.

citizen of India should enjoy freedom of conscience and the right to freely profess and practise any religion subject to public order and morality, that all citizens were equal before the law, irrespective of religion, creed, caste or sex, that no disability attached to citizens for these reasons in regard to public employment and in the exercise of any trade or calling, and that the state should observe neutrality in regard to all religions.

These provisions constitute the core of secularism as we understand it today. The resolution did not suggest that all religions had an element of truth or that all religions were true, but insisted that religion should have no role in public affairs and the state should be equidistant from all religions and not support any. The clauses were drafted in line with the thinking of Nehru rather than that of Gandhi. Once the leading political party in India was committed to this secular attitude, Nehru expected communalism to become a non-event. The masses had not been affected by it, and the communal parties, both Hindu and Muslim, derived their support from the feudal and upper classes, defensive of vested interests, seeking office and employment from the British, and pandering to myth and passion in their efforts to secure a base among the people.

To Nehru these parties seemed pygmies with feet of clay, who would lose relevance once the masses were provided with an ideology which would replace religion and who would fade into nothingness once the British were pushed out. He, therefore, in accordance with his favourite strategy of indirect approach, ignored the communal problem and concentrated his energies on the campaign against imperialism, and on the necessity of giving the national movement an economic orientation. The vast majority of the Indian people, whatever their religion, bore the common burdens of hunger and poverty, and if attention were given to the alleviation of these conditions, the curse of religion in politics would ipso facto diminish. Religious minorities should be of no political significance; the only minority which mattered and which had to be resisted was that of the rich exploiters in the town and the countryside.

Life, however, as Nehru himself often acknowledged, is different from and larger than logic. Communalism might have been a bodiless ghost but it was a ghost which, in the penultimate decades of the Raj, refused to vanish and continued to thirst for blood. So, setting aside his view that the Hindu–Muslim problem was an artificial contrivance which was not of vital concern to the masses, Nehru decided, during the latter half of 1933, when he was out of prison, for the first time to face the issue squarely and make a frontal attack on communalism as a cover for political reaction. He condemned the Hindu Mahasabha for its reactionary and anti-national policy of co-operation with the government and support of vested interests. This criticism applied equally of course to Muslim communal organizations, but Nehru rebuked them in milder terms. They seemed to him at least middle class and representative in some degree of the Muslim viewpoint; and its leaders behaved with greater dignity than those of the Hindu Mahasabha, who spoke only for capitalists, landlords, and a few princes and their hangers-on. Nehru also thought it understandable that the Muslims, being economically and educationally backward, would be apprehensive about the future. 'Honest communalism is fear; false communalism is political reaction.'[7] To distinguish between shades of communalism and to contend that it could sometimes be honest and therefore, presumably, legitimate, was to embark on a dangerous course. It at once jeopardized the position of the many Muslims in the Congress who participated in the national movement; and Nehru made this worse by stating that no other organization could successfully challenge the claim of the communalists to speak for the Muslims and that their aggressively communal character gave them an advantage over Muslims who were committed to nationalism.

What explains this attitude in the 1930s which ran counter to Nehru's general position and to his later efforts to combat the growing influence of the Muslim League? To some extent his slant in favour of Muslim communalism at this point was a reflection of his distaste for the efforts of M.A. Ansari and other Muslims in the Congress to reach a political settlement of the communal problem. To Nehru it was a futile endeavour to seek mutual adjustments, through formal negotiations and informal conversations, with Muslim communal leaders; unity conferences would never succeed because the British

[7] Interview to the press, 29 November 1933, *SWJN-FS*, vol. 6, p. 164.

could always outbid the Congress, and the Muslims in the Congress were constantly on the retreat and continuously offering concessions to which there could be no end. Far better, it seemed to Nehru, to accept that the Muslim minority in general was afraid for the future, and to exorcize this fear not by encouraging communal leaders but by granting linguistic and cultural safeguards on the lines of the Karachi Resolution and focusing attention on economic issues.

At a deeper level, Nehru's attitude was born of his conviction, which he shared with Gandhi, that the communalism of the majority community was far more dangerous than that of any minority in India. For Hindu communalism could masquerade as nationalism and could well degenerate into the Indian version of fascism. But if the Hindus rejected communalism and treated the minorities with generosity and as of equal status as themselves, irrespective of their religion, then there would be no scope for the communal virus to flourish among the minorities. It was the Hindu majority which had the greatest opportunity for divorcing religion from public life and for firmly entrenching this position.

All this seemed airy theorizing as, in the mid-1930s, communal rioting continued to scar the face of the country; and Nehru, languishing helplessly in prison, was plunged in gloom. 'What a disgusting savage people we are. Politics, progress, socialism, communism, science—where are they before this black religious savagery.'[8] But a chance for him to appeal directly to the people came in 1936, with him out of jail and election announced for the provincial assemblies with a wider franchise than before. Nehru undertook a countrywide campaign and in all his many speeches played down the communal issue, held up independence and better economic conditions as the first priorities, and concentrated his fire on the alien rulers, the capitalists, and the landlords. Speaking in the United Provinces on the same platform as Jinnah, Nehru referred to communalism as no more than a nuisance which made people petty-minded and hid from view the major problems. In his presidential address at the Faizpur Congress in December 1936 he did not refer to communalism at all.

The results of the elections validated Nehru's assessment that

[8] Diary entry, 17 April 1935, *SWJN-FS*, vol. 6, p. 348.

communalism was a shallow, skin-deep aberration. It had obviously not spread widely even among the middle classes. The electorate was still limited, with stringent educational and property qualifications; but even in the constituencies reserved for Muslims, the Muslim League could gain only 108 out of 482 seats, and 0.321 million out of 7.319 million Muslim votes. Nor could the League win enough seats to form the government in Bengal, the Punjab, and the North-West Frontier Province, where the majority of the people were Muslims. So it was logical for Nehru to support the refusal of the Congress to form coalition minorities with the Muslim League in the provinces where it had obtained clear majorities. Historians, basing themselves on hindsight, have criticized this decision; but it would have been suicidal for the Congress to throw away its credentials as a national, secular organization and, functioning as a Hindu party, to join hands with a Muslim communal party which had poor support even in a restricted electorate. It made better sense to move forward from the electoral successes of 1937 to an appeal to the masses rather than turn backwards and search for political agreements at an elite level.

Nehru was particularly eager to approach the Muslim masses. They had been too long doped with communal poison and were suspicious of the Congress; but he thought he saw a ferment among the younger Muslims and the rank-and-file which should not be ignored. Nehru believed that there was more freedom in social relations among Muslims than among the Hindus and, perhaps because of this, would accept a new thought if convinced of it. So in 1937 he initiated a Muslim 'mass contacts' campaign. This was an effort to implement his theory that the masses had no communal problem and could be led by an economic programme to forget this side-issue. But the opportunity was squandered. The 'mass contacts' campaign had some success in parts of the United Provinces, Bihar, Bengal, and the Punjab, but generally failed to make headway in the rural areas. Nehru's effort was broken by the lukewarm attitude of the right wing of the Congress rather than by the opposition of Jinnah and the Muslim League.[9]

[9] Mushirul Hasan, 'The Muslim Mass Contacts Campaign', in Mushirul Hasan (ed.), *India's Partition: Process, Strategy and Mobilization* (Delhi: Oxford University Press, 1993), pp. 132–58.

In fact, greater momentum was attained by Jinnah's counter-campaign, in reply to what he regarded as Nehru's challenge, to strengthen the position of the League among the Muslim masses by appealing to God and the Koran and alleging that Islam was in danger. Taking advantage of the error of the Congress in accepting office with little power in the provinces, Jinnah slid easily from attacking the Congress, representing majority opinion, to denouncing it as representing Hindu opinion. He complained of general harassment of Muslims in provinces with Congress ministries without clearly specifying his charges. Nehru had gradually and reluctantly to change his opinion that there was no real strength behind the League. Jinnah's demand that his party be recognized as the authoritative and representative organization of the Muslims was still unacceptable; but it was no longer enough merely to allay the fears of the minorities in matters of culture, language, and religious observances. Nehru was now willing to consider, in any scheme of provincial redistribution, the grant to important groups and minorities of territories within which they would have full opportunities for self-development. But the League, having little interest in non-political matters, paid no attention; and by the beginning of 1939 Nehru was forced to acknowledge that the communal problem had acquired a new and serious aspect. The fear of the Muslims that they might be swamped by the Hindu majority had widened considerably. Particularly in the United Provinces, there was more general ill-will among the Muslim masses towards the Congress than at any time before,[10] and fascist elements were becoming stronger in both the communal parties. Even so, Nehru still remained hopeful that economic issues would wither the communal problem if the provincial governments gave priority to such measures us the annulment of rural debt and the arrears of rent; but the Congress ministries were too conservative to move in such matters. By the time war broke out and these ministries resigned, Nehru had to accept that much ground had been lost. Even civil war seemed possible to him now.

The situation compelled Nehru to turn his attention to negotiations, by which he had never set much store, with the League. His

[10] Nehru to Rajendra Prasad, 7 July 1939, *SWJN-FS*, vol. 9, p. 471.

slender hopes for success were based on the League's commitment to independence; and it struck him that the League's attainment of a mass basis might prove helpful in bringing pressure to bear on its reactionary leadership. If the Congress and the League could work together in dealing with the British government in the war crisis, the communal grievances might fall into perspective. But Nehru, as he himself recognized, was not the man for such negotiations. 'I must confess to you', he wrote to Jinnah after a round of talks with him, 'that in this matter I have lost confidence in myself though I am not usually given that way. But the last two or three years have had a powerful effect on me. My own mind moves on a different plane and most of my interests lie in other directions. And so, though I have given much thought to the problem and understand most of its implications, I feel as if I was an outsider and alien in spirit.'[11] Nor was Jinnah interested during the war years in negotiations with the Congress. He was preoccupied in building up mass support with the co-operation of the British, which was now readily available. Nehru, on his part, became more concerned with giving assurances to other religious minorities, the Christians and the Sikhs, that the Congress was committed to secularism and that legitimate minority interests could be protected by a constituent assembly in which such questions would be settled not by a majority vote but by common consent, and differences referred, if necessary, to arbitration not by the British but preferably by the League of Nations.

However, much of these war years was spent by Nehru in prison, and he was able to think more deeply on his own attitude to religion. He was still critical of the way in which religions imprisoned truth in dogmas and encouraged empty ceremonials and practices. They had discouraged their followers from trying to understand the unknown and their philosophy of submission to supernatural powers frowned on social effort. Organized religion, allying itself to theology and often more concerned with its vested interests than with matters of the spirit, tended to close and limit the mind and to encourage a temper the very opposite of that of science. Reversing Voltaire's epigram,

[11] Nehru to Jinnah, 18 October 1939, *SWJN-FS*, vol. 10, p. 359.

Nehru suggested that if there were a God it may be desirable not to look up to Him. But his agnosticism and detestation of priests and their behaviour had never meant shutting himself off from the higher values. The influence of Mahatma Gandhi, with his emphasis on morals and ethics in public life, was alone sufficient to ensure this. In his autobiography, written in the mid-1930s, Nehru conceded that religion was more than blind belief and reaction; there was something else in it which catered to a deep inner craving of human beings. He quoted with approval John Dewey's statement that religion was whatever introduced genuine perspective into the shifting episodes of existence, and any activity pursued for an ideal end because of conviction of its general and enduring value. He was also in sympathy with Romain Rolland's definition of religion as a fearless search for truth at all costs with single-minded sincerity, for it presupposes faith in an objective to human effort higher than the life of existing society and even higher than the life of humanity as a whole.[12]

The extensive reading of Indian philosophy in Ahmadnagar Fort from August 1942 strengthened this inclination to see elements of value in the higher reaches of religion. The Buddha, of course, with his total commitment to finding the truth and his indifference to the other world, appealed to both the romantic and the rational sides of Nehru's nature. Reading Asvaghosha's *Buddhacharita* (written about AD 100) and coming across the Buddha's reply to the deputation that had come to beg him to return home, 'I would enter a blazing fire, but I would not enter my home with my goal unattained', Nehru recorded that when he read this sentence 'a thrill passed through me, almost an electric shock.'[13] But even the other schools of Indian philosophy attracted him as tracing the adventure of ideas. He was confirmed in his earlier feeling that religion supplied some deeply felt inner need of human nature and the vast majority of people all over the world could not do without some form of religious belief. It gave a set of values to human life, and though some of these values were outdated

[12] J. Nehru, *An Autobiography* (London, 1936, rpnt New Delhi: Allied Publishers, 1962), p. 380.

[13] Entry in prison diary, 11 November 1943, *SWJN-FS*, vol. 13, p. 282.

and even harmful, others were still the foundation of morality and ethics. Without some faith in spiritual tenets beyond the scope of the physical world, some reliance on moral and idealistic conceptions, there would be no anchorage or purpose in life. Whether we believed in God or not, it was impossible not to believe in something: some ideal or distant objective draws us on, though reason may find little substance in it. All human beings have a philosophy of life, vague or precise.

Nehru was also no longer as scathing about the other world as he had been. He now acknowledged the significance of the vast unknown surrounding us. Life did not consist entirely of the visible world; it was continually touching an invisible world which no thinking person could ignore, and the normal methods of science were not adapted to deal with it. But mysticism irritated Nehru as vague, flabby, and wallowing in a sea of emotional experience. He was more attracted by metaphysics which required hard thinking and, though based on premises which were assumed to be self-evident, thereafter required the application of logic and reason; but he was never fully at ease with it.

Nehru was still an agnostic, but a Hindu agnostic. He had grown up in an environment which took for granted the *atman,* a future life, the karma theory of cause and effect, and reincarnation; he had been affected by them and was favourably disposed towards these assumptions. But he did not believe in any of these theories as a matter of religious faith and they did not affect his life. He had a sense of mysteries, of unknown depths, as well as a desire to understand them; but he did not posit a God, and the idea of a personal God was alien to him. However, he could to some extent intellectually appreciate the concept of monism and was attracted towards the Advaita Vedanta philosophy. The diversity and fulness of nature stirred him and produced a harmony of the spirit, and he felt at home in the old Indian and Greek pagan and pantheistic atmosphere but without the conception of a god or of gods. He was also more impressed by what was essentially the Hindu idea that a human being could by self-effort rise to great heights rather than by the Christian notion that a superior power took the form of a human being.

Nehru had of course alongside been attracted, since the 1920s, to Marxism. But he found now that, while he could accept much of the Marxist philosophical outlook without difficulty, it did not satisfy him completely or answer all the questions in his mind; 'almost unawares, a vague idealist approach would creep into my mind, something rather akin to the Vedanta approach.' It was not a difference between mind and matter but rather of something that lay beyond the mind. Nehru still, while not ruling out intuition and other such methods of sensing truth and reality, clung to the anchor of precise objective knowledge based on reason and experiment; but he now saw much in common between the latest conclusions of science and the fundamental ideas underlying the Vedanta.[14]

Of greater immediate and practical significance was Nehru's understanding of India's heritage. He had always been aware that religious bigotry had little role to play in India's composite culture. In the early 1930s he had pointed out to his daughter that Mahmud of Ghazni, who destroyed the Somnath temple, was hardly a religious man and was no more than a successful soldier. More representative was Akbar, who might be considered to be the father of Indian nationalism, for at a time when there was little of nationality in the country and religion was a dividing factor, Akbar had deliberately placed the ideal of a common Indian nationhood above the claims of separatist religions. But such success as he attained in this endeavour was not due entirely to his own efforts. Akbar was a product of his times. The spirit of synthesis was abroad, and Akbar responded to it and became in fact its chief exponent.[15]

These scattered thoughts became a full-fledged analysis, over ten years later, in *The Discovery of India*. Nehru now worked out in detail, by a study of the country's long history, that the unity of India was an emotional reality rooted in history rather than a mere geographical creation or an imposed standardization of externals. Beneath the shared intellectual and cultural life among the educated

[14] J. Nehru, *The Discovery of India* (Calcutta: Signet Press, 1945), pp. 13–23, 622, 625–6.

[15] Nehru, *Glimpses*, pp.159–60, 317–18.

was a common popular culture of philosophy, history, myth, and legend. Existing traditions were accepted, adapted, and changed to meet new circumstances and ways of thought, and at the same time new traditions were developed. Every challenge of incursion of foreign elements was dealt with successfully by absorption and a new synthesis. Islam had come to India as a religion centuries before it came as a political force, and it had been received with the usual tolerance. When later the rulers happened to be Muslim, the essential continuity of Indian life was not vitally affected and the new rulers rarely interfered with the ways and customs of the people. A composite culture developed in such fields as architecture, food, dress, and music. Even the two religions, Hinduism and Islam, influenced each other.

In Nehru's view, the stable continuity ensured by the gradual growth of a varied culture resulted in a mellowness and gentleness which no amount of misfortune had been able to rub off. But this did not mean, as was often suggested, otherworldliness. The staying power of Indian culture was derived from a sound instinct for life. India had achieved an equilibrium between external activity and inner development by stressing both an acceptance of life and a detachment from it. The Buddha was the noblest example of this dual approach. Every period, during which civilization had flourished in India, witnessed an intense joy in life and nature, a pleasure in the act of living, the development of literature and the arts, and a highly sophisticated inquiry into relations between the sexes. Even in the earliest times, wrote Nehru—and the sentence is worth quoting because it obviously represents his ideal—Indians were 'a light-hearted race, confident and proud of their traditions, dabbling in the search for the mysterious, full of questions addressed to nature and human life, attaching importance to the standards and values they had created but taking life easily and joyously, and facing death without much concern.' Joy in the present and harmony with life and nature did not shut out the search for deeper knowledge; and this combination lay, as Nehru saw it, at the heart of the endurance of India's identity. Seeking the answers to essential questions was obviously the task of a small minority; but most people had some sense of purpose, of cause and effect, and of hope. Epics, legends, and traditions carried value to all levels of cultural development, held together a variegated society and provided a common background of ethical living.

Writing during a dark phase of Indian nationalism, Nehru was optimistic about the future. He was confident that, with greater opportunities, the inner failure which, rather than external attack, causes the decay of civilizations, could be arrested and changes moulded in line with the Indian heritage. The past of India, with all its cultural variety, belonged to all her people whatever their religion. If all Indians had been converted to Islam or to Christianity, their culture would still have remained the same. It was a living culture, with a firm foundation of principles but with a dynamic outlook. The spirit of inquiry directed to logical reasoning prepared the ground for scientific method. The philosophical ideal was the stress on truth, beauty, and goodness rather than on the acquisition of power and wealth. The general approach was one of the full acceptance of life, with asceticism the goal of but a limited few. The Indian heritage led naturally to scientific humanism even while it provided for the anchorage of faith. Their culture would in the future enable the Indian people to face life with the temper and approach of science, allied to philosophy and with reverence for all that lies beyond.

Coming out of prison in 1945, Nehru was forced to recognize that, whatever the long perspective eloquently outlined in *The Discovery of India*, in the last phase of the national struggle the dark shadow of communalism enveloped the scene. Gone was the buoyant optimism of the mid-1930s when he had asserted: 'The day on which India achieves her freedom, communal differences and jealousies will get solved of themselves.'[16] Jinnah might have thought of the demand for a separate Muslim homeland as a tactical move, but the Muslim masses had become so inflamed that the situation after the war, especially after the Calcutta killings of August 1946, was beyond control. Even had Jinnah wished to steer events, they had got out of hand and moved of their own momentum towards partition. Nehru and the Congress accepted the creation of Pakistan as a political necessity and not as recognition of the validity of the two-nation theory on the basis of

[16] Speech at Amritsar, 31 May 1936, *SWJN-FS*, vol. 7, p. 270.

religion. After the fierce frenzy of the riots of 1947, followed soon after by the murder of the Mahatma, independent India sought to move away from a sharp descent into savagery and to put together the broken pieces of national identity; 'We are building', Nehru asserted in a broadcast to the nation, 'a free secular state, where every religion and belief has full freedom and equal honour, where every citizen has equal liberty and equal opportunity.'[17]

With a large Muslim minority remaining in India, the categories of secularism as defined in the Karachi Resolution of 1931 became all the more important, for they form the only possible basis of a democratic, multi-religious society. The essential principles of national cohesion are not opposition to religion but the divorce of religion from politics and public life, the separation of the state from all faiths, the insistence on religion as a private matter for the individual with no bearing on civic rights and duties, and freedom for the profession of diverse forms of religious worship, provided they do not create problems of law and order. To act in any other way, as Nehru never tired of repeating, would be barbarous and medieval. But while these principles are the products of scientific, rational thinking and are integral parts of a civilized outlook, Nehru stressed that they were also inherent in India's composite culture. They were not, as has recently been contended, a gift to India of West European Christianity. They drew strength from their own logic but they also make India's historical experience meaningful. Nehru's analysis in *The Discovery of India* is corroborated by recent scholarship. Till about the middle of the eighteenth century, religion did not dominate public affairs in India but was almost one of several factors in a society, with 'a predominantly syncretic culture' and with no 'pervading sense of social separateness.'[18] Such tension and riots as occurred thereafter were the result of religious divisions coinciding with economic antagonisms or of local economic change being mixed up with religious disputes. Communalism as a distinct

[17] Nehru's broadcast from Delhi, 20 October 1948, *Selected Works of Jawaharlal Nehru*, Second Series (henceforth, *SWJN-SS*), vol. 7, p. 151.

[18] C.A. Bayly, 'The Pre-history of "Communalism"? Religious Conflict in India, 1700–1860', *Modern Asian Studies*, 19: 2 (1985), pp. 177–203.

phenomenon emerged only from the middle of the nineteenth century.

This was also in tune with Nehru's thinking on religion in these years. An adherence to basic values, a commitment to ethical conduct, and a sneaking sympathy for the Vedanta philosophy—these were all parts of Nehru's outlook throughout his many years as prime minister, and dispose of the contention that he was seeking to bind free India in the straitjacket of a Western ideology. The same trends of thought which surfaced in *The Discovery of India* may be seen in even sharper focus when he undertook a rethinking of first principles in 1958. Rationalism seemed to him inadequate for it appeared to deal with the surface of things without uncovering the inner core. More compelling was the Vedantic approach that everything, animate and inanimate, had its place in the organic whole, and a spark of the divine impulse, energy, or life-force pervaded the universe. So Nehru concluded that India should seek the objective of individual improvement and the lessening of inequalities without forgetting the ethical and spiritual aspects of life; 'and perhaps we might also keep in view the old Vedantic ideal of the life force which is the inner base of everything that exists.'[19] Over a year later he replied to a question about his religious beliefs: 'I am not attracted to the dogmas and conventions of religion, but I have certainly been attracted to the spiritual values in life and to the basis of Indian philosophy. I have no doubt that the great religions of the world contain vital truths. But unfortunately these vital truths are often forgotten and some superstructure is emphasized.'[20] He was impressed by a remark of Vinoba Bhave that the days of politics and religion had gone and the days of science and spirituality had come—understanding by spirituality the basic values common to the great religions. 'I am not exactly', he summed up to a British correspondent, 'a religious person, although I agree with much that religions have to say.'[21] Finally, in one of his last writings two days

[19] 'The Basic Approach', 13 July 1958, *A.I.C.C. Economic Review*, 15 August 1958.

[20] Nehru to J. Higgin, 18 December 1959, Nehru Papers, NMML.

[21] Nehru to J. Cook, 7 April 1964, Nehru Papers, NMML.

before his death, he emphasized that India should benefit by modern industrial processes and increase production; 'but in doing so we must not forget that the essential objective to be aimed at is the quality of the individual and the concept of *dharma* underlying it.'[22] Nehru was without religious faith but not without religious feeling.

Secularism in India, then, does not follow any definition in a dictionary but has evolved to suit a multi-religious society. The ideal secular attitude is also in India the most pragmatic policy. Only secularism of this type, derived from India's past and suited to the present context, can be the cornerstone of an egalitarian, forward-looking society, with religious pluralism, full civil liberties, and equal opportunities. It is the only possible social cement for a democratic community and the sole way to enable unqualified efforts at social and economic betterment. It provides every citizen with a sense of partnership and is more than tolerance; it is about equality. It underlay Nehru's thinking and functioning as prime minister. 'We are trying to evolve', he wrote towards the end of his days, 'a modem state within the framework of India's culture.'[23] Secularism coloured even his foreign policy. He could not contemplate transferring Kashmir to Pakistan merely because there was a Muslim majority in that state. Again, while Nehru was prepared on occasions to accept war with Pakistan on political grounds, he was reluctant to do so in 1950 because at that time the cause seemed to be purely communal.

To commit India to secularism and enact its essentials in the constitution was only the beginning of the struggle. The fact of Partition and memories of the migrations and the communal conflicts that came with it could not be easily forgotten. The consequent Hindu revivalism created, in Nehru's words, 'a crisis of the spirit',[24] and to start, as he hoped, a new chapter in line with India's heritage setting aside recent aberrations, was not going to be easy. Out of tune with

[22] 25 May 1964, Preface to Shriman Narayan, *Socialism in Indian Planning* (Delhi: Asia Publishing House, 1964).

[23] Nehru to T.A. Nizami, 6 May 1964, Nehru Papers, NMML.

[24] Nehru to Rajendra Prasad, 7 August 1947, *SWJN-SS*, vol. 3, pp. 189–91.

the communal mood which seemed to have general acceptance, Nehru at times considered resignation. 'All of us', he wrote sadly, 'seem to be getting infected with the refugee mentality or worse still, the RSS [Rashtriya Swayamsevak Sangh] mentality. That is a curious finale to our careers.'[25]

The destruction of Hindu communalism and the establishment of a secular state and society were therefore vital for the survival of a democratic India. Communalism, apart from its narrow and limited visions, was a cloak for reaction in all forms. To bring religion into politics meant the ruin of both. Throughout his seventeen years as prime minister, except for a few months in 1949 at the time of the Telangana rebellion—when he asserted that there was nothing to choose between communalism and communism in its violent phase—Nehru was never in doubt that Hindu political resurgence was the primary threat to a modern, progressive India. He felt even more strongly than before 1947 that it was the responsibility of the Hindus in India to provide the religious minorities with a sense of security. In particular, they had to make the large number of Muslims, who preferred after the Partition to remain in India, feel at home and not see themselves as second-class citizens existing on sufferance. There might be a few Muslims who were communal and out to make mischief; and they would have to be dealt with sternly. But most Muslims in India immediately after 1947 were down and out and on the defensive; and it served no purpose to question their loyalty which could not be produced to order. Winning the Muslims over was a problem of social psychology to be faced by the majority community. They should treat the minorities as a trust rather than as extraneous elements to be crushed or appeased. The test of success is not what the majority community thinks but how the minority communities feel. Full scope for the minorities is as important a criterion of a working democracy as the effective rule of the majority. A sense of grievance on the part of a minority demands self-examination by the majority.

So, when, in December 1949, some images were smuggled into

[25] Nehru to Mohanlal Saxena, 10 September 1949, *SWJN-SS*, vol. 13, p. 107.

the mosque at Ayodhya in Uttar Pradesh and proclaimed to be the manifestation of the avatar Rama, Nehru recognized the wider implications of this occurrence and urged the Uttar Pradesh government to take remedial action. That government, however, was reluctant to do so and Nehru, in face of this apathy, considered leaving all else and going on a crusade to combat communalism. But the authorities in Uttar Pradesh dissuaded him from proceeding even to Ayodhya, and the consequences of their impassivity are with us still. All that Nehru could do in this particular matter was wring his hands: 'The fact of the matter is that for all our boast, we have shown ourselves a backward people, totally lacking in the elements of culture as any country understands them. It is only those who lack all understanding of culture, who talk so much about it.'[26]

However, Nehru took decisive action on the general issue of the creeping paralysis of communalism which seemed to be overtaking even hardened Congressmen. In August 1950, Purushottam Das Tandon, who believed Muslims in India should adopt 'Hindu culture', was elected president of the Congress against Nehru's wishes. Nehru refused to accept this situation. If the argument were that in a democracy the decision of the majority on such an issue as communalism should be respected, 'then I say, to hell with such a democracy.'[27] He forced Tandon's resignation and committed a reluctant Congress to a secular policy. 'If any person raises his hand to strike down another on the ground of religion, I shall fight him till the last breath of my life, both as the head of the government and from outside.'[28]

Despite this ringing declaration, the battle for secularism was far from over. The inauguration of the rebuilt Somnath temple by the president, Rajendra Prasad, made this clear. Secularism demands the disestablishment of all religions. None of them can enjoy a privileged

[26] Nehru to G.B. Pant, Chief Minister of Uttar Pradesh, 1950, *SWJN-SS*, vol. 14, pt II.

[27] Speech at the Congress session at Nasik, 21 September 1950, *SWJN-SS*, vol. 15, pt I, p. 139.

[28] Speech at Delhi, 2 October 1951, *National Herald*, Lucknow, 4 October 1951.

relationship with the state while the government, on its side, should not be, or even thought to be, the agent of any type of religious revival. As prime minister, Nehru was always correct in this matter. He would not associate himself with any function that had a non-secular tinge, and took care to stress that the involvement of the Government of India in the 2500th anniversary celebrations of the Buddha in 1956 was not sponsorship of Buddhism but a tribute to the Buddha as India's greatest son. But not all of Nehru's colleagues, even the most senior of them, were as scrupulous in observing the secular ethic that the state should not promote any particular religion. K.M. Munshi, a member of the union cabinet, was the chief patron and promoter of the building of the Somnath temple; the Rajpramukh of Saurashtra wrote to Indian embassies abroad to collect waters and twigs and soil from various countries for the inauguration ceremonies; and the Saurashtra government sanctioned funds. Nor was Nehru able to dissuade the president from being present at the installation.

In promoting the secular idea, Nehru gave attention to all the religious minorities. The Christians created no major problem. While in the years before Independence Nehru shared the general feeling in India that Christianity and imperialism often behaved as partners,[29] after 1947 he opposed any hindrance to the practice and propagation of the Christian religion. There was no need to fear evangelical activity and Christians should not be given the impression that they were being suppressed in any way. Such a development, apart from being retrograde and weakening the confidence of a substantial section of the population, ran counter to official policies to integrate the Naga areas and to consolidate popular support in Goa against the Portuguese. He repeatedly pulled up the Congress government in Madhya Pradesh for seeming to be anti-Christian and to be concerned with Christian proselytization, even as later, in 1959 and again in 1962, he publicly disapproved of the interventions of the Christian clergy in the politics of Kerala.

There was, however, a special problem concerning foreign mission-

[29] *Autobiography*, pp. 374–5; 'Christian Missionaries in India', 27 February 1940, *SWJN-FS*, vol. 10, pp. 430–2.

aries. Their number nearly doubled soon after 1947. In particular, many American missionaries arrived, spreading out among the villages and projecting, in Nehru's words, 'quietly or aggressively',[30] the American viewpoint in politics at a time when India and the United States differed sharply on various issues. Especially worrying to Nehru and the government was the activity of foreign priests in the north-eastern areas, for they were reported to be fostering ideas of independence and advising the local Christians to keep aloof from the rest of India. Verrier Elwin, himself a British clergyman and Nehru's chief adviser in these matters, wrote that a 'Christian Mahasabha' was being formed.[31] So it was a problem not of missionaries who were foreigners but of foreigners who, though missionaries, were participants in non-religious and anti-national activity. Nehru's approach to the issue was to deal with the principal missionary institutions in India and abroad rather than with individuals and to grant visas liberally to doctors, nurses, and specialists. Such missionaries as were asked to leave or were turned away had such action taken on specific political grounds and not because of any general antipathy to evangelical activity. This too was not an approach shared by all those in authority and Nehru had to remind President Rajendra Prasad that, as the symbol of the secular state, he should not have permitted the holding in Rashtrapati Bhavan of a conference where missionaries were generally criticized.[32]

Size and history made the problem of integrating the Muslims more complicated. Aspects of Nehru's policy in this regard were to give special attention to the recruitment of Muslims in adequate numbers to the armed and civil services, and particularly the police, and to encourage their employment in the private sector. He took much interest in individual cases if they came up before him, and in March 1958 directed the chief ministers to send him quarterly reports of official recruitment, particularly when this was done without examinations.[33] Knowing also that Urdu, while not a monopoly of the

[30] Nehru to Amrit Kaur, 25 October 1953, Nehru Papers, NMML.

[31] V. Elwin, 'Note on Tribal People in Manipur', 24 January 1953, Nehru Papers, NMML.

[32] Nehru to Rajendra Prasad, 10 August 1953, Nehru Papers, NMML.

[33] Nehru to chief ministers, 26 March 1958, in G. Parthasarathi (ed.),

Muslims, was a language to which they attached much importance, Nehru pressed his colleagues, especially in Delhi and Uttar Pradesh, to give special consideration to the promotion of Urdu. If this language, which belonged more to Uttar Pradesh than to the whole of Pakistan, were denied its due, the Muslims would begin to feel that they were losing the symbols of their community and there was no honourable place for them in India. So this was more than a matter of language.[34]

Yet, it must be said that certain steps which Nehru, under pressure of circumstances, took, or failed to take, do not fit with his promotion of secularism. Special treatment of minorities and reservations for lower castes, while theoretically a violation of egalitarian principles, can be explained as temporary measures of affirmative action to redress long-standing toleration of injustice. But more serious is the acceptance of communal political parties. In 1948 Nehru committed the government to take action on a resolution of the Constituent Assembly calling for the ban of such parties. This decision, taken in the aftermath of Partition, was an obvious aspect of building a secular society. As the state does not interfere with religions, so religious organizations should not meddle in politics. But this resolution has not been implemented to this day. In 1961, Nehru, in the wake of communal riots in several parts of the country, directed the law ministry to examine afresh the matter of banning communal parties but was informed that communal parties were difficult to define and any such attempt might be questioned as an infringement of fundamental rights. But such difficulties could have been overcome more easily in Nehru's time than has proved the case since; and communal parties now flourish vigorously.

Another matter on which Nehru failed to act according to his convictions and in accord with secular principles was the banning of cow-slaughter. Nehru had always been opposed to such a ban. Even

---

Nehru: Letters to Chief Ministers (Delhi: Oxford University Press, 1989), vol. 5, pp. 34–7.

[34] Nehru to G.B. Pant, Union Home Minister, 9, 10,12 and 24 June 1958, Nehru Papers, NMML.

in 1923, as mayor of Allahabad, he had persuaded the municipal board to reject a proposal to ban cow-slaughter. In August 1947 he unhesitatingly turned down a suggestion favoured by Rajendra Prasad to ban cow-slaughter as symbolic of the attainment of freedom. He was not prepared to placate Hindu sentiment and viewed the issue as an aspect of the general problem of the breeding of quality cattle.[35] A concern for animal welfare was far more important than any particular measure to prevent the killing of cattle. Yet he allowed the listing of the banning of cow-slaughter as one of the directive principles of state policy in the constitution. He ensured that nothing came of it in practice. He suggested that any prohibitory legislation should be limited to cows and calves; but even this he discouraged and suggested alternative measures to protect the quality of the breed.[36] Any general ban on cow-slaughter would probably result in the best cattle being killed and the poorest being protected.[37] It would also flare up as a political issue in north-eastern India, where the eating of beef was common. While these valid arguments have ensured that nowhere in India has cow-slaughter been banned, by listing it in the directive principles a blow was dealt to secularism.

An even greater lapse in Nehru's implementation of secular principles was his restriction of the insistence on monogamy to Hindu men and the grant of the rights of divorce and inheritance only to Hindu women. In his keenness to win the confidence of the Muslim community, he failed to provide equality before the law to all Indian women and to sponsor the promulgation of a common civil law code. But there is no room in a secular society for inequalities which claim religious sanction. Religion has to be separated from the law as well as from politics. To deny rights to Muslim women which are available to women of other faiths is a violation of the provision in the constitution that the state shall not discriminate against any citizen on grounds of religion. The Constituent Assembly had declined, by a resolution

[35] Nehru to Rajendra Prasad, 7 August 1947, *SWJN-SS*, vol. 3, pp. 189–41.

[36] Nehru to Sri Krishna Sinha, Chief Minister of Bihar, 29 January 1953, Nehru Papers, NMML.

[37] Nehru to Rajendra Prasad, 30 July 1954, Nehru Papers, NMML.

in 1948, to accept that Muslim personal law was an inseparable part of the Islamic religion and had rejected attempts to exempt it from the directive principle advocating a uniform civil code. But Nehru felt, in the early 1950s, that the time had not yet come to impose on the Muslims in India such decisions taken by what was necessarily a non-Muslim majority. A start should be made with the Hindu code, thereby preparing the ground for the extension of its principles to all Indian women. But what Nehru postponed in the 1950s has now become even more difficult to carry out.

Nehru's efforts to promote secularism in India, on the basis not of Western ideas but of India's past, were not, therefore, an unqualified or enduring success. He had, in this as in many other matters, the right vision and the correct approach, but the implementation was inadequate and not vigorous enough in the face of entrenched conservatism. Communal rioting occurred throughout the 1950s and even increased during the early 1960s, and Nehru confessed that a sense of darkness was creeping over him. He had hoped that, as the economic condition of the people improved, religion would recede into the background and cease to be important in public life. He saw a precedent in Europe where the wars of religion, so prominent in the sixteenth century, were rendered irrelevant by economic progress. There was some validity in such an expectation; but he should also have given greater attention to the solvent of education. An educated democracy is synonymous with a secular society, overcoming communalism both of reaction and of fear. It is because of the failure to strengthen the human factor at every level and to foster a robust civil society that the problems which Nehru confronted are now grimmer than ever. But let Nehru have the last word. 'I believe', he wrote soon after independence when the horizon was dark, 'that India can only become great if she preserves that composite culture which she had developed through the ages. I confess, however, that doubts sometimes assail me as to whether this is going to happen or not. And yet at the back of my mind I feel sure that whatever might happen in the present, sometime or other, India will have to tread that path to self-realization and greatness.'[38]

[38] Nehru to the Nawab of Bhopal, 9 July 1948, *SWJN-SS*, vol. 7, p. 7.

10

India, the Suez Crisis, and the Non-Aligned Nations

The Suez crisis was the first major international test of non-alignment. Elaborated by the leaders of the newly independent countries of Asia after the second world war as the policy best suited for them from the viewpoints of both principle and advantage, it had worked to their satisfaction in keeping them out of the cold war as well as making the best out of it. Non-alignment had even, in the hands of its leading practitioner, Jawaharlal Nehru of India, been of some use to the world in maintaining a line of communication to the People's Republic of China and in reducing tensions in Korea and Indochina. But Suez in 1956, involving one of themselves in collision with a Western power and bringing in the United States and the Soviet Union, raised more basic and immediate issues. The non-aligned nations had greater opportunities; but their approaches faced greater dangers.

The crisis came to them without warning. While generally sympathetic to the Arab cause, Nehru had taken care not to involve India too deeply in the dispute with Israel. He agreed with reluctance to the Arab demand that no invitation be sent to Israel to the Bandung conference of Asian and African nations,[1] and accepted that this was an illogical surrender to Arab susceptibility.[2] At Brioni, where Tito, Nehru, and Nasser met in July 1956, an informal message was received

[1] Nehru's note, 19 December 1954, Nehru Papers, Nehru Memorial Museum and Library (hereafter NMML), New Delhi.

[2] Nehru's telegram to Indian missions, 4 January 1955, Ministry of External Affairs, Government of India, New Delhi (hereafter MEA Files).

from David Ben-Gurion saying that Israel had erred in leaning on the Western powers and the Israelis now realized more than ever that they were of Asia and must look to Asia.[3] The friendliness of this initiative suggested that there was no near prospect of war in West Asia, and the Arab–Israel problem was discussed by the three leaders of non-alignment in passing and in very general terms. On the flight back from Brioni to Cairo Nasser showed Nehru the text as it was being broadcast of the speech of Dulles announcing withdrawal of American assistance for building the Aswan dam; and Nehru found the speech insulting in tone—'These people, how arrogant they are.'[4] Nasser's own reaction at this stage, and during Nehru's two days in Cairo, was that he would abandon the Aswan dam project; and Nehru approved. It seemed wiser to distribute Egypt's resources among a large number of small projects yielding quick results rather than to concentrate on one major scheme which would not begin to function for at least another ten years and would vest any country providing the bulk of assistance with a commanding control of the Egyptian economy. In the conversations of Nehru and Nasser, the Suez Canal was not even mentioned.

The announcement by Nasser of the nationalization of the canal therefore came to Nehru as an unpleasant surprise. He liked Nasser as a person but, judging by his pamphlet *The Philosophy of Revolution*, did not think highly of his intellectual capacity; and now he felt that Nasser had acted in anger and in haste. Egypt had the right to nationalize the canal and had done well to give an assurance that the canal would continue as an open international waterway. But the language was intemperate and even war-mongering. Nasser seemed to Nehru to be undertaking more than he could manage and allowing himself to be pushed by extremist elements. In contrast, at this time Nehru was much impressed by Anthony Eden, who was passing through a phase of what Pineau described as '*une sorts de Nehru brittanique, en plus fragile*'. Nehru appreciated Eden's role at the Geneva Conference

[3] Nehru's note, 9 September 1958, Nehru Papers, NMML.

[4] M.H. Heikal, *The Cairo Documents* (New York: Doubleday, 1973), pp. 67–8.

on Indochina; they had got on well when Eden visited Delhi in the spring of 1955 on the eve of becoming prime minister; and the next year Krishna Menon reported after meeting Eden that there had been a real change in his views on the Soviet Union and his mind was now exercised about peace initiatives and competition in trade.[5] At the Conference of Commonwealth Prime Ministers in July, Eden spoke of changes of outlook and of direction in Soviet policy even if without any fundamental change of heart and referred to the new opportunities provided by a new element of flexibility in the internal situation in the Soviet Union.[6] The whole approach was highly acceptable to Nehru, who was confirmed in his opinion of Eden by a message from Moscow that Bulganin and Khrushchev were very appreciative of Eden after their meetings in London and had been impressed by his friendliness and readiness to listen to views different from his own.[7]

So, when the crisis broke, Nehru decided to make no public comment and to resist being swept away by a blind anti-imperialist feeling. He would not support Nasser uncritically for, however legitimate the nationalization of the canal, it had been done in a manner which would have far-reaching consequences and could add to international tensions. The non-aligned countries did not form a bloc and mutual support could not be taken for granted. Britain and many other countries greatly resented the action; and Nehru hoped that, as in 1953, he would be able to provide an emollient influence in Anglo–Egyptian relations. He was content, therefore, for the time being, with informing the Great Powers, Yugoslavia, and the Colombo Powers, that he had had no previous information that Nasser had decided to nationalize the canal.[8] He sought Tito's views; but other

[5] Krishna Menon's telegram from London to Nehru, 8 June 1956, MEA Files.

[6] Record of Eden's remarks at the Conference of Commonwealth Prime Ministers, 4 July 1956, MEA Files.

[7] Telegram of Indian ambassador in Moscow to Nehru in London, 10 July 1956, Nehru Papers, NMML.

[8] India, Burma, Sri Lanka, Pakistan, and Indonesia were known as the Colombo Powers because their prime ministers had first met at Colombo in 1954 and agreed to keep in regular touch.

non-aligned governments he intended only to keep informed. Nehru was instinctively inclined to play a lone hand, and in this crisis India's membership of the Commonwealth and close relations with Britain provided added justification for this attitude.

The deliberate silence and refusal to commit India to either side received Tito's approval. He, like Nehru, believed that Nasser had taken hurried action, and he directed the Yugoslav press, which had supported Egypt enthusiastically, to adopt a more cautious attitude. 'In my opinion, the whole issue, although very serious, is not so dramatic as some quarters want to present. The main thing now is not to be nervous, I believe that it is possible to act towards both sides with a quietening effect.' So he advised Nasser to be moderate and conciliatory and suggested that Nehru, in like manner, try to calm down bellicose sentiments in Britain.[9] Certainly Nehru's failure to react immediately had misled official opinion in that country. Eden thought it possible that Nehru might be willing to accept action against Egypt;[10] and the foreign secretary, Alec Douglas Home, asked Vijayalakshmi Pandit, the Indian high commissioner, if India would be interested in a conference to discuss international control of the canal and whether, in case a plan emerged, India would be prepared, in the final analysis, to enforce implementation.[11] This obliged Nehru to reveal his mind. He informed Home that what was of importance was to ensure the continuance of the canal as an open international highway and an agreement to this effect should not be difficult as Nasser had publicly committed himself to it. Any attempt to use force to secure this was, however, likely to defeat its own purpose and create widespread resentment in Asia.[12] The same day he wrote to Nasser a letter not brimming over with fraternal solidarity. He knew that his not

[9] Tito to Nehru, 2 August 1956, MEA Files.

[10] I. McDonald, *A Man of the Times* (London: Hamish Hamilton, 1976), p. 144.

[11] Vijayalakshmi to Nehru, reporting conversation with Home, 1 August 1956, Nehru Papers, NMML.

[12] Nehru to Vijayalakshmi, with message to Home, 2 August 1956, NMML.

giving prompt and public support to Egypt had bewildered opinion in that country as well as in the whole Arab world, where popular enthusiasm, whatever the attitudes of the governments, for Nasser's defiance of the Western powers had been general. Even now Nehru claimed to write, not as the head of a fellow anti-colonial, non-aligned country, but as the representative of a major user of the canal and one interested in a friendly settlement. Aware that Britain was thinking of convening a conference, he suggested that Nasser himself take the initiative and call together, on the basis of Egypt's sovereignty, all those interested in the international aspects of the canal. His own attitude he described as governed by a desire for a peaceful settlement and by due adherence to friendships and international usage.[13]

'In this letter it was Nehru the lawyer, the cautious elder statesman who was speaking.' It was thought that Nehru was annoyed because he had not been given prior information of the decision to nationalize; but if, at the time of his visit to Cairo, no decision had been made, then the speed with which the decision had been later taken showed irresponsibility.[14] But Nehru's position was not a result of pique, it was in accordance with the strict canons of non-alignment, uninfluenced by emotional sympathy, adopted with equal regard for India's friendship with Egypt and with Britain, and motivated with concern for the interests of both.

Nasser was worried by Nehru's clear warning that Egypt could not, in a crisis of her own making, take India's support for granted. It was not just that Nasser missed the comfort of India's backing; as important was the fact that many non-aligned countries could be expected to follow India's lead. When the British government sent out invitations to sixteen countries for a conference in London of major users of the canal, Sri Lanka and Indonesia sought India's guidance as to the reply that should be given. Nasser wrote to Nehru that Egypt would not attend a conference the result of which was a foregone conclusion. An international authority for the canal would be sought

[13] Nehru to Nasser, 2 August 1956, MEA Files.

[14] M.H. Heikal, *Cutting the Lion's Tail: Suez through Egyptian Eyes* (London: Andre Deutsch, 1986), pp. 135–7.

to be imposed, making the whole effort a fresh colonial move against a 'comparatively weak and an oriental people.' So he appealed to Nehru that India should also refuse to attend and suggested as a counter-proposal the placing of all international waterways under the regime of the United Nations. Egypt would also be willing to execute a fresh treaty with all concerned nations guaranteeing again the security of the Suez Canal and freedom of navigation; and such a treaty could be registered with the United Nations.[15]

Nehru was not impressed, particularly after he heard that the waterways Nasser had in mind were the Panama Canal, the Dardanelles, Gibraltar, and Aden;[16] for the countries concerned with these would obviously not agree to multilateral discussions at the United Nations, and this deprived Nasser's proposal of any touch of reality. So Nehru was inclined to consider participation in the London conference. Now that Egypt had secured physical control of the canal, attention should be given to the grievances of Britain and France, irrespective of their legitimacy. The demands of the two sides were not contradictory and the crisis could be settled by negotiation provided that rigid attitudes did not result in further unilateral decisions. There was scope for some institutional arrangements which did not violate the sovereignty of Egypt but which yet conformed to international requirements and commitments and were sufficient to create confidence. It was in India's own national interest that arrangements in regard to the canal should be such as to secure general acceptance.

Nehru, therefore, followed his lone path. He rejected the suggestions of Syria and Indonesia that the Colombo Powers should meet along with Egypt or even on their own. He did not request, as desired by Syria, that the conference should meet somewhere else than in London; but he did point out to Eden that the list of invitees was too restricted: Burma, Yugoslavia, Saudi Arabia, and Poland should have been asked. Nor should the conference be restricted to consideration only of an international authority to manage the canal. Attempts to

[15] Nasser to Nehru, 4 August 1956, MEA Files.

[16] Egyptian ambassador's conversation with Indian high commissioner in Pakistan, 4 August 1956, reported in telegram of same date, MEA Files.

impose a solution on Egypt would lead to armed conflict and powerful reactions all over Asia and large parts of Africa. If the conference was to have positive results, the whole approach would have to be different.[17] He then wrote to Nasser that if India participated it would be not to weaken Egypt's position but to work for conciliatory approaches and to prevent the conference from becoming a barrier to settlement. 'We wish', he added, in what was clearly a rebuke, 'to emphasize these aspects and not to support any unilateral action taken by one nation or any group of nations.' Then, in response to Nasser's request for advice, he suggested that Nasser should reply to the British government expressing surprise at the convening of a conference without reference to Egypt but affirming Egypt's willingness to attend if there were an agreed list of invitees and no prior conditions and commitments. While Egypt could not accept any challenge to her sovereignty, she would be prepared to execute a fresh agreement which would guarantee freedom of navigation. Himself disillusioned by the developments at the United Nations on the Kashmir issue, Nehru advised Nasser against any reference to that organization.[18]

Nasser rejected this advice. He was not prepared under any circumstances to participate in a conference convened by Britain. This deprived the London conference of the possibility of reaching firm decisions, for nothing could be settled in Egypt's absence. Nehru was also informed that the list of invitees could not be expanded. Yet, with an assurance from Eden that participation need not imply acceptance of the British demand for an international authority,[19] Nehru decided to send a delegation with Krishna Menon as its leader.[20] If nothing else, attendance could prove a check on the policy of intimidation and, by enabling a more balanced approach than was possible if only the Western nations discussed the issue, prepare the ground for another conference with which Egypt could be associated.[21] In this

[17] Nehru to Eden, 4 and 5 August 1956, MEA Files.

[18] Nehru to Nasser, 5 August 1956, MEA Files.

[19] Eden to Nehru, 7 August 1956, MEA Files.

[20] Nehru's statement in the Lok Sabha, 8 August 1956.

[21] Nehru to Prime Minister of Indonesia, 6 and 7 August 1956, MEA Files.

effort he hoped for assistance from the United States.[22] But he did not exaggerate the prospect of success. 'This is by far the most difficult and dangerous situation in international affairs we have faced since independence. I do not think we can do very much, but it is just possible that we might stop the rot. Probably we shall end by displeasing our friends on both sides.'[23]

To assure Britain that India was not Egypt's unhesitating champion and, provided that Britain refrained from the use or display of force, India would do her best for her, Nehru discouraged the Egyptian government from adopting the rupee as the medium of exchange for her trade with third countries and secured disallowance of discussion in the lower house of parliament of a private member's motion advocating India's withdrawal from the Commonwealth. Eden himself seems to have been still confident of Nehru's support, for he rejected Pearson's suggestion that the Suez crisis be discussed by the NATO Council before the meeting of the London conference, because this might antagonize and alienate Nehru.[24] Such friendliness to Britain made Egypt distrustful—and with some justification, for the Indian ambassador in Cairo was toying with the idea of an international authority excluding the great powers and perhaps presided over by Egypt.[25] To deal with these suspicions, Nehru directed Krishna Menon to break journey in Cairo on his way to London. But Menon was the wrong man for this. He patronized Nasser, whom he described later to Selwyn Lloyd as politically a beginner with a great deal to learn but gaining experience,[26] and started on the course—since described by Heikal and which prevailed right through the crisis—of being unable to get

[22] Message to US Secretary of State, John Foster Dulles, through Indian embassy in Washington, 8 August 1956, MEA Files.

[23] Nehru to C. Rajagopalachari, 10 August 1956, Nehru Papers, NMML.

[24] L.B. Pearson, *The International Years: Memoirs 1948–57* (London: V. Gollancz, 1974), p. 229.

[25] See telegram from British embassy in Cairo to Foreign Office, 7 August 1956, FO 371/119091, Public Record Office (hereafter PRO), London. I am grateful to Professor Wm. Roger Louis for copies of these PRO documents.

[26] Record of Selwyn Lloyd's conversation with Menon, 15 August 1956, FO 800/739, PRO.

on with Egyptian officials. To Nehru Menon reported that, while he found Nasser more mellowed and appearing to realize that perhaps he had been precipitate, he was unyielding on such issues as international control.[27] Menon's stance and tone were certainly not calculated to change this position.

In London Menon and his team assured the British government that India did not approve of Nasser's manner of nationalizing the canal and agreed fully that the canal should be placed under some form of international control. Informed that the British government were prepared to have recourse to force in the last resort, they advised Britain not to say so much and so often that she had it in mind, for Indian public opinion was well ahead of the Indian government and took a far less balanced view.[28] At the conference Menon sought to persuade the Western powers to negotiate with Egypt on the basis of her sovereignty, and was embarrassed by the Soviet Union taking the same line.[29] His compromise formula, tabled on 20 August, provided for a review of the 1888 Convention, particularly incorporating clauses regarding just tolls and maintenance, a conference of all signatories of the 1888 Convention and all user nations, association of international user interests with the Egyptian corporation for the canal without prejudice to Egyptian ownership, a consultative body of user interests, and transmission by Egypt to the United Nations of the annual reports of the Egyptian corporation.

Minority representation on the Egyptian corporation and a consultative body of user interests appeared inadequate to Britain and France and an appeasement of Nasser; but the formula as a whole was disliked by Egypt. So far from the Indian delegation virtually functioning, as Eden and Home later alleged,[30] as Egypt's spokesman

[27] Krishna Menon's telegram to Nehru, 15 August 1956, MEA Files.

[28] N.R. Pillai's conversations with Sir G. Laithwaite, 14 August, and Sir N. Brook, 15 August 1956, PREM 11/1144; Record of Selwyn Lloyd's conversation with Menon, 15 August 1956, FO 800/739, PRO.

[29] Menon's second telegram to Nehru, 15 August 1956, MEA Files.

[30] A. Eden, *Full Circle* (London: Cassell, 1961), p. 444; Lord Home, *The Way the Wind Blows* (London: Collins, 1976), p. 140.

and egging on Nasser, at the time Krishna Menon complained that the Egyptian government gave him no room for manoeuvre and pressed them to counter the growing impression that India had no influence in Cairo.[31] But Nasser could not be persuaded. Nehru was not surprised and, while urging Nasser to be a little more flexible and enable a revised proposal to be put forward,[32] he also directed Menon to formulate a 'more constructive' scheme,[33] implying that the earlier formula leant further to the British side than he himself would have wished. This lack of close accord between India and Egypt made it easier for the majority at the London conference to approve the Dulles plan for an international board of control. Only Indonesia and Sri Lanka, apart from the Soviet Union, sided with India; Ethiopia, Turkey, Iran, and Pakistan went along with the Western powers, although Pakistan, bearing in mind public opinion at home and in other Islamic countries, preferred to play a subdued role. Menon's suggestion that he walk out of the conference was overruled by the prime minister,[34] who had at no time attached much significance to a conference without Egypt. But he was unwilling to advise Nasser, as requested by Eden, to consider the Dulles plan. He told Malcolm MacDonald, the British high commissioner, that to him it was unthinkable to impose a solution on Egypt and it was politically impossible for Nasser to undo the act of nationalization. The first step was to get Egypt to negotiate and then, in the course of negotiations, to secure a reasonable settlement. The London declaration did not make such steps possible.[35]

The London conference, however, had at least, in Nehru's view, made any resort to force very unlikely, though, with neither the

[31] Menon's telegrams from London to Indian ambassador in Cairo, 20 August, and to Nehru, 21 August 1956, MEA Files.

[32] Nehru's telegram to Indian ambassador in Cairo, 21 August 1956, MEA Files.

[33] Nehru's telegram to Menon, 21 August 1956, MEA Files.

[34] Menon's telegram to Nehru, 22 August, and Nehru's reply, 23 August 1956, MEA Files.

[35] Telegram of British high commissioner in Delhi after meeting with Nehru, 22 August 1956, FO 371/119168, PRO.

declaration nor the Menon proposals being generally acceptable, the deadlock continued. India, therefore, as the leading non-aligned country on the stage, obviously had to think again. MacDonald saw this: 'I feel that he (Nehru) is doing a lot of hard thinking and perhaps some re-thinking.' But it was a thankless task. Along with the British government's efforts to recruit India's help to attain a settlement to their liking there was suspicion of her future objectives rather than appreciation of her present goodwill. 'I am convinced that we are finished if the Middle East goes and Russia and India and China rule from Africa to the Pacific.'[36] As for Egypt, she too was still chary of India.[37] So Nehru decided prudently to await developments. On 6 September, as the Menzies mission moved to its predestined end and the threats by Britain and France to use force became more open, Nasser wrote that he intended to appeal to the Security Council as well as offer to negotiate regarding freedom of navigation, tolls, operations, and management; and he requested Nehru to use his influence to secure favourable responses and start immediate discussions on the basis of safeguarding the legitimate concerns of user interests without acceptance of international control.[38] Nehru was willing to help. He again dissuaded Nasser from approaching the United Nations and suggested that the offer to negotiate be drafted in very general terms, opening the door for talks but making no specific proposals.[39] This was also in line with Tito's thinking. He felt that Egypt was in a difficult and dangerous position and Nasser should move cautiously; a peaceful settlement was still possible but the intentions of Britain and France were uncertain.[40]

On 10 September the Egyptian government announced, as advised by Nehru, their keenness for a peaceful solution without detriment to

[36] Home to Eden, 24 August 1956, quoted by P. Hennessy, 'Reopening the Wounds of the End of Empire', *The Listener*, 5 February 1987.

[37] Menon's telegram to Nehru from Cairo, 31 August 1956, MEA Files

[38] Nasser to Nehru, 6 September 1956, MEA Files.

[39] Nehru's message to Nasser, 7 September, and Nasser to Nehru, 8 September 1956, MEA Files.

[40] Telegram of Indian ambassador in Belgrade after interview with Tito, 8 September 1956, MEA Files.

their country's sovereignty and dignity and suggested as an immediate step the formation of a negotiating body representative of all views among the user nations. Nehru followed this up with a very friendly letter to Eden, arguing that the Egyptian memorandum provided a chance to establish some common ground from which a settlement on the points of difference could emerge. 'I need hardly assure you of my goodwill or of my awareness of your feelings and difficulties.'[41] He also wrote in similar terms to Eisenhower from whom he expected much,[42] for by now the United States had rejected the possible use of force, and Nehru thought that 'a harmony of peace' had been reached between India and the United States.[43]

The buoyant hopes which Nehru conveyed to Burma, Sri Lanka, Indonesia, and Yugoslavia were dissolved by Eden's speech on 12 September, announcing the formation of a Suez Canal association which would virtually take over the operational control of the canal and adding that other steps in assertion of British rights were being contemplated. Such threats of unilateral actions leading to imposed decisions drove Nehru to public criticism of the British government;[44] and he advised Nasser that the time had come to consider a reference to the Security Council, for this would at least delay a crisis.[45] But he had great faith in British common sense and could not believe that any British prime minister, let alone Eden, would use force on such an issue;[46] and he again appealed to Eden and to Lloyd not to turn their backs on negotiations. If necessary, an emergency meeting of Commonwealth prime ministers should be called.[47] He also requested Dulles to exercise the effective rôle of the United States.[48] But war

[41] Nehru to Eden, 11 September 1956, MEA Files.

[42] Nehru to Eisenhower, 11 September 1956, MEA Files.

[43] Nehru to Eisenhower, 7 September 1956, MEA Files.

[44] Speech in the Lok Sabha, 13 September 1956, Nehru Papers, NMML.

[45] Nehru to Nasser, 13 September 1956, MEA Files.

[46] See Krishna Menon's accounts of his discussions with Nehru at this time, M. Brecher, *India and World Politics: Krishna Menon's View of the World* (London: Oxford University Press, 1968), p. 65.

[47] Nehru to Eden and to Lloyd, 14 September 1956, MEA Files.

[48] Nehru to Dulles, 14 September 1956, MEA Files.

had come within the realm of possibility, and he directed the various ministries in Delhi to plan the measures which would be required in the event of hostilities.[49]

Was there anything more that the non-aligned nations could do at this stage? It seemed pointless for the prime ministers of the Colombo Powers to meet; by now Pakistan was the odd man out, and no purpose would be served by the four others repeating jointly what they had been saying separately. But Nehru continued trying to keep Egypt and the Western powers in touch at least informally with each other. The idea of an users association was a one-sided affair which obviously could not lead to negotiations; but Eden would go no further and ruled out the suggestion of a meeting of Commonwealth prime ministers. 'In any event we will maintain close touch with Commonwealth Governments by every means.'[50] The attitude of Dulles was as unhelpful. He recognized Egypt's legal title to the canal but asserted that an international easement had been created across her territory. No international regime that did not have the backing of the United Nations would be imposed forcibly on Egypt; but the easement had to be protected. The United Nations could deal with overt violations and the users association with covert ones.[51] Yet, as the days passed, India and Yugoslavia became more optimistic. The threat of war seemed to be receding a little,[52] giving time for fresh efforts by the non-aligned mediators.

The Soviet government made various suggestions; a reference by Egypt to the Security Council leading to the setting up of a group of six countries—Egypt, Britain, France, India, the Soviet Union, and the United States—to explore avenues of negotiation; the convening of a conference of the Bandung countries; a major international

[49] Nehru's minute for the Cabinet, 14 September 1956, Nehru Papers, NMML.

[50] Eden to Nehru, 16 September 1956, MEA Files.

[51] Dulles to Nehru, 16 September 1956, MEA Files.

[52] Nehru to chief ministers, 20 September 1956, Nehru Papers, NMML; E. Kardelj in conversation with Indian ambassador in Belgrade, 22 September 1956, MEA Files.

conference.[53] Nehru was for an immediate reference to the Security Council; the other suggestions could be considered later. But the Egyptian government only informed the Security Council and did not make a complaint before it. Nor were they prepared to formulate any constructive proposal.[54] Perhaps the personal dislike of Menon on the part of Egyptian officials, of which Nehru was unaware, contributed to these reactions; and Nasser and his advisers may also have been disappointed by India's continued lack of enthusiasm for their cause. The latest evidence of this was Nehru's refusal to sanction the supply to Egypt of bren-guns and spare barrels and fuses for mortar bombs: 'For us to supply arms to the Egyptian government at this stage would naturally be greatly resented by the United Kingdom and other Western governments and make them feel that we are supporting Egypt one hundred per cent in peace and war. Our capacity for playing a mediatory role would disappear.'[55] He also, finding that both Nasser and he were due to visit Saudi Arabia, asked Nasser not to stay on in Riyadh to meet him as this would suggest ganging up.[56]

A new phase of the crisis began on 23 September, with Britain and France asking the Security Council to consider the matter and Egypt filing a counter-complaint the next day. Nehru did not expect the Security Council to achieve positive results but at least it could provide an arena for negotiations. Yugoslavia, which was at this time the only non-aligned country to be an elected member of the council, helped, at the meeting on 26 September, to secure an adjournment; and Menon was busy again in Cairo and London trying to work out a formula acceptable to both sides. His plan was an amplification of his earlier proposal, with Egypt entering into an agreement for cooperation with an Users Association and regular joint sessions of

[53] Nehru to Menon in Cairo, reporting talk with Soviet ambassador, 17 September 1956, MEA Files.

[54] Menon to Nehru, 19 September 1956, MEA Files.

[55] Nehru's note to Foreign Secretary, 17 September 1956, Nehru Papers, NMML.

[56] Nehru's telegram to Indian ambassador in Cairo, 21 September 1956, MEA Files.

the Egyptian Board and the Users Association to discuss all matters in which users were concerned. Egypt would also agree to appoint United Nations advisers in the three main sectors of operations. To make this plan more acceptable to Britain Menon secured Nasser's assent to permit any question about the 1888 Convention, and particularly the right of Israeli ships to go through the canal, to be referred to the World Court.[57] Even so, the British government were not satisfied with this formula, especially as it lacked any clause providing a means of enforcement.[58] Yet Menon reported to Nehru that he thought he had persuaded Eden and Lloyd to accept these proposals and Nasser should now be pressed to do the same. 'For your information only we have got somewhere. If we can get over one or two smaller hurdles in Cairo, which should be possible with the weight of your backing, we would have turned the corner. Subsequent stages are largely methodological problems.'[59]

Such a misapprehension of the British attitude was soon corrected by Eden himself. He told Nehru that Menon had put some hypothetical questions and the British government could not commit themselves by answering these questions. They still stood by their earlier insistence on international control while Menon's proposals left Egypt in unfettered grasp of the Canal and provided no means of enforcing whatever arrangements might be reached.[60] But as the British Government were willing to consider alternatives to the idea of an Users Association as the basis of negotiation, Nehru thought there was still room for mediation.[61] Menon went even further and told Nasser, without showing him the text, that Britain had accepted his proposals with the addition of a provision for arbitration if differences arose over tolls or discrimination against particular countries. Nasser

[57] Brecher, *India and World Politics*, p. 68.

[58] Records of conversations of Lloyd and of Eden (on the telephone) with Menon, 28 September 1956, PREM 11/1102, PRO.

[59] Menon's telegram from London to Nehru, 29 September 1956, MEA Files.

[60] Nehru's note on interview with British high commissioner, 1 October 1956, MEA Files.

[61] Nehru to Eden, 4 October 1956, MEA Files.

was willing to accept this amendment and assumed that the plan which Menon would announce at the United Nations would reflect the Egyptian viewpoint.[62]

Menon's attempts to get his formula through by suggesting without authority to each side that the other would accept it might have led to confusion but for the fact that for the first time Egypt and Britain were dealing directly with each other at New York under the sponsorship of Hammarskjold; and one point on which all of them (plus the Soviet representative) seem to have been agreed was a dislike of Menon and his activities. The non-aligned countries were now not at the centre of the picture. Britain, France, and Egypt reached an agreement on principles whereby, according to Menon, Egypt had given in far more than she ever led India to understand she would, and on points which on the face of them were vital to her sovereignty.[63] Dulles thought that this was the best opportunity that they had had or perhaps ever would have for arriving peacefully at a reasonable and honourable solution.[64] Nehru too was confident that the problem had definitely reached a negotiating stage and it would be difficult to go back on this.[65]

Eden, however, was working out other plans. The secret arrangements with Israel necessitated a request for postponement of further explanatory talks with Egypt, scheduled to begin on 29 October. Nehru was as startled as most others by the Israeli attack and the Anglo–French ultimatum. With the invasion of Egypt, a balancing act was no longer possible. Nehru asked Yugoslavia and the Bandung countries to join him in public condemnation of the aggressors, assured Nasser of his full support, called on Hammarskjold to ensure that the procedures of the United Nations were swifter than those of invasion and aggression, and urged the United States to intervene. 'I cannot imagine a worse case of aggression. . . . The whole future of the

62 Nasser to Fawzi in New York, 7 October 1956, in Heikal, *Cutting the Lion's Tail*, p. 165.

63 Menon's telegram from New York to Nehru, 14 October 1956, MEA Files.

64 Dulles to Nehru, 18 October 1956, MEA Files.

65 Nehru at a press conference, 25 October 1956. *The Hindu* (Madras), 26 October 1956.

relations between Europe and Asia hangs in the balance.'[66] Towards Britain he remained 'not unfriendly and expressed his views more in sorrow than in anger',[67] but he did not conceal the strength of his feelings and his deep regret that Britain, with her record of liberal policies, should now have become again the symbol of colonialism. 'Unless these wrong courses are halted the future appears to me to be dark indeed.'[68]

Nehru's objectives at this point were to help Nasser, safeguard the sovereignty of Egypt, obtain a ceasefire and prevent the spread of military action, and save the Commonwealth. He regarded as impractical the proposal first made by the Soviet Union and then supported by Egypt and by China for a reassembling of the Bandung countries;[69] but he was willing to have a meeting of the Colombo Powers, as desired by Indonesia, if the other prime ministers could come to Delhi. Bandaranaike of Sri Lanka could not come immediately, and the position of Pakistan was ambivalent. She supported Nasser publicly and was concerned about the effect of the aggression on the Baghdad Pact; but her ministers resented Egypt's links with India and agreed privately with Britain that no satisfactory solution of the Suez crisis was possible without the use of force.[70] In the event, the Colombo Powers met (without Pakistan) in Delhi on 14 November after the fighting was over and reiterated general principles which they had all affirmed earlier individually.

Rather than build up an Afro–Asian or even a regional bloc, Nehru preferred to act through the special session of the General Assembly of the United Nations. He supported the idea, which was acceptable to

[66] Nehru to Dulles, 31 October 1956, MEA Files.

[67] Report of British high commissioner after interview with Nehru, 31 October 1956, FO 371/121785, PRO.

[68] Nehru to Eden, 1 November 1956, MEA Files.

[69] Bulganin to Nehru, 2 November 1956, and Nehru's reply of same date; foreign secretary to Indian charge affaires in Cairo, 2 November 1956; Zhou Enlai's message to Nehru, 3 November 1956, MEA Files.

[70] Feroze Khan Noon, foreign minister of Pakistan, to British high commissioner in Karachi, 31 October 1956, FO 371/121788, PRO; Heikal, *Cutting the Lion's Tail*, p. 219.

Egypt, of a contingent from the United States to re-establish armistice lines between Israel and Egypt and of an observer team manned by Czechoslovakia, Canada, and India. An international police force would be acceptable on the old Arab–Israeli armistice line for a temporary period but not in the Suez Canal area or anywhere else in Egypt. When the United Nations set up an emergency force, he was prepared for India to participate only if this were desired by the Egyptian government.[71]

Then came the Soviet proposal for a joint Soviet–American military effort to stop the fighting, coupled with the threat to use rockets. The British ambassador in Moscow, who did not dismiss the threat as an empty one, advised the foreign office to mobilize the United States and Nehru to warn the Soviet Union of the danger of such action.[72] But Nehru, even without prompting, appealed to Bulganin not to take any steps which might lead to a general war but to agree to act through the United Nations.[73] He also welcomed the Swiss proposal of a meeting of the heads of government of the United States, the Soviet Union, Britain, and France, and was prepared to attend if desired.[74]

The need for such a meeting dissolved with the British acceptance of a ceasefire. Home now requested Nehru to 'come in heavily and assist in bringing about a speedy settlement.'[75] Nehru's relations with Nasser at this time were cordial, but this was not reflected in the attitude of the Egyptian officials; and there was also sniping at India's position by Iran, Turkey, and Pakistan. Taking the main credit for Britain's acceptance of a ceasefire, they criticized India for not withdrawing from the Commonwealth and charged her with weakening Egypt by standing in the way of military action by the Soviet Union. Ali Sabry

[71] Sarvepalli Gopal, *Jawaharlal Nehru* (London: Jonathan Cape, 1979), vol. 2, pp. 286–7.

[72] Sir W. Hayter, *The Kremlin and the Embassy* (London: Hodder & Stoughton, 1966), pp. 147–8.

[73] Nehru to Bulganin, 6 November 1956, MEA Files.

[74] Nehru to the President of the Swiss Confederation, 6 November 1956, MEA Files.

[75] Home to Indian deputy high commissioner in London, reported in telegram to foreign secretary, 6 November 1956, MEA Files.

stated Egypt's willingness to accept an international force consisting of troops from India, Greece, and Colombia—and no one else.[76] But on 12 November Fawzi, the foreign minister, suddenly objected to India's participation on the ground that neither close friends nor declared foes of Egypt should be represented. The Indian ambassador attributed this unexpected cooling off towards India to either suspicion of the Commonwealth or the objection raised by the United States, at the instance of the British, to the inclusion of India and the exclusion of Pakistan, Canada, and New Zealand. But Nasser within hours overruled his foreign minister and explained away Fawzi's attitude as born of fears that India's presence in what many Egyptians would regard as an occupation force might damage India's popularity.[77]

Egypt now agreed to a force drawn from eight nations—India, Indonesia, Colombia, Yugoslavia, and the four Scandinavian countries. But Canada was keen to be included and sought Nehru's help in overcoming Nasser's objections.[78] Nehru argued Canada's case strongly. Despite her close links with Britain and France she had, from the start, opposed their Suez policy and had cancelled the contract with Israel for the supply of aircraft. With Egypt's acceptance of Norway and Denmark, Canada's membership of NATO could not be held against her and insistence on her exclusion would harm Egypt's interests.[79] It was added that India would have no objection to Pakistan's participation as well. Nasser agreed at first to a Canadian ambulance corps and air supplies and Hammarskjold was satisfied with this; but Nehru pressed for a Canadian contingent and Nasser finally gave way. But Nehru was less successful in persuading Nasser not to deport British and French nationals and persons of Jewish origin who had not taken part in anti-Egyptian activities. 'True wisdom', remarked a disappointed Nehru,[80] 'consists in knowing how far we can go, to

[76] Telegram from Indian embassy in Cairo, 9 November 1956, MEA Files.

[77] Indian ambassador's telegram to foreign secretary, 12 November 1956, MEA Files.

[78] Pearson's message to Nehru, 15 November 1956, MEA Files.

[79] Nehru's telegram to Indian ambassador in Cairo, 15 November 1956, MEA Files.

[80] Nehru to Indian ambassador in Cairo, 26 December 1956, MEA Files.

profit by the circumstances and to create a feeling of generosity which again results in a change in one's own favour.'

So, throughout the crisis, India, while keeping the other major non-aligned nations informed, acted mostly on her own, upholding Egypt's right to nationalize but regretting the manner in which it was done and striving to get Britain out of her predicament. The Egyptian government, especially the officials, were not always happy with India's approach; and this feeling was sometimes accentuated by Krishna Menon's personality and ways of functioning. But once Britain decided to employ force, India supported Egypt unreservedly, till Britain and France withdrew their troops without demanding any assurance regarding the canal. 'All they want now appears to be to avoid humiliation.'[81]

[81] Nehru to Tito, 2 December 1956, Nehru Papers, NMML.

11

De Gaulle and Nehru

France, with all that she stood for, was dear to Jawaharlal Nehru from his early years. She was 'the mother of freedom, at whose altar it was a joy to sacrifice',[1] and Paris was the symbol of liberty the world over. So not the defeat of France in 1940 but the grovelling of the men of Vichy before the Nazis hurt him greatly, as it suggested the surrender of France's glorious heritage and magnificent tradition. 'But there is another France, there must be one, for the heritage of a thousand years does not vanish in a night. That other France will rise again and assert the invincible spirit of freedom which made her great.'[2] In that sure belief he paid homage, in her darkest hour, to France of the Revolution, the breaker of the Bastille and of all the bonds that hold the human body and spirit captive. So naturally, throughout the war, his sympathy and goodwill were with General Charles de Gaulle and the Free French.

Yet Nehru was inclined to the view that de Gaulle's destiny had been fulfilled with the liberation of France, and he was not happy with the manner of de Gaulle's return to power in 1958.[3] But he was

[1] Letter to his daughter, 13 October 1932, *Glimpses of World History* (Bombay: Asia Publishing House, 1967), 383.

[2] 'Quatorze Juillet', *National Herald*, 16 July 1940, reprinted in *Selected Works of Jawaharlal Nehru*, First Series (New Delhi: Orient Longman, 1978), vol. 11, pp. 71–2.

[3] See Nehru's letters to chief ministers, 9 and 30 June 1958, in G. Parthasarathi (ed.), *Letters to Chief Ministers* (Delhi: Oxford University Press, 1989), vol. 5, pp. 53–4 and 66, respectively.

willing to give de Gaulle the benefit of the doubt if he could settle the Algerian problem. De Gaulle, on his part, does not appear to have concerned himself till this stage in his career with India, which he is reported to have once described as 'a dust of peoples living in misery and meditation.'[4] But these two representative figures had a line of communication in Andre Malraux, student of Indian civilization, friend of Nehru and minister of culture in de Gaulle's cabinet. De Gaulle told Malraux that his first diplomatic mission should be to India to ask Nehru not what France could give India but what India could give France. Doubtless influenced by Malraux, at meetings of the French cabinet de Gaulle would never permit mention of India and China in the same breath, for the two countries were not of the same dimension; while China was an empire, India was closer to France philosophically and culturally.[5]

So Malraux came to Delhi in the winter of 1958. He found, as expected, Nehru cherishing warm feelings for France, for to India France meant the Revolution, but wary of de Gaulle, whom Nehru felt, in spite of himself, to resemble Mussolini rather than Churchill. But Malraux steered clear of political problems and even Algeria was mentioned only once and briefly. He spoke instead of his deep interest in the spiritual side of India, to which he attached great importance and which in his view had significance for the whole world. He described de Gaulle as a new type of mass leader representing the spirit and soul of a nation—akin, Malraux added flatteringly, to Nehru in India—and asserted that under de Gaulle France was going through a new renaissance in which she would recover her soul. In the wider context, Malraux expressed his belief that out of the crises through which the world was passing a new civilization, based neither on modern capitalism nor on communism, would evolve, and France had a message for this new civilization. In this connection India became

[4] Quoted in Escott Reid, *Radical Mandarin* (Toronto: University of Toronto Press, 1989), p. 287.

[5] See Raja Rao, 'When Malraux met Jawaharlal Nehru', in S. Gopal, G. Parthasarathi, and R. Kumar (eds), *Jawaharlal Nehru: Centenary Volume* (Delhi: Oxford University Press, 1989), pp. 486–95.

important and had, according to Malraux, a very special role to play because India was the only country which could supply the spiritual foundation for the new system. India had a very special place in the minds of the French people, and this had nothing to do with politics. India represented to France a unique spiritual quality.[6]

Malraux, in his own way, had sought to smooth relations between de Gaulle's France and Nehru's India. A fresh chapter in relations between the two countries seemed to be opening, under leadership of men who could speak for their peoples and with mutual appreciation, in France of the essence of Indian culture and in India of the French commitment to human freedom and fraternity. After Nehru's talks with Malraux, the French ambassador in Delhi cabled to the Quai d'Orsay, 'The door of India has been opened to France—at last!'[7] But while Nehru maintained an attitude of cordiality to France, his personal relations with de Gaulle remained guarded. Even the settlement of the Algerian problem effected no material change. When Nehru and de Gaulle met in Paris in September 1962, the discussions were at an impersonal level. Nehru said that there were no problems between France and India and they could draw much closer in the economic and cultural spheres. The two leaders then talked about the Common Market and its possible effects on India, disarmament, the need to assure Cambodia against aggression, and Chinese incursions into Indian frontier areas.[8] Nothing in Nehru's record of the meeting hints that he and de Gaulle felt themselves to be kindred spirits—perhaps because Nehru was always suspicious of men with a military background, just as de Gaulle could never shake off his dislike of politicians. But of the two, it was de Gaulle's reaction

[6] Nehru's note to secretary-general, ministry of external affairs, on talks with Malraux, 15 December 1958, Nehru Papers, Nehru Memorial Museum and Library, New Delhi; A. Malraux, *Anti-Memoires* (London: Penguin, 1970), pp. 151–2.

[7] Quoted in Raja Rao, 'When Malraux met Jawaharlal Nehru'.

[8] Nehru's account of his talks with de Gaulle, 22 September 1962, File (101/66) WI/62, Correspondence, 47, Ministry of External Affairs, Government of India, New Delhi.

which was the more positive. He wrote a year later that he had been before a 'great man for whom the cause of mankind is the same as that of the Indian people'; Nehru embodied an independent and united India, and was untiring in his faith and in his efforts.[9]

However, despite this lack of a real personal rapport, these two outstanding personalities of the twentieth century had much in common, and their achievements bear comparison. At crucial moments in the destinies of their two countries, they voiced the feelings and aspirations of their peoples and had an instinctive awareness of popular moods. 'I listened', de Gaulle said once,[10] 'to the deep voice of our people as one hears the murmur of the sea.' Nehru too, for all his upper-class upbringing, had, second only to Gandhi, the capacity to discern and assimilate the responses of the Indian peasant. Both de Gaulle and Nehru nursed national self-confidence and, as a measure of sovereign independence, were distrustful of power blocs and carved out self-respecting foreign policies. Within their countries, they stood above factions and towered over their own political parties as national rather than partisan leaders. They placed before their peoples grand visions and not petty philosophies.

In their efforts to realize these visions they acted as pragmatists with a strong regard for national interests and not as doctrinaires circumscribed by outmoded theories. Nehru differed from de Gaulle in that he had a preference for socialism; but both rejected the notion of class war and recognized the prime importance of national unity and nation-building. Once Nehru had played his active role in securing Britain's abandonment of India, which to Malraux was the most significant fact of the century,[11] de Gaulle saw clearly that any idea of Algerie Francaise was stillborn. Both de Gaulle and Nehru gave their countries solid constitutional frameworks which, by and large, have

[9] *Memoires d'Espoir*, quoted in M. and C. Moraze, 'Nehru's Universal Significance', *Jawaharlal Nehru: Centenary Volume*, pp. 371–6.

[10] Quoted in A. Malraux, *Fallen Oaks* (London: Hamish Hamilton, 1972), pp. 32–3.

[11] Malraux's interview in 1974, quoted in Bruce Chatwin, *What Am I Doing Here*? (London: Penguin, 1990), p. 123.

stood the test of time and enabled the strengthening of democracy. Thrown up in very different contexts and emerging from sharply contrasting experiences, de Gaulle and Nehru remain of permanent interest beyond their own nations because of certain common approaches and aspirations which they embodied and carried a long way towards full realization. For these strivings are part of the upward ascent of humanity.

12

Nehru as Father

This is a deeply absorbing book,[1] but not perhaps as intended. The correspondence is between two persons both of whom evoke much interest in this country. Attention is sought to be focused on Indira Gandhi, to show the influences which moulded her in her youth and how by the age of 22 she is said to have come into her own. But there is nothing in these letters to hint even faintly at the splitter of Pakistan and the imposer of the Emergency. Indira Gandhi emerges as a lonely girl heavily dependent on her parents, an average student who took little advantage of an education which provided her with the best of all possible worlds, an in-drawn person reticent about her emotions. There is no inkling in her letters of the known tension between her and her father in 1938–9. The only letter written by her in this collection which is of any real significance is that of 29 August 1934 which, for once, pulls aside the curtain of effusive Anglo-Saxon endearments and throws open the window on Kamala Nehru's unhappiness in Anand Bhawan during Nehru's frequent absences.

> Do you know anything about what happens at home when you are absent? Do you know that when Mummie was in a very bad condition the house was full of people, but not one of them even went to see her or sit a while with her, that when she was in agony there was no one to help her? . . . with your release everything was changed—people flocked

[1] Sonia Gandhi (ed.), *Freedom's Daughter: Letters between Nehru and Indira Gandhi 1922–1939* (London: Hodder and Stoughton, 1989).

> from all directions, came to ask about her; sat with her. . . . As soon as Mummie is strong enough she should be removed to any place outside Allahabad and she is sure to improve rapidly.

These words cast a flood of light on the Nehru ménage and Indira's attitude to her close relatives. The letter as a whole stands out if only because it is the sole one of its kind.

On the other hand, Nehru's letters, most of them published for the first time because they were located too late for inclusion in the appropriate volumes of the *Selected Works of Jawaharlal Nehru*, add a great deal to our understanding of the mind and character of an already much-studied personality. Nehru regarded letter-writing as a genre in itself and devoted much care and time to it.

> What indeed are letters? Not surely just budgets of news, although they contain news. Not a record of illness and birth and marriage and death and humdrum domestic happenings such as are most of the letters that people write. They are something far more; they are, or ought to be, bits of the personality of the writer, quivering shadows of the real self. They are also, or they at least endeavour to represent and to mirror, something of the personality of the person written to, for the writer is full of the person writing to.

Over his letters to his growing daughter, especially after she lost her mother, Nehru took trouble and appears to have enjoyed writing them, as it gave him relief from other care and work. With simplicity and sincerity, he wrote of himself, his problems and his moods, of what he wished for Indira and how he would like her to shape her life but without imposing himself on her in any way. In difficult circumstances, he proved a sensitive father, trying to bring up his only child as neither spoilt nor neglected. The fact that he was perforce away in prison for long periods did not in itself worry him and he hoped that it would help her to be more self-reliant. That the pressures of home life were telling on her in his absence he knew and he gently advised her not to get hot and bothered over minor matters or to create conflict or imagine it where there was none. 'To mope and nurse a grievance secretly is a sign of weakness and folly. It is most undignified. Discuss the matter, have it out, try to understand the other party's viewpoint and tell him or her your own.'

Even when Indira was hardly 15, Nehru asked her to start thinking as to what she would like to do when she grew up. One could not merely loll through life; if one wanted to do anything it was worth doing it well and for this training was required. Indira had during these adolescent years no clear ideas on this subject; at one time she spoke of wishing to be a teacher, but there was no serious intention. So Nehru thought in terms of an education fitted to no specific purpose but planned for a future full of life and intelligence and activity so that she could distinguish herself in whichever sphere she functioned. Nehru was always careful not to thrust his own ideals on her and insisted that she should decide for herself on what would be her life-philosophy. While she had the advantage of a good hereditary background, the foreground had to be her own creation. But he did advise her that it was not good enough just to earn money, although some money had to be earned; it was far more important to do something that was worthwhile and did good to society. For this the right education was not examinations and the like but an all-round development of the human being, a harmonizing of internal conflicts and a capacity to cooperate with others, the strength to be true to what one considers to be right and the absence of fear.

In the two books of mostly impersonal letters published even at the time Nehru concentrated on the history of man, as he wanted his daughter to have the right perspective of the past and also because this topic was at that time of primary interest to him. But in the letters in this book Nehru draws Indira's attention to many other topics; for he was keen that she should develop into a cultured and interesting person, with some knowledge of the world and its problems and the capacity to fit in with any environment. She should be able to catch the attention of worthwhile people on an equal footing. For all this she should, whatever her particular bent, have some training in science, not only to understand the world she lived in but to secure a scientific outlook and apply the methods of reason and experiment in all her work. He urged her to learn a few languages without dabbling in too many of them. He sent her first to Pune and then to Santiniketan so that she could get to know the people in various parts of India and thought of sending her thereafter to some universities in Europe, to Oxford, and even for a while to the Soviet Union.

Even so, Nehru did not forget that education was more than intellectual training and reminded Indira that holidays were not meant for hard mental work and physical life was not to be ignored. Nehru's concern with health becomes more pronounced as Indira became increasingly prone to illness. He believed, on the basis of his own experience, that one could be aggressively fit by following some basic rules—exercise, good sleep, simple food, thereafter one should forget the body. Not to be physically fit was to him a major sin. It was rather silly to fall ill, but it was more likely if one thought too much about it. Illness only came as a rule when invited to do so. Regular mental occupation and companionship, healthy habits and surroundings were more important than doctors and tonics. With a normal, regular life and a proper state of mind, good health would come unasked.

Nehru also set out to encourage in his daughter the reading habit. Apart from his own educative letters, he chose books for her. Shaw's *St Joan*, for example, was sent to her when she was just over 15. Worried that she was inclined to read too fast, he suggested that she follow his own practice of summarizing worthwhile books in a notebook and writing whatever might strike or please her:

> There is a strange magic about good literature which is wonderfully refreshing and soothing. This magic comes to us solely as we make friends with good books, and when we have begun to feel it, we have found the key to the wonder land of books. They never fail us, these friends that neither age nor change. They have been dear companions to me, especially in prison, and I have got more pleasure from books than from almost anything. There is only one other thing which is, in its own way, more magical, more wonderful, and that is music. I have always regretted my ignorance of it. How much I have missed because of this! Literature, art, music, science—all make our life rich and deep and varied. They make us live.

Even when he had no time to read them, he liked to have books around him, for the mere sight of them gave him pleasure, standing there row after row, with the wisdom of ages locked up in them, serene and untroubled in a changing and distracted world, looking down silently on the mortals that come and go. In pure literature he normally avoided books less than fifty years old, but in other subjects he read whatever was necessary to understand the world. For the purpose of reading was to understand life with its thousand facets and to learn how to live life. Books lift us out of our narrow ruts, bring fresh vistas into view, extend our vision and bring a sense of proportion. He was particularly keen that his daughter should read widely, for he had high hopes for her; and those who cherish the thought of rising above the common head of unthinking humanity and playing a brave part in life's journey needed the vision and sense of proportion which would keep them on the right path and steady them when storms and heavy winds bore down on them.

To all this advice Nehru expected some response. He urged Indira to write to him from time to time as to what she was thinking. He wanted her to talk to him through her letters as he was doing to her. They should be friends and not just a father and dearly loved daughter. 'Of course you should write to me whenever you are troubled about anything. What am I for?' But gradually he was driven to accept that there was little communication between them even when they were together. 'For over five months', he wrote to her in September 1937, 'we were together—a long enough time—and no doubt we influenced each other as we were bound to do. And yet, is it not curious that during all these months we hardly had a proper conversation, apart from our brief talks about our day-to-day activities. I felt the gulf between two generations and I could not bridge it. No doubt you must have felt this way also.' Clearly this precipitated the melancholy and weariness which peep out of the letters written between 1937 and 1939. 'One part of me pushes out, the other tries to hide itself from the world. A Jekyll and Hyde existence.' Public life does not excite him while the idea of sanyasa appeals. He felt that he had lost the vivid desire to live and the keen incentive that drove him to action. 'Probably I am not a big enough man for the job that fate has thrust on me.'

Despite the one-sidedness of these letters which Nehru found so depressing, and although, unlike the *Letters from a Father to His Daughter* and those collected in *Glimpses of World History* the letters in this volume have an informal intimacy which suggests that they were not intended for publication, it is good to have them. They contain little about politics probably because Nehru knew that they were being read by the censor. There is also curiously nothing about religion, and the omission would seem to be deliberate. Nehru was in these days a determined agnostic but his wife was not; and in the circumstances he let his daughter decide for herself with not a word from him. But otherwise his letters range widely, with many splashes of brilliance, such as the account of his response at his first sight of the Trimurti at Elephanta. These letters of Nehru are of incomparable richness.

13

Tagore and Our Times

It is a great privilege for me to be here in Visva-Bharati this evening to deliver the first Prabodh Chandra Sen memorial lecture. My gratitude for having been asked to do so is enhanced by the fact that I have no special claims to this invitation. I have been in Santiniketan before but only as a visitor and have not the good fortune of personal bonds with this institution. Of Prabodh Sen's massive contributions to Bengali literature I have only hearsay knowledge, for I have no grasp of the Bengali language. The poet himself I had, in my youth, seen on a few occasions; but I do not belong to that generation of Indians who, for the greater part of their lives, felt, wherever they be, the impact of his presence.

For all these reasons, I was hesitant to accept your vice chancellor's gracious invitation. Moreover, speaking here, the natural theme is the thought, work, and creative output of Rabindranath Tagore; and in this year, which will mark his fiftieth death anniversary, we cannot avoid the brutal question—Does Tagore still mean anything to us today? All his poems and prose writings, as he himself recognized and has been firmly established by his interpreters, were imbued with a deep religious purpose. Tagore testifies to the assertion of Coleridge that no man was ever a great poet without being at the same time a profound philosopher. He was in essence a Vedantist, in line with the thinkers of the Upanishads, believing in the Absolute but extolling a personal God and revelling in a sense of joy in life and in the freedom of the spirit. Such an approach, however, is alien to our present agnostic and materialist age and leaves the average reader cold.

Fashions chart literary appreciation, and religious poetry nowadays evokes little response.

It is not, of course, necessary to agree with Tagore in order to recognize his genius. Yet, if one takes a second and careful look, it becomes clear that Tagore still has much to tell us, and it is this which has prompted me to accept the invitation to deliver this lecture. Tagore does not belong wholly to a past of which most of us have no first-hand memory, and his writings are not dated and expounding an outmoded view of life. Indeed, his thought and work, if read right, could be vital influences in our dismal present and even enable a better future. Thirty years ago, in 1961, when the centenary of Tagore's birth was celebrated, Jawaharlal Nehru reminded us that Tagore had tried to create an atmosphere in Santiniketan as well as in the whole of India; and Nehru had hoped that that living message would always be with us, guiding us in our life and our endeavours.

What is this living message, which Nehru, who was not religious in the conventional sense, had in mind? If he felt that, like the coming of the dawn in the mountains, it crept in and permeated his generation and was still alive long after Tagore had departed, it was born of the fact that Tagore did not isolate himself from what was happening around him in his own country and in the world. He was not impervious to the stirrings of nationalist sentiment in India at the turn of the century. He denounced the repressive policy of the colonial government and was active in collecting funds for the defence of Lokamanya Tilak. A few years later he opposed the partition of Bengal and composed songs which roused the popular spirit. Ezra Pound commented later that Tagore had sung Bengal into a nation. But the remarkable aspect about Tagore's songs in Bengali is that they became witnesses of Indian nationalism. They gripped the mood of the people throughout the country and their captivating lilt surmounted the hurdle of a lack of exact and detailed understanding. The same is true of his poems. The translations into English, even his own translations, cannot be expected to have the same power as the Bengali originals. Poetry, as Robert Frost is reported to have said, is what is lost in translation. Yet Tagore's verse has crossed linguistic boundaries, for in it India recovered her lost voice. It even crossed national frontiers, for Tagore gave utterance to the yearning for freedom of all the peoples of Asia. Indeed he spoke too, in one of his most moving poems, for the suppressed peoples of Africa. He gave tongue to the hopes of all the 'disinherited peoples of the world', who had lost both the harvest of the past as well as the present age.

George Orwell once remarked that an Englishman was either in or out, either a guilty imperialist or a person dedicated to bringing down the system; there was no third way. But an Indian in the years of the Raj could be a non-political nationalist, for there were other roads between collaboration and open resistance, and some of these intermediate roads are indispensable. Tagore came close to direct confrontation in 1919 when he renounced his knighthood in protest against the atrocities in the Punjab. He was as sensitive as any nationalist politician to the oppression of what he described two years later as 'the destitute and insulted humanity of India.' But he kept aloof from the non-cooperation movement which he regarded as too negative in approach and a form of political asceticism, and was especially critical of Mahatma Gandhi's call for the boycott of schools.

Gandhi and Tagore were obviously, in Nehru's phrase, two very different master-types of the Indian spirit. Yet Tagore recognized Gandhi as the one person whom India had produced in the last two hundred years who was possessed of the divine fire. The secret of his success was spontaneous self-giving, and the truth shone through his character in lucid simplicity. Gandhi too discerned that, though their spheres of action were not the same, Tagore was a vital element in the Indian scene. But, in fact, despite the contrasts in temperament and approach, these two figures had much in common. They shared a consuming love of India, a pride in her past, and a confident hope in her future. Though wounded by political subjection, they did not dislike the British. Tagore said it was hateful to hate; and Gandhi called on Indians to fight the sin but not the sinner. Tagore acknowledged that he could not help loving Britain, with some of whose people he felt an affinity: 'The fuel displays its differences but the fire is one.' Gandhi called on the British to get off our backs and walk by our side. Both Gandhi and Tagore, and indeed most of the leaders of our national movement, had a keen international sense, and their commitment to India, strong and unflinching, was yet poised on the broader platform of internationalism.

Tagore wrote with feeling of a subject India under British domination, 'broken in fortune' and 'in stained rags'; yet toward the end of his life he spoke with confidence of the temporary nature of their rules:

> I know their merchandise-bearing soldiers
> Will not make the slightest impression
> On planetary paths.

That India should be free was to Tagore a self-explanatory axiom. Self-government not only led to efficiency and a sense of responsibility but it uplifted the human spirit. For want of this opportunity every person in India remained a lesser human being; so, in spite of all the risk of error or mischance, India had to attain self-government. But what should Indians do to shake off their shackles? The answers of Gandhi and of Tagore were identical. Their objective was a straightened spine. Gandhi called on the starving and dispossessed peasantry to stand up for themselves, to develop self-respect and self-confidence. As he told the Indians in South Africa, 'If you behave like worms, others will treat you like worms.' Every Indian should display the strength and courage which have no use for force and question the legitimacy of the Raj whenever there was reason to do so. Tagore commended this psychological effort at liberation of the spirit and promotion of 'the immense power of the meek'. Political bondage was a symptom of inner decay. 'They who have failed to attain swaraj within themselves must lose it in the outside world too.' For those who remained weak invited subjugation. To illustrate this, Tagore tells the story of the lamb and God. The lamb, constantly attacked by stronger animals, complained to God in despair, 'Lord, why do all creatures seek to eat me up?' God replied, 'What can I do? When I look at you, even I am tempted.' Only the strong, Tagore concludes, can expect equality and justice. 'The only gift is the gift of strength, all other offerings are vain.' Strength must be sought peacefully but tirelessly. 'The English hurt our self-respect. They do so because we are paupers; when we are strong, they will be brothers. Till then, they will despise us and not fraternize.' Begging from the British would only invite further humiliation. 'Weakness is the traitor who betrays our soul.' Both Gandhi and Tagore stood for the self-respect of the individual—a lesson to be remembered even when India is free.

The emphasis on the innate dignity of the individual, the recognition that the right of being one's own master is the greatest of human rights, leads logically to the acceptance of democracy as the best form of government. But obviously the rights of any person cannot damage or weaken the rights of other persons in society and reaching a balanced accommodation in this matter is the prime task of a democratic government—that is, if society cannot reach its own adjustments. Tagore was of the view that one of the greatest achievements of ancient Indian culture had been the clear demarcation between the state and society and the definition of public welfare as largely a non-political function. The problem, in a society which has been multi-religious for centuries, emerges most prominently in the relations between those who belong to different faiths. Whatever the divergence in social habits, Hindus, Muslims, Christians, Parsis and followers of other religions lived together in general harmony. Irrespective of the religions of their rulers, they adhered to their own beliefs while influencing each other in architecture, dress, music, food, and even in their religions evolution. Society, in other words, had attained its own *modus vivendi*; and if the state sometimes acted in variance and rulers, in search of wealth or in pursuit of power, attacked the followers or institutions of other faiths, it did not affect the general balance. If there were at times conflicts between Indians of different faiths, there was also occasional hostility among factions and groups belonging to the same religion. But with the coming of the British, both the context and the approach changed. Regional imbalance in economic and social development resulted in the classes who gained most from British rule being drawn predominantly from among the Hindus; and the British themselves preferred to think of the Indian people as composed of religious communities who were antagonistic to each other. According to the imperialist viewpoint, as expressed by Sir Francis Younghusband in 1930, 'the animosities of centuries are always smouldering beneath the surface.' Communal rioting, so marked a feature of the Indian political scene from the late nineteenth century, was regarded by the British, not as the result of their policies or of recent economic factors but as a regular phenomenon of Indian society.

It is against this background that the development of Tagore's views on this issue has to be seen. In 1898 he wrote that an Indian nation could never emerge by leaving out the Muslims; and seven years later, during the swadeshi movement, he proposed that a Hindu and a Muslim should act as joint leaders of the organization to rally the country's force. But, alongside this awareness of non-religious nationalism, in keeping with the normal trends of Indian society till the advent of the British, there was a deference in Tagore's writings to a political version of Hinduism. 'Brahma', he wrote in 1885, 'is India's living God; Jehovah, the Christian God or Allah are not quite akin to our thought.' In 1898 he spoke of a Hindu nation; in 1901 he hoped for the rejuvenation of Hindu civilization; and in 1904 he commended his father for refusing to dilute 'our supreme national religion' with a vague universalism, and himself thought in terms of India achieving a 'peculiarly Hinduistic' harmony. It was only after the communal riots of 1906 and 1907 following the partition of Bengal that these parallel strands in Tagore's outlook disappeared. His mind now remained centred on all Indians, whatever their religion, working together. 'Today', says the hero at the end of *Gora*, 'I am, above all, an Indian. In me there is no conflict of communities, no struggle between Hindu and Muslim and Christian. They all belong to me and I belong to them all.'

In the years thereafter Tagore spurned ritual and ceremony as 'the fetters of blind observance' and had no use for any religion which claimed a monopoly of the truth. He repudiated the contention that certain peoples, races, or creeds had been specially chosen by God and hailed Zarathustra as the first prophet who emancipated religion from the exclusive narrowness of the tribal God, the God of the chosen nation. He disapproved of those who did not appreciate the religions of others and who brought the pride of acquisition and the worldliness of sectarianism even into the region of spiritual truth.

To the person genuinely moved by the religious impulse the ultimate truth is one, every religion bears some traces of it, and which particular creed more professes it is a matter of indifference. All religions aspire to the same goal and, while the externals of worship divide, the core of the religious quest is common. 'When religion has to make way for religious organization, it is like the river being dominated by its sand-bed; the current stagnates and its aspects become like a desert.' Love of God was best achieved in the service of one's fellow-beings. Initiation in the true religion was initiation in humanity. 'He alone sees, who sees all beings in himself.'

If this be the essence of religion, the fact that a society is multi-religious need pose no problems; and the state has no role to play in this matter. It is this idea, underlying the poems of Tagore and shared by Gandhi and other profoundly religious Indians, which forms the basis of the Indian understanding of secularism and which, after years of fostering since 1947, is today again hard-pressed. The logical attitude of getting rid of religion altogether is too utopian for human society. The more practical answer, in line with the recognition by Tagore and others of religion as a matter of individual experience and action, is the removal of religion from public affairs, the distancing of the state from all faiths and refusal to favour any one creed above all others, the insistence on religion as a private matter with no bearing on civic rights and duties, and freedom for the practice of diverse forms of religious worship provided they do not come into conflict with each other. Only secularism of this type, not defined in any dictionary or in accordance with Western precedents but enabling a modern outlook in the Indian context, can prove the cornerstone of an egalitarian, forward-looking country with religious pluralism, full civil liberties, and equal opportunities. Secularism is more than laws, concessions, and special considerations. It is a state of mind, almost an instinctive feeling, such as had existed in India for many centuries before being pushed into the background in recent times; and in our efforts to restore that ethos so that India may not be torn apart, Tagore's writings form a gushing source of inspiration.

It is not surprising that the poet, living at a time when India was stirring from the sleep of ages, was concerned with the necessity of ridding tradition of that which was stagnant. He who regarded even the lowliest of humanity as God's footstool naturally rejected a caste system which treated many as worse than animals and condemned them to indignity and humiliation. A social system which destroyed the self-esteem of millions and accustomed the people for centuries not only to submit to every form of domination but at times even to venerate the power that held them down could not be expected to retain and cherish freedom. Servitude in social life went ill with demands for political independence. 'The regeneration of the Indian people, to my mind', wrote Tagore in 1910, 'directly and perhaps solely depends upon the removal of this condition.' The real obstacles to progress in India lay in areas with which the British government had nothing to do—blind superstitions, the adherence to state customs, the maintenance of institutions which, whatever their purpose in the past, now only strengthened discord. He once asserted that he would even welcome a wave of atheism over India if, like a forest fire, it alone could sweep away the corruption and rubbish which clogged Indian life on every side. On another occasion he declared in a sentence which has particular relevance today, 'There is no one in all the world with whom it is so difficult to sympathize as with the narrower fanatics of our own particular faith.'

Tagore, as some of his poems and several of his novels and short stories testify, was particularly sensitive to the dependent and subordinate condition of women in Indian society. He denounced their treatment as chattels. In the poem *The Bride* the girl moans that she feels she is up for sale:

> I feel like a garland-seller, my ware examined
> Tested for quality, coldly.

In the short story *Victory* the description is stark: 'The bridegroom came with a friend to inspect the bride. Her parents were dizzy with anxiety and fear when they saw the God arrive to select the beast for his sacrifice.'

However, Tagore was confident that, if women were treated with the respect that was their due, they had a special contribution to make to the community. He did not think that they should merely seek to ape men, and he was amused that 'a large number of women are screaming themselves hoarse to prove that they are not women. He wanted men to respect women as mothers and as the recipients of love. 'The altar at which Women may be truly worshipped', he wrote in *Gora*, 'is her place as Mother, the seat of the pure, right-minded Lady of the house.' And then, in one of his articles, he says, 'As the Beloved, it is women's part to infuse life into all the aspirations of men; and the spiritual power that enables her to do so I have called charm and was known in India by the name of Shakti.' The domestic world, wrote Tagore, was the gift of God to women: but it was not only in personal life that he gave them a special role. They could bring strength and conviction in education as well as in politics. If women did not join hands with men, no institution could grow fully. India seemed to have been dead for ages, with the real truth receding through dead rituals; it was for women, like Savitri of ancient legend, to bring back India from the dead. In the world at large too, Tagore looked to women to set right the existing 'one-sided civilization', obsessed with power, and to rescue humanity from the oppression of materialism.

Much of this will not be palatable to modern feminists, who do not accept that women have unique roles to play or particular qualities to display, and resent what is termed 'pedestal treatment', romanticizing women so that they remain unaware of their subordinate condition. On the other hand Virginia Woolf, who regarded herself as a feminist in Tagore's time, said that 'the values of women differ very often from the values which have been made by the other sex.' A radical thinker long after Tagore, Jean-Paul Sartre also believed that the woman's role was on the emotional plane; it was a question not of inferiority but of different dispositions. Because of various material and social relations, women retained their sensibility unimpaired. Even Simone de Beauvoir, one of the patron saints of feminism, has argued that certain 'feminine' qualities, such as a healthy distance from hierarchies, tolerance of competition, patience, and a straightforward manner, though products of oppression, ought to be retained after liberation. Tagore's chief purpose was to raise the status of women in the household as well as to bring them across the threshold into the open air. But his views are not wholly circumscribed by the context of his times.

Even more striking is the convergence of Tagore's attitude, from its own starting point, with the present-day interest in ecology and the environment. The importance given today to the need to maintain a balance between humanity and nature is not a concept alien or novel to the Indian philosophical tradition. The oneness and unity of the universe is a primary doctrine of the Upanishads, which speak of the five stages of the cosmic process; matter, life, instinct, reflective consciousness, and spiritual consciousness. The Vedas are resonant with a strong sense of the beauty and grace of nature, and in the Chandogya Upanishad is found the story of Satyakama Jabala who learnt the truth about Brahman from a bull, from fire, from a swan, and from a bird. 'Who has taught you?' asks his teacher, and Satyakama replies, 'Others than men.' It is this harmony between God, nature, and humanity which, after a long gap, is voiced again by Tagore. 'I can feel', he wrote, 'the unity with the created universe of all animate and inanimate objects.' All things coexist, subsumed into one harmony. The story of Robinson Crusoe delighted him, for in it the solitary man is face to face with nature, coaxing and cooperating with it, exploring its secrets, using all his faculties to secure its help. Humanity's kinship with nature underlies the poet's joy when

> the sky opens, the wind runs wild,
> laughter passes over the earth.

Intimacy of companionship gives force to his appreciation of 'The wonder of the gathering clouds hanging heavy with the unshed rain, the sudden sweep of storms arousing vehement gestures along the line of coconut trees, the fierce loneliness of the blazing summer noon, the silent sunrise behind the dewy veil of autumn morning.' But there is more to nature than the appeal of beauty. 'The water does not merely cleanse his limbs, but it purifies his heart, for it touches his soul. The earth does not merely hold his body, but it gladdens his mind, for its contact is more than physical contact, it is a living presence. When a man does not realize his kinship with the world, he lives in a prison-house whose walls are alien to him. . . The trees, the stars and the blue hills' ache 'with a meaning which can never be uttered in words.' Even those today to whom God is dead and whose minds have turned away from the Upanishads feel able to respond to Tagore's affinity with nature and to work it into their own ecological concepts. Scientists have come round to what Tagore grasped intuitively over eighty years ago, that humanity and the environment form an integrated system.

Such deep sensitivity to his surroundings led Tagore to select Santiniketan, which he described as his 'tangible poem', as the site of his educational efforts. 'For our perfection we have to be vitally savage and mentally civilized; we should have the gift to be natural with nature and human with human society.' Living in simplicity and in communion with nature would produce a balanced outlook. Specific religious instruction would not be necessary, for if the environment were pure, religious feeling would grow of its own in the lives of the students. Noble strivings would intertwine with the beauty of the setting. 'Our temple of worship is there where outward nature and human soul meet in union.' It was not that Tagore neglected the more mundane requirements of society. Rural development received attention at Sriniketan. The future lay, in his view, with the promotion of community life in small towns rather than in huge cities or tiny villages. Large organizations reduced the role of the individual and therefore of human values. The same criterion led Tagore to deprecate wide disparities of wealth as vulgar and undignified, and, while converted to state ownership of natural resources, transfer of land to the cultivators, and cooperative or collective farming, he insisted that none of these steps should be taken at the expense of the individual. Democracy and socialism working in tandem formed the ideology of Nehru as well as the preference of Tagore, though they moved to this common conclusion from very different positions. Nehru was influenced by the European revolutionary tradition and by his recognition of the existence of the class war as well as by his commitment to the British nonconformist tradition of civil liberties. The prime elements in Tagore's thinking were the sanctity of the human personality and its rights to its own integrity and to its full flowering.

'Unity of truth', intellectual, physical and spiritual, or what President Havel of Czechoslovakia has recently described as 'living within the truth', was to Tagore the object of education. It was a search for integration and wholeness. He had a poor view of Indians who knew nothing of their own heritage and, educated with English as the medium, became 'barriers choking the stream that flows from the mountain peak of their ancient history.' They turned out to be not persons but shadows with slave minds and sounded like European brass bands. Instruction in a foreign language was like trying to act a play with a mask on one's face. The mother tongue was the obvious medium for Indians as for all others, but what was taught should include the best of what was known everywhere. Imitation alone was like dressing a skeleton with another person's skin; but it was the rejection of poverty to dwarf oneself by rejecting everything which was foreign. True modernism was freedom of mind, not slavery of taste, being true to oneself while accepting everything that was worthwhile from other sources. These aims of education remain as valid now as when they were formulated.

Living in a world 'wild with the delirium of hatred', Tagore felt that the chief lesson to be learnt was how to be rid of 'arrogant nationalism'. As it had developed in the West, a nation was 'an organized gregariousness of gluttony', with selfishness a necessity and therefore a virtue. He loved India and was eager to see her free; but he did not wish her to develop as a nation on the European model, and said there was no word for nation in his language. 'I shall', he wrote in 1917, 'be born in India again and again; with all her poverty, misery and wretchedness I love India best.' But the India he loved and believed in was not a piece of land but an idea, a tradition of assimilative synthesis of conflicting and contradictory forces. His understanding of history was astoundingly up to date and anticipates some aspects of the recent approaches of Fernand Braudel and the French Annales school. For Tagore marginalized the history of events and saw political turbulence as surface ripples on a slow-moving river whose course is shaped by natural forces. He probed beneath the skein of political affairs to discern the essential social and economic structures. To him history was the account of prolonged struggles and abiding rhythms between humanity, the soil, and the elements.

With such views, it was to be expected that Tagore spurned a narrow nationalist nostalgia and placed his faith in the long-term trends of Indian history. His declaration that he was not a patriot but sought his compatriots all over the world embodied his hope that India would not become inward-looking but would continue to mesh, as in the past, her own traditions with such outer influences as were acceptable. The atmosphere which, as Nehru said, Tagore tried to create in Santiniketan and in India was one in which East and West would meet in unity, peace, and understanding. Visva-Bharati was based on the premise that India accepts her obligation to offer to others the hospitality of her best culture and has the right to accept from others their best. It was such an India of which he was proud and which he wished to survive. His faith in his people, in humanity, and in the future, and the principles on which that faith was based, should help to keep up our spirits in these depressing times.

14

Gandhi

An Irrepressible Optimist

As the world staggers into the last decade of the twentieth century, it becomes increasingly clear that Gandhi was the greatest personality of these hundred years.[1] He took an interest in almost every aspect of human activity and all his efforts were for the good of humanity. During the freedom movement, he puzzled and exasperated many of his British adversaries. It was not only Winston Churchill who denounced him; Linlithgow, the heavy-handed viceroy of the war years, described him as 'the world's most successful humbug', an opinion shared by Willingdon before and Wavell after. To the military mind of Chetwode, commander-in-chief in the early 1930s, baffled by Gandhi's non-violent methods of warfare, he was 'as cunning as a cartload of monkeys'. But even at that time to those outside the fray between India and Britain the message of Gandhi to all men and women everywhere could not be hidden. Contemporaneous with the vituperation of British proconsuls came the ultimate accolade of jazz; and Cole Porter immortalized him in one of his best-known lyrics:

You are the top; you are Mahatma Gandhi,
You are the top; you are Napoleon brandy.

Nor has the glaring light of hindsight since his death in 1948 harmed Gandhi's reputation; indeed with the passage of time his fame has

[1] This is a review of Judith Brown, *Gandhi: Prisoner of Hope* (New Haven: Yale University Press, 1990).

increased and his name has become a household word in every part of the world. The white American singer, Joan Baez, in her autobiography published in 1966, reports a dialogue between her husband and their daughter aged 11:

> 'Did Gandhi have a penis?' she asked.
> 'Yes', he answered.
> 'Did he have a vagina too?'
> 'No', said Ira. 'He was a man, and men just have a penis.'
> 'Well', she said, pausing in the doorway, 'it's just that he was so nice . . . I thought he might have had both.'

In the United States, Gandhi inspired the blacks in their struggle for civil rights, and in the Soviet Union today Zviad Gamsakhurdia, the champion of Georgian independence, who has spent the past thirty years in and out of jail, advocates day-to-day rebellion in terms of civil disobedience. His elaboration of his approach echoes the voice of Gandhi: 'I don't see the point of fighting Gorbachev on Gorbachev's terms. I don't see why we should respect his constitution or his laws. They are the laws of empire and empire is dead.' Clearly, outside India at least, Gandhi is still very much of a live influence, and all for the good. As George Orwell observed soon after Gandhi died, which other world leader of this century has left such a clean smell?

It is not, therefore, to be wondered at that Gandhi is now an industry. Hundreds of popular writers, biographers, scholars, and graduate students have written about him. Research, shallow or in depth, of some aspect, major or minor, of Gandhi's life and work goes on incessantly in institutions round the globe. A man of wide interests and multiple achievements, of extraordinary energy and contradictory opinions, he provided, with his dislike of privacy, more material in his 79 years for scrutiny than any other person of his time. The fertile ground of his life has been gone over, ploughed, mined, dug up and assessed in detail and yet there seems no end to what can be discovered, retold and recast. If the Gandhi factories are ever closed down, it will certainly not be in our time.

A biography of Gandhi in a single volume, if it is to be more than a chronological account, would seem then to be a superhuman task, beyond the powers of a syndicate of historians, let alone a single individual. To have read everything written and spoken by Gandhi or about him, to have taken into account all research and analyses concerning him and his variegated efforts and then to provide a comprehensive and rounded interpretation by modern standards of biographical writing—even to state the requirements boggles the mind. Judith Brown handles the problem by making her own way through the thickets. A professional historian who is aware of all the writings about Gandhi, and herself the author of two earlier studies which examined in detail Gandhi's success in building up a political following in India, she sticks to Gandhi's writings, large enough in themselves, and her own knowledge, supplemented by consultation of the relevant official records and private paper collections. The book has no bibliography; the suggestions for further reading are very general; the notes provide a little more information but by no means give an idea of the vast literature centred round Gandhi. This is a blinkered book, but the approach enables the author to keep the task manageable and pushes us much further in our understanding of the subject.

For this method ensures the strength of the book, which is an analysis, on parallel lines, of the emergence and achievement of Gandhi as a public figure and the evolution of his inner life, which in Gandhi's case is so integral a part of his personality. The well-known facts of the early years are stated just enough to establish the growth in self-knowledge and identity and the pages on South Africa delineate the beginnings of commitment to public service, with the corollary of steady distancing from family life as normally understood. Brown stresses how the experience in South Africa contributed to the making of both the public and the inner life of Gandhi in ways which were to reach their full flowering in India. He organized the Indian community to resist unfair laws, worked to unify it, and launched a programme for raising its social consciousness. He developed what we would today call a keen sense of public relations, started journals for giving steady expression to his views, and appealed to as wide a public as possible across the world. He cultivated what he later termed the 'art of begging' and gained a reputation as an honest trustee of public funds. Above all, of course, he perfected the technique of satyagraha; non-violent resistance to injustice combined with a willingness to compromise provided basic principles were not damaged.

Alongside was the progress of the pilgrim spirit. Working within the Hindu tradition but open to outside influences, Gandhi came to the position that true religion, as against specific doctrines, was all-encompassing. The truth-seeker must strive for self-purification and find his God in compassion for fellow human beings. This necessarily presumed non-violence for this alone could safeguard the integrity of all involved. Brown rightly puts in this context *Hind Swaraj*, written in 1909. Noting the inadequacy of materialism and of modern civilization which was its product, Gandhi concluded that the ancient civilization of India was the best the world had ever seen. This was not xenophobia, a way of bolstering India's wounded self-esteem. Gandhi deplored that Indians also had lost their way and would have to recover these values and transform themselves before they could attain swaraj. Nor were these values solely spiritual; Gandhi laid emphasis on swadeshi, the right type of education, and the importance of good health and a proper diet.

On his return to the wider context of India, the three strands of Gandhi's life continue: the growing involvement in public affairs, the incessant effort to change Indian men and women, and the interest in his own self and conduct. Brown keeps hold of all three and follows how they weave together. Champaran and Khera had this in common, that the encounter with the Raj was at the level of legitimacy, raising the whole issue of government by consent; and this was to be the base of all later dealings of Gandhi with the British. He mobilized the peasantry by teaching them to cast off fear and to exercise their rights as citizens and, from 1920, when Gandhi concluded that British rule in India was Satanic, noncooperation became a civic duty. Most Indian readers will be familiar with the details of Gandhi's political leadership which Brown narrates with summary clarity, and will be more engrossed in the battle within on which depended the battle without. Spinning as a way of reaching out to the poorest Indians and work for Hindu–Muslim unity and the removal of untouchability were the means of generating the strength to acquire swaraj. But all these were also part of his effort to see God face to face; and now Gandhi was asserting not that God was Truth but that Truth was God, and such Truth was best found in the service of humanity.

That Brown does not fall victim to the obvious peril of losing sight of Gandhi's personal evolution in the crowded complex of events is demonstrated by the fact that she deals with the clash with Subhas Bose in about six lines, but devotes much attention to the individual civil disobedience of 1940, to which most students of political history attach little importance. For this was a carefully circumscribed campaign with limited objectives and planned and controlled by Gandhi from start to finish. Even if of little significance in the national movement—the *Statesman* of Calcutta reported it daily under the caption 'Cranks Corner'—it was a test-tube experiment in Gandhism and therefore earns careful analysis in a biography. But with the failure of the Cripps Mission and the Japanese advance Gandhi had to take more urgent decisions. The Quit India resolution was the decision of a leader with unflinching faith in non-violence accepting the risk of violence in order to end the calamity of slavery. The remainder of Gandhi's life has been gone over repeatedly by many and the tracks are well worn.

Judith Brown is a charitable writer and deflates criticism even when it is unavoidable. Of the inequities of imperialism she is well aware, but of the deliberate efforts—for instance, by the British to foster and take advantage of differences between Hindus and Muslims—all that she says are two passing references to the British tendency to see Indian groups in term of community and to their understanding of Indian society as a plural one of different peoples who needed special outlets in political life. On Gandhi too, while she steers clear of uncritical adulation, she does not consider seriously the various criticisms made of his leadership. Of the suggestion that Gandhi's style and idiom and his support of the Khilafat movement on the basis of Hindu–Muslim partnership rather than an overall Indian identity strengthened communal tendencies, she mentions the view but does not rebut or analyse it. She writes of Gandhi's 'moral economics' and states that the industrialists saw in it the promise of harmony and productivity rather than conflict. Surely it should be added that they also saw in it a way of strengthening their own position against that of the workers. It is true that Gandhi was far more concerned with changing people than reforming the economic order; but his philosophy assisted the landlords and the capitalists in maintaining their vested interests. Brown does not mention that in 1921 and again in 1931, in terms of peasant unrest in what was then the United Provinces, Gandhi, while prepared to consider at some stage suspension of payment of taxes to the government, refused to approve non-payment of all rents to the landlords. This was in tune with his lofty notion that no section of society should benefit at the expense of any other, but the immediate effect was to assist the rich against the poor.

What lifts this book above the ordinary level is the author's empathy with her subject. She clearly has in mind the non-Indian reader and, touching on every aspect of Gandhi's multiple activities and meshing closely the public and the personal themes, she seeks to establish that his efforts in so many directions make him a person for all times and places. The subtitle of the book is taken from a passage in the Old Testament, 'turn you to the strong hold, ye prisoners of hope', and the quotation is apt, for what sustained Gandhi through all the ups and downs of a long life was his hope grounded in religious conviction. To us in India, looking round us, Gandhi's plan to construct a new Indian polity and society infused with non-violence and godliness by transforming the nature of the human being seems very remote indeed. But Gandhi himself, however dark the horizon, was convinced of the ultimate success of truth. He was, as he often said, an irrepressible optimist; and it is that optimism that we now need most. Whether, without the sense of promise of the Nehru years and without, for many of us, Gandhi's religious faith, such optimism is possible, is the question.

15

Reappraising Sardar Patel

Forty-five years after his death, Vallabhbhai Patel, India's first deputy prime minister from August 1947 till his death in December 1950, is at last coming into his own. He willingly played second fiddle, first to the Mahatma from the time he came under his influence in 1917 till 1946 when he began to show signs of restiveness, and then not so willingly to Jawaharlal Nehru, when he could easily, but for the preference of Gandhi, have been Number One. He felt during these years that both Gandhi and Nehru were unduly soft to Muslims, thereby weakening India's integrity; but his stoic decency forbade him from revolt and he carried out, to the extent that he could, his own policy of impartiality between the two communities. Circumscribed by events and the prevailing leadership, he could not prevent the creation of Pakistan or heal the running sore of Kashmir; but he thwarted the balkanization of India and solved the problem of the Indian states by a proper mixture of firmness and friendship.

Now at last, with the vacillations of Nehru and the even worse drawbacks of his descendants clear, Patel's reputation is emerging from the shadows. As result, we have had a number of biographies.[1] Krishna has been working for many years, has been in touch with numerous officials, British and Indian, who served Patel and have given their recollections, is familiar with Gujarati sources, and has provided us with a comprehensive, if somewhat uncritical, life-story. Born poor

[1] This is a review of B. Krishna, *Sardar Vallabhbhai Patel.*

in a self-reliant Patidar family, Patel set up as a criminal lawyer in the towns of Gujarat and, at the age of 35, by now a widower, he spent four years in London and was called to the Bar. On his return he developed a flourishing practice in Ahmedabad and in 1917 entered municipal politics. Here he showed the qualities for which he later become well known: hard work, efficiency, impartiality in administration, courage, and a refusal to be overawed by the British.

The same year he came under Gandhi's sway and switched from a British to an Indian way of life. He was deputy commander in the Mahatma's Khera campaign and himself led, in the Nagpur flag controversy, the fight against dacoits at Borsal and the Bardoli campaign. He had by now become a national figure and paved the way for Gandhi's march to the sea at Dandi in 1930. He presided over the Congress session the next year and was chairman of the Congress Parliamentary Board during the years when the Congress was in office in some of the provinces. His handling of the Nariman and Khera episodes earned him the reputation of a strict disciplinarian. He was also seen as Gandhi's chief lieutenant in getting rid of Subhas Chandra Bose after the latter was re-elected president of the Congress.

With the outbreak of the war and Gandhi's sentimental attitude to British distress, Patel, for the first time, began to move away from the Mahatma; but as the war progressed, he reverted gradually to his earlier position and became once again Gandhi's chief spokesman and supporter. After three years inside the Ahmednagar Fort where negotiations with the British were on, he became more critical of C. Rajagopalachari than before and was scornful of Gandhi calling on Jinnah, thereby making the latter more influential. Jinnah was further strengthened by the viceroy Wavell's dissolution of the Simla conference on Jinnah's refusal to allow the nomination of a Muslim member by the Unionist Government of the Punjab. This marked the end of the Khizar Hyat Tiwana government.

In the years after 1945, Patel was repeatedly foiled in his efforts to deprive Jinnah of a united Muslim vote by his own colleagues—Gandhi with his pro-Muslim sympathies, Nehru with his secularism, and Abul Kalam Azad who wanted a Congress–League coalition. Patel could not make any headway in the Punjab, Sind, and the

North West Frontier Province. Wavell favoured the pro-League crowd with his decision to bring the League into the interim government and persuading Nehru to go to London, where the Clement Attlee government took positions favourable to the League.

Yet, with all this varied opposition, as minister of home and states from September 1946, Patel's firm and friendly attitude helped keep India unified without compromising on principles. He treated the rulers of the states as Indian and therefore not irreconcilable enemies. He foiled the efforts of Conrad Corfield of the states department to encourage the large states to declare independence and those of the Nawab of Bhopal, with his ambition to become the governor general of Pakistan after Jinnah, to balkanize India.

Patel confounded all his enemies, both British and Indian, as well as the pro-Pakistan manoeuvres of the nizam of Hyderabad and the unpredictable vagaries of the young maharaja of Jodhpur. He had his success when Baroda, Bikaner, and many others joined the Constituent Assembly on 18 April 1947; yet Jodhpur, Jamnagar, and Travancore still stayed away. With the lapse of paramountcy as envisaged in the plan of 3 June 1947, Jinnah expected accession to Pakistan of Kashmir, Hyderabad, Bhopal, and many other states. Even he did not hope to retain Travancore despite its vainglorious revolt and saw Sir C.P. Ramaswamy Aiyar sink to inglorious defeat. He had more hopes on Jodhpur and planned a Karachi–Jodhpur–Bhopal axis, which would have struck a blow at the heart of India. But Jodhpur was won over to India by Mountbatten and then by Patel. So too was the Jam Sahib (over lunch!), and the myriad states of Kathiawar were united under India's aegis. The intrigues of the nawab of Bhopal to divide the Indian states in the interests of Pakistan were thwarted with the aid of Patiala and Bikaner; so too was Junagadh's accession to Pakistan despite the hesitations and vacillations of Nehru and Mountbatten.

Two major issues still remained—Kashmir and Hyderabad. On Kashmir he took strong and immediate action to save Srinagar from Pakistani inroads. The maharaja was asked to shift from Srinagar to Jammu and a permanent all-weather road was built linking the state to India by July 1948. But further action was thwarted by Nehru who was blind in his support of Sheikh Abdullah, and by Mountbatten who committed India to a plebiscite and favoured referring the matter to the United Nations. The problem is still with us, after nearly fifty years, and in a worse form; and Kashmir has been sucked into the vortex of international politics. The reference to the United Nations was made without consulting Patel, who was then touring Assam. Had the problem of Kashmir been left to him, he would have driven out the Pakistani forces instead of agreeing to a ceasefire and effected a united subcontinent.

Patel had a freer hand in Hyderabad. His main obstacle was Mountbatten, who sought Nehru's help in preventing the Indian army from moving in. The nizam, with the help of Mountbatten's friend Walter Monckton, hoped to engage India in prolonged constitutional negotiations while purchasing arms from foreign sources and encouraging the Razakars to terrorize the Hindu subjects. Both Monckton and Mountbatten favoured the association of Hyderabad with India and not accession. A standstill agreement with India for two months was signed and the nizam utilized this period to strengthen his position. Mountbatten exploited his personal friendship with Patel to secure his consent to a draft treaty, with Hyderabad heavily weighted in the nizam's favour; but the latter came to Patel's rescue and rejected the government's own draft. The field was clear with Mountbatten's departure and, despite Nehru's instinct to postpone action, the Indian army moved into Hyderabad.

This was Patel's greatest achievement. The final success was bringing together the rulers of Rajasthan into the unions of Matsya, Vindhya Pradesh, Malwa, and Rajasthan. In two years Patel had solved in India's interest the problem of the Indian states which had threatened to split India. He first dissolved the Chamber of Princes, which enabled him to deal with the princes individually. He then merged the smaller states with neighbouring provinces, consolidated the larger states, and then created new unions, so that by the time India became a republic in January 1950 a new order had emerged with identical units constituting the Union of India. He died in December 1950 with his life's work accomplished.

Patel was an efficient administrator and the problem of integrating the Indian states was ideally suited to his temperament. He had an unshaken perception of the final goal and his friendly approach won over most of the princes. But whether he had a larger vision, which a prime minister should have, is doubtful. Nehru made mistakes and left India with problems which still remain unresolved; but this cannot cloud the fact that he was a statesman. Patel himself realized this and, while he often criticized Nehru, realized the limitations of his own virtues.

16

Tradition and Dissent

The Paradoxes of Subhas Bose

It is natural for a national movement, in its struggle against the alien ruler, to have recourse to tradition as an instrument for strengthening the self-respect of the people. In opposing the cultural hegemony which the colonial power seeks to impose, appeals are made to an imaginary golden past before the intrusion of the foreigner and to the glory of a culture pristine at the source before contamination by ideas from outside. Tilak and Aurobindo Ghose drew on the Indian tradition, as they understood it, without qualification, and were not abashed to allow their dissent to be coloured because of this by reaction and violence. Gandhi had, despite appearances, a modern outlook, and used tradition to build up his mass campaigns but without allowing it to swamp his progressive ideas. 'It is good to swim in the waters of tradition but to sink in them is suicide.'[1] Nehru was a more strident modernizer and, from the mid 1920s, stood forth as a revolutionary in the European tradition; but he did not claim to shake off his intellectual ancestry and was impressed by 'a majesty of soul' which had lingered in India despite centuries of vicissitude.[2]

The blend of tradition and dissent is far more pronounced in the case of Subhas Bose. Even now, more than forty-five years after his death, he still arouses great passions, and it is not easy to seek to assess

[1] *Navajivan*, 28 June 1925, *Collected Works of Mahatma Gandhi*, vol. 27, p. 308.

[2] *An Autobiography* (1936; Indian edition 1962), p. 429.

him without partisanship.[3] In the case of those who have achieved success in the worldly sense, the judgements of the historian are generally acceptable even when severe. But when someone with so many talents and such prodigious effort is deserted by conventional fortune, it seems unfair that the retrospective view should also appear to be harsh. Bose falls into this category. Twice president of the Indian National Congress, he held office without power. The path which he chose to secure freedom for India led into the sands of frustration. Then, as independence in some form or other became a certainty and Bose could have returned to his country to begin a new phase of his career, he died in an aircraft accident. All the dice seemed clearly loaded against him, and it is understandable that his admirers should be aggressive in defence and resent even the slightest hint of anything other than fulsome praise. Yet Bose does not need emotional sympathy and has earned objective scrutiny. Long years of hard life in prison or in exile, intense patriotism, a high measure of physical and moral courage, the strength to stand up to Gandhi—these are qualities which speak for themselves. Even the British recognized that, as the creator of the Indian National Army, he had protected Indians in lands under Japanese occupation and had been accorded by the Japanese greater respect and power than most other leaders in the same position; and his influence over those who had served under him was very considerable. 'It affects all races, castes and communities almost equally strongly.'[4] So to speak of him with detachment is, in a sense, to do him justice, and in no way to diminish him. For Bose is buried in the foundations of free India, and that honoured place no one can take away from him. He brings to mind Bukharin's last message to his wife: 'Know, comrades, that in the banner you carry forward there will be a drop of my blood.'

[3] For example, in Leonard Gordon's long and diffuse study of Sarat and Subhas Bose (*Brothers Against the Raj*, Delhi: Penguin Books, 1989) his judgements are weakened by his seeming all the time to be looking over his shoulder.

[4] Sir F. Mudie, Home Member, to Private Secretary to Viceroy, 23 August 1945, *Transfer of Power*, vol. 6, no. 571 and enclosure.

Progressive thinking, free of the shackles of tradition, seemed at the start to be distinctive of Bose. For many years he, with Nehru, was regarded as one of the leaders of the radical elements in the Congress, and perhaps even more to the 'left' than Nehru. For while Nehru was prone to be influenced, in Bose's phrase, by 'sentimental politics' and incapable of breaking away from Gandhi, Bose appeared as the hope of the stern and unbending socialists. But what precisely was the core of his ideological element? Did it consist of a clearly thought-out philosophy or was it, as Sumit Sarkar has described it, 'always extremely brittle and suspect'?[5] Bose certainly throughout spoke the right words. He defined freedom as implying not only emancipation from political bondage but also equal distribution of wealth, abolition of caste barriers and social inequities, and destruction of communalism and religious intolerance.[6] Though himself a believer in *mantra-shakti*, he was secular in politics and criticized Gandhi for strengthening the element of religion in public affairs. He demanded the establishment of a socialist republic in India with complete, all-round, undiluted freedom.[7] He supported the Karachi resolution on fundamental rights not for what it said but for its implicit potential and claimed to represent the group which stood between right-wing revisionists and the communists and strove for full-blooded socialism.[8] Above all, in his first presidential address at the Congress at Haripura in February 1938, he declared resoundingly that he had no doubt that the problems relating to the eradication of poverty, illiteracy, and disease and to scientific production and distribution could be effectively tackled only along socialistic lines. He was for planning, the abolition of landlordism, the liquidation of agricultural indebtedness, the extension of cooperatives, and industrial development under state

[5] Article in *Mainstream* (Delhi), 12 June 1976.

[6] Speech to the Punjab Provincial Students Conference, October 1929, quoted in Gordon, *Brothers Against the Raj*, p. 211.

[7] Presidential Address at the All India Naujawan Bharat Sabha, Karachi, 27 March 1931, *Selected Speeches of Subhash Chandra Bose* (New Delhi: Publications Division, Government of India, 1962), pp. 58–9.

[8] Presidential Address at the All India Trade Union Congress, Calcutta, 4 July 1931, ibid., pp. 64–7.

ownership and control.[9] It was, too, not just a matter of words, for, as a first step, Bose set up in 1938 the National Planning Committee.

Yet a further look is required to examine the nature of Bose's understanding of socialism. This is especially necessary in India where there are as many interpretations of the word as there are groups and even individuals espousing it. Many, flushed with the spirit of nationalism and eager to disown intellectual roots in European thought, have sought the origins of socialist ideas in the Hindu texts. The Advaita Vedanta was cultivated as fertile ground, and Gandhi has been acclaimed as an indigenous socialist. Jawaharlal Nehru looked askance at these efforts to blend left-wing thought with pride in the Indian heritage and, in the late 1920s, publicly declared himself to be a scientific socialist. But the idea of an Indian element in socialist doctrine infiltrated even into Nehru's mind and increasingly made itself felt. He who started by asserting that he was a 'full-blooded' Marxist went on to demand that Marxism be trimmed to the Indian context and adapted to the Indian genius. He accepted the Marxist analysis of the past but not its diagnosis of the future, was critical of the concept of the dictatorship of the proletariat, and sought a synthesis of Marxist solutions and Gandhian techniques. After becoming prime minister, the transformation of his outlook was even more rapid. He came near to proclaiming that he was no longer so much of a scientific as an utopian socialist, believed that the class war would be not so much resolved as dissolved, and later, while insisting on the basic approach of peaceful means, suggested that 'we might also keep in view the old Vedantic ideal of the life force which is the inner base of everything that exists.'[10]

This throwing together in the minds of so many of orthodox tradition and modern radicalism and leading to a welter of so-called socialist thinking in India encourages a more charitable view of Bose's gropings and predicaments. Allowance has also to be made for the

[9] Subhas Chandra Bose, *Through Congress Eyes* (Allahabad: Kitabistan, no date), pp. 1–51.

[10] 'The Basic Approach', 13 July 1958, *A.I.C.C. Economic Review*, 15 August 1958.

years of enforced residence in Central Europe. This cut him off from first-hand knowledge of Indian conditions and exposed him more than most Indian nationalists to the meretricious achievements of the fascist dictators. Exile in itself has a wearing effect on the mind and helps to explain the attraction which the discipline and authority of totalitarian rule held out to Bose. He appreciated the anti-British stance of Hitler and Mussolini without taking into sufficient account their deep contempt for Indian nationalism. Added to these distortions caused by long absence from his own country was the pragmatic cast of his mind, as evidenced by his attitudes even while in India. A disciple of Chitta Ranjan Das, he always veered between a commitment to total opposition to British rule on the one hand and a willingness to compromise on principles and work British institutions in the short term on the other. Thus he was always ambivalent on 'council entry'; and he was prepared to function over the years in the Corporation of Calcutta despite all the limitations of that institution. He was prepared for cooperation with the Hindu Mahasabha and the Muslim League,[11] and was ready to envisage coalitions with communal parties in forming ministries in Bengal and Assam. For achieving the last objective, he was even prepared to enlist the help of the Raj, and, as Congress president, requested the governor of Bengal to advise Fazlul Haq to form a coalition with the Congress in which Haq would be chief minister.[12] In December 1940, after he had left the Congress and was clamouring for immediate rebellion, Bose sought assistance from the enemy and wrote to the viceroy requesting him to withdraw the support of British officials and businessmen from the Fazlul Haq ministry.[13]

Bose's contention would no doubt have been that he should be judged by practical results and not by theoretical consistency. Any

[11] B. Chakrabarty, *Subhas Chandra Bose and Middle Class Radicalism* (Delhi: Oxford University Press, 1991), p. 62.

[12] See Lord Brabourne, Governor of Bengal, to the Viceroy 19 December 1938, Mss. Eur. F. 97, Brabourne Papers, vol. 56, India Office Library.

[13] L.A. Gordon, *Bengal: The Nationalist Movement 1876–1940* (New York: Columbia University Press, 1974; Indian edn 1979), pp. 286–7.

weapon was good enough if it would weaken British rule even for a little while. But some questions persist. Why, even as he denounced Gandhi and Nehru for temporizing, did he negotiate with British officials and communal parties? Why did he not seek to wreck the All-Parties Conference in 1928 and why did he not leave the Congress in 1931 rather than in 1940? Why, like Nehru and M.N. Roy, did he stay away from the Congress Socialist Party? Why, after his re-election as president of the Congress in 1939, did he reject M.N. Roy's advice to form a 'homogenous' working committee with Roy as general secretary and continue to search for compromise with Gandhi till he was broken and obliged to resign? These were issues of logic to which Bose attached no importance, and this viewpoint must be borne in mind while probing his theoretical position, even if, to do credit to Bose's level of leadership, such probing cannot be avoided.

Bose traced the roots of socialist endeavour in India to the teachings of Vivekananda and the customs among such people as the Khasis of Assam, who did not believe in private property. The new ideas emerging from the West had to be merged with local practice and a synthesis attained between modernism and India's past glories.[14] This was indiscriminate acceptance of tradition and pushing it within the contours of dissent from the status quo. 'Love', he wrote in his autobiography, 'is the essence of the universe and is the essential principle in human life. . . . This statement can be challenged when one can see so much in life that is opposed to love; but the paradox can be easily explained. The "essential principle" is not fully manifest yet; it is unfolding itself in space and time. Love, like reality of which it is the essence, is dynamic.'[15] This seems a traditional view at its most simplistic, with not a tinge of radical dissent. But what made it easy for Bose to take up such a position was the fact that the Western ideas to which he attached importance were more organizational than ideological, and what he sought to promote was party discipline, an

[14] Presidential addresses, Maharashtra provincial conference, 3 May 1928, and Rangpur political conference, 30 March 1929, *Selected Speeches*, p. 30 and p. 47.

[15] Bose, *An Indian Pilgrim: An Unfinished Autobiography and Collected Letters 1897–1921* (Calcutta: Asia Publishing House, 1965), p. 142.

active volunteer corps, unions of peasants and workers, and women's associations. It was this, coupled with direct exposure to events in Europe, which led him, in contrast to Nehru, to refuse to see any difference between fascism and communism and to stress the organizational similarities rather than the ideological gulf between them. He later recognized that his phrase 'a synthesis between fascism and communism' had not been a happy one and he tried to explain it away by saying that in the early 1930s fascism had not yet developed imperialist overtones and appeared to be merely an aggressive form of nationalism while communists in India had been adopting anti-nationalist postures.[16] But there is no getting away from the fact that Bose had never an intellectual abhorrence of fascism as a right-wing ideology, and this explains the ease with which he was able, as Congress president as well as during the war years, to seek support from the Axis powers. This can be well defended as the application of the well-worn thesis that Britain's difficulties should be India's opportunity; but it can hardly be fitted into the acceptance of a socialist ideology.

Moreover, as a proclaimed socialist, Bose should have been involved with the problems of the peasants and workers at least in his home province. At the Lahore Congress in 1929 he advocated undertaking immediately the task of organizing the peasants and other oppressed sections of the Indian people on their own grievances; but in Calcutta he, like others in the Swarajist Party, supported the rights of the zamindars as against those of the tenants. He had no deep commitment to the working-class movement in Bengal and, to the satisfaction of Indian capitalists, was more sensitive to their interests than to those of their employees.[17]

In his tussle with Gandhi, Bose put himself forward as the champion of left-wing policies against the entrenched conservatives, and in the Congress presidential elections he secured the support of almost all those among the rank and file who regarded themselves as 'leftists'. But here again Bose's leftism had meagre content. Unlike Nehru, who

[16] Interview with R. Palme Dutt, *Daily Worker* (London), 24 January 1938.

[17] Tanika Sarkar, *Bengal 1928–1934* (Delhi: Oxford University Press, 1987), pp. 18–21.

from the 1920s intermeshed nationalism and socialism and believed that they would strengthen each other, Bose saw no need to work out a socialist programme till freedom had been won. To him leftism was no more than the unceasing struggle for undiluted independence. It was only after such independence had been obtained that leftism would begin to mean socialism. So it was not for him essential, during the national movement, that a leftist should be a socialist, and socialism as an economic doctrine need be given prime attention only in the post-imperialist phase. If he set up the National Planning Committee, it was mostly as a sop to Nehru and others of that line of thinking, just as Gandhi was frequently agreeing to measures he did not think much of in order to appease Nehru. Indeed, paradoxically, Bose's mental attitudes had more in common with those of Gandhi than of Nehru. They were both sturdy, no-nonsense politicians as against the inward-looking, self-analysing, doubt-ridden Nehru. Bose's leftism was 'a philosophy of activism' and a protest against passivism.[18] His objective was an anti-imperialist front to oppose the federal scheme under the 1935 Act and to defeat those in the Congress whom he denounced as standing for constitutionalism and reformism. Gandhi would have agreed with the demand for an 'activist' outlook; where he differed from Bose was on the timing and on the acceptance of techniques of violence. Indeed, one may doubt if Gandhi took Bose's contentions seriously, for he knew of Bose's negotiations with Linlithgow and Brabourne even while he was objecting to policies of compromise. It was with Nehru that Bose's differences were more basic and ideological and, if Nehru was critical of Bose's conduct in 1938 and 1939, it was not solely for the elitist reason that he regarded anyone's effort to secure his own re-election to be vulgar. Merely to shout catchy slogans demanding instant battle with the government and to denounce the Gandhians in the working committee was no elaboration of left-wing views. There was weight in Nehru's rueful remarks that he could not make out whom Bose considered a leftist and whom a rightist, for many of Bose's so-called leftists were more

[18] See speech at the All-India Youth Congress, Calcutta, 25 December 1938, *Selected Speeches*, p. 44.

conservative than the so-called rightists. 'Strong language and a capacity to criticize and attack the old Congress leadership is not a test of Leftism in politics.' To contest the Congress presidentship on a personal basis and not on definite leftist principles and policies meant a setback for the real left.[19]

Bose's socialism or leftism-when broken down amounted, therefore, to no more than appropriate platitudes, political organization, and personal ambition. This made it easy for him to mix tradition and dissent without at any point concerning himself with the possible illogicality of his position. It is unnecessary to judge him solely on the basis of Nehru's criticisms or Gandhi's reactions. Nehru's clear-sightedness in this matter did not dim his affection for Bose and, till Bose left India, Nehru sought to save him from his own misjudgements and from the wrath of his antagonists. In Gandhi, on the other hand, Bose brought out all the latent harshness and, despite the lack of fundamental antipathy between them as personalities, the Bose episode showed Gandhi at his worst. He treated Bose as 'a spoilt child of the family', curtly told Tagore that the matter was too complicated for the poet to handle,[20] and destroyed Bose's political future. These tragedies of imperfect sympathies do not, of course, contribute the real evidence against Bose in assessing his ideology. But the lack of solid content in his seeming left-wing thinking speaks for itself and was clear to many even at the time. As early as 1928, *Kirti*, a radical journal of the Punjab, advised Indian youth to accept the ideas of Nehru rather than those of Bose, because while Nehru was a socialist revolutionary who strove to usher in a new epoch, Bose was a sentimental revolutionary who wanted only to overthrow the existing state.[21] And nearly eleven years later, *Forward*, the Calcutta newspaper, commented after Bose's resignation of the Congress presidentship:

[19] See Nehru to Bose, 4 February and 3 April 1939, *Selected Works of Jawaharlal Nehru* (First Series), vol. 9 (New Delhi: Orient Longman, 1976), pp. 480–5 and 534–49.

[20] Gandhi to C.F. Andrews, 15 January 1940, H. Tinker, *The Ordeal of Love* (Delhi: Oxford University Press, 1979), p. 303.

[21] July 1928, quoted in B.S. Josh, *Communist Movement in Punjab* (Delhi: Anupama Publications, 1979), pp. 80–1, footnote.

'The fact of the matter . . . is that Subhas Bose is no radical . . . when it became obvious that he had no lead to give and no plan of action to put forward, he could no longer keep his supporters together. In the last resort, his mainstay was Bengal's provincial feeling.'[22] This is a judgement not wholly to be dismissed as tainted by the factional politics of the Bengal Congress. The very strong claims of Subhas Bose on the attention of posterity have nothing to do with his ideology.

[22] 8 April 1939.

17

The Playgirl Transformed

Edwina Mountbatten

If the publication of a book of this size is any indication, Edwina Mountbatten rouses more interest than her very marginal role in history warrants.[1] Probably there is more interest in India than in Britain; the wife of the last viceroy and the personal friend of India's prime minister, glamour and gossip have combined to wrap her in the mists of romance and intrigue. Ironically, thanks to the latest restrictions on the import of books, Indian readers will have to be satisfied, for the time being at any rate, with excerpts in newspapers. But no doubt at some stage there will be an Indian edition, although it is only the last hundred pages which are of direct concern to this country.

The story starts as a conventional fairy tale. Ernest Cassels was a German Jew who settled in London, became a millionaire through his banking activities, and sought his way into upper-class British society, even becoming a trusted adviser of Kind Edward VII and regularly lending him large sums of money. The only child of Cassels married a dull conservative of aristocratic background whose only claim on our interest is that he was descended on his mother's side from Pocahontas, the Red Indian princess. Cassels was heartbroken by the early death of his daughter and lavished all his attention on his two grand-daughters,

[1] Review of Janet Morgan, *Edwina Mountbatten: A Life of Her Own* (London: HarperCollins, 1991).

of whom the eldest was Edwina. She had a lonely childhood, made worse by her father's remarriage to an unsympathetic character. But Edwina grew up a strong-minded girl with striking looks. Aware that she was a wealthy heiress, she liked having her own way and had no difficulty in getting round her grandfather's puritanical plans for her. From the age of 17 she was attracted to men and in 1922, when 21, she married, as in any fairy tale, not a prince but minor royalty, Lord Louis Mountbatten, an impecunious but conventionally handsome naval officer.

From here the fairy tale started to go wrong. All the fairies appear to have been at Edwina's cradle at her birth but some of them appear to have been a little drunk. The marriage had never a chance of success. This biography of Edwina has to be read as a companion volume to the much superior biography of Mountbatten by Philip Ziegler, published six years ago. Ziegler, while tactful, provided enough evidence to make clear that Mountbatten was a mediocrity who messed up whatever he handled, be it in war or in India. Janet Morgan tells us more in the same strain about his personal life. Lacking in all the superior qualities, he had all the inferior virtues. He was punctual and fanatically well-organized but obsessed with protocol and had neither a sense of proportion nor a sense of humour. He spent his spare hours drawing up his family tree with its links to diverse royal houses, reigning or deposed. He had a passionate craving for medals and ribbons. The shortcomings of the admiralty and the loss of a toothbrush were to him of equal importance. His request to Edwina, soon after their engagement in Delhi, was to recover a razor strip which he had left behind in the viceroy's house. After their marriage, his concerns were the management of his wife's immense fortune and the organization of her household. He wrote out the duties of housemaids and the precise responsibilities of the chefs, only to have these lists passed on without being read by Edwina to the housekeeper. His own bedroom in the vast mansion inherited by Edwina he converted to look like a cabin in a warship. A gadget created the sound of a ship's engines; and cutouts of the Mediterranean fleet twinkled Morse signals to each other. His bathroom was decorated with weeds, rocks, and fishes so that when Mountbatten took a shower he could make-believe that he was deep-sea diving. It is hard to remember that one is discussing the behaviour of an adult.

The consequences were not surprising. Within months of the wedding which caught the headlines round the world, Edwina was thoroughly bored. She found Mountbatten inadequate as a lover and tiresome as a husband. She had two alternatives: to plunge into non-stop social activity or to turn again to other men. Being Edwina, she did both. Throughout the 1920s and 1930s she led a life of what she herself described as one of 'complete hecticness'. She gave lavish parties and danced almost every night till the morning: 'You feel', she said, 'so much better afterwards.' She travelled round the world throughout the inter-war years to escape the British winters. She visited Paris every year to buy her clothes and throughout this period was a leader of fashion in the Western world. Cecil Beaton, the society photographer who drew a sketch of her for *Vogue*, described her in 1927 as 'with the highest heels, the most flashing bracelets and one of the most perfect complexions in London.' Even motherhood only meant brief, temporary pauses in the social whirl. Edwina left the upbringing of her two daughters to nurses and such parental attention as they received was only from the father.

All this wild carousing required companions. From 1925 till the mid-1950s Edwina had always at least one lover in tow. Janet Morgan, with a dogged perseverance worthy of a better cause, lists them all. I counted eleven and possibly may have missed some. Her sexual appetite appears to have been insatiable and in 1927 she was running three lovers at the same time. On one occasion, a servant announced that she had shown one of them to the drawing room and the second to the library; where, she enquired of Edwina, should she put the third? It was sometime in these years that she had once hurriedly to rush to Paris, not to buy clothes but for what sounds like an abortion. In the 1930s, there were insinuations in sections of the British press that Paul Robeson was one of her lovers. Edwina denied this and won a libel action. But her prowess as a liar was second only to that of her husband; and Robeson's biographer has maintained that the gossip was true.

What did Mountbatten make of all this? By 1931 he realized that

Edwina cared neither for him nor for her own reputation. He himself, apart from transitory affairs of his own, found emotional solace mainly in his children. 'There is always one woman in a man's life and darling—she's you.' That sentence was written by Mountbatten not to Edwina but to his daughter Patricia. But neither he nor Edwina thought at this time of divorce. He was dependent on her wealth and concerned about his career; she found Mountbatten tedious but was not interested in anyone else so deeply as to consider a permanent relationship. So husband and wife reached a working arrangement to stay together and lead separate lives. Edwina would help Mountbatten in his career and act as his hostess when necessary and if she was around; he would be friendly with the other men in her life and not make scenes. So the ramshackle marriage deceived nobody but did not collapse. There were even absurd situations when lovers were invited to wedding anniversaries and toasted the couple, or Mountbatten had to cheer up Edwina when she had been jilted by a lover. There was generosity as well as self-interest in his complaisance.

Then came the war. Rejected by all the women's auxiliary services because of her notoriety as a pleasure-lover, Edwina turned to the Red Cross and St John's Ambulance Services. She took intensive training courses and, as the war spread, she sped round the world inspecting and organizing health and welfare centres. There was little slackening in the queue of men receiving her favours, but she had now found other outlets as well for her energies. She worked hard with an unexpected determination while taking care of her appearance and looked, in Janet Morgan's phrase, 'a cross between a film star and Florence Nightingale'. Princess Alice, the wife of the governor general, seeing Edwina in Canada in 1941, was close to the mark when she commented, 'I think that she is a hard worker and clever, though one always feels that she has a hard streak in her character.' Mountbatten also, thanks to Churchill's support, could appear as more than a pompous if somewhat inefficient martinet and by 1945 was treated as a war hero.

Two years later came the Indian viceroyalty. By the time Mountbatten landed in India in February 1947 all parties concerned had reconciled themselves to Partition and Mountbatten took it on himself to implement the decision swiftly and ruthlessly. Neither he nor Edwina understood India; but in Jinnah Mountbatten confronted a person of almost equal egocentricity and the viceroy perforce lurched on the side of the Congress. On her part Edwina developed a personal attachment for Nehru and, as a corollary, for Nehru's country. She first became aware of her emotional feelings in September 1947, after the transfer of power; but it was not till May 1948, on the eve of the departure of the Mountbattens from India, that Nehru responded and became conscious that he himself might be involved. Clearly Edwina had no influence on the shaping of events and of India's policies before or after the advent of freedom. Janet Morgan reports that V.P. Menon had said that Edwina had played a significant part in influencing Nehru to accept Dominion Status. But this was in May 1947 when neither Edwina nor Nehru were aware of any interest in each other. The decision to remain a Dominion was taken by Nehru and Patel on purely political grounds, to prevent total balkanization of the country.

'You have brought me', Edwina wrote to Nehru in May 1949, 'all I was yearning for, happiness, balance, misery even!' She still had, for a few more years at any rate, the music conductor Malcolm Sargent following her around; but from now it was Nehru who really mattered. She visited India every year from 1950 till her death in 1960, and faithfully echoed Nehru's views in all matters. She does not seem, at any time in her life after her school days, to have read a book; and Nehru's gift to her of his *Autobiography* was a waste. She had no political sense whatsoever. She opposed the General Strike in Britain in 1926 because she could not bear the thought of London coming to a stop. She approved of the Munich agreement in 1938 because she wished for peace at any cost. After the war she supported French action in Indochina and also influenced her husband to do so. So it is not surprising that when, on her return from India, she had turned completely around in her outlook and canvassed British generals and cabinet ministers in favour of Nehru's opinions, she was not taken seriously.

If for Edwina, without inner resources or mental horizons, the relationship was rewarding, to Nehru the gains were very different.

Tickled at first by the idea of the viceroy's wife showing a personal interest in him, he later found the companionship not intellectually satisfying but an emotional release in the drab desert of Indian politics. He agreed at first to write to her every day because it gave him a chance of expressing his love of words; and, though later, because of the pressure of business on his side the correspondence thinned out, letter-writing to Edwina was his only opportunity of gaining solace from the talent which had found voice, years earlier in prison, in his three major books. But he had never any intention of letting the relationship get out of hand. He warned Edwina at the start that they must take care not to hurt each other nor (a vain hope) should they disclose their feelings to other people. In June 1948 he made her promise that nothing they did or felt should ever be allowed to come in the way of the work each of them had to do. Then later, 'I need you always', he wrote, 'but I am convinced that we have to function in our respective orbits or else either or both of us will lose our roots and feel terribly unhappy.' So it was unnecessary for Edwina to speak constantly in the early and mid-1950s of divorce and to secure Mountbatten's acceptance that he would never stand in the way. It was also ridiculous for a jealous woman in Delhi (obviously Padmaja Naidu) to smash the photograph of Edwina in Nehru's drawing room. There was at no time any question of a permanent link between Nehru and Edwina.

Now to the question that always crops up. Was there a physical side to the relationship and did they sleep together? Edwina told Mountbatten that it was a 'strange relationship—most of it spiritual.' She could, of course, have been lying. Janet Morgan believes that Nehru would have considered it disloyal and bad-mannered to sleep with his friend's wife. True, even though we know that Mountbatten had reconciled himself to his wife's habits and did not regard the men involved as guilty of disloyalty. No one can say for certain whether the relationship between Edwina and Nehru went beyond the occasional clinch. But who cares, and does it matter?

Janet Morgan's biography has been severely mauled in such reviews in Britain as I have seen. It is certainly poorly written and over-detailed. But there are more serious inadequacies. Any biography to be worth the name should both seek to probe the mystery of the individual concerned and use the subject to open up areas of social and political history. That is the secret of the success of such books as Christopher Hill's on Oliver Cromwell and Isaac Deutscher's on Trotsky. Janet Morgan does not attempt the second task and, as Edwina was so unimportant a character, this can be explained away. But the main point of interest in Edwina's own personal history is what, in the early 1940s, changed her from a rich playgirl into a socially committed person. In the blunt language of *The Economist*, what transformed her 'from whore to saint'? The answer cannot be the outbreak of war and the call of patriotism, for even in early 1940, fearing a Nazi invasion of Britain, she was planning to sail with her children for the United States, and only dropped the idea at the last moment. The clues to the basic change in her conduct and character have to be sought with the help of psychology. Could it be, at least, partly, that disillusioned with her marriage, she was seeking to break out of her loneliness by leading a wild life, but later found relief, first in working for the war effort and then, at a deeper and more satisfying level, in India and with Nehru? Janet Morgan makes little effort to delve into the possibility of such answers. She does not seem to be even aware fully of the question.

PART III

History and the Present

18

History and the Search for Identity

[illegible]

history is now a recognized [illegible] fifty years before [illegible] French revolution of 1789 [illegible]

[illegible]

18

History and the Search for Identity

While I have, in my earlier years, taken some interest in the history of our country during the last two hundred years, my present concerns are developments and trends of more recent date—of the first years of India's freedom. I hope that it will not for long remain a fact that the chair of contemporary history, which I happen to hold, is the only such chair in our universities. For contemporary history is now a recognized branch of the main discipline. It was over fifty years before any professional historian attempted to assess the French revolution of 1789; but a multi-volume study of the Russian revolution of 1917 was begun within thirty years of the event and reaches completion this year.

Such recognition of the academic study of recent history has not, of course, been attained without resistance; nor has such resistance ceased. Professor Elton, for example, argues that it is a mistake to concentrate on the history of the last two hundred years because it is too near our own world and does not help to show up the variety of human experience, with the frequent result that the student conjures up imaginary utopian or golden ages in the remote past.[1] The danger of historical phantasies is real enough, but it is not necessarily a consequence of the study of recent history; and there is surely an intrinsic advantage in attaining a better understanding of the world in which we live.

[1] G.R. Elton, 'Putting the Past Before Us', *Times Literary Supplement*, 8 September 1978.

This is especially so because our world is qualitatively different in many ways from all that went before. History today has become world history, with the primacy of Europe destroyed and Asia and Africa playing their rightful roles. Geoffrey Barraclough, writing primarily for an European audience, stresses this change which, though manifest, has not been easily accepted in the West.[2] But to us in India what is of importance is not the change, which seems obvious and natural enough, but the new orientations which the nature of the change imposes. The end of a particular phase of imperialism and its merging into our past colour our view of ourselves and of other peoples who passed through a similar experience as well of those who were its authors. Such a view, shaped by a shared colonialism, can be pushed backwards as well as forward. Greater attention to the precolonial histories of the countries of Asia and Africa would help to set contemporary history in proper perspective. We could then go on to comparative studies in Asian and African history.

The study of contemporary history runs counter to the view, widely prevalent today, that the primary task of the historian is to assess long-term trends; but this in itself may be a healthy development. One does not always wish to miss the trees for the wood. Short-term events do not obviously comprise the whole of the past; but while recognizing their limitations, they are not wholly to be ignored. However, methodologically also, the examination of the immediate past has inherent and well-known drawbacks—all the documents are not available, passions often still run high, partisanship is not buried. The lack of comprehensive source material makes writings in contemporary history more tentative, and the conclusions more provisional, than in any other sector of historical analysis: but it does not follow that, therefore, the effort is of little worth.

Moreover, to set against this relative paucity of documentation, the student in this field has some positive advantage—the abundance of oral testimony and participant observation, the lack of hindsight which deflects the common accusation that history is the version

[2] Geoffrey Barraclough, *An Introduction to Contemporary History* (London: Pelican Books, 1967).

of the victor and enables a better comprehension of the hopes and fears of the time, the opportunity for fieldwork, the greater scope for utilizing the methods and conclusions of allied disciplines like economics and sociology. When Descartes said that the most eminent scholars of Roman history knew less about what had happened in Rome than Cicero's housemaid, his intent was to denigrate the discipline of history as a whole: but in a way he was, without meaning to do so, recognizing the value of contemporary history. He was, one may say, echoing Thucydides, who had held that the historian could write with confidence only about events that he himself had experienced. Descartes was also, and again without deliberation, stressing the importance in historical testimony of such lowly creatures as housemaids. Great men, being prone to emphasize their role in the destiny, tend to exaggerate their own importance both in their private papers as well as in their oral record; but ordinary men and women, by just being themselves with no self-deceiving memories, help in the building of social and economic history. Especially in our country, where illiteracy robs us of documentation at this level of society, oral evidence is of added value and provides a dimension to contemporary history which is lacking for the history of other periods; for illiteracy is not inarticulateness.

As for the need for objectivity, it is possible, as much in dealing with the recent past as with any other period, to adopt a scientific approach, to collect and collate the evidence systematically, and to assess such evidence by rigorous and recognized methods. To the extent that a historian is aware of and can, in the examination of evidence, subdue his subjective elements, he can do this as much in contemporary as in any other history. Detachment is a mood born of self-discipline and not a matter of remoteness in time. Some of the most partisan historians in India and the world today are those writing of centuries long gone by. A fierce controversy raging now in Europe, with accusations of bias being hurled from both sides, concerns ancient Athens; while the most common criticism of the leading historian of the Bolshevik Revolution is that he is too dispassionate. Indeed, it can be contended that the student of contemporary history, if only because he is aware that his field of study is within touching distance, as it were, and he has perhaps even lived through it, is particularly sensitive to the possibility of non-academic influences in weighing his evidence and is especially careful to try and set such influences aside.

In a sense, the mood of detachment has been made easier in India for the study of the histories of all periods by the end of the imperial connection. No one disputes that the studies of Indian history undertaken by some British scholars and administrators during the years of their rule have often been of considerable value. Indeed, it has even been argued that social studies by outsiders gain in understanding from the culture shock suffered by the authors. But any such gain can only be secured if the culture shock goes along with a basic empathy with the people studied; and empathy, if it did exist, was more often than not smothered, in the case of British studies of India, by the demands of imperialism. For example, many British writers sought to justify imperial rule to others and to themselves by asserting that India was not a nation because it did not fulfil what were regarded as being the basic criteria of nationhood. Language, asserted the historian Freeman, was instinctively accepted by mankind as the badge of nationality; if so, then it followed that India, with an abundance of languages, was a non-nation. Seeley elaborated this to contend that India has no jealousy of the foreigner because there was no India and therefore, logically speaking, no foreigner. The vast majority of British historians regarded as meaningless the fact that some Indians claimed to give expression to a national consciousness. These theories rationalizing foreign rule are obviously untenable, but it is well to remember that they are still part of a living tradition. They inspire a school of historians which is influential in Britain in our own day; and they even evoke supine echoes among a few Indian writers.

To counter these theories, Indian historians, writing in the years of the national movement, laid stress on national identity being a matter not of a common language or religion but of a shared feeling and outlook. India had had for centuries a unity of spirit and continuity of culture and the men who were giving renewed articulation to this were but revivifying a dormant cohesion and not struggling to create something novel. Hegel might have treated the countries of the East with contempt, and James Mill and Macaulay condemned the religions and philosophies of India as decadent; but European scholars of a later age had acknowledged the depth and vitality of Indian culture. It was such a heritage which was claimed to be the source of recent Indian national awareness; and this conformed to the concept of nationalism as formulated by such diverse thinkers as Mazzini, Acton, Renan, and Weber. Political subjection could not destroy 'national character', and changing circumstances were enabling fresh expression of a perennial feeling. This argument too, however unhistorical, has had a long life, for it appeals to sentiment and nostalgic romanticism. Even Jawaharlal Nehru, who prided himself on his rationalist stance, succumbed to its attractiveness in the dark years of the early 1940s, when the situation suggested that the British might well stay in India indefinitely. He wrote with passion of India being more than a geographical entity, of the Idea of India which originally took shape at the dawn of civilization and had survived for thousands of years.

Now, over thirty years after the departure of the British, we do not need to take sides or to set out to establish preconceived conclusions. We can see the gaping holes in the models of the posthumous defenders of imperialism; we can also see that narrow, obscurantist nationalism cannot survive the scrutiny of scholarship. A nationalist attitude is understandable during a freedom movement. At the time when the mood of opposition to British rule was beginning to expand in India, a British judge remarked, 'A subject country has no politics.' To that the reply was promptly given, 'A subject country has nothing but politics.' Historical writing also was often a continuation of nationalist politics by other means. But, in a free country, politics is not the expression of a basic patriotism. At best, it is the rivalry of ideologies, but, more often than not, it is the clash of groups in the search for power, and such politics, however normal and inevitable, can have no place in academic concerns. The attainment of independence implies that our efforts in historical writing are no longer compulsorily afflicted with environmental pollution. The colonial experience has been integrated into our past and ceased to be an obsession. Our historians can afford to come into their own, taking advantage of, and contributing to, the latest advances in method and research.

This is not in any way to assert that, in this new atmosphere, good historical writing is a virtue of the cloisters. It may be possible for an artist to cut himself off from society. Picasso has told us that before entering his studio he would, in traditional Indian fashion, take off his shoes as a token that he was leaving the attractions and pressures of society behind him—though, as the painting 'Guernica' reminds us, he was not always successful in forgetting the context of his existence. But the historian, like every other social scientist, cannot, even if he could, afford to insulate himself from the world in which he lives. His task is not to explore in isolation a past which is done with and finished. The study of history is, by its very nature, an incomplete discipline with ever-fading margins, not just in the shallow sense that new evidence is always coming to light, but that every generation has fresh interests and is putting new questions to the past. It is in this sense that Croce's oft-quoted epigram, that all history is contemporary history, should be understood. The task of the historian is perpetually to re-examine, and even to re-judge, the past in the changing light of the present. He suggests novel hypotheses, establishes new connections, poses fresh problems. He does not seek an illusory finality but opens the way to further discussions. Acton, it will be remembered, set out to write a definitive history and ended by writing a few articles. On the other hand, because the civil war of the seventeenth century is still being waged in England, research and writing on the subject continue in an unending flow.

The discipline of history is the constant restructuring of the given elements in new generalizing patterns, the imposition of organizing concepts on the historical process to open fresh vistas of understanding. It is a form of intellectual crystallography, whereby the formation of the past changes incessantly according to which of its features the present is emphasizing because of its current interests. Concepts, interpretations, the selection of facts, even the nature of facts which, as Lucien Febvre has said, are often mere operational constructs—all will vary with these constant shifts in focus. No historical analysis is without a point of view or a commitment to particular values. Those who claim, with baseless pride, that their approach is value-free are either guiltily and shamefacedly concealing their values,[3] or, even worse, unaware

[3] Compare the observation of Sir Herbert Butterfield, whom no one would regard as a subversive radical, that those who imagine that they are 'writing

of them. It can indeed be said that conscious subjectivity is an asset in the approach to the social sciences.

It is this continuous recasting of the data which, more than anything else, makes the work of the historian an exciting effort. The writing of history is not just a matter of getting a few facts right, the spelling out of an unbroken narrative based on intensive research, or even an absorbing evocation of times gone by. It is more than clear exposition, a flair for nuances, an intuition for character and the re-creation of atmosphere. These are much; but historical analysis which is worth the name goes further and seeks to interpret the facts in relation to an internally consistent, theoretical, generalizing explanation. It takes in research and professionalism and goes beyond them to form an intellectual construction. Perhaps in India we have been too content treading water, happy to be writing history mechanically and unquestioningly according to set patterns. There may have been some excuse for this thirty years ago; but now we must move out of the shallows of traditional methodology, redefine our concepts, work out new models, cross the frontiers of the other social sciences, set forth on fresh comparisons. How far behind we in India generally are can be seen from the fact that while in our country the debate still goes on as to whether history is a social science and what its relations with other social sciences should be, elsewhere in the world not only has this been taken for granted for years but a reaction has also set in to the over-enthusiastic emphasis on the methodology of the social sciences.[4] Like all academic disciplines, history is basically an exercise of thought. Because the nature of the subject makes it easier for us to forget this, it is all the more necessary to stress the need for it.

By being aware of contemporary interests and confronting the past

---

history without any presuppositions at all' are sometimes merely refusing to examine their presuppositions. *History and Human Relations* (London: Collins, 1951), p. 99.

[4] For example, Lawrence Stone, 'History and the Social Sciences in the Twentieth Century' in Charles F. Delzell (ed.), *The Future of History: Essays in the Vanderbilt University Centennial Symposium* (Nashville, TN: Vanderbilt University Press, 1977), pp. 38–40.

with such questions as are of relevance to those interests, the historian, in addition to his commitments to his subject, fulfils his obligation to society. The answers which he obtains, however provincial, are more than contributions to scholarship; they could be of valid concern even outside the profession. To those who desire its companionship, history will then grant an expansion of awareness, a means of understanding the world rather than an escape from it. It will provide not dry compensation but an added measure of comprehension.

But if society is to derive these gains, it also has some obligations. The historian at work should be left severely alone. Scholarship is one of the few remaining areas where any other attitude than laissez-faire becomes a betrayal. Especially for authority to strive to impose conclusions from any ideological viewpoint is to render the intellectual effort meaningless. There have been in recent times too many instances of this for me to have to argue this point at length. Europe in the 1930s saw the dictators ordering historians to pull the past out of shape in order that they could thrust themselves into its forefront. This very year there has been published in Moscow an official biography of Mr Brezhnev which makes no reference to Stalin or Khrushchev. The shadow also looms in our country of politicians and officials looking over the shoulders of the historians and trying to secure analyses and conclusions which meet with their approval. Were this shadow to become a major reality, the consequence of our discipline could be catastrophic. Historical writing is, and must remain, a free enterprise. The interventions of those who appear to regard themselves as unacknowledged historians, although they lack the knowledge and training of mind essential for what is now a severe and demanding discipline, serve only to muddy scholarship and to foul the atmosphere.

The importance of a point of view in historical research makes it all the more crucial that such an approach should not be the victim of either blandishment or bullying. History is a highly individualist study, and no two historians share an identical outlook. Even when scholars adopt a broadly similar position and have in common a set of general philosophical ideas, the differences between them are usually so acute that sharp controversy rages. There is a point to the observation recently made in Europe that there is no school of Marxist historiography but only a number of Marxists writing history. We lazily speak of collectives of scholars, but this is a semantic convenience which quickly loses precision. If it does not, and a total uniformity does prevail, then we should worry; for a clash of opinion is the sign of normal health in any discipline. Every historian, working with the accepted and the latest tools, but deciding on his own point of departure, questioning the assumptions and the conclusions of others and cutting his own trail, can illumine sectors of the past. What we want among historians is neither cold war nor detente but a clear-eyed give-and-take; and it is from such academic polemics, exciting and rewarding in themselves, that society too can secure benefit.

But the rivalries of concepts and exchanges of ideas have to be grounded in professional analysis. If extraneous elements attempt to influence such debate by proffering incentives or menacing harassments, then corruption can enter. When official weight is placed behind a particular viewpoint, the door has been opened to disaster. The threat is specially sharp in our country as financial support for research can be drawn, in the main, only from official sources. This is, in a way, an advantage, for private foundations, as we see in other countries, frequently and expectedly extract a price for their gifts. When scholars or institutions proclaim that they wish to be free of the state, it is mostly to conceal that they wish to be subservient to someone else. But when academic work is dependent on public funds, it becomes all the more incumbent on those who dispense those funds, in justice both to themselves and to those whom they wish to encourage, that they make arrangements for decision-making on academic grounds alone, and on the advice of those professionally qualified.

Centuries ago, Bacon claimed that history makes men wise. Such a claim appears grandiose to any gathering of historians in our own, more cautious and more cynical, age. Even when the historian and the society in which he lives serve each other as they should, neither expects that the interaction will result in any great measure of wisdom. Nor can history offer any practical contribution to knowledge. We historians cannot save a life or prevent a war. Of all the social sciences, it is history whose dividends are seemingly the least useful. But if utility is defined in other than superficial and immediate terms, history has much to offer. It is not necessary to stress that it is of help in evaluating the policies of states. When considering, for example, the attitudes of the United States, it is worth remembering the American society as a whole has no past that stretches beyond two hundred years; and American policy is best understood if it is borne in mind that it does not carry the burden of tradition. In contrast, the permeations of revolutionary ideology in China have to be seen in the context of a long and continuous history. Chairman Mao always prided himself on the fact that he knew little of the world outside China; and his willingness to regard the revolution as open-ended was sustained by his belief that he was more deeply rooted in his own country than most of his colleagues. This was, however, a weakness as well as a strength, for inwardness is no ally of progress.

History has also been often harnessed to social purpose in a deeper, and sometimes more dangerous, sense. It has been utilized and even distorted to legitimize dynasties, classes, and religious and other elements in their pursuit of power; and it has also been resorted to by various groups in their search for identity. Such a search for identity is fair enough; the danger lies in setting out to discover a preconceived, false identity inspired by a narrow ideology. Perhaps the prominence of historical controversy outside professional circles in our country today is caused by the widespread search for a renewal of identity in a post-colonial society. Many, resentful of the influences which have gained root in India during the nationalist period, strive to go back, beyond these years, and revive what they believe to be the traditional forces in Indian society; others, more realistic and not just living in the twentieth century but belonging to it, recognize that historical understanding suggests a national identity which is not atrophied but encompasses the past as well as looks forward. It is an identity which has developed and is developing naturally, rather than one which has been imposed.

If the compulsions of the present lead us to fresh awareness of the past, that knowledge in turn conditions our view of the present; and it is in such interactions that the historian's work is of the best value to society. The past is not all that has merely happened but what has survived to a later age, and perhaps still influences situations. It is by the incessant, rigorous but not rigid, examination of such a past that the historian can best hope to serve not only his subject but also his contemporaries.

19

The Fear of History

Of all the social sciences, it is history which rouses the greatest interest in the minds of the politicians. There are various reasons for this. It has always had an inventive and purposive use. The line between history and mythology is thought to be thin; the past can be used to lend legitimacy to any aspect of the present and, especially in the years of resistance to imperialism, history could be utilized to strengthen the forces of cultural nationalism.

But, the use of history did not depart with the foreigner, though the nature of the problem changed. In the first place, the discipline of historical analysis has itself been transformed. In the last thirty years the study of the past has become scientific, and is as different from mythology as astronomy is from astrology and chemistry from alchemy. It goes without saying that history is not, and cannot hope to be, a science in the sense of experimentation and re-creation of the conditions which are being examined. No precise laws which can be checked are possible. But the study of history can be scientific in the sense of rational approaches and analyses and the careful and methodical scrutiny of source material. It has moved away from the projection of the historian's identity and from the search in the past for current aspirations, and is a specialized discipline with a recognized and verifiable methodology and the proper use of proper evidence. The historian, of course, is still aware of the present and on this basis formulates the questions which he poses to the past; but he would regard it as a betrayal of his task if he utilized his present requirements to secure the answers which he seeks from the past.

However, this in itself worries the politician who, even in a free country, hopes to utilize history in the interests of his ideology and, especially if the latter is retrograde and backward-looking, finds that scientific history is of no use to him. He would seem, indeed, to be even more than worried by the fact that the 'new' history is an obstinate discipline. Unlike the other social sciences, such as economics and sociology, which are, in a sense, reactive studies and seek to solve problems rather than be content with assessing them, history seems to stand apart, as a kind of judge; and the discipline is so deeply embedded in the popular consciousness that it cannot be ignored.

This explains why all totalitarian regimes seek to harness history in their support and have it rewritten according to their needs. Hitler secured the elimination of the Jewish element and contribution in the German past. An almost exact parallel with what is happening in India today happened in Germany in the early twentieth century. Gustaf Kossinna argued for the primacy of German prehistory in a study published in 1912 where the German people were described as the most superior and the cradle of world civilization. The 1941 edition quotes Hitler at length and Kossinna's chauvinism was a deliberate support of racism. Himmler used these arguments to back Nazi policy and stated that 'Prehistory is the doctrine of the eminence of the Germans at the dawn of civilisation.' Mussolini ordered the revision of Italian history to serve as a precedent for his own foreign policy. Historiography in the early phase of communist societies also distorts events and personalities on the ground that the new history represents the aspirations of a new class whose role has not been considered before. History to dictation is a natural ally of authoritarianism.

There is, alongside this desire to exploit history, a widespread fear of scientific history. This is not peculiar to India. In recent months we have had in Britain academic mugging of Marxist historians and in Greece invective poured on French scholars who dared to minimize the glory of ancient Athens. But what is novel and particularly alarming in our country is the manner in which non-historians have decided to intervene in what should, at best, be historiographical polemics amongst professionals. One can ignore presumptuous editors who publish in their dailies lists stating which historians should be given what jobs. But the situation becomes more serious when politicians, especially those in authority, decide to pronounce on purely academic matters.

The Janata party has been swept into power primarily to safeguard civil liberties. Manifestly one of these liberties most to be cherished is the right of scholars to free thought, unimpeded research, and the untrammelled expression of their conclusions. But this academic prerogative is the first to be challenged by the Janata party, or at least a section of that party, the Jan Sangh and its ally, the RSS (members of which have publicly defended the move to ban certain books on history). The Janata government would appear to be providing official sanction to this assault; and, as was perhaps to be expected, the historian is the first of the social scientists to come under fire. Those among the economists, political scientists, and other academics who publicly supported the Emergency have either clambered on to the new bandwagon or been forgotten; but even the historians who declined to support Mrs Gandhi in her last two years of power have now to deal with fresh onslaughts both on themselves and, even more seriously, on their discipline.

The prime minister has been reported to have said, at a widely publicized function in the capital, that a particular type of approach to our national past is the 'correct' type of history. As this report in the press has not been denied, we may take it that the prime minister did say this. The report raises many questions. There is, first of all, no such thing as 'correct' history. Information can be correct or incorrect but not history. There can only be views of the past, some of which approximate more clearly to the reality because of the evidence they draw upon and the quality of their logic and analysis.

Besides, while I have regard for Morarji Desai and respect for his achievements, I am not aware that he has any special qualifications for expressing a conclusive preference for a particular approach to history. I am sure that Morarji Desai would think many times before stepping forward, even in his newly acquired status as head of the government, to proclaim that Newtonian physics were superior to those of Einstein; it is odd then that he should venture into history, which is today as technical a branch of knowledge as physics.

It is said that on the same occasion, Dr V.K.R.V. Rao called upon the new government to translate the history of India, compiled by Bharatiya Vidya Bhavan, into all the Indian languages. Dr Rao would rightly regard me as out of my mind if, in twenty years' time, I, as an outworn academic and discarded careerist, ascended the platform to demand that the writings in economics of J.C. Coyajee be translated into our fourteen languages. I wonder if our politicians realize that when they deliberately trespass into specialist fields of scholarship and seek to lay down the law, they are, in the minds of all thinking persons, making fools of themselves.

Even worse; for who is he whom the prime minister and Dr Rao are commending? Dr R.C. Majumdar, who even thirty years ago was twenty years out of date and writing, at length and in profusion, traditional, blinkered history. His only claim today to our esteem is that he is 91 years of age. His longevity has earned him the right to be preserved in cotton wool by either the Janata government or the Bharatiya Vidya Bhavan (at times one feels that these days the Bhavan is becoming a part of the government).

But, all this would be merely laughable were there not lurking behind it a serious danger. For, Dr Majumdar is the doyen of a Hindu chauvinist view of Indian history. He and his followers see the history of our country only in terms of the achievements of the Hindus; and any questioning of their analysis of the medieval period or of the national movement in terms of 'Hindu heroes' is said to reflect a pro-Muslim communalism. Obviously, there were some events which were closely related to Hindu–Muslim relations and have to be analysed as such. Religion as a factor in historical explanation is not to be ignored; and the existence of religious tensions at various times and places cannot be underplayed. But no historian would today regard religion (or any other element for that matter) as the sole factor in explanation. To interpret the history of medieval India or to study Indian nationalism only in terms of Hindu–Muslim relations leads into the blind alley of limited explanations based on communalism of either the Hindu or the Muslim variety.

Modern Indian historiography has been influenced by the context in which it has developed and, with the changing context, has passed through various phases. Initially, the modern study of Indian history, in the period of Western imperialism, was dominated by British and European opinion as expressed through the interpretations of Orientalists, Indologists, Utilitarians, administrators, proclaimed imperialists, and other camp-followers of the *raj*. The hangover of this type of interpretation of Indian history is still to be found, with varying degrees of subtlety, in a few lingering academic pockets in Britain with some less subtle echoes among Indians.

But, in India itself, parallel with the evolution of the national movement and influenced by it, Indian historians began to question the European interpretation. This healthy development was gradually a victim of some distortion under the pressures of cultural chauvinism and communal politics. With independence, these pressures lost much of their emotive force and Indian historians, in a sense, came into their own. They could adapt and apply the new methods of analysis which were increasingly coming into vogue in the world. They could question the prejudiced conclusions of imperialist historiography without succumbing to the narrowness of cultural nationalism or basking in its comfortable atrophy. They could do justice to the size and complexity of India and involve themselves in studies of its regional structures. But all this in itself has called forth the opposition of communal politicians who wish, for ideological reasons, to restore the outmoded and simplistic framework of cultural nationalism.

It would be bad enough if this group in the Janata party was concerned only with fostering a species of unscientific history which was suited to its political activities. But in fact this group has mounted an offensive on independent practitioners of the discipline and thereby posed a threat to the foundations of our intellectual life. They have blundered into the position of assuming that historians who write as they will and with proficiency are in fact supporters of the former regime.

Take the episode of the time capsule. Mrs Gandhi's government, for reasons best known to itself, decided to inter this capsule and to include in it, along with a very detailed list of personalities and a chronological catalogue of events, an assessment of the first twenty five years of free India written by a non-official historian. The whole idea of a time capsule is a nonsensical gimmick and no historian would take seriously either the idea of placing in it an interpretation (apart from a catalogue) of history or giving any such draft serious consideration. It is a commonplace that each historian has his own interpretation and no two historians agree. The new government has taken what can only be termed a ridiculous decision to spend as much time, effort, and money in lifting this capsule as had been spent in entombing it; and, in the bargain, seems to foist on one historian the responsibility for another historian's analysis. Nor is the rank and file of the Janata party short of bumptious bounders who cannot comprehend the professional ethic that one historian will not revise the viewpoint of another.

There are, however, more important issues than the time capsule to worry about. Three text books, *Medieval India* by Romila Thapar, *Modern India* by Bipan Chandra, and *Freedom Struggle* by Bipan Chandra, Amales Tripathi, and Barun De are under attack. The first two have been published by the National Council for Educational Research and Training and the third by the National Book Trust, both organizations financed by the ministry of education; and the withdrawal of these books is being seriously considered on the suggestion, it is believed, of the prime minister. A fourth book, brought out by a private publisher, *Communalism and the Writing of Indian History*, by Romila Thapar, Harbans Mukhia, and Bipan Chandra, was being translated into some Indian languages by the Indian Council for Historical Research; and it is known that this project has also been put in abeyance.

It appears that these actions have been initiated on the basis of criticisms from anonymous sources. The academic level of the criticisms is so low as to rouse the suspicion that the motivation is more personal and ideological than scholarly. Those who have written in support of the criticisms have made such comments as to suggest that they have not even read the books in question.

Interestingly, three out of the five authors under attack are my colleagues at the Centre for Historical Studies in the Jawaharlal Nehru University; and this naturally rouses the thought that a concerted attack on the centre, known from its inception for its independence and resistance to all forms of pressure, may be part of the strategy. It is paradoxical that a section of the Janata party may be holding against the Centre for Historical Studies the very fact that most of its members publicly demonstrated their opposition to the Emergency and signed the representation protesting against the 42nd amendment of the constitution. If the objective is to give official recognition to one approach to our country's history and to suggest that this approach is superior to all others, obviously the first step in such a monstrous strategy would be to weaken those departments of history which are likely to take an independent intellectual position.

Whatever its academic inadequacies and its long-term dangers, as a political act the attack is shrewd, for it seeks to stir both Hindu sensitivity and liberal fears. Quite apart from the questions of interpretation and emphasis, historical facts which go against a 'Hindu' view of history are brushed aside. No note is taken of the recent worldwide process which has seen a shift of interest in historical research from personalities to social and economic trends. The stress now is not on the roles and actions of individual rulers but on the wider context and background. Beneath the policies and day-to-day activities of men lie more significant, impersonal developments. So the interrelations between religious sects and the social and economic conditions of the time become more pertinent, and it is shallow to explain any phase of Indian history in terms of a single theme—that of the relationship between Hindus and Muslims.

Those who wish to remain on this simplistic level of explanation are deliberately narrowing the focus of their vision and ignoring both the research and the methodology of the last thirty years. The Centre for Historical Studies at the Jawaharlal Nehru University was started with the intent of taking these new trends in historical explanation into account and concentrating its attention on social and economic history. If, as part of this enthusiasm to block all new approaches to historical knowledge, this centre be weakened, then we shall have in India only the occasional topic on social and economic themes in the traditional syllabus of dynastic history and no major drive to develop new forms of research in the discipline. In other sciences, new knowledge is welcomed; in history it is feared and sought to be smothered. Obviously, in the long run, this cannot hope to succeed; but, in the process, a great amount of time would have been lost and considerable effort frustrated.

The specific flaws in the criticisms levelled at these textbooks rise from this approach. If historical analysis were as easy as this, everyone can claim professional expertise and happily make authoritative pronouncements. For example, that Aurangzeb was a bigoted and communal Muslim is thought to be beyond dispute, and scholars who do not describe him as such are blamed for secular partisanship. It is not grasped that the honest historian has to come to terms with the fact that there are a number of documents of Aurangzeb's reign referring to cash and land endowments made by him to individual Brahmins and to Hindu temples.

Aurangzeb was obviously not a mere communalist but a careful manipulator of religious groups. So the problem spreads out from a narrow study of Aurangzeb's religious convictions and policies to a consideration of the politics, the economic necessities, and the social environment of the various religious groups accepting patronage from Aurangzeb. In attempting such a broader consideration of the forces and patterns of that time, historians are not trying to promote Hindu–Muslim harmony for non-academic reasons. They are only, in line with current professional thinking on the subject, extending the framework of analysis.

The effort to denounce these textbooks also aims at frightening people who would otherwise instinctively take a liberal stand, by hinting both that these authors project the views of the former government and that these books are part of a widespread communist conspiracy to infiltrate educational institutions. There is no reason why Mrs Gandhi's regime should be given gratuitously a monopoly of scientific historical writing; it certainly does not merit this gift.

Work was started on the three NCERT books in 1964 at the invitation of the then editorial board, consisting of Nilakantha Sastri, Muhammad Habib, Bisheshwar Prasad, B.P. Saxena, and P.C. Gupta with Tara Chand as chairman. I took over the chairmanship in 1966 at the request of the then minister for education, M.C. Chagla; and the other members of the board were Nurul Hasan, Satish Chandra, and Romila Thapar. All the three books were written and published by 1970; and the next year, when Nurul Hasan became minister and the board was reconstituted, I declined to continue as chairman and Romila Thapar gave up her membership.

These facts should indicate that the books had nothing to do with the Emergency. They also show that the books passed through a wide range of expertise, ensuring that the final text would be regarded as reliable by historians. Apart from the scrutiny provided by the two boards, the manuscripts were also sent to other historians for their comments and these were considered in detail by the authors and the editors, and the texts modified where necessary. Even after publication, when comments were received from scholars and educationists, changes were made in later editions. The purpose was to ensure that the textbooks did not express idiosyncratic or wholly subjective viewpoints but stated what might be termed a consensus of modern research and analysis. For, the whole purpose of such textbooks is to provide schools and colleges, which are aiming at high academic norms, with books which are regarded by professionals in that discipline as maintaining a respectable level of quality, incorporating the most recent trends of research and comprehensible to the age group for which they are intended.

The basic structure of a textbook in history should have standard material acceptable to historians. Textbooks, which are after all the technical literature for teaching a particular subject, can only be written by experts, although their general comprehensibility can certainly be commented upon by other educationists. A proper textbook in history should not provide information to be memorized but indicate ways in which the past can be understood. It is therefore essential that historians involved in and familiar with ongoing research and current methodology should be made responsible for the preparation of textbooks.

Textbooks at one level are a public issue, but at a more important level they are the responsibility of those professionally involved in the subject since the general intellectual level of work in the subject is dependent upon the quality of textbooks used throughout the period of training. Not only teachers but the students themselves are interested in this, for the serious student today has a fuller awareness of intellectual requirements and makes greater demands on the academic framework of his life than his counterpart of an earlier generation.

Competition for a place in the sun adds to this. Today's student cannot be lobbed off with substandard knowledge masquerading under various guises. So the writing of textbooks should not be left to those who are mere compilers of outdated and often incorrect information or money-rakers who are not historians but professional textbook writers. History textbooks are not intended primarily to teach the child patriotism, loyalty, morality, mythology, or whatever; they are meant to teach the child history. Such virtues can be taught through other, preferably extracurricular, means.

The other allegation of communist infiltration can hardly be treated seriously. I have been attacked in parliament by name from the government benches as a supporter of communist causes. Marxist fellow-historians will no doubt squirm to find me placed, however involuntarily, in their midst. The specific charge is that I had a share in recommending the purchase of the P.C. Joshi archive by the Jawaharlal Nehru University. This is an invaluable collection for the study of international communism since the First World War, and very high bids were received for it from both Europe and the United States. Joshi himself gave priority to retaining these papers within India, although it meant financial loss; and I am proud of even the minor role I played in seeing to it that those papers were not lost to our country.

Such attacks are facilitated, and confusion in the public mind made easier, by the denunciation of the 'new' history as Marxist. It is, indeed, incredible how easily the bogey of communism is raised and what a wide multitude of thought and concept is covered at the popular level by the label of Marxism. A serious consideration of social and economic factors, which the scientific approach to history entails, is seen as the thin end of the Marxist wedge. The fact that some of the world's leading anti-Marxist historians are economic historians is clearly beyond the comprehension of these self-styled saviours of the discipline in our country.

This sense of insecurity is so acute that all trace of Marxist thought is sought to be wiped out. There is obviously no justification for a crude and vulgar Marxism of a populist variety; but of this even serious Marxists would be ashamed and they can be left to deal with it. But

Marxism in itself is a major intellectual influence in the world and throwing a *cordon sanitaire* round the Indian mind is not the answer. We need to have a dialogue with Marxism and not to suppress it. Naive Marxism will have to be out-argued and not smothered by unbridled authoritarianism. Without some Indian scholars writing serious Marxist history, Indian historiography would be much the poorer. It is worth remembering that the richness of the French intellectual tradition of recent years in contrast even to the Anglo-Saxon one is explicable to some extent by the need to formulate an intellectual attitude to Marxism.

There must be many in the Janata party, among both the leaders and rank-and-file, who are disconcerted by this whole string of events concerning history and historians, and the mental outlook which it denotes. Not merely are textbooks denounced, but a book which has been privately published is recommended for withdrawal, and it is stated that the prime minister desires a review of similar books from a similar viewpoint. This leaves it open to the government to secure withdrawal on a large scale of books which do not meet with official approval.

There is in fact, underneath this whole controversy, a general principle involved, namely, the academic rights of the academic community. The government's actions and threats indicate contempt for scholars. Withdrawal of serious, prepared literature is considered by ministers and bureaucrats on the basis of anonymous complaints without any explanation being offered or any known process being followed. It has been said that a decision is pending. It is mystifying as to why the whole matter is being treated as being strictly confidential. To this day neither the authors nor the editorial board have been informed that their books have been criticized or what is the nature of the criticism. The minister for education has stated that some historians are examining these books but nothing has been disclosed as to who these historians are. Such secrecy suggests that the proposed withdrawal of these textbooks is no mere academic matter.

If textbooks can be arbitrarily condemned and their withdrawal considered because they do not happen to suit the ideology of a particular political group within the ruling party, the same can happen to other publications; and one is well set on the road to the indiscriminate banning of all kinds of books. Freedom of expression is as much an issue as academic freedom in this whole affair. Independent thought is not a hang-up from the past but the life blood of a democratic society. It is frightening that one should even need to say this.

In developed countries, where universities have access to private affluence and research is supported to a considerable extent by non-official foundations, the academic community can keep away from government. This is not so in India, and scholars, academics, and research workers are heavily dependent on official support for their employment, salaries, and most other requirements for their work. This makes it all the more incumbent on our government to ensure that their control of the financial levers is not exploited to restrict the independence of the academic community and, what is even more reprehensible, to interfere with the processes of thought and the conclusions of research. So the issues raised by this attack on a few historical works are very wide and concern not only the authors of these books and other historians but all members of the academic community and indeed every person interested in the maintenance of civil liberties and in the free play of the mind.

Unimpressed by shabby authority and refusing to bow to social and economic pressures, the Indian academic community have, on the whole in recent years, a fairly commendable record; and no doubt they will resist this latest onslaught by a few Janata extremists till wiser counsels prevail in the Janata party as a whole. There is certainly no possibility that the large majority of practising historians will surrender their understanding of their discipline. If history is to be a rational study of the past, historiography must break away from its own past. This has happened in India as elsewhere in the world; and there is no scope for retracing these steps. The new trends and insights in historical analysis transcend differences in politics and environment. The demarcation today is not between American and Soviet historians but between scientific historians in every country on the one hand and the old-type historians on the other. Of such scientific history our politicians, save those with a distorted outlook, have nothing to fear.

20

Democracy

India is today facing the most intense crisis since it became free in 1947. Assassination has become a routine method of political activity, terrorism is rampant in various parts of the country, there is a minority government at the centre, federalism demands a firm grounding, communal rancour and caste unrest are on the increase, the economy is in a crisis, and the government has been obliged to go cap in hand to the International Monetary Fund. It is not a wild fantasy to wonder whether, like the Soviet Union and Yugoslavia, India too is on the road to disintegration. 'Things fall apart, the centre cannot hold.' Are the words of the poet a grim warning to us? To gain some understanding of what is happening to us, it is not enough merely to study the immediate present. The foundations of our contemporary culture—political, economic, and social—were laid down in the first years of freedom when Jawaharlal Nehru was prime minister and the inspiring and driving force; and we need a sense of the recent past if we are to confront our problems sensibly and get through the current crisis. The present has roots in the past and the past influences the present. So it seems worthwhile to look again at the fundamentals of independent India and to ask ourselves did we set out on the right lines and, if so, where did we go wrong and what should we do now to rectify matters?

A basic commitment of India in 1947 was to the democratic process. The ideological shape of the nationalist movement, the influence of Western liberal thought, and the teachings of Indian philosophy all combined to provide unanimous support to democratic values. Democracy was an end in itself and not just a means to an end. It was the most acceptable form of government because, in the final analysis, it promoted the growth of human beings and of society. 'Nothing can be worse for the world, I think, than a deprivation of human freedom of the individual.'[1] It has been argued that democracy was compulsive in India; given the size, the manifold problems, the entrenched pluralism, the cultural diversity, the regional pulls, and the conflicting pressures of religions and languages, India could only be held together in the long run by a democratic structure. But, in fact, as humanity knows to its cost, authoritarian grips are possible over even large societies; and for nearly two hundred years the British had ruled India largely by executive government, with a hollow façade of seemingly representative institutions. This tradition could have been followed by the government of free India, as had been done in other newly free countries of the third world. Indeed, it was even suggested that democracy was a luxury which India, whose central fact was backwardness, could ill afford. Liberal democracy had developed gradually in the West, after long years of capitalist industrialization; and it was anti-historical to impose it on a society where the primary concerns were the basic economic needs.

However, no one in free India was prepared to consider an alternative to democratic government. But what type of democracy? Mahatma Gandhi had not favoured parliamentary democracy and his mind had run along lines of village autonomy and trusteeship. But Nehru and many others preferred the parliamentary system; and their views prevailed. Along with the sovereignty of parliament, corollary institutions were nurtured—cabinet government, a free press, and an independent judiciary; and the constitution incorporated a list of the rights of the citizen that has proved a model to the world. Lord Scarman, an eminent British judge who supports the growing demand in Britain for a written constitution, has said recently that the Indian constitution is the only one that really covers social and economic rights as well as civil liberties and fundamental rights. He described it as 'one of the most elaborate and brilliantly drafted bill of rights that I know.'[2]

[1] Jawaharlal Nehru, *Visit to America* (New York: J. Day, 1950), p. 136.
[2] *New Statesman and Society*, 28 September 1990.

Above all, bearing in mind the political mobilization achieved during the freedom movement, the framers of the constitution introduced adult suffrage. This was very much a leap in the dark. Even in countries with widespread primary education, universal suffrage has been introduced relatively recently; would it work in an underdeveloped society like India? One primary purpose of Nehru's ceaseless tourings of the country as prime minister was to teach the people to cherish the privilege of the vote and exercise it with responsibility. His speeches made hard issues vivid and plain to a people who for the most part were illiterate. He tried to explain problems to his audiences in as simple a language as possible and to get them to think and to understand. All his speeches were part of a sustained programme of adult education. And the response has not been inadequate. Over the years India has strengthened herself as a nation by transforming herself from a passive and traditional society into an open and participant one. This unseen revolution is Nehru's most lasting monument and his most striking contribution to the process of nation-building in India.

As a support to the base of the parliamentary system Nehru looked first to community development and later to panchayat raj. Local, participatory democracy would provide a scaffolding to the constitution. The real meaning of democracy was the forward movement of a whole people: 'it is not good enough to work *for* the people, the only way is to work *with* the people and go ahead, and to give them a sense of working for themselves.'[3] They had all to be involved in the building of a new India, and a measure of equality in opportunity and fulfilment progressively produced. Active citizenship would promote social cohesion. The programme has not produced the expected results in economic development; but it has helped to strengthen rural India at the roots and intensified the social and political consciousness of the villagers. The point is made by the peasant in Uttar Pradesh who is quoted as having remarked in the late 1950s: 'There is but one difference between yesterday and today; we no longer have padlocks on our mouths.'

Political democracy in India, however, has had its shortcomings,

[3] Nehru to B.C. Roy, 25 December 1949, Nehru Papers, Nehru Memorial Museum and Library (NMML).

some noticeable even in Nehru's time and others which have gained prominence in recent years. The fact that, except for two years in Kerala, the Congress party was in power in all the states as well as at the centre throughout Nehru's primeministership, permitted the inherent problems of a federal system to remain in the background. Moreover, as Upendra Baxi has pointed out, Nehru, despite his democratic instincts, sometimes acted outside the bounds of legality. He would not deprive the princes of their privy purses although he revoked the principle of compensation to the expropriated zemindars; he condoned the pardon given by Vinoba Bhave to the dacoits who claimed to have undergone a change of heart; and his response to charges of corruption against some of his colleagues was, at best, ambivalent.[4] But these transgressions seem minor when compared with the downhill slide in the decades after Nehru. The Congress party, which Nehru had hoped would help to hold the people together at least until other unifying factors took root, has declined in character and discipline. Institutions like the civil service and the judiciary have had their integrity continuously corroded, while corruption has proliferated without serious check. The climax of the decline of democratic principles was the Emergency, which for two years set aside the concepts of the rule of law. The electoral rebuff to this aberration demonstrated that the Nehru inheritance could not be uprooted; but political democracy in India has yet to cure itself of other debilitating weaknesses.

A healthy democracy can help much in the problem of nation-building. We are seeing in the world today that nationalism, far from being an outmoded concept, is still a powerful influence. But when India attained freedom in 1947 it was at the heavy cost of the partition of the country on the basis of religion. Indian nationalism was still obviously brittle and free India had to pick up broken pieces to put together the jigsaw of nation-building. In 1871, at the first meeting of the constituent assembly of a united Italy, Massimo d'Azeglio commented, 'We have made Italy; now we must make Italians.' So too India had to set about creating a fresh sense of nationality which

[4] Upendra Baxi, 'The Recovery of Fire: Nehru and Legitimation of Power in India', *Economic and Political Weekly*, 13 January 1990.

would erase the animosities that had flourished in the last decades of British rule. The subject of secularism demands separate treatment. Another source of tension, though weaker then religion, has been the question of language. Nehru had no liking for linguistic provinces and in this matter drifted to decisions rather than initiated them. But the principle does not necessarily weaken the nation, especially in the context of democratic functioning; and within the national borders there should be room for individuality and various levels of association. A democratic society is not necessarily a homogeneous society; the right to belong and the right to be different within that belonging are not contradictory. As the years have passed, the question of language has cooled down as a political issue. But the removal of language from the arena of controversy may have provided space for other issues, such as the process of caste mobilization, to intensify.[5]

Both religion and language are contributory elements to the wider problem of ethnicity, which is a prominent issue not just in India but in many other parts of the world. Several developed countries have also recalcitrant minorities or are faced with the necessity of absorbing large numbers of immigrants; but the problem has intensified in the new-born states and threatens to tear their national fabrics. As collective memories of resistance to colonial rule recede, group loyalties and sub-national identities gain prominence. Some of these groups resent what has been described as 'official nationalism',[6] a national identity that has not been generated from below but is imposed from above by those at the heart of the power structure of the country. In the north-east, the wide measure of autonomy just short of independence granted to the Nagas has helped to subdue the rebellious elements; but now Assam has become an acute problem. Kashmir is a specific issue, it being the only state in India with a Muslim majority and the problem having assumed international dimensions. Religion, language, and a subjective feeling of being treated unfairly have all combined to make many Sikhs in the Punjab aggressively defiant. There are no

[5] Paul Brass, *The Politics of India since Independence* (Cambridge: Cambridge University Press, 1990), p. 206.

[6] Benedict Anderson, *Imagined Communities* (London, 1983).

easy solutions; but clearly terrorism has to be exterminated, the states insulated from foreign pressures and, in a democratic society, the wishes of the people have to be ascertained.

Democracy is not just a matter of political organization. It has to be supported by equality and equity, distributive justice, and social fairness. Otherwise even the political processes get weakened. It is not enough that the vote is cherished by the Indian people. For it to be utilized properly simultaneous advance is required on the social and economic fronts as well. Universal franchise can, in theory, be a powerful instrument of social and economic change. A majority vote can being about marked transformation. But as Marx had noted, the right to govern is not necessarily the power to govern. An unequal, hierarchical society in India has managed to subdue the political vote. A wide network of caste and kinship ties comes into play. Vote banks are created. At first these were formed on the basis of the economic and social dependence of the lower castes and the rural poor; more recently mobilization has been by political leaders along caste and community lines. So, despite increasing politicization, till now the major beneficiaries of democracy have been the well-placed and the well-to-do in the towns and the countryside.

The arrest of the social change so vital for the proper functioning of a democracy is particularly marked with regard to the status of Harijans and of women. A year after the enactment in 1955 of untouchability as a criminal offence, Nehru was optimistic enough to claim that untouchability had broken up, had no life in it and, except in odd areas, had disappeared. But the law is one thing and the facts are another. Nehru believed too much in the power of reason, the strength of the law, and the leverage of the vote. This hindered full awareness of the rigidity of tradition in India, the endurance of conservative resistance, and the propensity to violence. India's major problem is social backwardness, the failure to reduce inequality, exploitation, and caste differences. Whether the solution to this problem, which is becoming increasingly more acute, is in the direction of the reservation of official jobs, is debatable. Other long-term solutions seem to be required.

Gender discrimination is a large aspect of social injustice. As far back as in 1928 Nehru had quoted with approval the statement of a French philosopher that the test of a civilization is the way it treats its women. Much later, towards the end of his life, asked what he regarded as the greatest real advance achieved in India under his leadership, he had no hesitation in referring to the enactment of measures for improvement of the status of Hindu women. They had been granted rights of divorce and inheritance and monogamy was enforced on Hindu men. But this was partial and piecemeal reform, leaving Muslim women outside the pale and dealing only with certain aspects of personal law. But even of these partial measures of reform the enforcement has been always slack; and India's face is still darkly smudged with such sporadic horrors as dowry deaths and the burning of widows.

Democracy also demands progress on the economic front. Though India began the experiment in political democracy in an economically backward society and worked it astoundingly well, at any rate at the start, for the democratic processes to take root and continue to work with a fair measure of genuineness the political system has to be associated with economic growth and equity. As a Vietnamese communist leader remarked, 'You cannot walk with one long leg and one short leg.' But as it is in India, there is some truth in the dismissive observation of Lee Kuan Yew, the former prime minister of Singapore, that all we have is the mechanics of democracy; it is a parlour game that we play, who takes power, who gets what spoils.[7] But can Indian move on from its present condition of what seems a soulless democracy to an assault on poverty in conditions of freedom, to economic prosperity for all sections of Indian society achieved by participatory and persuasive means? Three general presumptions are now widely believed: that only rich, developed countries can afford freedom and civil liberties;[8] that in underdeveloped countries authoritarianism is required for growth—China, South Korea, Taiwan, Singapore,

[7] Interview in *The Economist*, 29 June 1991.

[8] Cf. Sergei Stankevich, a close adviser of Boris Yeltsin: 'Never and nowhere has a transition of society to a qualitatively new status been accomplished during, let's say, a flourishing parliamentary democracy . . .' Quoted by Dimitri Simes, 'Is Boris Good Enough?' *Guardian Weekly*, 20 October 1991.

Indonesia, and Hong Kong; and that democracy, capitalism, and a market economy go together and are indivisible. Can India, as Nehru had hoped, prove the exception to all these three axioms?

When Nehru talked of socialism, it was an explosive word, especially as in the 1930s he claimed to be a scientific socialist. But in fact Nehru's socialism was a matter of purpose and principle rather than of dogma and definition. His approach was ethical and humanist: the rejection of vulgar greed and exploitation, the social organization of decency, the strengthening of a humane culture. Every sensitive Indian cannot but be outraged by the social cruelty, the blighted lives, and the waste of talent that disfigure our country. In economic terms the socialism that Nehru had in mind was equality and sharing: the creation of equal opportunities for all Indians and the raising of their minimum standards of living. Lech Walesa, the president of Poland, spoke in a similar strain when he described a few years ago what socialism meant to him: 'The bakery with the freshest, crispest rolls is socialism. A system which allows anyone to run for president, that is socialism. And unions which genuinely defind the rights of workers, that, to Lech Walesa, is socialism.'[9]

If socialism was once an explosive word, it has now, with the collapse of the communist parties in the Soviet Union and Eastern Europe, become a dirty word. But recent developments in the world cannot efface the importance of human and social values. Indeed, the changes in the Soviet Union, by removing the model to which so many looked up in the years since 1917, force us in India to think in terms of working out our futures in our own way. Not doctrinal socialism but a social ethic inspiring our economic development could knit our nation closer and reduce the dimensions of ethnic disharmony. It is worth mention, in this connection, that in China recent economic reforms and a swing to the market economy have boosted agricultural production but deeply undercut rural health services. Agricultural output has boomed; mortality rates have also gone up and life expectancy at birth has declined.

The strategy of development adopted by India in 1947 was not

[9] Quoted by David Selbourne, 'Poles Apart', *New Statesman and Society*, 4 August 1984.

solely the outcome of Nehru's ideological predilections. There was general consensus that the state had a considerable role to play. The Bombay Plan, prepared in 1944 by leading businessmen, regarded massive public investments in the infrastructure and the basic industries as necessary to facilitate the growth of the private sector and to set the country on the road to rapid development. Both the United States and the World Bank urged the governments of the third world to draw up five-year plans. There was also agreement among the policy-makers in India on the need to give priority to programmes of industrialization. Patel supported Nehru on the importance of building a self-reliant economy; and, as Nehru remarked to Gandhi in 1940, if you sit on your industries then other countries will not sit on you.[10] Gandhi and his followers looked forward to an India of village communities with a heavy agricultural bias. But Gandhi did not reject industrialization outright. He accepted the need for key industries but was opposed to large-scale production of items which could easily be produced in the villages. Their self-sufficiency assumed the utilization of such tools and machines as the villagers could themselves make and afford to use.

Nehru's economic strategy was certainly successful in the years when he was prime minister. Manufacturing output in India rose at an annual rate of 8 per cent during the years 1955 to 1965. The imported proportion of gross domestic fixed capital formation, which was extremely high in 1947, has been dropping continuously since then. But there were some intrinsic weaknesses in the approach which gradually manifested themselves. Greater economic growth had the paradoxical consequence of intensifying inequality in both the urban and the rural areas and widening the gulf between the rich and the poor. It was thought that production had to come before distribution; economic development had to precede social justice. Abundance is needed before poverty can be expelled. It was not grasped that such over-phasing corrodes democracy. Growth and equity are parts

[10] See Amrit Kaur's notes of a discussion between Gandhi and Nehru, *Selected Works of Jawaharlal Nehru*, First Series, vol. 15 (Delhi: Orient Longman, 1982), p. 647.

of a single model, production and distribution must be linked, technological productivity and structural changes in society need to go together.

Moreover, the low emphasis to agriculture was not set right by the collateral advantages gained by the peasants from the development of heavy industry. The application of scientific methods to agriculture did result in a considerable increase in production; but this did not lead on to widespread distribution of the agricultural yield. Indeed, with the advantage taken of better techniques and greater facilities by landlords with medium-sized estates and by the richer peasantry, a new elite developed in the countryside. The green revolution, carried through in the years after Nehru, has further strengthened this trend. A reverse, and healthier, process could have been initiated if programmes of land reforms had been taken seriously. But because such reforms are a matter for the states and not the union government and with that government more concerned with food production, little has been done about land reforms below the level of the large zamindari estates. Everyone in India favours land reforms but it is a rhetorical rather than a real consensus. So we have an incessant expansion in the extent and levels of poverty among the landless poor; and the problem is intensified by the failure to check the menacing increase of the population.

Basically, the failure in building a strong democracy in India by supporting the political system with social advance and economic equity is a failure of political will. Radical social and economic goals can be achieved by democratic, accommodative methods of functioning if, with the backing of a strong political movement, the desired objectives are pushed through. A unique opportunity was lost in the 1950s when Nehru did not exploit fully his power and his popularity to pursue his agenda. His openmindedness and undogmatic temperament, attractive in themselves, led to ambivalence in several essential choices, political, social, economic, and administrative. He brings to mind Machiavelli's observation that rulers should seek to be feared rather than loved.

There has also been the failure to give the same emphasis to primary as to higher education, despite the proviso in the constitution that every child should have free and compulsory schooling. If there is one shortcoming of free India that now stands out as a disaster, it is surely the vacillations in education policy and its persistently low place in national priorities. Even now, the proportion of funds devoted to primary education is relatively low and has been declining as a proportion of the total expenditure in the five-year plans. The share of elementary education in the amount allotted to the education sector was 56 per cent in the first plan and 44 per cent in the seventh plan. Nor has the growth in the number of schools kept pace with the growth of population. Education is still seen largely as a means of producing trained manpower rather than as a cultural and nation-building activity. It is imperative to stress that primary education provides a wide and firm social basis for democracy and trains the people to apply reason and logic in public affairs. But extensive public investment in education, health, and housing is also both a matter of social justice and a way of securing high-term dividends. Most fast-growing countries show a high adult literary ratio. Countries with a better educated population have higher economic growth. Unless a population is literate, other investment projects may well fail. So, from every point of view, it is deeply worrying that one-half of the number of illiterates in the world are to be found in India. An effective democracy assumes an educated electorate, a secular society is an educated society, and economic and social change achieved by democratic means requires an educated people. It is not yet too late to give the highest priority to a crash programme which provides a minimum of education for all our people, and for women in particular.

If there is any lesson to be drawn from recent events in the world, it is that democracy is not a luxury which only the rich nations can afford but the right of all peoples. Glasnost and perestroika, leading to the collapse of the communist party in Eastern Europe and the Soviet Union make this clear, just as the brutal suppression in Tiananmen Square in China establishes, if only by negative affirmation, that the desire for civil liberty never dies in the human spirit. Development with participation as an integral factor, liberty as a vital element of progress, and openness to the outside world as the fundamental right of every man and woman—this is the democratic core of the Indian experiment since 1947. It is sad and paradoxical that even as the world is coming round to the view that the public ethos of India is the most satisfactory and acceptable model even for underdeveloped countries, in India there has been chiselling away at the collective social morality which our leaders established for us—unity, self-reliance, social dignity, secularism, and growth with equity; and all within a democratic framework. The early decades of free India have today sometimes the nostalgic fragrance of a dead age. But what Hegel described as 'the cunning of history' may yet prove that the ideas associated with Jawaharlal Nehru were not, like the red rose in his buttonhole, purely for ornamentation. His hopes for India have not been blown away by current tempests and could, if adapted to present reality without weakening their intrinsic principle, lead us into better times.

21

The Crisis of Secularism in India

An issue horrifyingly prominent on the Indian scene is the sharp recrudescence in recent years of political aggressiveness among diverse groups of Hindus, Muslims, and Sikhs claiming religious sanction. This has culminated, in the last six months, in a rich carnival of hate. The focus of the belligerence of the Hindu group was the Babri Masjid in Ayodhya in Uttar Pradesh. Alleging that this mosque had been built in 1528 by a general of Babar, the first Mughal emperor, after destroying a Hindu temple on the site where the avatar Ram was believed to have been born, on 6 December 1992 the mosque was demolished. The evidence brought forward in support of this allegation, that a temple had been destroyed, is flimsy and unconvincing. Even if it be true that a temple had been destroyed over four hundred years ago, that is no argument for now razing a mosque to the ground; but even that contention about the destruction of a temple cannot be substantiated. However, in the present inflamed atmosphere a genuine search for the truth seems of little account.

The demolition of the mosque has had its repercussions and its aftershocks rumble on. Communal riots have taken place in various parts of the country with over a thousand dead and much property destroyed. High-explosive bombs, aimed at disrupting normal life, have caused hitherto unknown levels of destruction, especially in Bombay. Set afoot in 1947 when freedom came to India along with secession of those parts of the country where Muslims formed a majority and wished to cut adrift, it would appear that this effort to divorce religion from public life has come to a standstill, and that secularism is in its last throes and may well be strangled.

This continuing crisis has deep implications. The necessity of ending the abuse of religion for political purposes leads on to a more basic question: Can people in a multi-religious society like India live together in harmony? A country where religious beliefs are not generally non-existent or shallow, and where religious rituals are not to most people empty, can only survive in such a country if religion is kept out of public life and regarded as a personal matter for each citizen. In other words, India, as we have known her and as we hope she will continue to be, cannot afford to be anything but secular.

It has, however, been argued that secularism cannot thrive in India because it is an alien cultural ideology imposed on a country to which it is not suited, primarily by India's first prime minister, Jawaharlal Nehru, who was beguiled by science and technology and thought in terms of rational understanding and a scientific temper. It is true that Nehru had no use for conventional or organized religion and refused to participate in temple-going and rituals. A mild agnostic who prided himself on a pagan outlook, he had scorn for the priests and theologians who took firm positions on what was unknown and quarrelled fiercely with each other. He believed that there was enough work to do in this world without bothering about the next. But what appalled him was the exploitation of religion by political and economic interests and the spread, in the penultimate years of the Raj, of both Hindu and Muslim communalism and the consequent frequency of communal rioting in various parts of the country.

However, even at this time Nehru had respect for the high principles of true religion as against the asserted certainties of dogma and doctrine; and he was in accord with Gandhi's insistence on religion and politics going together because by religion Gandhi meant the primacy of truth. In his autobiography Nehru went along with Romain Rolland's definition of religion as the search for truth at all costs with single-minded sincerity. The influence of Gandhi was supplemented by Nehru's readings in Indian philosophy while in prison in Ahmednagar for three years from 1942. The Buddha's emphasis on ethical action without concerning oneself with God and the hereafter appealed to him. He acknowledged that religion as generally practised was distasteful to him for it was closely associated with superstitious practices and its approach was unscientific. Yet he realized that religion catered to some deeply felt need of human nature and gave a set of values to human life. He was irritated by mysticism and, while metaphysical thinking provided a certain intellectual fascination, he was never at ease with it. But he accepted that all men have some vague or more precise philosophy of life, and he himself appreciated the concept of monism and was attracted to the Advaita Vedanta. The dialectical materialism of Marx explained much but did not satisfy him completely or answer all his questions.

The same trend of thought may be seen when, as prime minister in 1958, he undertook a rethinking of first principles. Rationalism seemed to him inadequate, appearing to deal with the surface of things without uncovering the inner core. More compelling was the Vedantic approach that everything, animate and inanimate, had its place in the organic whole, and a spark of the divine impulse, energy or life force pervades the universe. So Nehru concluded that India should seek the objective of individual improvement and the lessening of inequalities without forgetting the ethical and spiritual aspects of life. And in one of his last writings, two days before his death, he emphasized that India should benefit by modern technical processes and increase production: 'but in doing so we must not forget that the essential objective to be aimed at is the quality of the individual and the concept of *dharma* underlying it.'[1]

An adherence to basic values, a commitment to ethical conduct and a sneaking sympathy for the Vedanta philosophy—these were all parts of Nehru's outlook from the time he became prime minister in 1947 and they dispose of the contention that he was seeking to bind free India in the straitjacket of a Western ideology. The secularism in which Nehru and his colleagues placed their faith was not, as has been said, 'a gift of Christianity'—that is, of West European Christianity. Dictionary definitions of secularism do not apply in any particular situation. Culture and context provide secularism with various manifestations which move well beyond what the lexicons tell us. In

[1] Written on 25 May 1964 and published in the Preface to Shriman Narayan, *Socialism in Indian Planning* (Delhi: Asia Publishing House, 1964).

Western Europe, as a result of confrontation between the state and the church, secularism has come to mean the separation of the two, and particularly laicization in education. In the erstwhile Soviet Union, secularization denoted atheism and an assault on religions as agents of exploitation. In India, with several religions and the religious element deeply embedded in the human psyche, and with two centuries of foreign rule, the secular idea has taken shape in ways which have no parallels elsewhere.

The present and future of secularism in India should be seen in historical perspective. As Tagore wrote, the muffled steps of the past are felt in blood. India has, from time immemorial, been the home of several religions. Christianity came in the early centuries after Christ and long before it was accepted in Europe. Jews and Zoroastrians settled in the country without difficulty. Muslims came to India several centuries prior to their becoming a political force. But varying religious beliefs did not form a source of social tension. Alongside the maintenance of private identity, and often even enclosed social habit, there was also mutual influence and adaptation among people of different faiths. Converts to Christianity from Hinduism carried with them several customs, caste privileges, and a faith in horoscopes. The impact of Jewish and Hindu traditions can be seen in Syrian Christian church architecture in Kerala.[2] Similarly, mosques in Gujarat show the influence of Jain temples in the neighbourhood. Hindustani or Urdu is a language with Hindu and Muslim lineage; and the interaction of Hinduism and Islam can also be seen in music, dress, and food. Nor could the two religions evolve in India in isolation. An inscription of the year 1264 found in Junagadh, written in Sanskrit and issued by a group of Muslim traders, refers to Allah as Viswanatha. This strand strengthens with the development of the Sufi and Bhakti movements and the emergence of figures like Ramanand and Kabir.

Was this background of popular culture acceptable to the rulers? It is easy to find instances in the history of ancient and medieval India of the desecration or demolition of institutions of religious significance.

[2] Susan Visvanathan, *The Christians of Kerala: History, Belief and Rituals among the Yakoba* (Madras: Oxford University Press, 1993), p. 3, p. 9.

But such actions were not the monopoly of the followers of any one particular religion. A Hindu ruler of the eleventh century, Harsha of Kashmir, melted images in Hindu temples, and a Hindu general cut down the Bo-tree in Bodhgaya. Shaivites and Vaishnavites, Hindus, Buddhists, and Jains, Sunnis and Shias quarrelled and frequently pillaged each others' shrines. When the Sikhs conquered Sirhind in 1764, they deliberately destroyed all buildings, including the mosques. There is no room for generalizations about bigotry applicable only to Muslims.

Nor were such actions the result solely of mindless fanaticism. If Mahomed of Ghazni demolished the temple at Somnath, he also destroyed mosques in Central Asia; and he had in his service a Hindu general who helped him to lay hands on the immense wealth to be found in these institutions. Akbar was, of course, an enlightened monarch. But he drank, wherever he was, only water from the Ganga and married a Hindu wife because he sought to derive political advantage rather than to demonstrate devotion to Hinduism, just as Aurangzeb believed that his religious zeal would secure him not just merit in heaven but the loyalty of his restive Muslim subjects. In parallel actions he sought to win over the Hindus in his empire by land grants to temples.[3] Such temples as he did destroy were located mostly in areas which were in political revolt. Religious institutions, be they temples, mosques, or gurdwaras, were also symbols of dynastic dominance. The main interest of rulers, then and now, is the pursuit and maintenance of power, and bigotry or tolerance, as the case may be, was linked to political interest. Ranjit Singh in 1801 had Muslim learned men present at his court not just to show his broadmindedness but to get these men to validate his claim to be king of the Punjab. Human motivation is complex, and all historical events have plural explanations.

To establish authority in India over people of several faiths, rulers had perforce to keep religion in its place. Babur, with the help of Rajput allies, defeated at Panipat the Muslim sultan of Delhi. The number of

[3] Satish Chandra, 'Reassessing Aurangzeb', *Seminar* (December 1989), pp. 35–8.

Hindus in Mughal service continued to rise till in Aurangzeb's time they formed a third of the total. In later Mughal campaigns special provision was made for the prayers of both Hinduism and Islam, and a Jain temple was constructed close to the Red Fort at Delhi for the benefit of Jain soldiers in the imperial service.[4] In South India, in the fifteenth century many Syrian Christian churches were built or sponsored by Hindu rulers in return for military service by the Christians; and Christians were donors at Hindu temples. A Maratha ruler built one of the five minarets of the *dargah* at Nagore. A Muslim ruler was the benefactor of the temple at Madurai, and the nawab of Arcot was the protector of temples at Chidambaram and Tirupati. Tipu Sultan of Mysore in 1793 bore all the expenses for the restoration of the *math* at Sringeri which had been destroyed by a Maratha chief. To this day there are shared traditions and ceremonials in the temples, mosques, and churches of South India.[5]

In these years, then, religion did not dominate public affairs but was at most one of several factors in a society with 'a predominantly syncretic culture' and with no 'pervading sense of social separateness'.[6] Tension and riots, such as would today be termed communal, can be noticed occasionally from the eighteenth century onwards, but were the result of religious divisions coinciding with economic antagonisms or of local economic change being mixed up with religious disputes. Certainly there was no sense of a religious community functioning as such in politics. A change, however, occurred with the coming of the British. The fact that they landed in the coastal areas, where the majority of the local population happened to be Hindus, meant that it was primarily the Hindus who took advantage of the avenues of trade and employment opened by the British and of education in the English language. We can imagine how very different the situation would have been if the British had come in as a land power and if, like

[4] C.A. Bayly, 'The Pre-history of "Communalism"? Religious Conflict in India, 1700–1860', *Modern Asian Studies* (1985), no. 2, pp. 177–203. I have drawn much from this article.

[5] Susan Bayly, *Saints, Goddesses and Kings* (Cambridge: Cambridge University Press, 1985).

[6] Bayly, 'The Pre-history of "Communalism"?'

all their other predecessors who came into India, they had come in from the north-west. If they had found themselves say on the North West Frontier and in the Punjab and the UP, where Muslim influence was considerable and where also the Muslim population was greater than in the coastal areas, the situations would have been different. But the fact remains that they landed in the coastal areas, and by the time the British moved into the interior of the country where lay the zones of Muslim influence, a regional imbalance in economic and social development had been created.

This slotted smoothly into the British understanding that India was not a nation, as she did not conform to nineteenth-century European thinking that blood and language were the criteria of nationhood, but a cluster of peoples with separate religious identities. These 'imagined religious communities',[7] moreover, were seen as traditionally hostile to each other. British policy was based on this assumption that India was permanently fractured by religion.

Ironically, the Indian National Congress, the party claiming to speak for the growing nationalist sentiment, was inclined to the same illusion. Its leaders too acted on the basis that Hindus and Muslims were separate entities. At its fourth session in 1889, for example, the Congress resolved that no subject would be discussed if the Hindu or Muslim delegates as a body objected. In 1916 politicians claiming to represent Hindu and Muslim interests met to frame a joint representation to the government. Leading figures in the Congress, not excluding Gandhi, spoke increasingly in a Hindu idiom.

So British policy and Congress shortsightedness, working in a context of British policy and lopsided development, nourished the religious element in Indian politics; and this culminated in the partition of the country. The counter-efforts of Nehru and others to build a national identity failed to make headway. Little ground was gained by their attempts to point out that communalism was shallow, skin-deep, and of relatively recent origin; and that priority should be

[7] Romila Thapar, 'Imagined Religious Communities? Ancient History and the Modern Search for a Hindu Identity', *Modern Asian Studies* (May 1989), pp. 209–31.

given to the problems of poverty, hunger, and illiteracy which concerned most Indians and overrode differences in religion. But Nehru at least succeeded in getting the Congress in 1931 to accept that in a free India there would be freedom of conscience, all citizens would be equal before the law irrespective of religion, creed, caste, or sex, no disability would attach for these reasons in regard to employment, and the state would be neutral in regard to all religions. These were the building-blocks of Indian secularism from 1947.

After the fierce frenzy of the riots that accompanied Partition, followed soon after by the murder of the Mahatma, independent India sought to move away from a steep descent into savagery and to put together the broken pieces of national identity. The categories of secular practice enunciated in 1931 were incorporated in the constitution of 1950. The principles of national cohesion would be the divorce of religion from politics and public life, the separation of the state from the churches of all faiths, the insistence on religion as a private matter for the individual with no bearing on civic rights or duties, and freedom for the profession of diverse forms of religious worship provided no problems of law and order were created. These secular values derive from no borrowed ideology but, apart from drawing strength from their own logic, make Indian historical experience meaningful. Integral to a civilized outlook, they also provide the policy best suited to India. They form the social cement required by a multi-religious society striving to become a healthy democratic community. They provide the only way of making certain that no one is treated as a second-class citizen on the ground of religion.

What is worrying is that secularism of this type has not as yet taken firm root in India. The state itself has to bear some responsibility for this, for its policy in this regard has, from the start, been faltering. The Constituent Assembly resolved in 1948 that communal political parties should be banned; but no action has been taken till now on this resolution because of legal difficulties in defining a communal party. The banning of cow-slaughter was made, despite the resistance of Gandhi and Nehru, one of the Directive Principles of State Policy. Though no action has been taken in this matter, a principle was jettisoned as a concession to a chauvinist section of Hindu opinion.

Above all, while the reform of Hindu personal law was initiated, a common civil law for all Indians was not enacted, despite a pledge to this effect in the constitution. This is a violation of the principle of equality before the law, for Muslim women are at present being denied the rights given to Indian women of other faiths. There is no room in a society which declares itself to be secular for inequalities which claim religious sanction. Religion should be divorced not only from politics but also from the law. Indeed the Constituent Assembly had, by a resolution in 1948, refused to accept that Muslim personal law was an inseparable part of the Islamic religion and rejected attempts to exempt it from the Directive Principle favouring a uniform civil code.

If the Government of India were reluctant, in the early years, to act on this resolution and impose a common civil law, it was because of the conviction of Nehru and his colleagues that, on the morrow of Partition, the minorities required special consideration. There might still be a few Muslims in India who were communal, and any efforts of theirs to make mischief would have to be dealt with sternly. But more attention should be given to winning the Muslims over and making them feel at home in a free India. The problem of minorities was basically one for the majority community to handle. The test of success was not what the Hindus thought but how the Muslims and other communities felt, just as, while minorities might turn communal out of a sense of grievance or insecurity, communalism of the majority community was dangerous and, masquerading as nationalism, was in fact a form of fascism. The minorities might sometimes be driven by fear to be communal; but there could never be any justification or rational explanation for majority communalism. Only if the Hindus were secular could the minorities be helped to become secular.

A problem which goes to the root of rational life can only be solved by raising the broad level of society and building up the human factor at every level. A secular state can only be grounded in a robust civil society. Even in the matter of personal laws, the way is open for liberal opinion among Muslims, after living in a free India for so many years, to utilize the precedent of changes in Islamic personal law carried out by the British before 1947 without much protest and to follow up the resolution of the Constituent Assembly. It is true that in 1986 a statute set aside a judgment of the supreme court by which a divorced Muslim woman without any means of subsistence was granted maintenance till she remarried. Yet that statute itself has been questioned by several high courts. But for the present crisis one could have hopefully awaited an initiative to arise within the Muslim community in an India committed to secularism for reforms in the personal law in the interests of gender rights.

However, will the present crisis be overcome? The outlook today is dark, but the past gives hope. Secularism is more than laws, concessions, and special considerations. It is a state of mind, at best almost an instinctive feeling, such as India has known for many centuries. With the impetus of democracy and the spread of education, that traditional sense of a common bond which subdues communal feeling can be restored and made stronger. As far back as in July 1948, in the wake of months of communal frenzy, Nehru looked forward with confidence to a brighter future. 'I believe', he wrote, 'that India can only become great if she preserves that composite culture which she had developed through the ages . . . whatever might happen in the present, sometime or other, India will have to tread that path to self-realization and greatness.'[8] That note of optimism can strengthen us still.

[8] Jawaharlal Nehru to the Nawab of Bhopal, 9 July 1948, *Selected Works of Jawaharlal Nehru* (Second Series), vol. 7 (Delhi: Oxford University Press, 1988), p. 7.

22

Secularism: From Rammohun Roy to Jawaharlal Nehru

Secularism is a moral ethic analysed by philosophers and social scientists; and it is also a political perspective considered by policy-makers. Culture and context therefore provide it with various manifestations which move well beyond theoretical definitions. In Western Europe, as a consequence of confrontation between the state and the church, it has come to mean the separation of the two; and in countries with Communist regimes it has denoted an assault on religion as an agent of exploitation, though even in those countries the governments have, more often than not, had to reach working arrangements with the churches. The setting in India has been very different. Unlike Western Europe, which is predominantly Christian, India is a multi-religious society; and the religious element is deeply embedded in its culture. On such a people was imposed alien rule, distorting politics, the economy, and every aspect of social life. Influenced by these factors, the secular idea has developed in India in ways which have had no parallels elsewhere.

Rational criticism of narrow religious dogma and defiance in action of obscurantism claiming the authority of religion were known in India before the nineteenth century; but it is from that time that we can trace the problem with the orientations that are still with us. In Rammohun Roy we can assess both an effort to deal with the problem and the circumstantial influences which coloured most of such efforts, giving rise to ambivalences and even contradictions. A product of the composite culture of India, Rammohun was influenced by Islam much before he was exposed to ideas from the West, and he used reason to lay bare the weaknesses of all religious doctrines. He did not denounce belief but felt that the best form of worship was the promotion of 'the union of human hearts, with mutual love and affection for all one's fellow-beings, without distinction of caste or creed, race or colour.'[1] So right at the start, independent of Westernization, sound lines for developing a secular society in India were formulated: not a denunciation of religion or the search among the different faiths for a common religious base or the reform of existing religions, but stress that religion should draw people together with a practical aspect of concern for all men and women. But even Rammohun drifted away from this initial assertion of correct principle. Religion as tested by its contribution to 'social comforts' failed to remain in the forefront of his mind; under the provocation of Christian missionaries he fell on the defensive and, while commending the 'ideal humanity' of Christ rather than the teaching of the Bible, justified his own faith in a dogmaless theism on the basis of the Upanishads. However convincing to himself, this immediately weakened his persuasiveness with the followers of non-Hindu religions; and Rammohun drew further away from Muslims by suggesting that tolerance came particularly easily to Hindus and proclaiming that British rule in Bengal was much better than that of the nawabs which had preceded it.

The rejection of Hinduism by Derozio and his followers appeared to swing them close to secularism on godless lines; but the position was at no time clear-cut. Even their move from one religion to another was not always with total severance. Krishna Mohan Banerji, for example, became a Christian but argued that the Bible had been anticipated in the Vedas.[2] A more effective, if indirect and less fierce, approach was that of Vidyasagar. He looked to British authority for reform in Indian society and he shared the general view of educated Hindus of the time that the British had done a service by ridding the country of centuries of Muslim tyranny. But against these limitations of outlook stands the

[1] In Rammohun Roy's tract *Tuhfat-ul-Muhawaddin.*

[2] S.K. De, *Bengali Literature in the Nineteenth Century* (Calcutta: Firma K.L. Mukhopadhyaya, 1962), pp. 588–9.

fact that Vidyasagar showed the way to a secular future by emphasizing education as the means of raising the level of society and creating a public opinion which would insist on right action. Perhaps the greatest tribute paid to him was the complaint of a British missionary that the textbooks prepared by Vidyasagar for elementary schools were secular and that he had struck out deliberately the command to worship God and the passages about the immortality of the soul.[3]

The Brahmo Samaj, though theist, held out promise in that it was committed to no particular religion. To Keshub Sen, it followed from the belief that God is one and had created all humanity that one should look upon all, whether Parsis, Hindus, Muslims, or Christians, as one's brothers. He encouraged one of his disciples to study Islam from the primary sources and to translate its texts into Bengali,[4] and he compiled for his services extracts from the scriptures of all the major religions. His criticism of caste and *sati* from the viewpoint of the brotherhood of man formed a natural prelude to the promotion of Hindu–Muslim unity. But working the other way was the quest for a universal religion, for any such search for a synthesis is unacceptable to the believers of religions founded on revelation.

The trends were healthier in western India. There too at first the stress was on finding a religion to which everyone everywhere could subscribe. The Manavadharma Sabha, the Society for Human Religion, was followed by the Paramahamsa Mandali, promoting universal brotherhood and looking for a universal religion. But the Prarthana Samaj, while holding that God was one and without form, did not set out to establish a religion on that basis. Such a religion was left to evolve on its own, round the core of mystical experiences shared by devotees of all religions. The leaders of the Prarthana Samaj gave their prime attention to social reforms, with current religion, as Chandavarkar defined it, being the practice of civic virtues.[5] There is a

[3] Quoted in Amales Tripathi, *Vidyasagar the Traditional Modernizer* (Calcutta: Longman, 1974), pp. 91–2.

[4] David Kopf, *The Brahmo Samaj and the Shaping of the Modern Indian Mind* (Princeton: Princeton University Press, 1979), p. 252.

[5] Quoted in C.H. Heimsath, *Indian Nationalism and Hindu Social Reform* (Princeton: Princeton University Press, 1964), p. 106.

touch of chauvinism in Ranade's argument that the rise of the Maratha power represented an effort of a Hindu nationality to assert itself. But generally his was a dedicated mind undiminished by religious narrowness. His boast in 1893 that 'This race of ours is the chosen race' was about not Hindus alone but all Indians of whatever faith, for he added immediately that he was speaking of one-fifth of the human race. But even more important for the future than the social concerns of the Prarthana Samaj was the offensive in this part of India on Brahminical Hinduism. Lokahitawadi denounced caste and wished to preclude religion from taking any part in temporal activities. Jotirao Phule trod the same track with even greater vehemence, condemned the hierarchical values associated with orthodox Hinduism and, like Vidyasagar, placed his hopes in non-religious education.[6] Such attacks on caste in the cause of human equality could not but lead to rejection of discrimination between the followers of different religions. The Satyashodak Samaj did not preach a universal or natural religion but favoured the worship of a Supreme God who transcended all religions including Hinduism. Non-Hindus were free to join the Samaj though unfortunately it is not known how many, if any, Muslims, Parsis, and Christians had become members.

In sharp contrast was the Arya Samaj in the northern part of the country. Here the assaults on caste and other forms of social degradation were made as parts of a campaign for a purer Hinduism. Once, in Gujarat, Dayanand recited and discussed the *gayatri* mantra before an audience that included Muslims; but such an instance cannot minimize the insistence on the infallibility of the Vedas, thereby placing all non-Hindus beyond the reach of the Samaj. Resurgent Hinduism was less aggressive at the religious level in Bengal. Ramakrishna, being steeped in mysticism, looked beyond creed and doctrine. He compared religion to water which assumed the shape of the vessel into which it was poured. Once, for a few days, he lived like a Muslim and turned away from all Hindu forms and places of worship. Vivekananda was more concerned with the world, and he spoke of the one religion which would harmonize the Vedas, the Bible, and the Koran. It was

[6] Rosalind O'Hanlon, *Caste, Conflict and Ideology* (Cambridge: Cambridge University Press, 1988), pp. 233–4.

good to be born in a particular creed but it was terrible to die in one. While the Vedanta was to him the science of religion, he thought the time had come to make Advaita practical and he saw in Islam practical Advaitism. A combination of Vedanta brain and Islam body was the only hope for India and he admitted Muslim boys into his ashram. Yet the Hindu viewpoint in Ramakrishna and Vivekananda could not be missed; and it became even clearer in others. Rajnarain Bose gave a public lecture in Calcutta in 1872 to prove the superiority of Hinduism to all other religions. The Tattvabodhini Sabha stated that its aim was to demonstrate that India was a symbol of righteousness and to establish that among all Indians Hindus should be given a superior position.[7] Nivedita, thinking along the lines of Vivekananda, spoke of Hindus and Muslims serving as 'converging artillery' to create the motherland and advocated the spirit of science; but she also wrote books on *Aggressive Hinduism* and *Kali the Mother*. All these claims and statements, though intended primarily to counterattack the Christian missionaries, had an adverse impact on those Indians who were not Hindus.

Nivedita was also interested in politics; and it was the merging of Hindu revivalism with nationalist sentiment that created the element of danger for India's future. In western India the outstanding exponent of this was Tilak. In Bengal the terms Hindu and nationalist were becoming synonymous. From 1867 Hindu *melas* were organized for the widening of national awareness. 'The Hindus', wrote Nabagopal Mitra in 1872, 'are destined to become a religious nation.'[8] Bankim Chattopadhyaya defined religion pragmatically as being that which preserved living beings; religion could not be separated from utilitarianism.[9] He accepted that it was wrong to generalize about Hindus and Muslims,[10] and admired Akbar without reservation. But the general drive of his writings was to exalt a purified Hinduism, with which to him

[7] Quoted by K.N. Panikkar, 'Culture and Ideology', *Economic and Political Weekly*, 5 December 1987.

[8] Quoted in Heimsath, *Indian Nationalism and Hindu Social Reform*, p. 137.

[9] In Bankimchandra Chattopadhyaya's *Krishnacharitra*.

[10] In Bankimchandra Chattopadhyaya's *Rajsinha*.

Islam could not compare. The great principles of Hinduism were good for all ages and for all mankind,[11] and Bankim favoured action for the enforcement of these principles. 'I am a Hindu . . . must do what is good for all the Hindus and abstain from doing what is bad for any Hindu . . . There are many nations in the world besides the Hindu . . . In many cases what is good for them is bad for us. In such cases we must so act as to deprive them of the good.'[12] Writing of the wretched condition of the peasantry in Bengal he spoke of a typical peasant who was a Muslim; a decade later he withdrew the criticism. He also revised *Anandamath* to make the Muslims and not the British the enemy.[13] The tyranny of the Muslim kings is a theme which occurs repeatedly in his novels.

The exaltation of Hinduism at the political level in Bengal reached its climax in the writings of Aurobindo Ghosh. He pointed out rightly that all Indians, of whatever caste, class, or religion, had been brought to a certain level of equality by equal inferiority to the British, and he pleaded for a communion of hearts between the Hindus and the Muslims. But essentially his case for political freedom was based on Hindu premises. Self-knowledge and self-realization were, according to Hindu philosophy, the ultimate objectives; but these could not be attained if foreign influences disorganized and stifled growth.[14] The nation that looked up to Sri Krishna as the ideal hero could never submit to autocracy in any form.[15] If the existing state of things was allowed to continue, the Muslims would be the inheritors of the future and the Bengali Hindus would disappear from the list of nations; but fortunately the national movement had come in time to save him if he consented to be saved.[16] Though Indian nationality was composed of

[11] *Letters on Hinduism.*

[12] Article in Bengali 'The Disgrace of India' (1872), translated by and quoted in R.C. Majumdar, 'Political Thought of Bankim Chandra', *Hindustan Standard*, 17 June 1962.

[13] Hiren Gohain, 'Dialectics of Defeat', *Economic and Political Weekly*, 20 February 1988.

[14] *Bandemataram*, 9 June 1907.

[15] Ibid., 25 November 1907.

[16] Ibid., 6 March 1908.

many races and Indian culture of more than of world civilization, the Hindu formed its base and centre and the dominant note of Hindu culture, its sense of the spiritual and universal, would be the peculiar feature of the composite Indian nationality.[17] Such primacy given to the Hindu element reflected itself in practice too. Bhawani Mandirs were the points of political activity and, while Jugantar of Calcutta placed no ban on Muslims, Anushilan of Dhaka would not permit them to join.[18]

Such an approach could be found also in southern India, where Annie Besant was preaching that India and Hinduism were one and without Hinduism India had no future. But in Bengal itself the reaction was not long in coming. The British were expectedly active in fanning discord between Hindus and Muslims. But as Tagore observed, 'Satan cannot enter till he finds a flaw.'[19] The social disharmony between the two religious communities had been spanned by a popular culture but this was seriously weakened by Hindu nationalism. The Muslims too had begun to look for a distinct self-consciousness and, while Muslims were to be found in the *swadeshi* movement, that was later disfigured by communal rioting. The lesson was not lost on Tagore. Till then parallel strands had run in his thought. In 1898 he had written that an Indian nation could never emerge by leaving out the Muslims; and seven years later, during the *swadeshi* movement, he had proposed that a Hindu and a Muslim should act as joint leaders of the organization to rally the country's forces. But more prominent than this awareness of non-religious nationalism had been commitment to Hinduism. 'Brahma', he wrote in 1885, 'is India's living God; Jehovah, the Christian god and Allah are not quite akin to our thought.'[20] In 1898 he spoke of a Hindu nation; in 1901 he hoped for the rejuvenation of Hindu civilization; and in 1904 he commended his father for refusing

[17] Ibid., 14 June 1908.

[18] A.C. Guha, *Aurobindo and Jugantar* (Calcutta: Sahitya Sansad, 1975), 37.

[19] Quoted in Sumit Sarkar, *The Swadeshi Movement in Bengal 1903–1908* (Delhi: People's Publishing House, 1973), p. 83.

[20] Quoted in Susobhan Sarkar, *Bengal Renaissance and Other Essays* (Delhi: People's Publishing House, 1970), p. 161.

to dilute 'our supreme national religion' with a vague universalism and himself thought in terms of India achieving a 'peculiar Hinduistic' harmony. But after the riots of 1906 and 1907 the bias in his thinking shifted to Indians of various religions working together. 'Today', says the hero at the end of *Gora*, 'I am, above all, an Indian. In me there is no conflict of communities.'

If the dual tones in Tagore's thought had sorted themselves out and placed him firmly on the side of a secular approach, the seeming contradictions in Gandhi's many utterances over a long spread of time all resolve themselves into a coherent attitude. He did not develop secularism into a full-fledged theory but practised it and his life speaks for him even better than his words. The famous comment in his autobiography that those who said that religion had nothing to do with politics did not know the meaning of religion suggests a rejection of secularism in the accepted sense. But by religion Gandhi meant not any belief or creed but the values of truth, love, and justice. He strove to bring into politics compassion and activity to improve the living conditions of men and women. 'To a people famishing and idle, the only acceptable form in which God can dare appear is work and promise of food as wages.'[21] But religion as conformity to church and ritual had no place in politics. 'If I were a dictator, religion and state would be separate. I swear by my religion. I would die for it. But it is my personal affair. The state has nothing to do with it.'[22]

Were all his other achievements in diverse fields set aside, Gandhi's efforts for a communion of hearts between Hindus and Muslims, especially in the last months of his life, alone ensure him a place among the immortals. But a religious outlook in politics, however noble and sophisticated the concept of religion might be, could not but, as Nehru saw,[23] give the national movement a revivalist character as far as the masses were concerned. Moreover, while Gandhi insisted on respect for all religions, felt that though all religions had an element of truth none could claim a finality of truth, and insisted that he was at heart

[21] *Young India*, 13 October 1921.

[22] *Harijan*, 22 September 1946.

[23] *Autobiography* (London: John Lane, 1936), p. 72.

a member of all religions, it was emphatically clear that Hinduism was the dominant force in his life. It coloured his ways of action and inspired his commitment to universal brotherhood. He himself acknowledged this. 'My religion is Hinduism which for me is the religion of humanity and includes the best of all the religions known to me.'[24] He also permitted the intrusion of conventional religion into nationalist politics. In the Khilafat campaign he planned joint action by the Hindus and Muslims rather than integrated action by Indians. He wanted Hindus to be better Hindus and Muslims to be better Muslims and all of them to be better Indian citizens. He told the Muslims, for example, that they should feel particularly ashamed of what the Mapillas had done and it was for them to ensure that such things did not happen again.[25] Gandhi was against the exploitation of religious beliefs for political purposes but he was prepared to use them for effective and improved political behaviour.

This attitude of Gandhi was to Nehru an embarrassment, for he had, by the 1930s, shed the traditional Hindu faith of his early years, was disgusted by the attitudes which enabled widespread communal rioting, and had been converted to the Marxist analysis of the social evils of religion. He himself planned not so much for the solution as the dissolution of the communal problem by the spread of industrialization and education. By such means had religion been taken out of politics in Europe and he saw no reason why this should not also happen in India. His conception of the role of religion in free India was spelt out in the resolution on fundamental rights at the Karachi Congress in 1931. Every citizen would enjoy freedom of conscience and the right freely to profess and practise any religion subject to public order and morality, all citizens would be equal before the law irrespective of religion, creed, caste, or sex, no disability would attach to citizens for these reasons in regard to public employment and in the exercise of any trade or calling, and the state would observe neutrality in regard to all religions. Set against the background of

[24] Article in S. Radhakrishnan (ed.), *Contemporary Indian Philosophy* (London: George Allen & Unwin,1935).

[25] *Collected Works of Mahatma Gandhi*, vol. 21, p. 321.

India's composite culture, of whose existence Nehru was convinced and which is one of the themes of *Glimpses of World History*, the Karachi resolution formulated secularism as it should develop in the Indian context.

This positive approach pushed the communal problem to the back of Nehru's mind. To him Hindu–Muslim differences were artificial and kept alive by parties which were props of political reaction. This suited the British, and Nehru, like Gandhi, was confident that once the British departed communal antagonism would disappear. Hunger, poverty, and illiteracy were common to all Indians and much more basic than religious differences. Meantime, to stem the growing communal stridency, he, again like Gandhi, expected the Hindus to be generous and, dangerously for the future, distinguished between shades of communalism. The fact that the Hindus were in a majority made their communalism a version of fascism, while that of the minorities might have a core of genuine concern about the future.

The Congress under Gandhi and Nehru was unable, in a colonial context, to exorcise communalism of either type. The compromise of office acceptance and the failure of the mass contact campaign gave Jinnah a vantage position which he exploited to the full during the war years to push the country into partition. But with large religious minorities still living in India after 1947, secularism was an indispensable prerequisite for the creation of a democratic, egalitarian society. Nehru committed India to this and saw to it that the principles of the Karachi resolution were incorporated in the constitution. Throughout his primeministership, except for the short period of the rebellion in Telengana, Nehru regarded Hindu communalism as the greatest threat to the survival of India as a free and forward-looking country. The Muslim outlook might often be worse but after 1947 it had no weight behind it in India. It was for the Hindus to win over the minorities by making them feel that they were equal citizens.

Although Nehru had placed secularism high in his pattern of priorities it cannot be said that he always measured up fully in the implementation of this ideal. The special concern for minorities, to which he gave so much attention, is in itself a breach of the secular principle of the equality of all; but it can be justified as an interim policy, unavoidable till the minorities are fully integrated. But serious were the failure to ban communal political parties, to which the government were committed, the inclusion of the banning of cow-slaughter among the directives of state policy in the constitution and the delay in introducing a common civil code for all the people of India.

Secularism, in the sense of every citizen enjoying freedom of conscience, religion a private matter with no part in public life, and the state supporting no particular faith and not discriminating against anyone on the basis of religion, is an integral part of a civilized outlook in public life. In India the concept is crucial for the building of national identity, the strengthening of the sense of belonging to the national community. But secularism, if a constituent part of every modern nation, takes different forms in different societies. In India the problem, as Nehru told Malraux,[26] is that it is a religious country and the religion of the large majority is not founded on an inspired book. Even in the days when religion in any sense had no strong appeal for him, Nehru recognized the magnificence in theory of Hinduism; and in his later years he came round to feel an affinity with the Vedanta. But what always concerned him were the social practices of Hinduism, which are rigid, narrow, and exclusive. To change these is essential, for secularism is about equality. A secular state cannot be rooted in a non-secular society, and a secular society can be promoted, as Nehru had realized even before independence, not solely by statutory enactments and political manoeuvring but by economic development, social justice and, above all, by education. An educated democracy is the environment best fitted for secularism to flourish. Nor does secularism in India need to be anti-religious or even non-religious, if religion is interpreted, as Gandhi and the noblest of our thinkers have done, as the acceptance and pursuit of certain values. Nehru described the highest values of our age as humanism and the scientific spirit, and if applied religion fosters these ideals in public life and, as Gandhi hoped, spiritualizes politics, no denial of religion

[26] Andre Malraux, *Anti-Memoirs* (London: Harcourt Brace, 1968), p. 145.

is required. Even Marx's demand for freedom from religion had in view mostly the socially reactionary side of religion, the device of the exploiters to reconcile the oppressed to their lot. Religion as private and personal belief is incompatible with the philosophy of materialism but it does not run counter to the Marxist analysis of historical change. But what does hinder the entrenching of the secular concept in India is the tendency to link it with Hinduism, to claim that Hinduism has all the ingredients to provide the world with a universal religion, to assert that Hinduism is the guarantee for the tolerance which is needed for secularism. These contentions, true or not, themselves seem dogmatic to the followers of other religions; and they are not required. Respect for other faiths is not dependent on a common base. The principles of secularism can stand on their own and have stood for centuries in India. Asoka proclaimed that by honouring other faiths one exalts one's own faith and at the same time performs a service to the faith of others. But tolerance as the final goal is a passive interpretation of secularism. India has to move on from tolerance and, with an active social conscience, develop a society neither theocratic nor hostile to religion but rational and scientifically minded, building, in Tagore's words, a *mahajati* based on a broad humanism and the repudiation of all sectarian barriers and prejudices, 'so that high and low, Hindus and Muslims and Christians, all without exception can come together, mingling heart with heart, effort with effort.'[27] There is an echo in this of Rammohun's earliest writing.

[27] Quoted in Sarkar, *The Swadeshi Movement in Bengal*, p. 84.

23

Women and the Law

This is a revised, updated version of a remarkable book which should be read by all who are concerned with the present, and interested in the future, of India.[1] Vasudha Dhagamwar is a scholar who draws on the disciplines of law, history, and sociology; but this book is more than an academic exercise. The writer is driven by an intense commitment which will stir all but the wilfully blind among her readers. She establishes how the law in India during the last two hundred years has been limited by the background and prejudices of the law-makers—British and Indian. But even well-meaning laws are perverted in their implementation by the social norms, often retrograde, of the judges, the police, and the people, and distorted by powerful sections and pressure groups to thwart justice. That this warps our democracy and stands in the way of our achieving social dignity and fairness is the conclusion which should shake us out of the complacency born of our normal platitudinousness.

The British in the nineteenth century, even the best of them like Macaulay, knowing little about India and hardly meeting any Indians, made laws for the Indian people on the basis of their own experiences in Britain and of ideas drawn from their upper-middle-class background. Such laws made paltry sense to the vast majority of Indians who were sunk in poverty and whose social attitudes had nothing in common with those prevalent in elite circles in Britain. This

[1] Vasudha Dhagamwar: *Law, Power and Justice: The Protection of Personal Rights in the Indian Penal Code*, revised edition (Delhi: Sage Publications, in association with The Book Review Literary Trust, 1992).

gap between the ethos of the foreign rulers and that of millions of their local subjects became particularly clear in respect of offences against the person—rape, kidnapping, abduction and slavery—because these crimes, and the laws concerning them, impinge most on ordinary people.

The British law-makers, and the judges who enforced these laws in the years of the Raj, saw the problem of rape in India in terms of men of low caste violating women of higher castes, although far more common were cases of wealthy men of the upper castes forcing themselves on helpless women servants and labourers, and on the wives of those beholden to them for employment. No attention was paid to the character of the rapist, but it was readily assumed that if a woman was proved or suspected to be of loose character, she had consented to rape, kidnapping, or abduction. It was very much a law tilted in favour of men. Nor did the courts take account of social realities, of the timidity of illiterate women and the likelihood of their yielding not just to physical force but to the force of circumstances, and of the difficulties presented by testifying in their own languages and having the evidence translated into English.

In cases of kidnapping and abduction, the Indian Penal Code of 1860 was more concerned with the violation of the property rights of the state or guardian than with the deprivation of the individual's freedom; and this bias was sustained in the attitude of the courts. As for slavery, the British did not abolish the institution of slavery but only made it an offence to carry out any transaction in slaves. It was presumed that, as the man was theoretically free and able to choose, he had chosen to be enslaved.

All this should be of interest only to the sociologist of the day for the laws and the attitudes of the courts could be expected to alter drastically with the coming of Independence. But in fact there has been no marked change since 1947. The laws regarding the person are still interpreted and administered in a manner weighted heavily against women. The comment of Dr Johnson in the eighteenth century about Britain is still valid in present-day India. 'Nature has given women so much power that the Law has very wisely given them very little.' In 1949, the Allahabad high court acquitted several men charged with repeatedly raping a girl aged 12 years on the ground that she was a 'fast' girl and had shown no signs of struggle. In 1970, the supreme court treated lightly a proven case of abduction because the woman concerned had previously had a liaison with the abductor. It was assumed that the fact that he had seduced her earlier gave him the right to do as he liked with her thereafter.

More judgments in rape cases where the supreme court took into account the character of the women involved led ultimately to public agitation. The government thereupon referred the matter to the Law Commission which, in 1980, proposed several amendments which would have tightened the law. But the Act of 1983 failed to incorporate many of these suggestions. It has not been accepted that a woman's character should have no bearing on the case and that silence cannot be interpreted as consent, which must be free and voluntary. The provision that rape cases could be tried *in camera* was intended to protect the women but in fact secrecy has, more often than not, helped the defendants.

So, unimpeded by this act, our courts, headed by the supreme court, have continued on the course of undermining the rights of women and the rule of law in this regard. In 1985, the supreme court reduced a death sentence to life imprisonment as the murdered woman had once been married to the accused. In another case of murder the court again lightened the sentence on the ground that the accused had been upset because his sister had been abandoned by one of the men murdered. In 1987 the sentence of death was changed to life imprisonment because the deceased had been having an affair with a woman related to the accused. It is possible that the judges were on principle opposed to capital punishment. Such an attitude is commendable in itself. But it is deplorable if this position is sought to be cloaked by the assumption that a man has a proprietary interest in an ex-wife or women relatives, and private vengeance is therefore to be treated as a ground for compassion.

The sexual ethic widely prevalent in our country is also disclosed in the attitude to sati. This is one matter where the Indian Penal Code promulgated by the British fully covers the crime, for it stipulates that not the widow but all those involved, be the sati voluntary or involuntary, should be charged with murder. In 1987, Roop Kanwar died on her husband's pyre. One would expect most, if not all, Indians to have been outraged. In fact, members of all political parties, except the two Communist parties, visited the site and even participated in the twelfth day ceremony. Yet there was sufficient protest in the country for the central government to take notice. All that was required was to enforce rigorously the relevant clauses in the Indian penal code. But the government decided on fresh legislation which took no step forward but two steps backward from the penal code. For it was enacted that the woman who was to be a sati shall be punished and the persons involved charged only with abetment to murder. So the poor woman who is almost always pushed on to the pyre and forcibly held down will be the chief accused, and the killers organizing the murder will be held only on a lighter charge. Such is our march into the twenty-first century.

Perhaps it is unfair to cast the blame primarily on the laws and the courts, for their faults and inequities are made possible by social thinking and social morality which in India are grossly backward and inadequate. Slavery, or bonded labour as it is euphemistically termed, is yet to be eradicated in India and takes various forms and is accepted by public opinion. Though there is now a keener conciousness of human rights than before, we still find, scattered round the country, children working long hours in wretched conditions for a miserable pittance, or men and women binding themselves to toil without wages in order to pay off loans. Still extant in the Gwalior area is the old *dhareecha* practice of remarriage of women who are not divorced and whose husbands are alive. On the face of it this suggests an advanced stage of women's rights, but in fact this practice is now exploited by men to arrange the sale of their wives. It is accepted in the area as a part of everyday life and the transactions are written out by lawyers in documents and registered by government servants. That the sale of a human being is a crime and the registered documents have no legal validity appear to deter no one. Rather, these documents are utilized to terrorize the women sold, for they are usually illiterate and a seemingly legal document has an aura of binding legitimacy.

Another variety of cases showing the dichotomy between law and morality in India is provided by the dacoits of the Chambal valley. In 1960, Vinoba Bhave secured the voluntary surrender of some leading dacoits, but soon after dacoity surged again and continues till today. The dacoit has a recognized place in local society and even the victims find excuses for such robbery with violence. There is an established nexus between the dacoits and the police and corruption is the counterpart of robbery. A local saying, popular right down to the 1960s, suggested that one should have three sons: one would be a dacoit, one should join the police, and the third would look after the joint earnings of his brothers. When a dacoit surrenders, he is paid handsomely for rehabilitation, but no compensation is ever given to those who have been robbed. Nor is dacoity confined to the Chambal valley. The current case of Veerappan, who with his gang roams the forests of Tamil Nadu and Karnataka, requires careful scrutiny. Are links with politicians, civil servants, and policemen the prime reason for the immunity he has enjoyed so long and the ease with which he murders so many?

Vasudha Dhagamwar's book is a massive indictment of Indian society and of the men and women who provide leadership to that society. Can it be that, beneath a thin veneer of modernization, a purposeless state functions among a primitive people? Children are sold into prostitution, brides are burnt for dowries, daughters are killed because they wish to marry as they please, women are stoned to death as witches, and activists are gangraped by landlords and policemen. When some prisoners were blinded, the chief minister of Bihar claimed that the action had 'social sanction'. Our laws regarding the person serve power and arrest justice. Even on the occasions when the law wakes up to its real purpose of ensuring fairness, powerful forces, strengthened by backward social norms, see to it that the law fails altogether.

A hundred years ago in Paris, Emile Zola, by the power of his pen, forced a reluctant people to face reality, correct injustice, and behave like decent human beings with a proper scheme of values. One can only hope that Vasudha Dhagamwar will, with this book, render, even in some small measure, a similar service to contemporary India.

24

The English Language in India since Independence—and its Future Role

The place of the English language in India since Independence has to be seen against the background of developments in the years of British rule. Education in the English language had been introduced both to provide recruits for the subordinate services and to teach Indians the rudiments of a culture which was commended as superior to their own. Apart from the question of the impact of foreign influences, the use of the language itself became an issue. The fact that the nationalist idea was being fostered in India by the use of the English language was sufficient evidence to imperial apologists that India was not a nation. To many theorists of nationalism in Europe in the nineteenth and early twentieth centuries language was the crucial test. But to Indians this was a restricted definition based on European experience. They preferred to think of a nation, in Acton's phrase, as a moral and political being and, far from regarding expression of their sentiments in the English language as demeaning, saw an advantage in strengthening their case by utilizing the resources which knowledge of English opened up.

There is no instance in India of such an incident as that of Jean Joseph Rabearivals, the poet of Malagasy who killed himself in 1937 because he could not reconcile his nationalism with the French language and culture in which he was obliged to work. Indians, perhaps because for centuries bilingualism had been the accepted norm among the educated, with knowledge of Sanskrit or Persian along with their own mother-tongue being expected, in the days of British rule saw no contradiction between commitment to their own country and culture and total ease in a foreign language. Tagore was primarily a poet in Bengali but himself translated many of his poems into English. Gandhi transformed the national movement by drawing the illiterate masses into politics and he laid down even in 1921 that one of the essentials of India's freedom was to get rid of what he described as the infatuation for English. But he himself wrote in English clearly and forcefully; and the British authorities in India recognized soon enough to their chagrin that Gandhi expressed himself well in excellent English and had a fine appreciation of the words he used. Nehru took trouble to attain sufficient proficiency in Hindi so as to be able to communicate with large numbers of his people; but it was primarily in English that his thoughts were formulated and expressed. Widely read in English literature, he wrote with tense elegance and control of phrase, was capable on special occasions of superb flights of English prose, and hailed the coming of India's freedom with a passage that has moved into anthologies of English writing.

Yet Nehru awaited with equanimity what he believed would be the quick and natural decline of the English language in a free India. Apart from the small Anglo-Indian minority whose mother tongue it was, to all other Indians English was a foreign language which had spread only because the British had made it the medium of instruction. Like Latin in medieval Europe and Sanskrit and Persian in pre-British India, English had been learnt by a small number in various parts of the country. A new linguistic caste had evolved, isolated from the millions of ordinary men and women. After 1947, Nehru and his colleagues rid themselves of any prejudices born of the feeling that English was the language that had helped the British to hold the empire together. The first generation of independent India's leadership had no such complexes and were of the view that a language belongs to all those who speak it. As language communicates experience, it can transcend the boundaries of the culture of its origin. When, in 1954, an old Irish revolutionary started a letter to Nehru in Gaelic and then switched to English with the remark, 'Forgive me for using the language of the enemy', Nehru's reaction was one of mild and amused surprise. But to him language was a part of the history of a people, each word calling up images, and yet alive and expanding to take new circumstances into account. If a language, while basing itself on its ancient roots and associations, was also receptive to growing needs, it would be strong and vigorous and be an index of the national character. As the whole background of the English language was different and its history unknown to the Indian people, Nehru did not think that it could ever become a living language widely spoken in India. For the educational and cultural development of the masses only the regional languages were suited. Among them the one with the widest range, covering, with its variations, a large part of northern India, was Hindi, and Nehru felt that it should be promoted as the language linking up the whole country. Basic Hindi, with about five thousand words, and borrowing from Urdu, English, and other languages, should be developed and could be picked up easily by most Indians, for the Indian languages are allied to each other.

So Nehru was for gradually abandoning the use of English as an official language. He also expected and even desired it to fade out as the link language in India. He felt that there would be a psychological value in this, for, though not worried about its past ties with imperialism, it had hurt him, in his tours as prime minister to other parts of the world than Britain and the English-speaking countries, to note the surprise and contempt with which the use of English by Indians in conversing with each other was received. It was regarded as a sign of mental degradation. But Nehru conceded that it would be foolish to drop English altogether. It had already gained ground in India, was becoming an important world language and was indispensable for the advance of science and technology to which Nehru attached such importance in building a modern and forward-looking India. So Nehru wished English to be studied as a second language and for most people as a language of comprehension rather than as a language leading on to the study of English literature. Even from the 1930s Nehru had been an exponent of Basic English.

In accord with this reasoning, Nehru supported the provision in the constitution that Hindi would be the official language of the union but English could also be used as the official language for the next fifteen years, that is, till 1965. He, like most others, thought that during that period Hindi would gain general acceptance as well as the strength and suppleness to serve as the common language of India. But the expected did not happen. Hindi perforce made some headway. In the armed services, for example, where even in British days a pidgin Hindi had been in vogue, the words of command were now converted to Hindi, as only the officers understood English. But in most areas of public activity the English language stood its ground. In fact, the enthusiasts for Hindi, finding fifteen years far too long and seeking to displace English well before 1965, achieved the contrary result of giving it new life. Hindi itself did not develop in a way that could be understood by the masses and Nehru was driven to complain that it was often beyond his comprehension. Even government agencies like All India Radio used a very stilted and artificial language, and English words, instead of being incorporated into Hindi, were translated in ways that sounded ridiculous. The non-Hindi-speaking people began to fear that a ban on English even before they had acquired a sufficient knowledge of Hindi would mean that they would be handicapped in the search for employment. The economic dimension of the language problem soon spread out to become a political issue and the agitation against Hindi in southern India posed a threat to Indian unity.

To Nehru it was clear that any decision on this question of Hindi replacing English could not be hustled and would have to emerge on the basis of consent; and the maintenance of national unity was more important than anything else. The tensions that encompassed the demands for linguistic provinces and the problems that followed their creation in the mid-1950s made this clearer than ever. The passions roused in all parts of the country by a narrow love of language and the local languages rather than Hindi providing the challenge to English lessened the sense of community and endangered the national fabric. This was a problem alien to Nehru's understanding, for to him, while language was important, the administrative boundaries of provinces were a marginal problem. But he realized that linguistic rivalries had become a pressing political issue and the stress on regional languages, however justified in itself, was weakening the concept of

India. So he was all the more eager to leave alone the matter of Hindi versus English. If, in their anxiety to hasten what would have been a natural development the supporters of Hindi had adopted poor and self-defeating tactics, Nehru was not pleased with the result but did not regard it as a severe setback. Hindi as it was evolving was neither graceful, artistic, nor generally understood; enthusiasm for Hindi was often a cloak for revivalism and Hindu chauvinism; and if, because of resistance to Hindi the regional languages were to become predominant with no link language at all, it was better to adhere to English as an official language for the whole country, the more so as English was establishing itself as the leading language of the world and was India's main means of access to scientific and technological research. So in 1959 Nehru promised that there would be no imposition of any language by decree and English would remain an associate, additional language for an indefinite period. The final decision on the replacement of English by Hindi would rest with those sections of the Indian people who did not know Hindi. Four years later this assurance was translated into permissive legislation, providing that English 'may' continue to be used after 1965, in addition to Hindi, for the official purposes of the union and in parliament. In 1968 this was further spelt out to stipulate the use of English in addition to Hindi for certain specified official purposes. No time limit was placed for the supplanting of English by Hindi and it could be used indefinitely unless the legislatures of all the non-Hindi-speaking states by resolution demanded otherwise.

Nehru had not been willing to provide an explicit commitment that English would continue as an official language forever. That seemed to him unnecessary and even constitutionally improper; but the supporters of English need have no cause to worry. A mature people acted by consensus on such issues and no government would be so foolish as to create the problem and difficulties which would follow from seeking to secure the acceptance of Hindi by force. Nor did his functional compromise seem to him weighted against Hindi. It was only through the Indian languages, which had deep roots in the minds and hearts of the people, that the national awakening which had taken place in the years before 1947 could be consolidated. But the regional languages, with their limited provenance, would have a restrictive effect. The promotion of Hindi was part of the effort of building the nation, and the life of the nation was much longer than one or two generations. So Hindi could afford to wait.

The result has been that, while Hindi has waited, the number of Indians with a knowledge of English has expanded and amounts to over 4 per cent of the total population. It is now reckoned that about 35 million Indians speak and write English of some type or other. This English-speaking population is spread across the whole country. So English, besides being an associate official language everywhere and the dominant language in the north-eastern states of Nagaland, Meghalaya, and Mizoram, may be described as the only non-regional language in India. It is a link language in more than an administrative sense in that it counters blinkered provincialism. Though there are at least twenty regional variations of English in India, those who speak and write in these slightly different ways can understand each other and form a cultural constituency of their own. It is the language of communication of the civil services, of the managers and senior employees of the public and private sectors of the economy, and of the professions. A uniform law for the country means that it will continue indefinitely, given the state of development of Hindi, in the high courts and the supreme court. The need to avoid intellectual isolation within India as well as from the rest of the world obliges its retention by the academic community. It is the principal medium of higher education and of advanced research in all fields. While Hindi has been introduced as an optional medium in examinations for recruitment to the civil services, its limited vocabulary and the lack of adequate textbooks in that language leave the advantage with candidates opting for answering in English.

That knowledge of English is the passport for employment at higher levels in all fields, is the unavoidable avenue to status and wealth, and is mandatory to all those planning to migrate abroad has meant a tremendous enthusiasm since Independence to study it. Schools which teach in English from the start have proliferated and admission to them is more prized than to those where English is only the compulsory second language. In the years immediately after the British left, standards of English teaching not surprisingly fell; and a quip of those times was that the official language of India was incorrect English. To remedy this, in 1958 an institute for the training of teachers of the English language was set up. Nehru's only proviso in this matter was that the institute should not be headed by an American. Textbooks for teaching in English, adapted to the local context, are now produced in India. Nehru also laid down the policy, which has by and large continued to this day, that no restriction should be placed on the import of books. He overruled recommendations based either on the need to conserve foreign exchange or on the desirability, even on rare occasions, of censorship on moral grounds. He was not happy with the wide circulation in India of *Lady Chatterley's Lover* but vetoed the proposal to ban *Lolita*. There is also today the practice of importing sheets and binding them in India so that many books are much cheaper in India than they are in Britain. The government also subsidizes the reprinting of standard textbooks. To add to all this, piracy, primarily of pulp novels, is rampant. No traveller by air within India can fail to notice the popularity of Mills and Boon and James Hadley Chase, while children with a knowledge of English depend heavily on Enid Blyton and Western comics.

Indian publishers also are not inactive. India ranks as the world's third largest producer of books in English, after the United States and Britain. More books are published annually in English than in all the regional languages taken together. Penguin's have this year started publishing in India two books a month, on Indian themes or by Indian authors. Serious journals of science and scholarship manage to survive despite limited circulation and magazines of popular interest multiply. Of over 20,000 registered newspapers nearly 4000 are in English and are second in number only to those in Hindi. Both radio and television have regular programmes and news services in English and the University Grants Commission sponsors educational features in English daily for one hour on television. Consumerism is promoted by advertisements in English. The film industry caters to the large majority in Hindi and the regional languages; but a film in English produced in India with Indian actors could be seen in London this summer and Mr Keating's Inspector Ghote and other characters bring home vividly the nuances of Indian English as it is spoken. Amateur theatricals, so prominent in the days of the British in India, survive in the big cities; but more widespread is rock music. In India today, the words of these songs are better known than the works of Shakespeare.

All this wide and varied use of English cannot cloud the fact that it is essentially the language of the Indian establishment. In India's history language has been a marker of the culture, and of the 'higher' culture: first Sanskrit, then Persian, and, for the last 150 years, English. It has been associated with modernization, though, as the example of Japan proves, knowledge of a European language is not necessary for this purpose. Even today, English in India is the badge of privilege of a small minority dispersed over the entire country. It can be said that English is the carrier of a national culture as against the limited stretch of even Hindi, let alone the other regional languages; though even here there is a problem. Any such national culture in the English medium in India tends to get weakened at the roots; for there is a tenacious indigenous culture that goes back to pre-British days, and there are inherent difficulties in understanding one culture in the language of another. Philosophers, for example, have found it not easy to translate precisely into English terms like dharma and nirvana. Perhaps I might also cite an example from history, where transfer of ideas has given rise to novel situations. At Amritsar the worship is of the Granth Saheb, the sacred scripture of the Sikhs; and the temple was known as the Durbar Saheb. But it was the dome of the shrine that caught the British eye, and the whole complex came to be known as the Golden Temple. The name has continued to the present day, with the result that attention has shifted to the buildings rather than remain with the texts and the sanctum where they are housed. English has also helped to extend the dimensions of the regional languages. Many creative writers in the Indian languages have a knowledge of English and have taken advantage of this. The forms, structure, and content of contemporary literature in these languages show the impact of the English language and writing, old and new. Even the novel is an imported literary form. But these assets are heavily shadowed by the division in India—which the use of English consolidates—between the few who govern and the many who are governed. English is no longer the language of empire or of a culture which claims to be superior. But it is the language of the ruling class. While the Indian culture in the English language provides all those responsive to it with a sense of community, it cuts them off from the vast number who do not know the language. The separation is constantly deepened, with the medium of English leading to better schools and colleges, greater opportunities, and a higher economic and social status. This is an unnatural situation in a working democracy based on adult suffrage. With politics in India broadening down from Delhi to the states and the increasing involvement of the population in the rural areas, English-speaking India and politically-conscious India diverge more and more. In itself a healthy development, this adds to the tension between the minority at the top who know English and the many millions, armed with the vote, who do not.

This would soon spell the end of English in India—if politics provided all the answers. Nehru himself believed that English would not so much be atrophied by the democratic process as wither because of malnutrition. A living language has its roots in the masses and any language without such sustenance would rapidly lose vitality. Certainly, to many Indians before 1947 English was an alien language in which they were compelled to study a foreign literature. Skylarks and daffodils, sceptred isles and country churchyards, meant very little to them and stirred no memories; and it is partly this which Mr Muggeridge has in mind when he speaks of enraged and unemployed graduates chasing the British out of India, hurling after them curses and copies of *The Oxford Book of English Verse*. But with Independence, English, even if it could not be expected to become a language of mass communication, began to sink roots into the upper layers of the Indian soil. A few Indians still write English as it should be written and do so with skill and grace.

Why do they wish to do so? Yeats was sure that only in one's own language could one write with music and vigour. Joseph Conrad, among the greatest of those novelists who have written in English which was not their mother tongue, has a chilling story called *Amy Foster*. Here a Slav peasant, shipwrecked on the English coast, lives for years in a village in Kent. Everyone shuns him except a dull girl who marries him; but even she takes her child and leaves him when, in a fever, he speaks in his own language. Bertrand Russell, who knew Conrad, thinks there could be something of Conrad himself in this story: the loneliness in his life, and the strong will rather than the aptitude which underlay his work. If, then, writing in a language which is not their own does not come easily even to the best, why do so many persevere in this effort? Joseph Brodsky has placed such writers in three categories: necessity, superhuman ambition, and the need for further estrangement. The best Indian writers in English do so out of necessity, not because English was once the imperial and is now an official language, nor because they are in exile in Britain, but because it is in that language that they can best express themselves. They are not even aware that they are writing in a foreign language. Published recently was a distinguished novel in verse, set in California but written by an Indian; this year we have had some highly rated novels by Indians; and most of these authors are very young. So it is not just the old generation, educated in the days of the Raj that finds English easy to handle. The other two categories of Mr Brodsky claim some Indians. Eager to secure a world audience or distance themselves from their own country, they seek to write what may be called British Standard English and sometimes do not quite succeed. These bring to mind Gordon Bottomley's sneer of Matthew Arnold in a sari. They give up an inherited identity for a literary tradition in which they are not fully absorbed. But most Indians who today speak and write English do so with an authentic Indian voice. To them English is no longer an uncompromisingly foreign tongue. An Australian writer, Sylvia Lawson, has defined what she terms the paradox of her country's culture: 'To know enough of the metropolitan world, colonials must, in limited ways at least, move and think internationally; to resist it strongly enough for the colony to cease to be colonial and become its own place, they must become nationalists.' This paradox becomes even sharper for Indians using English, for most of them have a language of their own; but the best of them combine a distinctive feel of the Indian experience with a loyalty to the best traditions of English literature, bring a worldview to bear on their home country, and keep exclusiveness under control but without betraying their inheritance.

India is not a country with a large community of British settlers who might have resisted the influence of the local context. Nor is English in India, as in the Caribbean, the sole means of communication. The languages of India have a history which, in most cases, goes back over a thousand years; and, just as English has influenced them during the last hundred years, they now influence English. They give it an indigenous flavour and promote a new idiom. Gandhi, for example, spoke of a Himalayan blunder. A character in one of R.K. Narayan's novels says how fond he is of the sound of curds falling on warm rice. An Indian author based in the West has told us that, in a novel published this year, he first wrote of a peg to hang ideas on and then, realizing that a peg had no meaning to Indian readers, revised it to read a bamboo pole to hang ideas on. Some politicians in India are described as crocodiles in loincloths, a phrase that would evoke no real image in Britain. Glossaries are now being published of words of common usage in Indian English, such as bedsheets, shirting, suiting—the list is constantly growing. Many such words, and even the grammar often used, rouse associations with the Indian background. The load of English literature is put down and there is no servitude to Fowler. The inability to keep in touch with the changes taking place in English usage in Britain is compensated by accord with changes taking place in various parts of India. It is Indian literature that is written in the English language. It is also a new chapter in English literature.

In 1901, when Queen Victoria died, an anonymous loyalist published a couplet in an English newspaper in Calcutta:

Dust to dust, ashes to ashes,
Into the grave the great Queen dashes.

Here a knowledge of words is combined with a total lack of sense of the English language. Over seventy years later an Indian poet, capable of writing correct idiomatic English, published what he termed a 'Very Indian Poem in Indian English':

You are all knowing, friends,
What sweetness is in Miss Pushpa,
I don't mean only external sweetness
But internal sweetness,

Miss Pushpa is smiling and smiling
Even for no reason
But simply because she is feeling . . .

There is, of course, an element of parody in this, reminiscent of a performance of Peter Sellers; but the poem also conveys the confidence of Indians capable of writing Standard English while deliberately using English not for Western audiences but to talk to each other, drawing vigour from Indian life and extending English, as James Joyce had done, to convey their own experiences and consciousness. Perhaps there is an advantage in this even for readers in Britain. Graham Greene has said that it was by reading R.K. Narayan that he knew what it was like to be an Indian; for it could be that no one can write in depth about a foreign country. Even E.M. Forster could only write about the effect of India on his fellow countrymen and women.

What of the future? It is manifest that English with its variants has found a permanent place in India. There will always be a few who will speak and write it by the highest standards, with a full understanding of English literature and an awareness of the historical and social contexts. These writers and scholars ask for no concessions. But many more will use English as a matter of convenience, for communicating across the country, keeping in touch with the outside world and remaining abreast of developments in all fields. Indians find English pliable enough to convey their own moods and approaches. Recourse to English no longer suggests deracination or cultural displacement. There is no strong counterpart in India to the growing feeling in parts of Africa that writing in English is irrelevant to African culture. Plenty of Indian writers of talent and passion find English a language in which they can deal adequately with the special realities of the country. Standard English it may not always be, but alive it is and will continue to be.

The demand for knowledge of English will increase and, to cater to this—in addition to convents, international schools, and private schools with English as the medium of instruction—the government has begun to set up model secondary schools in every district, with teaching in both Hindi and English. Over two hundred such schools have already been opened and the rest are expected to start functioning within the next two years. If the scheme works well—and it is too early yet to say that it will—it will ensure the spread of English to the rural areas and bring within its reach bright students who could not normally afford an English education. In the schools already established, nearly half the number of pupils are on scholarships and from families below the poverty line. The English language taught here is a language of comprehension, to enable the students to read quickly, speak with facility, and write with accuracy rather than to make them conversant with English history and literature. The effort is to move away from the British cultural background, relate the English language to the Indian setting, and concentrate on the learning process. Like the teaching of foreign languages in the European Economic Community, teachers of English in India are encouraged to attach greater importance to fluency than to proficiency in grammar. The main purpose of knowing English is to understand and to be understood. So, in consequence, while Standard English is taught, the drift of the students is towards Indian English.

However, even Indian English is not, and can never be, the first language in India, and no one expects that at any time all the millions of the Indian people will speak and write it. English is, and will remain, the pan-Indian language of the elite; it cannot function as the vehicle of mass culture. This in itself restricts the scope for the growth of English, for it cannot develop in the ordinary circumstances of the day-to-day life of the common people. The contrast is clear when one looks at the vitality of the regional languages. It is also these languages, the mother tongues of the masses, that form the best media for primary as well as adult education. That a child is best taught at the start in its own language is now not disputed. Lord Bullock, in his report in 1975 on education in Britain, has stated this clearly: 'No child should be expected to cast off the language and culture of the home as he crosses the school threshold.' A language is most easily learnt when it is in tune with the social context. To teach an Indian child in English at the primary stage perpetuates a segregative system of education, strengthens distinctions of class and status, and warps the mind. Failure to resort to regional languages in literacy campaigns also hampers their success. The oral tradition of learning is very strong in India, in the not limited sense of memorizing texts, but the open oral tradition of transmission of epics, myth, and social meaning, with constant additions and amendments in tune with historical change. English cannot fit into this form of oral tradition. If priority be not given to the regional languages at the primary and adult levels, one may well find that, by the year 2000, while those speaking English in India are almost as many as the total population of Britain, more than half of the world's illiterate population in the age-group of 15 to 19 will be in India.

English will continue to be spoken in the two houses of parliament and some legislatures in the states; but it will gradually give way as the main medium of Indian politics to the local languages. The natural culmination of democracy is the general use of the mother tongues. But paradoxically, even as English recedes as the language of politics, the question of language is cooling down as a political issue. The radio, and television even more, are diffusing knowledge of English, Hindi, and the language of the area and thus achieving imperceptibly what governments and politicians had struggled in vain to do. Hindi as the single official language of India is a receding goal; but its spread through the air and on the screen does not arouse aggressive antagonism. Basic Hindi, or Hindustani, spoken in films is now being understood throughout the country. Nehru was right not to seek prompt and permanent solutions but to let events shape themselves. Political, economic, and social developments determine the spread or arrest of languages. So India moves pragmatically and quietly to the greater use of the regional languages in democratic politics, primary education, and the battle against illiteracy; and basic Hindi becomes more widely known in areas where it is not the mother tongue but does not oust English. With languages not competing with each other, English comes into the picture as a compulsory second language at the stage of secondary education, and children come to its study with the added advantage of familiarity with their own language and literature. Indians will also continue to use English, with their own accents and idioms, as an additional official language, and as the language of higher education and advanced research. It will serve as a vehicle for transcultural understanding and as a catalytic agent for other Indian literatures; and it will remain the chief means for the growing middle class of communicating among themselves across the vast expanse of India.

These possibilities need also to be set in the wider context of the future of English in the world—and in Britain. We live more and more in a visual age. With computer programmes, cognitive revolutions, and artificial intelligence, non-verbal language may grow in significance. Already in India young film-makers tend to rely more on images than on words; and recently a popular film has been made which dispenses almost wholly with a script. The silent movies are with us again. An organization in the United States is today campaigning to have English made the national language by an amendment of the constitution and the campaign is meeting with resistance. And in Britain itself, now a multicultural society, with a variety of ethnic groups, some of them speaking their mother tongues and each developing its own version of English, notions of British identity are changing; and Standard English may itself suffer marked changes and its use contract. For, as Raymond Williams repeatedly pointed out, it is the spoken rather than the written language which is the real source of authority, and the other derives from it. Who knows—sometime in the next century a speaker in Cambridge may be struggling to deal for one hour with the topic: 'The English Language in Britain—and its Future Role'.

PART IV

LIVES, LITERATURE, AND CRICKET

25

25

The Fairy Tale of Ramanujan

The broad outlines of the life of Srinivasa Ramanujan are well known throughout India. His story has all the ingredients of a tragic romance and haunts the imagination of everyone who has heard it. Yet, till now we have had no satisfactory biography, thoroughly researched, placing Ramanujan firmly in the shifting contexts and entering into his mind so as to explain why he functioned as he did.

One cannot say this latest effort by Robert Kanigel fulfils these requirements.[1] Kanigel, a journalist specializing in science subjects and, we are told, a university lecturer (in what?), has certainly worked hard. He has spent years accumulating material in Tamil Nadu and in Cambridge and speaking to everyone with even the remotest connection to Ramanujan. But he is not familiar with the background in India and in Britain; and he does not expect his readers to be.

The bloated book is intended for American audiences, and unsophisticated ones at that. He instructs us how to pronounce names like Ramanujan and Pachaiyappa's and words such as Michaelmas. Pages are devoted to explaining the game of cricket and the Cambridge tripos examination and a beginner's guide is provided to the customs and traditions of Indian society. At the slightest opportunity Kanigel goes off at tangents to discuss in detail events and personalities with only a marginal bearing on Ramanujan's life. The book cries out for a competent copy-editor.

[1] Robert Kanigel, *The Man Who Knew Infinity: A Life of the Genius Ramanujan* (New York: Scribners, 1991).

On Ramanujan himself Kanigel meanders often into shallow psychoanalysis. A subject which is a gift to biographers has been handled in an unmemorable way and the book is more akin to a movie script than to an intermesh of life, work, and settings which would increase our understanding of an unusual personality who has been variously described as the greatest mathematician of the country, the greatest pure mathematician since Isaac Newton, and the greatest mathematician produced by India in the last thousand years. Maybe it is a film which Kanigel has in mind for he says that Ramanujan's life seems 'the stuff of cinema'. So this book may at some stage be transposed on the screen and we may have a product on the lines of the lives of Louis Pasteur and Emile Zola. It is a pity Paul Muni is dead; he had the build for the title role.

Yet, from the masses of material, relevant and irrelevant, thrown together in this book, one can extricate enough to form our own picture of this genius with the dark burning eyes who set aside all norms. There is of course in India a long tradition of creativity in mathematics. As far back as 500 BC Vedanga Jyotisha asserted that 'as are the crests of peacocks, as are the gems on the heads of snakes, so is mathematics at the head of all knowledge.' Since then the discipline has remained alive in our country, making contributions such as the numerals and the concept of zero, which the world has adopted, and occasionally producing giants in the field.

But there was no genetic reason to expect the muse to favour a lower-middle-class family in Kumbakonam, into which Ramanujan was born in December 1887. He did well at school but, once he came to college, became so obsessed with mathematics that he neglected other subjects, with the result that he twice failed what was then known as the First examination in Arts (F.A.). With the aid of an outmoded textbook which he had come upon by chance, he spent long hours working out for himself on a slate results which had been established much earlier in Europe.

This and not his early death was the real tragedy of Ramanujan. Mathematicians are usually at their best in their twenties. So at the zenith of his powers Ramanujan was wasting his time, 'pitting his brains' as Hardy, who later discovered him put it, 'against the accumulated wisdom of Europe.' But it may have served the purpose of honing his genius, for Ramanujan went on to fill several notebooks with what were to prove his own contributions to knowledge. But what was repetitive and what was original he was not himself aware.

Mathematics on its own, however, while solacing to his mind, brought in no cash. Ramanujan's strong-willed mother saw to it that he married, when 21, a girl aged 9; and the family now looked to him for an income. He tried private tuition, but his mind moved at levels so far above examination standards that his pupils did not take long to cry off. It looked as if his bubbling genius would be smothered by poverty and the mindless officialdom and educational system of the *raj*. But there was one Indian member of the provincial civil service in Madras whom chance brought in contact with Ramanujan and who deserves to be remembered. R. Ramachandra Rao, the collector of Nellore district, was interested in mathematics and felt, after seeing some of Ramanujan's work, that he deserved to be encouraged. So he paid Ramanujan out of his own pocket Rs 25 a month for three years—which in those days was enough to sustain Ramanujan—and then saw to it that he was provided with the post of a clerk in the Madras Port Trust. It is for this, more than anything else, that that institution will be remembered by posterity.

Meantime, the outpourings of formulae and theorems continued and came to the notice of British officials, who passed them on to some academic colleagues for appraisal. Was Ramanujan a fraud, a crank, an autist—or a genius? Was he purloining ideas and equations from published works and, in the welter of his confused calculations, passing them off as his own? Was he an eccentric playing round with numbers and, by the law of averages, proving sometimes right and sometimes wrong? Was he one of nature's freaks, not uncommon, an 'idiot savant', whose mind could work out in a twinkling the most complicated sums but which was substandard in almost everything else? Or was he that rare phenomenon, an untutored genius who, given the opportunity, would blaze new trails and take the discipline forward by unimaginable lengths?

Nobody, British or Indian, in Madras who studied his notebooks was quite sure. One British mathematician could not set aside the nagging thought that Ramanujan might be no more than a 'calculating boy', while another came to the cautious conclusion that Ramanujan was 'evidently a man with a taste for mathematics and with some ability.' There was clearly no hope of a breakthrough in India and Ramanujan, egged on by some friends, sent excerpts from his notebooks to recognized mathematicians in Cambridge. The first two recipients, to their later embarrassment, made no response; so Ramanujan, unshaken in his self-confidence, mailed the excerpts to Godfrey Hardy at Trinity College.

From this point Kanigel's book becomes virtually a dual biography and with some reason, for without Hardy there would have been no Ramanujan as the world knows him. Hardy was a younger man than his two colleagues who had ignored Ramanujan, had no racial prejudices, tended to radical views, and was probably a sexual dissenter. He studied carefully the material sent to him by Ramanujan and, not wishing to rely solely on his own judgement, called in Littlewood, a fellow mathematician at Trinity. They found that some of Ramanujan's conclusions were well known in Europe, while others were presented without proof. It has been suggested that Ramanujan deliberately withheld the proof for fear that his work would be stolen by others. But this interpretation does him an injustice.

In fact, Ramanujan's mind functioned in a manner which is by no means uncommon. As every creative thinker knows, after hard toil conclusions often spring out seemingly from nowhere. Intuition is not in contrast to the intellect, but the crown of the mental process, a completion of its labour. To Hardy, trained in Western systems of thought which give emphasis to critical intelligence and step-by-step analysis, Ramanujan's ways of work at first sight appeared bewildering. But the continuity between intellect and intuition, while accepted more easily in India, is not unknown in Europe and it is generally recognized that the deepest truths are frequently known through intuitive apprehension, after much previous study. Intuition does not supplant reason but supplements and rounds it off. Sir Peter Medawar, for example, the Nobel prizeman who scorned what he termed 'philosophy fiction' and described it as an 'elevated kind of barminess', yet conceded that the necessity of reason did not mean the sufficiency of reason and recognized that in science a creative imagination was the privilege of the rare spirit who achieves in a blaze of intuition what the rest strive for by analytic industry. Ramanujan was one of those rare spirits.

Indeed, Ramanujan's orthodox Hindu background ensured that unfamiliarity with known knowledge and reliance on insight posed no problems. He played with numbers, each one of which, as has been said, was his personal friend, with the certainty that he was unravelling the mysteries of the Vedantic universe. He dwelt in a realm where the mathematical and the philosophical worlds were one, and his thought and his beliefs flowed into each other. Like Newton, he saw no conflict between astrology and pure mathematics. An equation, he is said to have observed, had no meaning unless it expressed a thought of God. The zero he saw as the representation of Absolute Reality and Infinity was the myriad representations of that Reality.

When Hardy asserted that Ramanujan was no mystic, he was right in the sense that Ramanujan had had and sought no mystical experience more positive than the conviction that the deity appeared in his dreams pointing the ways in which, it must be said, Ramanujan himself was inclined to go. But Hardy went too far when he claimed that Ramanujan's religion was a matter of observance and not of faith and that religion, except in a strictly material sense, played no important part in his life. In addition to his strict adherence to ritual and prescribed practice, Ramanujan was content, till almost the very end, in the unbroken cocoon of his Vedantic beliefs. When he remarked to Hardy that all religions seemed to him more or less equally true he was not denying religious creeds of every kind but stating a basic concept of Hinduism that there are many paths to God. So too, because a commitment to non-violence was an inherent part of his inherited outlook, he declined to act on the suggestion of his British sponsors and undertake any work related to the First World War. It was only in the last months of his life, when he resented a fate which had doomed him to an early death, that he moved away from conventional Hinduism and replied sharply to a mention of gods and temples that 'it was foolish talk and they were only devils.'

'Indianility', to use the quaint word coined by Ramachandra Rao, was at the core of Ramanujan's personality. In the case of Mozart, another young and tragic genius, an understanding of his life does not help much in the interpretation of his music; but with Ramanujan his life is relevant to the assessment of his achievement. His study of mathematics was integrated with his philosophy of life. So too his inborn confidence saved him from complexes created by the colonial situation and he took almost for granted, and as his due, the support of Englishmen like Hardy. That support came when Hardy, convinced that Ramanujan's work merited further investigation, first requested a colleague on a visit to Madras to seek out Ramanujan and give a first-hand report, and then arranged for Ramanujan to move to Cambridge.

The five years at Trinity College, from 1914 to 1919, are as much the story of the vindication of Hardy as the triumph of Ramanujan. Hardy was by nature withdrawn and Kanigel is persuasive in contending that there was not between these two men, especially at the start, the considerate cordiality such as would have made Ramanujan feel fully at home in strange surroundings. But from the point of view of his work Ramanujan could not have hoped for more. Hardy, whatever his doubts earlier, now recognized that he had imported to Cambridge a raw mind of astonishing individuality and power. Years later, when shown the only photograph of Ramanujan that exists, that taken in 1919 for his passport, Hardy observed: 'He looks rather ill but he looks all over the genius he was'—and of that he had always been certain from the time he met Ramanujan. He collaborated with Ramanujan, encouraged him to work on his own lines, bolstered his self-confidence, and did not smother the fires of intuitive insight by insisting on detailed proof. He knew by now that there was much to be said, even in mathematics, for 'thinking vaguely' and taking at times leaps of the imagination. As for recognition, Hardy first secured for the failed student from Madras a degree from Cambridge and then the Fellowship of the Royal Society and, on the second attempt, a fellowship at Trinity College. The unknown scribbler of numbers on a slate in India had in five years established himself as a world figure. Yet, despite this unprecedented acclaim, during these years depression was for Ramanujan never far away. He rarely left his rooms and was not very comfortable in them. Being for long unaware that one slept under and not on top of blankets, he shivered at nights unnecessarily from the cold. He never got on personal terms with British families whose habits, as he understood them, he found repellent. Once an Englishwoman remarked to him that the trouble with the working classes was that they never bathed. On Ramanujan looking disgusted, she added that the English people he mixed with were sure to be having daily baths. 'You mean', asked Ramanujan, 'you bathe only once a day?'

Indian students at Cambridge, proud of his growing reputation, sought him out and a few, knowing his strict vegetarian habits, even offered to cook for him. But Ramanujan, sensitive and touchy, declined these offers. Trinity College, which has always boasted of one of the best kitchens in Oxbridge, would gladly have provided him with special, sumptuous meals; but Ramanujan hardly if ever ate in college. He obviously liked good food, though his tastes were bizarre. Stuffed aubergines fried in oil are a South Indian delicacy but Ramanujan, we are told, liked to eat them raw. However, such treats were beyond reach in wartime Cambridge. Ramanujan's diet consisted usually of rice with pickles or chilli powder; and sometimes, when immersed in work, he lived for days on poppadums. He even occasionally invited Indian friends to meals cooked by him and was greatly offended if their enthusiasm after such repasts was not great. On a visit to Liverpool he with great courage drank a cup of Ovaltine; caught immediately after in an air raid, he regarded it as divine punishment for consuming a beverage which contained egg powder.

On top of all this, throughout these years Ramanujan received hardly any letters from his wife. His possessive mother intercepted all correspondence between the married couple. So loneliness, malnutrition, and a feeling of being neglected led to a sickness which was diagnosed as tuberculosis, and Ramanujan spent the last years of the war in and out of hospitals and nursing homes. In a mood of hypochondriac despair, early in 1918 he threw himself in front of a train on the London underground and was saved only by an alert guard switching off the current and the train stopping a few feet ahead of Ramanujan. Arrested for attempted suicide, his release was secured by Hardy's double lie—that Ramanujan was a Fellow of the Royal Society (he was elected only a few months later) and that Fellows were immune from arrest. The police were not taken in but, aware that Ramanujan was a distinguished mathematician, let him go.

Back in Madras in 1919, Ramanujan at last stood up to his mother, insisted that his wife stay with him and, though critically ill, continued to work on mock theta functions, which were to be his last distinctive contribution to the subject. He was now free of financial problems and even wrote to the University of Madras, which was paying him a regular stipend, that it need not give him as much as it was doing. But, to quote Aldous Huxley's words about D.H. Lawrence, the miracle was at an end, the flame guttering to extinction. On April 26, 1920, it was quenched.

Today, over seventy years after his death, Ramanujan still evokes a sense of unmeasurable loss. There is always a tinge of sadness to the departure of young genius even if, as Hardy has consoled us, Ramanujan's best work had probably already been done. Past the peak perhaps; but his mind had continued to function far above ordinary standards. What he did achieve is still being studied as suggesting new lines of thought; and his work has been found useful in a variety of ways—the development of computers, the treatment of cancer, and the making of blast furnaces, plastics, and telephone cables.

So who knows what more Ramanujan would have done? A sense of incompleteness will always hang around Ramanujan. To fellow-Indians he provides feelings both of pride and of shame. In an era of colonial rule, he gave his people reason for self-esteem. With an awareness of his powers and a boundless confidence, he secured commendation which was universal and without a trace of condescension. But his people, barring a few individuals, would have let him remain a forgotten victim of circumstances, and it was no thanks to them that he had worked out his destiny. Ramanujan is a symbol of national pride—and of guilt.

26

The Pursuit of Science

This biography of Subrahmanyan Chandrasekhar, generally regarded as the most distinguished living theoretical astronomer, deserves to be read widely and not just by professional scientists.[1]

Chandrasekhar's researches during the last sixty years in physics, astrophysics, and applied mathematics are laid out in eight books and six volumes of selected papers; and it has been calculated that if all the formulae, equations, and texts in his books and articles are put end to end, they would cover the distance from the earth to the moon. All this is obviously beyond the comprehension of most of us; and, while Wali necessarily touches on the various aspects of Chandrasekhar's work, laypersons need only grasp the core of his major contributions to knowledge. This he announced to the world in 1935 and for it he received the Nobel prize nearly fifty years later. A densely-packed star is known as a white dwarf. Chandrasekhar discovered that all stars do not become white dwarfs, for if the mass of a star exceeds a certain limit—the Chandrasekhar limit—the star becomes unstable, collapses under the pressure of gravitation, and creates a black hole. This conclusion he reached not by observation but by mathematical calculations; and its validity has been borne out by later research by others.

Wali's biography, however, is more than a mere record of Chandrasekhar's achievements. What makes the book of interest to the

[1] Kameshwar C. Wali, *Chandra: A Biography of S. Chandrasekhar* (Delhi: Viking, Penguin India, 1991).

general reader is that it spreads out into an effort to trace the evolution of Chandrasekhar's working style, the development of his personality, and the influences which have affected his life. He is not a scientist working on the frontiers of knowledge and opening up new fields for study. Rather, he moves into a known area, outlines the present state of our understanding, tries to add to it and round off the subject. Having mastered one field, he then moves on. He has described himself as a lonely wanderer in the byways of science, searching for completeness and perspective. In science, it has been said, there are two kinds of persons, those who write the first sentence and those who write the last. Chandrasekhar belongs to the second category. He is a systematizer more than an explorer. He is not so much a pioneer as a provider of coherent accounts with form, order, and structure.

What give Chandrasekhar's work special attractiveness are his literary graces and allusions and his aesthetic sensitivity. His single-mindedness in scientific research has not meant isolation from humanist influences. He is familiar with English poetry and the Russian novel, takes trouble about writing even the most severely technical pieces, and once gave a lecture comparing aspects of creativity in Shakespeare, Newton, and Beethoven. He is also captivated, as are many other scientists, by the beauty produced by harmony in nature, and he wound up his address accepting the Nobel prize with the translation of two Latin sayings: 'The simple is the seal of the true', and 'Beauty is the splendour of truth.'

Like most seekers of knowledge, Chandrasekhar set out on his long trek with a deep sense of inadequacy. 'I feel at times', he wrote in 1931, 'that my heart will break by the oppression of my ignorance.' Thereafter the steady pace of his intellectual efforts has at no time slackened. He has, for more than half a century, dedicated himself to scientific endeavour without thought of what it may bring him, working steadfastly with an overawing sense of purpose solely to gain knowledge. A mentor and friend, Edward Milne, himself a distinguished astrophysicist, summed this attitude up in words which could be a paraphrase of the Bhagavad Gita: 'It is right to have ambitions; life would lose its savour without them; but that man really achieves who can continue to work whether his ambitions show signs of realization or not.' So, while all the top honours of science have, over the years, come Chandrasekhar's way, he has not lost his head over them or at any point rested on his successes. Even the award of the Nobel prize led him to remark that it was the judgement of posterity that really mattered and there was in general no correlation between the judgement of future generations and that of one's contemporaries.

A strong sense of detachment has developed in Chandrasekhar as the years have passed; but along with this, and more surprisingly considering his stature as a scientist and the magnitude of his achievements, he confesses to a feeling of disappointment. From the start he had known that the sustained intensity of his labours would exact its price. 'I have learned to realize', he wrote to his father in 1936, 'more and more that scholarship demands its own sacrifice and the intellectual interests outgrow—rather, necessitate the sacrifice of—other considerations.' The epilogue of Wali's book, which consists of a record of conversations with Chandrasekhar in recent years, ends on a similar, sad note. All that he has done does not seem to him very much, and his hope in his youth for contentment and a peaceful outlook on life as a result of pursuing the goal of knowledge has remained unanswered. He admits that the sense of harmony, which had been his objective in earlier days, has eluded him. Now he is even doubtful if his goals were the right ones. The pursuit of science at the expense of other personal aspects of his life might not have been justified, not so much for himself but more for those close to him. Surrounded by a sense of solitude despite a glittering career, he concludes that a fulfilled life is not necessarily one in which you pursue certain goals; there must be other things.

To understand better this feeling of desolation amid resounding success, one should perhaps look at Chandrasekhar's personal background. Born in a middle-class family of Tamil Nadu, he was brought up in an atmosphere where primacy was given to intellectual achievement and scientific research. C.V. Raman was his paternal uncle but Chandrasekhar was taught to stand on his own feet and not to seek to blossom under Raman's patronage. Studying in Madras at the Hindu High School and later at the Presidency College, Chandrasekhar stood out as a mathematician of brilliant promise and, while still an undergraduate, published a paper in the *Proceedings* of the Royal Society in London. He then went on to Cambridge, to Trinity College where, a few years earlier, Ramanujan had blazed a trail of glory and whose memory Chandrasekhar helped to foster and whose widow he rescued from dire poverty. For six years at Cambridge, from 1930 to 1936, the emotional centre of Chandrasekhar's life was science. But no Indian of that generation could escape the pull of politics. Jawaharlal Nehru was a compulsive hero, and Chandrasekhar was among those students who in 1927 was fined for missing classes in order to be at a public meeting addressed by Nehru. Three years later Chandrasekhar came in direct contact with the seamy side the Raj when an Englishwoman refused to travel in the same railway carriage with him. In Britain too he could not escape racial prejudice; and in Cambridge, while fellow-scientists treated Chandrasekhar as an intellectual peer, there was not much support among them for India's right to freedom.

For the most part, therefore, Chandrasekhar kept his views on this subject to himself; but it is a pity that Wali does not spell out these views in detail. We learn that, on a visit to the Soviet Union in 1934, Chandrasekhar was impressed by the sight of the Red Square in Moscow at midnight, and Wali suggests that the favourable impression was created at least in part by Chandrasekhar's political leanings at that time. Does this mean that, in addition to his sympathy with the Indian nationalist struggle, Chandrasekhar was also inclined to left-wing views, so prevalent in Cambridge in the 1930s, on economic and social matters? A comment to his father in November 1935 hints at this. 'In the real world', he wrote, 'the poor are always punished, the idealists are always stoned, and students always caricatured and justice never wins.' But it would be worthwhile to know more and for certain.

Clearly, despite the recognition he had received, Chandrasekhar was not enamoured of the civilization and the material attractions of the West. He was conscious, as he phrased it, of the 'very fine cultural atmosphere' which had wrapped him since his childhood, and in 1936, when he came to India and married someone whom he had known for long, it would seem that, though he had planned only a short stay, he would have settled down in India if he had been made an offer suitable to his talents and aptitudes. Cambridge had not given him a permanent post; Eddington, at that time the leader in the field of astronomy, while personally friendly, had ridiculed his work; other European scientists agreed privately with Chandrasekhar, yet were unwilling to say so publicly; and in the United States he had accepted only a temporary assignment. But India at that time had nothing to offer and Chandrasekhar went to Chicago for what was to prove a permanent exile.

This, for a person of his cast of mind and spirit, has not proved easy. He was hurt by some episodes of racial discrimination; and then, with the war in Europe and the British government and Indian nationalism set on a collision course, India was much maligned. Chandrasekhar and his wife tried, with no great success, to build a mental wall of self-defence. Once the United States was directly involved in the war, Chandrasekhar devoted considerable time to ballistic research and reluctantly agreed to join the atom bomb project. But the fact that he was an Indian citizen raised problems of security; and by the time clearance was obtained Chandrasekhar had changed his mind and pulled out. Here again one wishes Wali had told us more. Was it merely because the war was drawing to an end and Chandrasekhar did not wish to disrupt his work at Chicago that he did not go to Los Alamos—or did he, as one suspects, have objections on principle to the making of an atom bomb?

Even in Chicago Chandrasekhar was subjected to administrative pinpricks and minor humiliations; and when he came on a short visit to India in 1951 Homi Bhabha offered him a post at the Tata Institute of Fundamental Research. Chandrasekhar did not pursue this and, years later, said he was not absolutely certain he had been right in not having done so. This would certainly seem to be one of the turning points in his personal history when history, in Taylor's phrase, failed to turn. It is instructive to compare the careers of Bhabha and Chandrasekhar. They were virtually of the same age, worked at Cambridge in the golden age of science in the 1930s, and were both elected to the Royal Society at about the same time in the early

1940s. Then their ways separated. Chandrasekhar lived abroad a life dedicated to pure science, reached the heights, and has confessed to a sense of disappointment. Bhabha returned to India, moved away from research and the prizes that that offered, and spent his time in building up the Atomic Energy Commission and providing scope for fundamental research in his own country. He died suddenly in an air crash with his work in a sense half-finished; but there is no reason to believe he was in any way frustrated. In contrast, Chandrasekhar has acknowledged that he would have been satisfied with half his scientific work if he could have served the Indian scientific community at least to half the extent he had served the American scientific community, because in total terms for the future it would have meant far more for Indian than for American science.

In 1952 Chandrasekhar and his wife decided to become American citizens. His father was not happy; nor, it would appear, was Chandrasekhar. 'Life here', he had written to his sisters a year earlier, 'in spite of its wholesome climate for my intellectual work, has the quality of distilled water, and I feel curiously desiccated.' His decision was dictated mainly by the practical considerations that he and his wife were putting down roots in the United States and becoming involved in its domestic politics. Offers still came to him from India—the vice-chancellorship of the Jawaharlal Nehru University (which Wali does not mention), and the chairmanship of the Atomic Energy Commission in the late 1960s and a research position in the early 1980s; but administrative responsibilities had no appeal for Chandrasekhar and he was clearly losing touch with developments in India. He felt, for instance, that the Emergency had by and large been justified. But there was no corresponding affinity with, even if there was grateful acceptance of, the United States. Always a very private person, his long tenure, for nearly twenty years, of the editorship of the *Astrophysical Journal* has meant, because of his severe ethical standards, a self-imposed isolation from his professional colleagues; and his support of Oppenheimer and opposition to Edward Teller's war-mongering have led to his cutting himself off from governmental activities. He took much trouble over his students and in return they have been devoted to him. During the war he drove hundreds of miles twice a week to take a class of just two persons, both of whom later received the Nobel prize.

But, on the whole, his has been a long life of loneliness, yearning for India. It is an acute ache that he was abroad at the times when his mother and later his father died. He disapproves of Indians who settle down in the West in jobs much below the level of their talents and experience merely for the comforts afforded by life abroad. He has adhered to vegetarianism, is a strict teetotaller, and refuses to make any concessions to popular mass culture. He dresses elegantly in well-cut sober suits and sticks to pen and ink, disdaining the use of ballpoints. He has got no final satisfaction from his distinguished work; nor has he fallen back on the consolations of religion. When his mother died, his response was to assert that 'the only thing we can perhaps do is to shake our fist against Him who has shown his sport with us.' He considers himself a Hindu atheist, leading a rational way of life without belief in God. To him can be applied, even more perhaps than to Nehru himself, Nehru's well-worn words about his being an odd mixture of the East and the West, 'out of place everywhere, at home nowhere.'

It is true that a biography of a living person is unlikely to draw attention to the warts. But Chandrasekhar does seem to be a person without major flaws. And so we leave him in his eighties, not looking back on the pinnacles of his life or living the serene existence to which one would think he was entitled but awaiting death with equanimity and concerned only about his wife were she to survive him. Wali's biography will appeal to large numbers outside the fields in which Chandrasekhar has toiled. Certainly I have not read a more moving book in recent years.

27

E.M. Forster, *The Hill of Devi*

A new book by E.M. Forster is a literary event.[1] He is one of the few living masters of English prose; but never perhaps has so great a reputation been built on so meagre an output. Thomas Hardy, a writer who overwhelmed us by as much the quantity as the quality of his writing, once remarked that Mr Forster takes seven years to write a book. Clearly, the output is small because the standards are high; sensitive writing is the result of arduous effort. But even so, as the years passed many of us regretted the unpublished masterpieces. So now everyone will be grateful for what Mr Forster has given us. *The Hill of Devi* is an account of his association with Dewas State in India. It includes the letters written home to his relations and friends during his two visits in 1912–13 and 1921; but ever since his first visit Mr Forster kept in touch with his Indian friends and he uses his extensive knowledge of the inner workings of Dewas State to link up the letters and give a connected account. Like all letters written from afar Mr Forster's main aim was to amuse; the thought and beauty come in unawares. But *The Hill of Devi* is more than a work of art; it is one of the most revelatory descriptions we have of life in an Indian 'native' state in the twentieth century. This was perhaps not Mr Forster's aim; but this is certainly the impact that it has on Indian readers. Mr Forster writes without condescension but with great perception, and the general result is a flood of light on princely India.

[1] E.M. Forster's *The Hill of Devi*, of which this is an undated and possibly unpublished review, appeared in 1953. The original is in typescript, which suggests it was written for publication.

Mr Forster was introduced by the well-known Punjab civilian Sir Malcolm Darling to Dewas State, which Darling called 'the oddest corner of the World outside *Alice in Wonderland*.' Due to an old arrangement between two brothers there were two ruling families, the senior and the junior branches and their rights and jurisdictions crisscrossed in such a manner as to endanger all efforts at ordered administration. The town of Dewas, the capital of both branches, lay at the foot of a hill about 300 feet high and was known as the Hill of Devi, because at its top was a temple to the Hindu goddess Devi. Mr Forster first came out to Dewas on a short visit as the guest of the senior maharaja, and was so captivated by his personality that he agreed eight years later in 1921 to serve for six months as his private secretary. It is the fortunes of this maharaja that are traced in this book, from the first promise of his youth to the catastrophe which finally engulfed him. To the detached reader he seems merely a charming but weak personality corrupted by circumstances; but Mr Forster heaps adjectives over his hero—he is said, among other things, to be brilliant, lovable, witty, versatile, resourceful, subtle, able, and irresistible. Mr Forster even goes so far as to state, 'He was certainly a genius and possibly a saint, and he had to be a king'. Now there is nothing in the facts placed before us to warrant such a statement and when it is made by a person of Mr Forster's experience and judgement, it demands an explanation.

After all, few Englishmen came out to India with a wider background of culture and fewer still created for themselves in those days the opportunities to establish friendly relations with Indians. Untrammelled by official harness and free of all racial prejudice, Mr Forster's deepest wish was to be alone with Indians; uninhibited enough to dress in Indian clothes for the sheer fun of it, he was soon accepted by the people of Dewas as one of themselves, and saw much of the side of life hidden from most English residents in India. But on the other hand Mr Forster is not of the type who can find nothing wrong in this country. He is frank enough to deplore the absence of beauty in Dewas and to observe that except in matters of religion the Indian people do not seem to move towards anything important. How, then, could such a constant, sensitive, and detached observer reach such a seemingly far-fetched conclusion about one particular individual? Mr Forster, as we know from his other works, is a protagonist of personal relationships, and he found in the maharaja a fellow-believer in the heart. Affection was the only force to which the maharaja responded; otherwise he was no better, and in many respects worse, than his neighbour the ruler of Chattarpur, whom Mr Forster describes as 'mystical and sensual, silly and shrewd.' If the maharaja had any attributes of genius at all, it was a genius for human relationships. To this others also bear witness; Lady Darling, for instance, describes him as 'one of the sweetest characters upon this Earth' and talks of his 'usual angelic sweetness'. But it was Mr Forster who responded with the greatest eagerness to this capacity for friendliness. It must have been almost as if he were living a chapter in one of his own books. *The Hill of Devi*, indeed, though it is not a work of fiction, has all the atmosphere of a novel.

The maharaja, then, was a good friend. But that was about all. Both his wife and his son ran away, the latter in the firm belief that his father had tried to poison him. Even Mr Forster admits that he misgoverned his kingdom. And finally on top of domestic scandals and administrative chaos came economic collapse. In 1933 the state became bankrupt and the Government of India was obliged to intervene. Relations between the maharaja and the paramount power were unhappy, and Mr Forster writes with subdued bitterness of the officials of the political department who, he says, were on the whole 'an unattractive body of men' lacking courtesy, kindness, and sympathy. The maharaja finally fled to Pondicherry in French India, defied all orders of the Government of India to return, and in 1937 died in self-imposed exile and poverty. For this Mr Forster, ever a critic of the world of officialdom and power, blames the Government of India. 'They were', he says in a magnificent sentence, 'impeccably right and absolutely wrong.' But it is difficult to see what else the government could have done. A refusal to face an enquiry regarding the charge of attempted murder brought by his son and a flight that was not perhaps unpremeditated to foreign territory left them no other option. There were, in fact, flaws in the maharaja's complex character. If he was loving and lovable, he was also, as Lady Darling acknowledged, 'one of the . . . most unwise men I have ever met.' It is true that society does not often tolerate personal values but it is also true that personal values can rarely solve the problems of society.

But even if Mr Forster's estimate of the maharaja cannot be unqualifiedly accepted, *The Hill of Devi* remains a book of intrinsic worth. It is written—this goes without saying—in prose of gossamer quality. To the social historian it is a valuable study of an India that has now disappeared. An interaction of private and public history, it gives vivid pictures of life in an Indian state, with its servility and intrigue, its backwardness and obscurantism. The description of Gokul Ashtami, the festival of eight days in honour of the birth of Krishna, is remarkable for its delicacy and imaginative understanding. Reared in the agnostic tradition, yet Mr Forster can appreciate the religious sense in whatever form it may appear. Every detail, he says, was almost without exception fatuous and in bad taste; only one thing was beautiful—the expression on the faces of the people as they bowed to the shrine. Hinduism did not appeal to him; Islam exercised a greater attractive power. But he recognized that the festival touched something very deep in the hearts of the worshippers and was no more illogical than Christmas. But above all *The Hill of Devi* is valuable for the unintended portrait of a refined Englishman. Mr Forster has written a noble book; and in the opinion of one reader at least it is the author, and not the maharaja, who is its central character.

28

The Indo-British Love Affair

Fiction [about India] written in English by non-Indians is the subject of Sujit Mukherjee's latest book.[1] He deals in an appendix with American novelists and there are passing references in the text to European authors; but basically he is concerned with British writers. This has engaged Mukherjee's interest for many years. He has sat in the dusty stacks of libraries in various parts of the world, has read many thousands of pages, and has spent long hours brooding over his wide erudition. The final result of this long-drawn and varied effort is a balanced work, with considered judgements cleverly concealed beneath a lightness of touch and a wry sense of humour.

The British liked to regard India as more than a colony ruled and exploited by them and which contributed to their prosperity. It was, in Paul Scott's words, every English person's home, even of those who had never visited it, and was mysteriously in their blood. But British novels about India cannot be regarded as an important genre of English literature. It is spread out over two hundred years and is of massive bulk; but much of it is pulp fiction. Kipling received the Nobel prize for literature, created an undying character in Kim, and wrote some short stories which will live; but his work is too enveloped in imperial ideology and pride of race for him to retain the primacy which he enjoyed in his lifetime. Paul Scott's sustained writings, without touching the heights, raise key questions about the penultimate years of British rule and convey the slackening of tension

[1] Review of Sujit Mukherjee, *Forster and Further: The Tradition of Anglo-Indian Fiction* (Bombay: Orient Longman, 1993).

for the British in free India. There are other stray instances of novels of some literary quality, such as Christine Weston's *Indigo*; and one of the pleasures of reading Sujit Mukherjee is that he brings these forgotten memories back to mind. But, on the whole, Anglo-Indian fiction is an arid zone.

In fact, the sole Anglo-Indian novel which can even today stand on its literary worth alone is E.M. Forster's *A Passage to India*. Mukherjee is justified in incorporating Forster in his title and, though his main purpose is to cast a forward glance from that vantage point, he looks both before and after. There is also reason for this. Forster is not in the main tradition which makes the case for British rule or delineates British presence and influence in independent India—a tradition which is petering out in the sands. But there were others before him, like William Arnold and Edmund Candler, who engaged in the more rewarding search of trying to find out what went wrong with the Indo-British encounter. If the historian has the advantage of hindsight, these novelists, as Mukherjee points out, had the rarer qualities of prescience and insight. Indeed, the works of Forster, Thompson, Orwell, and others with a similar approach are of great value to the historian in recreating the intellectual climate of those years.

Forster was not concerned with the Indian nationalist movement, which had taken off under Gandhi by the early 1920s when Forster was writing his novel. Nor does he denounce in forthright terms, as Orwell was to do much later, the humbug of the white man's burden and the corruption which lying about exploitation involved. Forster was impatient with Indians, who he thought did not seem to move towards anything important except in matters of religion; and he did not claim to understand or to be influenced by India. In his letters to his friends he speaks of India's 'incomparable fatuity' and describes her as an 'unexplainable muddle'. He is not concerned so much with Indians as with the British in India, the clash between liberalism and empire and with the British failure to build with Indians the personal relations which to Forster were the most important aspects of life. For this he blames the British lack of imagination and their undeveloped hearts. They might act correctly and be competent administrators, but their stiffness and insensitivity rendered their results barren. Love and

Truth were constantly at war. British officials in India, says Forster in a magnificent sentence in *The Hill of Devi*, were 'impeccably right and absolutely wrong'—a contrast which his friend Auden unknowingly echoed a few years later in his line, 'How wrong they were in being always right.'

A lesser novelist but as concerned with relations between the British and Indians and with a sharper sensitivity to Indian public opinion was Edward Thompson. His novels, stories, and plays deserve reprinting by some enterprising publisher. Confronting the same problem that worried Forster, Thompson also gave up hope. 'The job has got beyond us', says one of the characters in *A Farewell to India*. Gandhi heard of this title and remarked to Thompson, a few years later, that there was no question of a farewell, for he would always be a prisoner of India. But Thompson could not shake off a sense of personal failure and in his case a sourness takes the place of the puzzlement which was Forster's. Nehru could not understand this dejection, for to him Thompson was a real peace-maker between nations and peoples. He wrote to Thompson in the summer of 1946, when Thompson was on his deathbed, that he had been one of the very few persons who had made India understood by a number of English people and England understood by many Indians. This was no hollow platitude. Thompson belied in his life what he wrote in his novels. It would seem that he recognized that Nehru was expressing no empty sentiments, for his son, the well-known historian E.P. Thompson, has told us that after reading Nehru's letter his father let it drop with the words, 'Oh Lord, now let thy servant depart in peace.'

Mukherjee imposes order on his voluminous subject by disentangling the various strands which surface in Anglo-Indian novels. British rule was supported, from the time the Crown took over the administration in 1958, by the prop of the princes. With their wealth, love of sport, and proneness to loose living, the princes are tailor-made for the romantic novel; but surprisingly they hardly figure in such a setting at British hands. But perhaps reality leaves little room for the imagination. Vivid accounts of the maharajas are to be found in J.R. Ackerley's *Hindoo Holiday*, which, as Mukherjee says, is based largely on fact, and in Forster's diary with letters, *The Hill of Devi*. Forster had a poor opinion of the princes as a whole but this does not come through because he liked his maharaja as a human being. Apposite is the comment in Paul Scott's early novel, *The Birds of Paradise*, that what gave these birds of gorgeous plumage their special power was the fact that they were dead; their deadness was more disturbing than the restlessness of a cage full of living birds.

Alongside the princes, the British sought to line up the Muslims. Soon shaking off their suspicions after the revolt of 1857, the British encouraged the Muslims to regard themselves as a separate entity and to shy away from the growing spirit of Indian nationalism. They appear in the British novel as mutineers, hardy Pathans (the Lochinvars of the east), and loyalists. The hero of *A Passage to India* is a Muslim; but this was because most of Forster's friends happened to be Muslims. Probably because he found it easier to understand Islam than the bewildering pantheism of Hinduism, one finds that most Muslim characters in novels written by the British emphasize their commitment to their religion than to any wider secular ideal. Even Christine Weston, who is by no means a diehard imperialist, comments on her Hindu and Muslim characters that, much as they learned to understand each other psychologically, they remained unreconciled and, like cloth which has been dyed deep, their separate traditions clung to them. So it is no surprise that we hardly find any depiction—with one exception—of a nationalist who happens to be a Muslim. But that exception goes far to redress the balance. The stance of Mohammed Kasim in Paul Scott's *Raj Quartet*, and his dealings with his two sons, bring into focus all the problems of a sensitive Indian of Islamic faith on the eve of Partition.

Little attention is also given in novels by British writers to attachments between British and Indians and to the products of such relations, the Eurasian community. That the Indian woman was always at hand, especially to British soldiers and planters, that the British woman was sexually threatened, and that for her to be voluntarily attracted to the Indian male was demeaning not only for her but for the British rulers as a whole—these were the stereotypes of British thinking that lasted well into the twentieth century. The British soldier's contempt for Indian prostitutes is stated explicitly in *Five Finger*

Exercise, the novel of Brain Aldiss written during the Second World War. But the other two stereotypes have become blurred. There has emerged a new category of the Indian spiritual preceptor who does not close the door on physicality; while Paul Scott deals with both rape and mutual attraction. Parvati Manners is the better type of Eurasian who will have no difficulty in feeling at home in India. But in *The Alien Sky* Scott portrays also the more usual Eurasian who faces the predicament of belonging neither here nor there. Better known (thanks to the film) is a similar character in *Bhowani Junction* by John Masters; and worthy of mention in this connection, if only because of the literary skill of the author, is Francis King's *An Act of Darkness*, where an Eurasian governess gets entangled in the passions of an English family and finally migrates, as many Eurasians in reality did, to Australia.

Given the Englishman's love of cricket and the hold the game has taken in India, it is odd that these are not more widely reflected in Anglo-Indian fiction. I know of only one such novel, Mike Marqusee's *Slow Turn*, published recently by Michael Joseph. It deals with a test match at Chepauk in Madras and the murky politics of international cricket. But Mukherjee, though himself an accomplished cricketer, does not mention this book or draw our attention to any other. The only aspect of sport in British fiction about India that interests him is tiger-shooting, perhaps because he sees in it deeper meanings. He believes that the lure of the jungle was part of British search for privacy; the experience of India was at times so overwhelming that the Englishman tried to get away from it all and be by himself. Mukherjee also suggests that the tiger represented some enduring spirit of India which the British felt they had failed to subjugate; no matter how thoroughly they had conquered the country and imposed their authority and administration, some basic fear of India continued to haunt them and, to excise their fear, the tiger had to be shot again and again. However this be, the result was that, by the time the British left India, the tiger had been nearly exterminated. But tiger-shooting has certainly added to the volume of British fiction-writing, particularly if, as Mukherjee thinks possible, much of Jim Corbett's hair-raising accounts are drawn more from the imagination than memory. However, tales about shooting tigers are not the monopoly of British authors. One of the best of them is written by an Indian. David Davidar's *Mist* is a splendid product of the Indo-British encounter.

What of the future? The unique love affair between the two countries is over. The British no longer think of India as their home, even though there will always be some persons of British origins staying on or, as Paul Scott would prefer to have it, hanging on in this country, with no imperial overtones clouding their vision or limiting personal relations. The world of Forster and Thompson has gone, and Mukherjee has provided it with a noble epitaph. India will doubtless continue to figure in the British novel, but in no way different from any other part of the world. Anglo-Indian fiction will belong, at its best, to the historical novel, such as Leo Myers' *The Near and the Far*—and to Inspector Ghote.

29

The Spell of Cricket

Anyone who is interested in cricket and enjoys reading good English prose has the best of two worlds.[1] For cricket, more than any other game, seems to attract literary elegance. A.G. Gardiner on Ranjitsinhji, Neville Cardus on Frank Woolley and Mushtaq Ali, and John Arlott on Hobbs—the roll-calls of polished stylists and exciting cricketers are intertwined, continuous and, fortunately, ongoing. To me, as no doubt to many others, the game and the English language have helped each other to increase the sum total of fascination. I still remember, for example, reading a long time ago a comment of Cardus on Duleepsinhji. 'It is one of the delights', wrote Cardus, 'of an English summer afternoon to watch Duleep's bat flash in the sun.' That sentence, with all that it leaves unsaid, has haunted me through the years.

Can Indian cricket add to the lore of the sport as well as to the sparkling patches of prose? Certainly it started with a bang at the international level. There had been before 1932 both English sides coming to India and our teams going abroad. But the first official test at Lord's that year, with England 19 for 3 after an hour's play on the first morning, showed that a new, glowing star had emerged in the East. Since then there have been ups and downs, but cricket has outlasted the *raj* and become an enduring object of public interest.

[1] Review of Ramachandra Guha, *Wickets in the East: An Anecdotal History* (Delhi: Oxford University Press, 1992); Ramachandra Guha and T.G. Vaidyanathan (eds), *An Indian Cricket Omnibus* (Delhi: Oxford University Press, 1994); and Sujit Mukherjee, *Autobiography of an Unknown Cricketer* (New Delhi: Ravi Dayal, 1996).

Indeed frequently—too often alas—it is the brightest spot of the Indian scene. When we despair of our politicians, Sachin Tendulkar keeps up our spirits. But have our prose-writers kept pace with the achievements of our cricketers? There have certainly been in the English language—of which alone I am competent to speak—no dearth of commentators; and several write attractively and with knowledge. There is Sujit Mukherjee for one.

Now comes Ramachandra Guha. He is a young historian of much promise, he has played cricket with seriousness and has watched most of the Indian stars of the last twenty years, he has read widely and has kept his ears open, and he writes with clarity and wit. *Wickets in the East* is a book which all connoisseurs of cricket will enjoy. My only complaint is that it is too short. There are quite a few throwaway lines which leave you wanting to know more. We are told, for instance, that Stanley McCabe played three of the greatest innings in the history of Test cricket. I can think of two straightway, but would like to know which is the third of which Guha is thinking. The relatively unknown George Tribe is described as the greatest ever left-arm wrist-spinner. More evidence to support this claim would be welcome.

Guha begins the book in the time-honoured way by giving us his selection of the best Indian eleven of all time. There is an in-built problem here, for the area from which one is picking changes with the formation of Pakistan in 1947. Even so, there are about three hundred names to consider. Some, like C.K. Nayudu and Gavaskar, pick themselves, but thereafter every reader will have his or her own favourites. Guha, of course, intends to set off arguments; the thrill of this effort lies in the discussion. Even if one takes into account only the figures of the past and not the players of today, the debates will be interminable. To me, for example, it is unthinkable that Mushtaq Ali should be omitted. But then, I have watched him bat at Chepauk, and Guha is too young to have seen on the field the man he describes, presumably from hearsay, as indisputably the most stylish batsman between Ranji and Viswanath. Mushtaq was more than what the score-books tell us; his lean and languid brilliance had to be seen to be believed. But Viswanath is clearly Guha's hero. He devotes pages to his brilliance, his sporting instincts, and his charm and courtesy on and off the field. He even rates him higher than Gavaskar. So we need not question Guha's choices too severely and can content ourselves with drawing up our own lists.

With the best Indian eleven out of the way, Guha gets down to a novel approach to his theme. Instead of recounting chronologically the achievements of Indian cricket, thereby running the grave risk of trespassing into tedium, Guha starts from what he terms the local roots and brings back to memory the exploits of many long-forgotten heroes just below the national level. Drawing on folk histories and Ranji Trophy matches, he wanders round our provinces and the erstwhile princely states and gives us lists of elevens for all of them. The lists in themselves are disputable and are not important. They are merely pegs which enable the author to tell us stories about not only the titans like Ranji, Duleep, and Nayudu but also about those who deserve to be better known, like Benjamin Frank of Karnataka, Ram Singh of Madras, and Ghulam Ahmed of Hyderabad. It is good to read of the ageing Nayudu being hit on the mouth by a bouncer, sweeping with his bat three front teeth off the pitch, and lifting the next ball for a six; and of Ghulam Ahmed, surprised to find that he was bowling short of length on a matted wicket having the mat measured to establish that it was longer than the specified requirements.

There is nothing in this book of the murky world of politics and intrigue in which the selectors seem to live; and even when Guha is forced to criticize, he does so with a cheerful generosity. We are told fondly of Lala Amarnath, known to be 'quick to love and quick to fight', of Pataudi and Jaisimha reaching a stage when they were batting from memory, and of the Gaekwad family eight of whom played first class cricket and of whom at least six were cricketers.

Guha loves the game and those who starred in it in India, and he can communicate this feeling to his readers. Even those who come to the book with no knowledge of the game should find their interest kindled.

~

This is, as far as I know, the first anthology of cricket in India. It is too short for an omnibus and is really a miscellany; accounts by writers, Indian and English, of twenty distinguished Indian cricketers and descriptions of some outstanding matches played by India, rounded off with some varied pieces on such themes as the Bombay cricket club, the Indian crowd, cricketing terms in Indian languages. There are even extracts from a novel of R.K. Narayan and a short story. The assortment, as a whole, makes good reading.

The editors of this book had in mind three objectives. They looked for well-written and evocative essays which might help to turn Indian cricketers into legendary figures and 'humanize them in literary terms'; they sought to pay tribute to the greatest of Indian cricketers; and they tried to track down choice items hidden away in old journals and newspapers. The result succeeds, better than any video, in providing a panorama of Indian cricket history to the eve of our own times and will bring back to life some memory or other to almost every reader.

The book appropriately starts with Ranji, the first of the illustrious and, even if a part of what we are told is true, perhaps the greatest of all Indian cricketers. The Jam Sahib of Nawanagar, who, in the heyday of the *raj* in Victorian years, fawned on viceroys and on Englishmen generally, is well forgotten; but history remembers the cricketer of genius, the inventor of the leg glance, the batsman who scored in one day two centuries against Yorkshire, the fielder of quicksilver brilliance. There is no one alive today who has seen him play; but Neville Cardus, no lavish dispenser of superlatives, has written that Ranji brought a light with him that never before was seen in cricket and never will be seen again. Ranji's nephew, Duleep, was more of this world and trained himself to be an accomplished batsman. He did not dazzle the crowds with his instinctive wizardry. But we of the older generation do not need to grieve too much at our misfortune in not having seen Ranji. For, as Cardus hints, there was a shade of Ranji in Mushtaq Ali. He too was a primitive genius. Those of us who have seen Mushtaq bat can comprehend what Cardus had in mind when he wrote of Mushtaq's shooting stars of strokes. A short innings of 39 runs at Chepauk shines in the memory of all those who were privileged to watch it long after the double hundreds of others in more recent times have paled. One of the glories of Indian cricket is the partnership of Merchant and Mushtaq in the second innings of the Test at Old Trafford in 1946, vividly recounted here by Ray Robinson.[2]

Merchant himself, though he was the anchor of this combination and indeed for long of the Indian team, has tended to be forgotten. That is the unfair fate of solidity. The scoreboard, said Cardus, is an ass; so too, in many ways, is history. But John Arlott makes some amends. Merchant's eye, wrist, and footwork were better than those of many others more spectacular at the crease. Like all superior batsmen, Merchant played the ball late. He did not take chances with his readings of the bowler's action and decided on his stroke after the ball had pitched. A characteristic incident was in a match in England, also on the tour of 1946. Being ill and knowing that the match was petering out into a draw, Merchant went in to bat on the third day and intended to be out quickly. But such was his ingrained skill that he was unable to sacrifice his wicket despite all his efforts.

The captain of Merchant and Mushtaq Ali on this tour was the senior Nawab of Pataudi. A.A. Thomson speaks of him as being only a rung lower than Duleep, who himself stood lower than Ranji. But the senior Pataudi was no more than a well-trained batsman. His century for England against Australia in 1933 was one of the slowest on record. In fact, his son, to whom only incidental references in this book are made, is more gifted. I recall the Oxford coach, who watched over both father and son, remarking in the late 1960s that while the senior nawab was assiduous in placing bat to ball, his son had an inborn flair for batting. But the father deserves recognition if, as is believed, he ruined his English test career after scoring his century by defying his captain and refusing to be a party to bodyline bowling.

Merchant and after him Hazare got runs when they were most needed by India and held the side together; but they could never capture the imagination of the crowds. That was left in the 1930s to the more glamorous figures, apart from Mushtaq, of Nayudu and

[2] Not to be confused with the test match played precisely ten years earlier, in July 1936, when Mushtaq scored his famous century (the first by an Indian overseas), mentioned in the Introduction.—Ed.

Amarnath. Ranji once remarked that no one is sooner forgotten than a successful cricketer. This year (1994) we are celebrating the centenary of Nayudu; but he is now no more than a distant memory to a few. Nayudu who? The description in this book of Nayudu's hurricane performance at Bombay against Gilligan's team in 1926 suggests that he was only a great hitter. But surely Nayudu was more than that. His late cuts off fast bowlers bore testimony to a wonderful eye and superb grace; his cover drives demonstrated the power of his wrists; he moved on the field like a panther; he was the first of India's noteworthy captains. Amarnath is more fortunate in this collection. A short analysis written after his retirement brings him to life and touches on all his varied contributions to the game in India.

And so the roll call goes on. Sujit Mukherjee, as knowledgeable about cricket as about literature, does justice to Vinoo Mankad, one of India's great all-rounders, whom Cardus describes as having honoured the art and nature of cricket in all that he did. Then follow chapters on other stalwarts, the stout-hearted batsmen 'with the welfare state of the mind', the bowlers Phadkar and Gupte, and the spin quartet. The essay on Gavaskar does not tell us much of his batting skills, and it is difficult from this book to compare him with the other master, Viswanath, of whom there is a glowing account.

The book, as it is, is a joy, with the second, lighter half establishing how widely cast is the spell of cricket in our country. But it leaves us wanting more. What of the pioneering bowlers, Nissar and Amar Singh? What of the great players of our own times, Kapil Dev, Azharuddin, and Tendulkar? One awaits a thicker, revised edition.

The memoirs of an Indian cricketer are rare if not non-existent, and Sujit Mukherjee's book is welcome for that reason alone. But the author has other qualities as well; he is the only Indian who has played cricket of a high standard who can also write good English prose.

Cricket is a game which has attracted eminent writers. The names of A.G. Gardiner and Neville Cardus spring immediately to mind; and there are more recent writers who, if not such masters of flourishing prose, still make the game readable. Mukherjee is the only Indian who qualifies to join this select group. His title, *Autobiography of an Unknown Cricketer*, is obviously a spin-off from the well-known *Autobiography of an Unknown Indian* by Nirad Chaudhuri, itself a reaction to Nehru's *Autobiography*; but whereas Chaudhuri's book is sour and cynical, Mukherjee's book is light, joyous and carefree. The result is that no one would even re-read Chaudhuri unless he or she is a misanthrope; but Mukherjee can be turned to again and again, especially by those with a love of the game and not just of the scores and the statistics.

There is no grim competitiveness here, no stark determination that has coloured the batting of, say, Bradman. A love of cricket for itself has always been the mark of great Indian cricketers like C.K. Nayudu. Mukherjee is a spin bowler of competence, but is satisfied with playing in Ranji Trophy matches, and has no consuming ambition to appear for his country. Spin bowling requires intelligence; but such a bowler takes fairly long to ensnare even an average batsman in his coils. It is not as spectacular as fast bowling; nor can it compare with a dashing batsman. A Grimmet does not have as many hero-worshippers as a Lindwall or an Archie Jackson; but Grimmet's skill was what often won matches.

Mukherjee was such a bowler. A Bengali born in Bihar, his account of cricket in Patna in the British days is replete with tales which, to an ageing lover of cricket, bring back his own memories of youth. There is a figure like the Irish clergyman Father Clearey in each state of British India, a European missionary who was keen about cricket and imparted his obsession to those around him without any obvious political overtones. Mukherjee's trips with the Patna college side to the neighbouring state of Bengal makes for rollicking stuff, uncontaminated by the politics and platitudes which were, to most of us young Indians in the 1930s and 1940s, of the greatest interest. There is no touch of Hindu–Muslim rancour and rivalry in these pages. After Independence, provincial cricket continues on its untrammelled way with the game remaining as one of the few lasting and refreshing legacies of the *raj*.

Mukherjee then moves on to spend two years at the National Defence Academy in Khadakvasla where cricket was played with more discipline and reserve. Then another two years as a Fulbright scholar in Philadelphia in the United States, where the game was regarded as of British ancestry and played only with a few on weekends. But throughout Mukherjee communicates an infectious love of cricket as a sport in stimulating and light-hearted prose of quality.

This is a book which should be savoured because it is so rare and out of the way. We are used to books by test cricketers, full of scores and victories and defeats. This book by Mukherjee brings out the joys of cricket as it is played in Indian towns and villages by those to whom the game is primarily a sport. It will be enjoyed by all the unknown cricketers who are so plentiful in India.

30

Israel Diary

2 July 1973

I get to Tara Hotel in Kensington with my luggage. El Al town terminal is at this hotel. As I arrive at 11.20 and the bus to the airport leaves only at 12.40, I leave my luggage and go to the coffee lounge. When I return at 12.45 my luggage has disappeared. I find it outside the terminal. A young man comes up and says he has removed two things from my box—an electronic calculator and the transformer. Discloses himself as an Israeli security officer and shows me his card. I ask him how he opened my box and he shows me his bunch of skeleton keys. Says when he saw my luggage unattended, he couldn't take the risk of some Arab planting an explosive in the luggage and disappearing in order to blow up the terminal. He had taken out all the electronic goods as possibly dangerous. (That morning the newspapers carried the story of the shooting of the Israeli air attache in Washington. So obviously feelings are tenser than ever.) I am worried that he might be a double agent who planted something in my luggage (though if he had been he wouldn't have disclosed himself to me).

Anyway, when we got to the airport at 2 p.m. I asked the people at the El Al counter to search my luggage again, but they were polite and did so only cursorily. Obviously they have instructions from their government to treat me courteously.

We took off at 3 p.m. and after a short trip at Paris when we are not allowed out we reach Tel Aviv after a five-hour flight at local time 10 p.m. one hour in advance of London. Nothing much to report on the flight. Food was quite good, but according to Jewish religious customs (Kosher)—no milk in coffee for example after dinner. Service not very good. Plane full of security men. I had heard in London that El Al hijackers are summarily shot with flattened bullets and their bodies quietly dropped into the Eastern Mediterranean as the plane approached Tel Aviv. Certainly the security arrangements are best on their planes and I am glad to be travelling on one of them. But I am scared to do anything which might land me with a bullet—like picking up the fork with the right hand for example. So I sit quietly not moving more than I need to and reading Agatha Christie's ominously worded *Appointment with Death*. The security chaps on the plane have not been tipped off by the foreign office and are obviously suspicious of a dusky Indian on board.

Daniel Argov receives me at Tel Aviv airport and sees me through passport formalities. We drive to Jerusalem and get here at about midnight. Comfortable air-conditioned hotel with a lovely view over Jerusalem. Argov, in charge of Indian studies at Jerusalem Hebrew University and an old friend, has been deputed to look after me and the foreign office have placed an air-conditioned car with chauffeur at my disposal.

So here I am in Israel—why am I here? The Israelis are modern, socialist, democratic; on the other hand they are squatting on land which is not their own, are arrogant and racist, with relations with South Africa—'an outpost of Europe'. Where does the truth lie and will one's feelings always be ambivalent about Israel. Can India's relations with Israel be improved without modifying the broad realpolitik policy of supporting the Arabs? And can Israel help in this?

3 July, Tuesday

I have told Argov that I don't want publicity and that I would like to avoid speeches. Fortunately, because my trip was postponed by two days as I couldn't get a seat on El Al on 30 June, the lectures and seminars at the university have had to be cancelled. Still, it is a heavy programme. We have an Israeli breakfast—no cooked food—orange juice, bread, butter and marmalade, *dahi*, coffee. I avoid the large assortment of salads. I decide to keep a diary but no ink in my pen. Spend the whole day looking in vain for ink at the hotel, university, etc. It is a ball-point state, so in the evening take to my ball-point pencil.

See the model of the temple of Jerusalem at the hotel—quite impressive with taped guides for which you press buttons. Then first go to Yad Vashem—the memorial for the Jews killed in concentration camps—ghastly pictures of the mass deaths and atrocities. Israel keeps these memories alive. It is a masochistic state with a strong foundation of self-pity—the state is bound together by the horrors of past history—both to evoke sympathy from outsiders and to keep their young from forgetting. The Eichmann trial had this purpose.

Then sight-seeing: the Wailing Wall, the Laka mosque, and the mosque of Omar. The place teems with Americans and you can hear nothing but American accents—Israel is New York's Mediterranean resort—American Jews getting quite weepy at the Jewish religious sites. After the mosques, a long walk through the Arab quarters of the city—the market with its steps going up and down. I walk along the Via Dolorosa and then to the Church of the Holy Sepulchre. I am rather moved with the plaque said to mark the spot where Jesus was whipped, and the various stations of the cross.

Then come back to the hotel to change and go to the university for lunch. Meet President Avraham Harman and my host Deputy President Dr Bergmann, a chemist. Others present: a foreign office man, an American sociologist Schiffrin, and a Canadian South East Asia specialist Rudner. They want to promote ties with Indian universities and exchange scholars and students. I ask them to write to the UGC. Otherwise conversation rather dull—usual stuff about why India is interested in Iraqi oil and not South East Asia; can you have change with stability? Bergmann a nice man who was a friend of Bhabha, Schiffrin has a pleasant manner, Rudner rather tiresome. Schiffrin says he told his class the fact that I had been friendly with Maxwell though totally disagreeing with him was a striking example of Indian democracy. [1] It could never have happened in China.

[1] The reference is to Neville Maxwell, correspondent of *The Times* (London) in New Delhi in 1960s. Maxwell wrote a controversial book, *India's China War* (1970), which blamed India for both the boundary dispute with China and for the onset of the war. Gopal was a friend of Maxwell and was thanked by

After lunch, walk round the university campus: the centre for Asian and African studies, the library. Then off again to Rachel's tomb on the road to Hebron and the church at Bethlehem. This is perhaps the oldest church in the world and in the basement is what is claimed to be the manger where Christ was born. Back to the Garden Tomb and Golgotha and the place of Crucifixion. Was this where Christ died or near the Church of the Holy Sepulchre? The British colonel in charge of the place thinks it was here. No one is sure if it was even either. Still all this is worthwhile and I, being sentimental, find it moving. We then go to the Mount of Olives, Gethsemane, Mary's tomb, King David's tomb and the hall above, which is said to have been the scene of the Last Supper.

6 p.m., the Israel Museum. We are shown around by an American Jewish girl who has settled down here. First the Shrine of the Book with bits of the Dead Sea Scrolls. Then we see an exhibition of the life of the Morocco Jews, then replicas of old European synagogues, and some finds from archaeological diggings. They have a random collection of Impressionist, Picasso, and modern art—but we have no time for it.

8.30 p.m., dinner at a French restaurant Chez Simon given by Mauss, the director of the Institute of Asian and African Studies. Michael Brecher, Shimoni the 'Mr Asia' of the foreign office, Olsbansky the professor of comparative religion, and Rudin a philosopher are the others present, apart from Argov. They are bitter about Jawaharlal Nehru and India's attitude to Israel and I try to explain both. Make it clear that there is no chance of any change in policy in the near future. Home by 11.15 p.m., dead tired—but start this diary and complete it on the morning of 4 July.

4 July, Wednesday

Up by 6 a.m. An interesting feature of the conversation last night was the attitude of semi-contempt for the Christians which the Israelis

---

him in the book. Gopal, however, wrote a devastating review of the book (*The Round Table* 245, January 1972, p. 117). Although they remained in touch, their friendship did not recover from the book and the review.—Ed.

have. They stress the fact that they do not regard Christ as 'Our Lord' by using not the standard BC but CE, meaning Common Era, so it is BCE, Before Common Era and not BC. They talk of the Holy Christian places as meaningless but useful to bring tourists. Christ had not been born in Bethlehem—that was a myth to associate him with King David; Nazareth was not the village of Biblical times; there was nobody in David's tomb; neither of the two places claimed was the site of Calvary.

There is a strong feeling between European-Ashkenazy Jews and Sephardi-Spanish and Arab Jews; even a Black Panther movement which talks of violence. Nothing as yet of significance, but it is clear that non-European Jews are second-class citizens—not to mention the Arabs of whom there are many in Jerusalem and who are the helots: all the waiters and servants in my hotel, for example, are Arabs.

I did a little shopping this morning—shirts, a pair of trousers, coasters, and table mats—and then to the foreign office for a talk with Shimoni. I told him Israel shouldn't worry about improving official relations but they should send some non-European Jews to India, not be associated with right-wing Indian parties, and improve Israel's image in India. He wanted periodic contacts with Indian ministers and senior officials. They did not like being associated with Jana Sangh and Swatantra but were helpless as these were the only persons interested in coming to Israel. All their Congress contacts had found themselves on Congress (O). Mrs Gandhi had expressed an interest in 1962 in Israeli youth activities. I told him to invite journalists like Verghese, Mulgaonkar, Kuldip Nayar, G.K. Reddy, Dilip Mukherjee, and non-officials close to the prime minister like Pupul Jayakar and Shanta Gandhi. He took down the names. Let us see.

Then lunch with foreign office officials and Michael Brecher hosted by the foreign office at the Jerusalem theatre. Sheshnon, director of Asia Department, and Aram, consul in India, and Trigor, his successor-designate, present. First, a long discussion on India's policy *vis-à-vis* the US, Russia, and China. Then on Israel's image in India. I said it was bad. Israel was regarded as a theocratic state, consorting with right-wing parties, regarding herself as an European element located in Asia. Sheshnon justified her Europeanness. Brecher and Art Isenberg (who was also there) agreed with me. Nothing can explain away the fact that Israel with an Asian population of 60 per cent had a ruling class which was 98 per cent European.

Tea at the Van Leer Foundation. Segre, Mrs Aram, and one or two others. General conversation. Segre drove me back to the hotel. Wants me to help him with the *Jerusalem Journal of International Relations* of which he is to be the first editor. He wants to give it an Asian orientation. He is worried that Israel behaves like the 52nd state of the USA and has a Bronx-orientation. I told him I would gladly help, only my name couldn't appear on the masthead as one of the advisers.

Dinner with Michael Brecher and his wife and Argov at a French restaurant. My first relaxed meal since getting here. We decided to keep off India–Israel relations and talk about Jawaharlal. He thinks my talking might have some impact on the foreign office.

5 July, Thursday

Argov and I had breakfast at 6.30 and set off at 7. First to Mount Scopus in Jerusalem and then to the Dead Sea. I paddle in it and swallow deliberately a mouthful to see what it tastes like. Bitter-salty. Then to Masada. Up to the site by cable car and then wander all over Herod's palace. They have not made an effort at full reconstruction and work on excavation is still going on. Then down again and back to the Jordan river and the border point at Allenby bridge. A young soldier who has been deputed to explain the position to us struggles to talk to Argov in Yiddish who then translates it back to me in English. After a while the soldier tells Argov he can just manage in English. When Argov translates this to me I tell the soldier not to worry and do the best he can in English. He then breaks forth into fluent English with a marked American accent and says he is a migrant from Boston. There is considerable movement of Arab petty traders and visitors across the border.

We proceed to Jericho. See the ruins of the Biblical fort and the later Hashim palaces. I can only think of trumpets, Satchmo Armstrong, and Kathleen Kenyon.[2] We have lunch at an Arab restaurant and drive

[2] The reference here is to the musician Louis 'Satchmo' Armstrong's 'Joshua Fit the Battle of Jericho'. Kathleen Kenyon was a British archaeologist best known for her excavations in Jericho. She was the principal of St Hugh's

up to the lake of Galilee. I again paddle and taste the water which is almost sweet. After sitting for a while on the bank we go for long drives on the Golan heights and look at two half-destroyed Syrian posts. Considering the way they are developing these occupied areas it does not look as if Israel has any intention of anything more than border rectification anywhere else except in Sinai. If this is all she is willing to bargain with, why should the Arabs negotiate at all? So prospects of a settlement don't seem to me promising.

At 8.30 we arrive at Ayelet Hashakar Kibbutz where we are to have dinner and spend the night. There are over 200 guest rooms and the place is chockful of Americans. The Israelis should remember their proverb more—'Go nowhere near the bee either for its honey or its sting.' But the vegetarian dinner is the best I have had in Israel.

6 July, Friday

After breakfast wander round this kibbutz which specializes in fruit-growing and has just started a small industry—making car tyres. Then drive to Nazareth. There the new church is like the Lakshmi Narayan temple. Tapes of hymns and then priest spoke through a mike to kneeling Americans in the gallery. As girls in shorts were not allowed into this 'holy place', a few had wrapped towels around themselves and this added to the bizarre atmosphere. The old church next door was in disrepair, but it was more worth looking at.

We went on for lunch to another kibbutz, Ein Hachtofer—The Judge—called after Justice Brandeis who gave money for its founding in 1936. This had more atmosphere than the other kibbutz—no guests or tourists in the first place. It specializes in making screws. The food was not as good as in the other kibbutz—a more serious and committed atmosphere here. After lunch a drive along the sea to call on Daniel Argov's wife; and then to Tel Aviv airport for take-off by TWA 5.15 local time for Bombay.

There seems no prospect of Israel withdrawing from old Jerusalem

---

College at Oxford from 1962 to 1973 and knew Gopal from his time at St Antony's.—Ed.

and the Golan heights, or of the Arab countries being able to push her out of these areas; so there is hardly any hope of a settlement between Israel and the Arabs. The latter will have to live with Israel even if they do not accept her; and the world will have to live with the Arab–Israel problem. But Israel itself will have to change her stance if she is to become an integral part of modern Asia. The country is still basically a colonial, settler, 'white' society, and the socialism, though it is genuine and ideologically sound, is of the 'top drawer' variety and of a limited compass. It serves the needs of the Europeans, and the few non-Europeans who are drawn into it are only there to be brought forward to counter allegations of racism. But there are other factors which are emerging and it is these which have to be watched. Future interest lies in internal developments within Israel and not in Arab–Israel relations which preclude any major shift. The growing clash between 'first-class' and 'second-class' Israelis, and the movement for a radical Marxist programme, which though led by 'white' Israelis, seeks support from the Arab and Asian population and attacks the present government as racist and oppressive. These are the signs to watch.

Copyright Statement

Part I. The British Empire in India

1. Gladstone and India. In Donovan Williams and E. Daniel Potts (eds), *Essays in Indian History: In Honour of Cuthbert Collin Davies* (New York: Asia Publishing House, 1973).
2. Lord Curzon and Indian Nationalism. In S.N. Mukherjee (ed.), *The Movement for National Freedom in India,* South Asian Affairs, no. 2, St Antony's Papers, no. 18 (Oxford: Oxford University Press, 1966).
3. 'Drinking Tea with Treason': Halifax in India. In William Roger Louis (ed.), *Adventures with Britannia* (London: I.B. Tauris, 1997).
4. All Souls and India: 1920s.
5. All Souls and India: The 1930s and After. In S.J.D. Green and Peregrine Horden (eds), *All Souls and the Wider World: Statesmen, Scholars, and Adventurers, c. 1850–1950* (Oxford: Oxford University Press, 2011).
6. Churchill and India. In Robert Blake and William Roger Louis (eds), *Churchill: A Major New Assessment of His Life in Peace and War* (New York: Oxford University Press, 1996).
7. The 'Cambridge School' and South India. Review of C.J. Baker and D.A. Washbrook, *South India's Political Institutions and Political Change 1880–1940, Indian Economic and Social History Review*, vol. 14, no. 3, July–September 1977.

Part II. Jawaharlal Nehru and His Contemporaries

8. The Mind of Jawaharlal Nehru. In *Heras Memorial Lectures 1977* (New Delhi: Sangam Books, 1980).
9. Nehru, Religion and Secularism. In Sarvepalli Gopal and R. Champakalakshmi (eds), *Tradition, Dissent and Ideology: Essays in Honour of Romila Thapar* (New Delhi: Oxford University Press, 1996).
10. India, the Suez Crisis and the Non-Aligned Nations. In William Roger Louis and Roger Owen (eds), *Suez 1956: The Crisis and its Consequences* (Oxford: Clarendon Press, 1989).
11. De Gaulle and Nehru. In French, *Revue Espoir*, no. 45, December 1982 (Institut Charles de Gaulle).
12. Nehru as Father. Review of Sonia Gandhi (ed.), *Freedom's Daughter: Letters between Nehru and Indira Gandhi*, in *Book Review*, vol. 13, no. 6, December 1989.
13. Tagore and Our Times, Prabodh Chandra Sen Memorial Lecture 1991.
14. An Irrepressible Optimist. Review of Judith Brown, *Gandhi: Prisoner of Hope*, in *Book Review*, vol. 15, no. 4, July/August 1990.
15. Reappraising Sardar Patel. Review of B. Krishna, *Sardar Vallabhbhai Patel*, in *Frontline*, 12 July 1996.
16. Tradition and Dissent: The Paradoxes of Subhas Bose.
17. The Playgirl Transformed: Edwina Mountbatten. Review of Janet Morgan, *Edwina Mountbatten*, in *Frontline*, 31 August–13 September 1991.

Part III. History and the Present

18. History and the Search for Identity. Presidential Address at the Indian History Congress, Hyderabad, 28–30 December 1978, in *Mainstream*, 3 March 1979.
19. The Fear of History, in *Seminar*, January 1978.
20. Democracy.

21. The Crisis of Secularism in India. Shastri Indo-Canadian Institute, Silver Jubilee Celebrations, 1993.
22. Secularism: From Rammohun Roy to Jawaharlal Nehru.
23. Women and the Law. Review of Vasudha Dhagamwar, *Law, Power and Justice*, in *Frontline*, 21 May 1993.
24. The English Language in India since Independence—and its Future Role. In John Grigg (ed.), *Nehru Memorial Lectures 1966–1991* (Oxford: Oxford University Press, 1993).

Part IV. Lives, Literature, and Cricket

25. Fairy Tale of Ramanujan. Review of Robert Kanigel, *The Man Who Knew Infinity: A Life of the Genius Ramanujan*, in *Frontline*, 31 January 1992.
26. The Pursuit of Science. Review of K.C. Wali, *Chandra: A Biography of S. Chandrasekhar*, in *Frontline*, 20 July 1991.
27. Review of E.M. Forster, *The Hill of Devi*.
28. The Indo-British Love Affair. Review of Sujit Mukherjee, *Forster and Further*, in *The Book Review*, vol. 17, no. 12, December 1993.
29. The Spell of Cricket. Review of Ramachandra Guha, *Wickets in the East*, in *Frontline*, 19 June 1992; review of Ramachandra Guha and T.G. Vaidyanathan (ed.), *An Indian Cricket Omnibus*, in *The Book Review*, vol. 18, no. 10, October 1994; review of Sujit Mukherjee, *Autobiography of an Unknown Cricketer*, in *Frontline*, 1 November 1996.
30. Israel Diary.

Index